Free Men Are Fighting

THE STORY OF WORLD WAR II

By Oliver Gramling

AP—THE STORY OF NEWS

FREE MEN ARE FIGHTING

FREE MEN
ARE
FIGHTING

THE STORY
OF WORLD WAR II

BY

OLIVER GRAMLING

AND

ASSOCIATED PRESS CORRESPONDENTS

AROUND THE WORLD

FARRAR AND RINEHART, INC.

NEW YORK   TORONTO

To Newsmen Everywhere

"*On the desert sands of Africa, along the thousands of miles of battle lines in Russia, in New Zealand and Australia, and the islands of the Pacific, in war-torn China and all over the seven seas,* FREE MEN ARE FIGHTING *desperately—and dying—to preserve the liberties and the decencies of modern civilization. . . .*"

FRANKLIN D. ROOSEVELT, July 4, 1942.

CONTENTS

ix

LIST OF MAPS

Meet the Correspondents

TWO TIRED, worn American correspondents arrived in Berlin one day in 1940. Neither had had a hot bath recently and neither had enjoyed the luxury of a good double bed. The hotel clerk was not encouraging.

"We allow hot water only on Saturdays and Sundays," he said, "but even then, our guests do not use it. You see, Der Fuehrer has a coal fund and all of our guests donate their share of hot water so that Der Fuehrer will have more coal for next winter."

The dejected correspondents tossed their bags into their meager rooms and went out to call on Berlin acquaintances. Maybe they could get a hot bath that way. But word promptly got around that the two reporters were in Berlin. Nazi bigwigs heard about it. A dinner must be staged. A party must be arranged.

The two men were wined and dined most of the night. They were regaled with the sterling qualities of Nazidom. Then, behind a sleek-uniformed chaffeur, they were delivered to their hotel. Although the echo of all the Nazi virtues rang in their ears, what they still wanted most was a hot bath.

They started up to their diggings. In front of them stood the manager of the hotel himself, clicking his heels and beaming.

"I beg your pardon, gentlemen," he said, "but one of our most distinguished guests unexpectedly left us and we have his suite for you. I myself will show you the way."

He opened the door to the hotel's best.

"I hope, gentlemen," he smiled, "that you will sleep well."

He started to leave, but came close.

"And, by the way," he whispered, looking around to be sure that no one overheard, "if you try the taps, I believe you will find some hot water!"

The luxury of hot baths, champagne, or parties, could scarcely

influence American correspondents. Hitler and all his hot water—
or all of his hot air—could not change that. What correspondents
generally have written about World War II, as well as what they
continue to write, is what they saw and heard.

Today, I began looking back over what correspondents of The
Associated Press, Wide World, and their allies have written in the
past three years. The idea is that, fitted together, their stories may
help to highlight the world's most tragic conflict.

So this will be a book by men who have been on the scene.
At one time or another, their stories may have been printed in
member newspapers or heard over affiliated radio stations. However, the identity of the correspondents may not have been known
at the time because the stories did not always carry bylines.

Some of the men have been in the thick of the war since it
began. Others have been mustered out because of illness, wounds—
even death. A good many are now interned in enemy countries. But
where one has had to stop, another has taken his place. You will
meet them in considerably more detail in this book. Sketches of
them also will be carried in an appendix. You will find them all
human beings.

One was born of a coal mining family in western Maryland—so
poor that he had to wear his sister's shoes to school. In 1941 he
won the Pulitzer Prize for foreign reporting with his stories of
the British Fleet in the Mediterranean.

One was born of American missionary parents in China. In
1942 he was the last correspondent to leave Singapore before it fell
to the Japanese.

One came from Oklahoma, little realizing that his career would
be in striking contrast to the quiet-sounding name of his home town
—Stillwater. In the Pacific he was given up as lost, but escaped
Bataan and lived to tell the story.

One was graduated from the United States Military Academy
and decided that writing about war might be even more exciting
than fighting it. Since the beginning, he has seen action on the front.

One came from a family of eleven children in Montana, and
got through college by typing and waiting on tables. He "volunteered" when war was declared and helped cover the Battle of the
Coral Sea.

One came by his reportorial instincts naturally—his mother,
father, and sister all being newspaper people. In 1940 he followed

General Chiang Kai-Shek; in 1941 he was with MacArthur, and in 1942 he was in the middle of the Pacific.

Some were born with silver spoons. Some were born without any kind of spoons. Some have Phi Beta Kappa keys. Some never went to college. They all are American-trained and they all are on the same assignment—news.

Space limitations will prevent actual, first-hand meeting with all of their active colleagues, of which there are approximately 7,200. But these colleagues also are scattered over the world—from Harrisburg to Hankow, from Miami to Minsk. They also contributed to this story.

Day in and day out, messages of encouragement, assignment, and reassignment go out to all these men from "the news center of the world"—AP headquarters in New York City—and day in and day out, replies come back to "Kenper, New York." That is the cable address of Kent Cooper, General Manager of The AP. He directs the world's largest news staff from an office in which there is no desk—only chairs and telephones—and wherever newsmen meet he is affectionately known as "The Managing Editor of the World."

The task of the author of this book is that of selection, correlation, and editing to meet space requirements. He also is responsible for the connective material, most of which, however, is based on the dispatches of the correspondents. Should the connective material contain any suggestion of opinion or conclusion, the author assumes full responsibility. The correspondents themselves reported only fact.

Since there are so many facets to human activity, there will be some stories that do not deal directly with the war. Their purpose is to reflect the interests of everyday people in wartime. Their inclusion should be understandable—because all people over the world have not always been concerned with the same problems of existence at the same time. Also, I know it will be impossible to recreate all the events of so grave a period between the covers of a single book.

But there will be something for the record of human sacrifice and suffering—as well as for the record of the men who have reported it—if what follows helps in any way to portray what *has* happened and what *is* happening to people all over a world in which we all want to live.

The date selected as a starting point for this narrative is August 28, 1939. I do not know where it will end . . . or what will have happened before it ends.

O. G.

New York, N. Y.
April 21, 1942

Free Men Are Fighting

THE STORY OF WORLD WAR II

CHAPTER 1

The First Blitzkrieg

August 28–September 3, 1939

I

ON AUGUST 28, 1939, in the Bronx Zoo in New York City, a baby deer—just born into a world of trouble—was given the name "Crisis." An Atlanta motorcycle cop clocked a brother officer and hauled him into court for exceeding the speed limit. In Selby, Ohio, an angler claimed some sort of a record for piscatorial efficiency by landing what he described as a live "canned" fish because its head was imprisoned in a discarded soup tin. A farmer in Pineville, West Virginia, exhibited a stalk bearing ten ears of corn, and his superstitious wife said it meant "war within ten months." A transcontinental bus skidded to a stop in Manhattan, Kansas, and two sailors were hauled off—both seasick.

From all over the world there was news—all kinds of news.

Perhaps two stories that day, better than any others, reflected what many people were thinking. They came from across the Atlantic.

The first was from a young foreign correspondent, Drew Middleton. Normally stationed in London, he went to the English countryside to find out what ordinary, everyday people were thinking. He wrote from West Mill, Hertfordshire, England:

This is England, forty miles but 100 years from London.

This is England dropped in the midst of a lush farming country. These are the English, solid, unimaginative farmers who have fought England's battles since Crécy, holding to the English idea that no alien sun shall set on their fields, no alien ideas disturb their lives.

The man on the street in London is a worried fellow.

3

The man in the country is less worried on the surface, for he fears no air raids. Underneath he is perhaps more worried about what war will do to his ideas, his home, his government.

In this village of 400 they gather in the "pub" evenings just as they do in London. But the talk is less spirited and perhaps more thoughtful.

"Aye, we may find peace by bargaining, but it won't last," said one farmer. "I don't look forward to what'll happen then. I was out last time.

"But things will be good for a while. Wheat prices'll go up which'll help us. But then they'll come down again hard. My boys'll go. Can't keep 'em. They're like colts wanting to run."

He paused and sucked on his pipe.

Another spoke:

"It ain't likely we'll get anything out of it. People like us never do. But we'll fight it.

"What worries me is what's going to happen to us when it's over. We had hard times after the last one. Hard times in it, but harder afterwards."

Another farmer began:

"It ain't no use bargaining. God knows I don't want no war. But them kind. They don't understand. I don't want no war. I have four sons."

I went into the street. In the churchyard the Vicar was walking. We stood and talked. I told him what the men had said.

"They mean it too," he said sadly. "I don't think they mind Germany getting stronger. But they think Hitler broke his word when he took Czecho-Slovakia. They've been angry ever since and they don't cool easily."

That was what ordinary, everyday people along the English countryside were thinking. Across the English Channel, several hundred miles away, other ordinary, everyday people also were thinking. Another young foreign correspondent, Edwin Shanke, talked to them in the streets of Germany:

Tears filled her eyes and trickled down upon the steel fragment in her hand.

Moved by the tenseness of the world situation, this German World War widow was showing some of the mementoes of the last war—mementoes that she had found in the garden of her home in Western Germany, close to the French frontier.

There were rusty shell splinters that had fallen to the ground; a battered part of an English warplane that had been shot down.

She is a proud woman, proud of the fighting ability of the German soldier and convinced they don't come any better.

The war took her husband. And now, she knows, if war comes again chances are fifty-fifty it will take her "war baby." He is somewhere on the Polish Front.

"If I only knew where," she says.

The change that has taken place in her within the last twenty-four hours is remarkable—and she is typical of millions of German men and women today. It is a change all the more remarkable because the Nazi-inspired press and the government-controlled radio are working overtime to show that the "calm of the German people is unbreakable."

It required Germany's extensive mobilization to shake her full faith in another bloodless victory, in which the Poles, as the Czechs before them, would bow before the mighty German nation.

Now, like the others, she watches tight-lipped. Around the corner, automobiles and motorcycles are being commandeered. In the school yard, hundreds of horses are being examined and assigned to the Front.

A policeman explains: "We need the horses because those lazy Poles haven't got the roads we have. There's nothing but mud and sand over there."

The German World War widow nods understandingly when I talk about the possibility of another conflict. She says: "In the twenty years since the World War I've never really known what peace means."

She passes signs reading "To the nearest air raid shelter" on the way to the grocery, to the milk and dairy products store, to the butcher, and to the market. In her hand she crushes the new rationing slip and tries to figure out how she can best take care of her family. She doesn't come back with much.

"Imagine! A thimbleful of milk," she exclaims.

She watches silently as crews of men with acetylene torches cut down iron fences. Steps like these have awakened the German people—almost overnight—to the danger of another war. It has made them nervous and irritable.

Friends call on friends, to comfort each other, to talk over chances of war or peace.

"We went through one World War and haven't recovered yet," one says, "and now we face another. God, I hope everyone can get together again as they did last year and settle it over the conference table."

Someone turns on the radio to catch the last-minute news. But only martial music blares forth, as it has almost constantly for the past three days.

2

THESE two stories—one from the village of West Mill, Hertfordshire, England, and the other from Berlin, Germany—told something of what ordinary, everyday people were thinking on August 28, 1939. They still felt the same way three days later, but by that time the thing they dreaded had arrived.

Louis Lochner stood in Berlin's Kroll Opera House to catch the words that plunged the world into another war. The setting was not new to him. A special meeting of the Reichstag at 10 A.M. . . . Hitler screaming . . . Hitler prancing . . . Hitler flailing the air on a stage built for music and laughter . . . Hitler, self-hypnotized . . .

The one-time Austrian paperhanger's words brought the rubber stamps of Nazism to their feet and provided Lochner's story:

Adolf Hitler declared to the German nation today that he would achieve the return of Danzig and the Polish corridor and halt Polish attacks on Germans or die fighting.

As a sign of determination to "live henceforth more than ever for Germany alone," the Fuehrer and his adjutants appeared at a momentous Reichstag session in gray uniforms. Greeted by a great ovation, he plunged directly into his subject. He declared:

"We meet to solve the problem raised by the Versailles treaty."

Then the deputies rose to their feet and "heiled" as he cried:

"I have never desired anything more than to serve the State as a soldier. I am putting on the uniform and I shall take it off only in victory or death!"

Hitler disclosed that he had picked his successors as leaders of the Reich in case anything happened to him. Field Marshal Hermann Goering and Rudolf Hess, deputy fuehrer, were first and

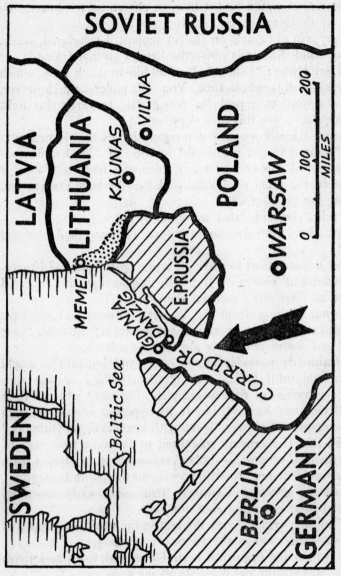

Map 1—Hitler's first move, opening World War II, was a thrust to regain the Polish Corridor (arrow), taken from Germany by the World War I settlement and included in a reconstituted Poland. The drive also sought to recapture Danzig, the German port that was made a Free City under international control following World War I. The Corridor cut Germany into two parts and Hitler said he would close the gap or die fighting. Earlier in 1939, Germany had taken over Memel (dotted area), lost in the first war.

7

second choices respectively. If something happened to both of them, he said, the nation would be led by men chosen as the bravest by the senate of the Nazi party.

Germany will not count on Italian support, he declared, while, on the other hand, Russia is now "the Reich's eternal friend."

Said Herr Hitler: "I should above all like to thank Italy, which has supported us this whole time. You will understand, however, that I do not want to appeal for foreign 'aid to carry this fight through. We shall solve this task ourselves."

In essence Hitler's speech was a reiteration of the German plea that every attempt to get a peaceful revision of "intolerable conditions" had failed. He said Germany's demands had been "modest and loyal" but the reply of Poland and the Western Powers had been nothing but provocation.

"It is a lie," he said, "that we do all by force."

[NOTE: More than five hours before, Germany had marched on Poland.]

In a last-minute effort to stave off action by Britain and France, Hitler renounced all claims on them. By implication, this included renunciation of Germany's colonial claims.

"We want nothing from the Western Powers and we have formally declared we have no claims against them," he said. "Our West Wall (of fortifications) is also our west border."

He refrained from declaring war on Poland, but said he would continue to fight until Poland's government yielded or was supplanted by a government that would yield. Germany will not fight women and children, he said, but if its opponent resorts to such warfare, Germany will answer "bomb with bomb and gas with gas."

He said that if Germany submitted to Poland's treatment of his latest settlement proposals—Poland refused even to discuss them —Germany would deserve to withdraw from the political stage.

He told the cheering Reichstag that, since early morning, Germany had been returning shot for shot.

He called the German Army the best in the world—equipped at a cost of 90,000,000,000 marks ($36,000,000,000).

Hitler was at his oratorical best. He looked worn and tired, but his voice was strong and his gestures vigorous.

He was followed on the rostrum by Minister of the Interior Wilhelm Frick, who proposed a law that decreed Danzig was a part of the Reich and that its citizens had German nationality. The measure was adopted unanimously. Then Field Marshal Goering, on behalf of the Reichstag and the German people, pledged Hitler unswerving loyalty and unquestioning obedience.

3

HOURS before Hitler began his Reichstag tirade, fighting had started at Danzig. It began at the Polish munitions depot at Westerplatte in Danzig Bay. Lynn Heinzerling was there and heard the first shots:

In a Danzig hotel lobby I heard a German officer who usually slept late leave a call for 3:15 the next morning—Friday, September 1. I realized then that it was coming.

It was 4:47 A.M. by my watch when the firing started. I ran down the hotel stairs several steps at a time.

The night watchman said:

"Es geht los." (It's started.)

I ran toward the Vistula River. There I saw what it was—the German warship *Schleswig-Holstein* firing on the Polish munitions depot at Westerplatte.

[NOTE: Although the firing started at 4:47 A.M., Hitler's order of the day instructing the German Army to "meet force with force" was not timed until 5:30 A.M.]

Already the warship's white sides were blackened from the powder of the shells she was pouring onto the heavily wooded Westerplatte peninsula from 18-centimeter and 28-centimeter guns. Surprisingly enough, I found a taxi that took me to the former Customs House. From there I climbed a hill behind the lines.

Below, German soldiers were guarding all approaches to the waterfront and clearing the entire harbor district of thousands of civilians to make way for the air raids that were to come. Windows all through the district were smashed by the force of the explosions of the shells from the cruiser.

The *Schleswig-Holstein* was standing out in the harbor, not far off shore. Beyond the peninsula, in Danzig Bay, were other ships of the German Fleet. Between the two forces lay the little peninsula, completely surrounded by enemy territory and offering no chance for retreat or escape. The Poles seemed to be drawing back, strictly on the defensive, and their firing apparently had no definite objective.

After an hour of shelling from the *Schleswig-Holstein*, I saw a

German landing party set out, but the attempt to storm the Poles failed. A cross fire of machine guns, the Poles' chief armament, drove them back with heavy losses. As the battle progressed, my movements were restricted sharply. Still I had a chance to see the wreckage of the Dirschau Bridge, which the Poles had mined in advance, then blown up to cover their retreat.

This fighting that Heinzerling saw in Danzig Bay marked the start of Hitler's long-threatened conquest. While Hitler had harangued the Reichstag on September 1, Nazi planes also were swarming toward Warsaw. His first blitzkrieg was on. Lloyd Lehrbas, like thousands of inhabitants of Warsaw, heard the roar of Nazi motors and saw the bombs come down. With a telephone in one hand and a gas mask in the other, he stood by and told what he saw over a line to Budapest:

German warplanes swooped over Warsaw this afternoon in an air attack in advance of three Hitler armies invading this country.

From where I am I can hear the wail of power-diving fighting ships and can see fourteen German bombers slowly, steadily following the course of the Vistula River, Poland's outlet to the sea. Apparently they are attempting to destroy all bridges.

The raid began at about 4:30 P.M. (11:30 A.M. N.Y. time) and is still continuing more than an hour later. Now they are coming back after making a wide circle. They are apparently heading toward government buildings in the center of downtown Warsaw. I can see puffs of anti-aircraft fire.

Although the raid is still on, there is no panic. Across the street from me hundreds of inhabitants are watching fascinated on rooftops. Tremendous explosions are shaking the city and rattling windows. Anti-aircraft shells are bursting around the bombers, which are coming over at an altitude of about 6,000 feet.

Warsaw had little warning. Elmer W. Peterson, Associated Press chief of bureau here, and I heard the anti-aircraft guns before we heard the scream of air raid alarm sirens.

If the bombers have tied up traffic over the steel railroad bridge spanning the Vistula, it is a serious blow for Poland's traffic from here to the coast and to the west. The Germans apparently tried for definite military objectives.

Reports have started reaching here of air attacks elsewhere

in Poland. A large number of women and children were killed when Nazi planes bombed a refugee train from Poznan at the Kutno station, seventy miles west of Warsaw. A hospital for feeble-minded Jewish children also was hit.

4

THIS Lehrbas story by no means told all of what happened in Warsaw and elsewhere that fantastic day. Hundreds of colleagues, stationed like sentries over all the trouble spots, added the details. It was undeclared war—dictator style.

Puzzled, unenthusiastic Berliners looked at each other and resigned themselves. French civilians began to evacuate Paris. A million children, each carrying a gas mask, trekked out of London. Half-naked English laborers piled up sandbags.

President Roosevelt issued a plea against the bombing of non-combatants.

A 70-year-old grandmother in Bellingham, Washington, had her picture taken with her newest catch—a 47-pound salmon. Thirty Washington admirers of John Nance Garner announced formation of an "Evil Old Man's Club" after labor leader John Lewis had dubbed the Vice-President of the United States an "evil, whisky-drinking old man." The British Association for the Advancement of Science canceled its meeting.

Britain and France already had parried too many threats with too many conciliatory words. A year before there had been "Munich" and Europe's "War of Nerves." Appeasers Chamberlain and Daladier had handed over Czecho-Slovakia (without even her consent), naïvely seeking to establish "peace for our time" after another Hitler promise:

"The Sudetenland is the last territorial demand I have to make in Europe, but it is a demand from which I never will recede."

And as far back as March—five months earlier—the Western Powers had pledged aid to Poland in the event she had to resist a threat to her independence.

Now blitzkrieg had come in spite of millions of "diplomatic" words and innumerable conferences. But Britain and France still did not declare immediate war. They followed the 1914 pattern and issued an ultimatum: "Withdraw from Poland or we will fight." It was delivered even as stricken Warsaw smoldered and border cities lay under siege of German troops. It went unanswered.

Spain announced strict neutrality. Yugoslavia, Rumania, Denmark, Latvia, and Bulgaria did the same. Portugal took a similar view. The Argentine Government urged its people to keep calm. Finland said it would keep out. Ditto Lithuania. Ditto Cuba. Ditto helpless or semihelpless countries around the world.

While a sad-faced news statistician was figuring that 8,500,000 were killed in World War I, Britain and France, their ultimatum still unanswered, rushed complete mobilization. That same night of September 1, the largest city in the world looked like this:

The lights of London went out tonight, not alone by air raid precaution orders, but in dread of a winged terror that might fly in the dark.

Three weeks ago London had a "blackout rehearsal" but it was nothing like this.

In the streets tonight you ran your head into lampposts and whistled vainly for taxis that were only wavering shapes in the fog and drizzle that swept in from the Channel. No one treated the blackout as a joke and there was little traffic.

In cavernous railway stations, covered windows kept the light in as families gathered to leave the city and as reservists with rifles in one hand and umbrellas in the other wandered about looking for trains.

The pubs were comparatively empty and stores did little business. Firehouses, air raid precaution centers and police stations were the busiest places. The one aim seemed preparedness.

That represented a free people's first real experience with "blackout." It also represented a new problem—a new technique in war. There had been practice blackouts, all of them an incongruous, ironic note in twentieth-century living. Englishmen had squirmed under them—in Folkstone one test had drawn the complaint that it interfered with the traditional Saturday night bath— but England was facing stupefying reality, and the famous London fog now had ominous, terrifying competition.

5

SEPTEMBER 2 came and the Nazi fighting continued. More places bombed . . . more people killed . . . more property blown to bits and thrown with crushing, obliterating force on helpless people.

Then Britain and France issued their last ultimatums. Hitler had a matter of hours to withdraw from Poland. The time for reply terminated at 11 A.M., London time, Sunday, September 3. The deadline approached. How was the average Londoner feeling about it? Fred Vanderschmidt found out:

Ten minutes to eleven o'clock . . . two old women walk serenely down a Kensington side street on their way to church. The church bells ring deeply and mournfully. But the street is sunlit and quiet.

Five minutes to eleven o'clock . . . a decrepit London taxi wheels placidly around Trafalgar Square. A few men doze on the benches in the sun. The big clock says it's five minutes to wartime. A little girl in a green coat and her nanny stroll along in intimate conversation. Wonder why they haven't moved her out of London.

There are sandbags around the buildings and the sunlight glances off the tin hats of blue-coated bobbies. There is enough sand piled up here and there to make a little seashore, and the soldiers in khaki battle dress are hurrying everywhere with their neat little knapsacks with service gas masks inside.

Two minutes to eleven . . . plain people line up across from Downing Street. They are very quiet. There is Home Secretary Sir Samuel Hoare walking slowly from Number 12 Downing Street, the office of the conservative whip in Parliament, to Number 10 where Neville Chamberlain is waiting.

11:15 in London . . . faces in Downing Street strain toward the wide black door of Number 10 and there is scarcely a whisper as Big Ben booms. Down on the broad Victoria Embankment men in civilian clothes and steel helmets hurry quietly along.

The radio plays soft symphony music, and at this hour Great Britain and the Third Reich are at war.

11:15 o'clock . . . the sad voice of Chamberlain falling almost to a hush: "I am speaking to you from the Cabinet room at Ten Downing Street. . . . This country is at war with Germany. . . . Now may God bless you all and may He defend the right. . . ."

Buckingham Palace . . . a handful of tired-faced people outside, sentries in tin hats and battle dress, and conical steel sandbagged sentry boxes in a great cement yard. Inside, a youthful, earnest couple bending over the radio . . . the King and Queen.

11:32 in London . . . the wail of sirens echoes through the empty Sunday streets. Men with flags and whistles and steel helmets spring into the streets. Stray pedestrians run for shelter. Anti-gas trucks stand at the curbs. It seems that every doorway has its air raid warden. They are courteous and calm but they make you get off the streets and into comparative safety of ground floors and basements if no orthodox shelter is in sight. Yet many cling to doorways and peer upward if they can.

11:40 . . . a long note of the sirens' "all clear," the signal blows at intervals, and then the Air Ministry explains the alarm was caused by an airplane, which later proved "friendly," off the South Coast.

Noon in London . . . "all clear" signals echo around courtyards of Buckingham Palace. The sovereigns and their household are in a brief service of prayer. In Fleet Street the cables come to life again. The air raid wardens go back to their machines and more news goes out. Men with relieved faces swish into pubs in tall rubber boots and shout for their pints. Their gas masks swing unused from their belts.

That was London. In many parts of the world, due to time differences, people were still asleep. In New York it was only a little after 6 A.M. and the streets were deserted in the Sunday dawn, except for a few people en route to St. Patrick's Cathedral and other places of worship. In many of the earlier time zones there was the usual stir, and in the churches of Wales benedictions were pronounced and congregations sang:

> Praise God, from Whom all blessings flow!
> Praise Him, all creatures here below!
> Praise Him above, ye heavenly host!
> Praise Father, Son, and Holy Ghost!

Along the cables under the Atlantic, through the ether and over telephone lines, sped the news which all newsmen knew would come. Britain finally had declared war on Germany. France quickly followed.

6

THE PATTERN of United States reaction came from many sources. In Washington, Kirke Simpson, who wrote the famous Unknown Soldier stories of 1921, had just finished an estimate of U.S.-German relations:

The outbreak of war in Europe finds German-American relations far less cordial than in 1914 when the World War began.

The capitals of both countries are without their respective ambassadors. Already nine months have passed since President Roosevelt called Ambassador Hugh R. Wilson home for report and consultation after a severe anti-Semitic outbreak. He has not been returned, and there seems no intention of sending him back. German Ambassador Dieckhoff has been absent from his post for the same length of time.

In the last year and a half the United States and Germany have found it almost impossible to settle problems that rose between them.

A series of notes passed between them on the subject of Austria's debts to the United States Government (around $24,000,000 plus about $20,000,000 in debts to private American investors), but no settlement has been reached. Germany alleges she cannot pay the obligations of the country she took over unless the United States takes into account the unfavorable trade balance with this country. This, Secretary of State Cordell Hull will not do.

Another series of exchanges has taken place on the subject of mistreatment of American Jews in Germany.

German exports to this country not only pay higher duties than the products of other countries because she is on the American economic blacklist, but they also pay punitive customs because countervailing duties of 25 per cent were levied on the grounds that Germany subsidizes exports. With different systems of trade dividing them, commerce between the two nations has declined markedly in the last several years.

Two points of difficulty have been eased slightly in recent months. An agreement was concluded whereby American citizens who receive inheritances from Germans will have a little less trouble getting their heritages out of Germany. And Hitler agreed to a more orderly exodus of Jewish refugees.

Two recent developments in this country have concerned German-American relations. In June a mixed-claims commission decided that the explosions that occurred at the Black Tom and Kingsland arsenals, New Jersey, in 1916-1917, were the result of German sabotage. American claims against Germany for $50,000,000 were validated. This was a reversal of a decision made by the commission at Hamburg in 1930, which accepted the industrial accident theory.

A second development was the investigation by the Securities

Commission into the issue of $73,000,000 in German bonds in this country. The SEC ruled that, before the bond issue could be approved, the commission must have information concerning the German budget, the German public debt, gold and foreign exchange, etcetera. The German Embassy declared that the demands for information were such that no sovereign government could comply with them.

German activities here have been investigated by the House Committee on un-American activities. German spies were convicted in a spectacular trial some months ago. The United States, after granting an export license for helium for the new German dirigible, refused to sell the gas to Germany. This government also refused to recognize Germany's acquisition of Czecho-Slovakia.

President Roosevelt has repeatedly condemned European dictators and appealed indirectly to the German people on several occasions. Reichsfuehrer Hitler did not even deign to reply directly to Roosevelt's appeal to him in April. Instead, he made a public speech in which he derided the democracies and shot many shafts of sarcasm at Roosevelt.

The Simpson report reflected a more or less official estimate. Around the country quick reaction and comment varied.

The leader of the German-American Bund in New York announced his organization was for neutrality. The wizards who count money said $50,000,000 in gold had arrived from Europe in two days. A German citizen, visiting New York, rushed to his local consulate and enlisted with the Nazi forces. An American invalid embarked for the Shrine of Miracles at Lourdes in spite of the European hostilities.

At the World's Fair, built on the marshes of New York's Flushing, people crowded in to see a bathing beauty encased in a block of ice, and at still another concession eager crowds paid their money to make synthetic parachute jumps.

Everything considered, the conflict appeared a long way from home.

CHAPTER 2

Bloody September

September 3–September 30, 1939

I

FORTY thousand words of war news poured across AP cables the day Britain and France declared war. They dealt with every conceivable angle of war effort—from a reminder that it was the 156th anniversary of the signing of the treaty of peace that gave the U.S. its independence, to the jailing of fifty merchants in Rumania for profiteering on food. They all crossed the desk of one news analyst, and late that day DeWitt Mackenzie wrote his reaction:

This war was bound to come sooner or later. It wasn't inevitable that it should grow out of the German-Polish controversy—for that was incidental to the main issue. But the lines of the dispute were so drawn between Herr Hitler and the Anglo-French Brotherhood that there had to be a showdown in the long run.

Europe couldn't serve two masters.

This terrible eventuality gradually had sunk home in the minds of the unhappy general publics as the "War of Nerves" progressed. And when the break came, many people in all countries found themselves in agreement with the famous British Labor Leader, Arthur Greenwood, who expressed relief in a dramatic speech in the House of Commons that the "agony of suspense" was at last over.

As another possible general war started, both sides taxed each other with aggression and laid down their aims. The Anglo-French Allies, charging that Herr Hitler is out for world domination, are bent on smashing him and his creed.

"I trust I may see the day," said British Prime Minister Chamberlain to a tense House of Commons, "when Hitlerism has been destroyed."

17

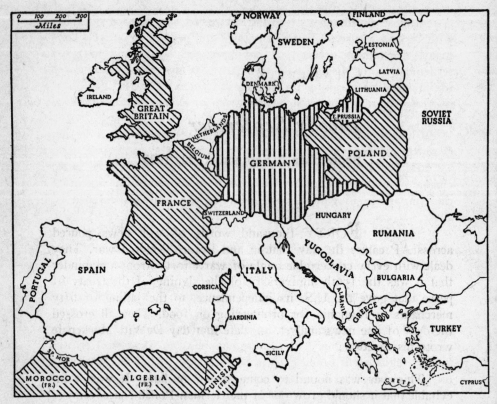

Map 2—Europe lined up like this when Germany invaded Poland on September 1, 1939. Great Britain and France allied themselves with Poland against the Nazis.

Almost simultaneously Hitler answered by charging England with "trying to use all European states and peoples to encircle Germany." Britain is accused of having egged on Poland to resist settlement of the dispute with Germany. So now Nazidom declares its intention of breaking up this alleged encirclement, to give Germany freedom to carry out her program of expansion and development.

Chamberlain summed up the British viewpoint when he declared in his radio proclamation announcing war:

"His (Hitler's) action shows convincingly that there is no chance of expecting that this man will ever give up his intention of using force to gain his will. And he can only be stopped by force."

The first time I heard almost those identical words they were spoken by another great official of the Anglo-French Alliance. The occasion was last December, not long after Czecho-Slovakia went to the sacrificial altar at Munich. I then learned that England and France had decided to crack down on Hitler. I had said to this statesman:

"I have not come to you for an interview, because I know you cannot grant that, but I need your help. I seem to sense a change in the Anglo-French policy towards Germany. I can't put my finger on it, however, and I shall be grateful if you will tell me whether there has been any change and, if so, what it means."

The statesman weighed this unusual request for an instant and then said:

"We have decided after long experiment that the policy of appeasement is useless. We have come reluctantly to the conclusion that Hitler isn't susceptible to any moral suasion, but only to force.

"The man is mad—"

My informant caught himself quickly and with obvious concern at his remark.

"I mean," he corrected himself, "that he is a man with a dangerous obsession. He must be smashed."

The Reich is widely held to lack the foodstuffs, raw materials, and other supplies vital to the prosecution of a long war. Herr Hitler is said to have been banking on a quick, decisive smash of his opponents.

The Soviet Union, which has just signed a nonaggression pact with Germany, possesses most of the things which Germany lacks. Very recently, though prior to the signing of the nonaggression pact, Russia and Germany made a trade agreement for a huge exchange of materials and goods. Should Russia now decide to provide Germany with the necessities for a prosecution of war, it will have a marked bearing on the trend of hostilities. This most certainly must be a matter of deep concern to France, England, and Poland.

In this connection, Germany is making every effort to get Russia and Japan to conclude a nonaggression pact. The point is, of course, that if Russia and Japan should become involved in war— and there always is a chance of that, so long as relations continue as unfriendly as at present—this would hamper Russia in providing Germany with supplies.

Japan has been looking this proposition over with a weather eye. It is said she isn't very enthusiastic over the idea.

The present position of Italy—one of neutrality so far as concerns the actual bearing of arms—was wholly expected. It has been well known among observers for some time that the general public of Italy has no stomach for war on behalf of Nazidom whose policies are decidedly out of favor with the average Italian. For this reason, among others, it would have been surprising to see Signor Mussolini try to lead his country into war in support of Herr Hitler.

Also, it was understood that Britain and France intended to concentrate in a drive against Italy, both by land and by sea, if Il Duce entered the conflict. That presumably entered into his calculations as well. At this juncture there is much speculation as to whether Mussolini will continue to maintain a "hands off" attitude.

Who wins at war? A striking commentary on the vicissitudes of fate on the battlefield is contained in a little dispatch by The Associated Press from Doorn, Holland.

There in the quiet of this old-world hamlet sits an aged German exile. His white head is bent over a big map of Poland, and he is placing different colored pins to indicate the positions of the opposing armies. In spite of his extreme age, he works with the sureness of one long-accustomed to military movements and maps. He is the former Kaiser Wilhelm—the "all-highest" who once ruled the great German Empire, but lost his throne in the World War.

2

On the first night of the war apprehensive crowds gathered at the tomb of France's Unknown Soldier. Daladier read the French declaration. London was cloaked again in fog and blackout. The patriotic Poles were still cheering the promise of Allied help. One of their first communiqués announced the killing of at least 1,500 of their citizens by Nazi blitzkrieg.

The ink on the British and French declaration was scarcely dry. The new British war cabinet had just been formed. It included Anthony Eden as Dominions Secretary and Winston Churchill in his old post as First Lord of the Admiralty.

Somewhere in the Atlantic the $20,000,000 German *Bremen* was sneaking home from New York, passengerless. The Cunard liner *Carinthia,* indistinct in its recent dull camouflage, was at sea under sealed orders. The $25,000,000 *Queen Mary,* greatest single booty among all the fifty-four liners ploughing the dark ocean, was due at her American port. It carried J. P. Morgan and 3,384 other passengers, many of them fleeing the European debacle. The palatial *Normandie,* $60,000,000 pride of the French merchant marine, was tied up at her New York pier, departure indefinitely postponed.

The British liner *Athenia,* with 1,400 passengers, some of them Americans, slipped along her course 200 miles off the Hebrides. The first-class passengers were dressed for Sunday dinner.

There was a flash on the port side and the *Athenia's* lights went out.

The next day, and the one after that, rescue boats hurried into port. At Galway, Ireland, and Greenock, Scotland, weary and half-naked survivors were hauled ashore. There was plenty of news on the first real "incident" since the declaration of war. From Galway and Greenock came word of the survivors:

The master of the *Athenia* said that his ship "was hit by a torpedo that went through the galley and into the engine room, causing heavy loss of life."

The captain, James Cook, was brought to Galway by the Norwegian steamship *Knut Nelson,* with 430 other survivors of the first submarine disaster of the war. The survivors included about 250 Americans.

Captain Cook said that immediately after the torpedo was fired, the submarine rose to the surface and shelled the *Athenia.*

"One shell carried away the main mast. It was evidently aimed at the wireless room, but missed its mark."

Maxine Robinson, 16 years old, of Austin, Texas, member of

a party of sixteen college girls who had been on vacation in Europe, said that all her party was saved.

"We were just finishing dinner," she said, "when we felt a jolt and the ship was plunged into darkness. All of us jumped up on the tables. Then we went up on deck and slid down the ropes to the lifeboats. We were in the lifeboat only a few minutes when there was a flash and we felt something whiz past us going in the direction of the liner. We were four hours in the lifeboat before help arrived. My hands are all blistered from rowing."

Captain Cook said he did not know how many were dead and injured.

Members of the *Knut Nelson's* crew said that many of the *Athenia's* passengers were killed when the ship's boiler exploded after the torpedo had struck.

Because there were only twenty berths on the *Knut Nelson,* some of the injured had to lie on improvised beds on deck. A number died en route to Galway.

Six hundred of the shaken and weeping survivors arrived at Greenock. Two hundred of them were injured.

Mr. and Mrs. W. H. Cox of Neepawa, Manitoba, said they had just got into a lifeboat when the rope broke, throwing them into the water. Mrs. Cox added: "We were soon taken back into the boat, but we had to bail it out with shoes. While we rowed during the night, we were almost submerged by the swell from the submarine as it passed under us."

Children who had lost their parents were carried weeping into the Adelphia Hotel at Glasgow. Some had lost their voices. There were wives without husbands, husbands without wives. All were desperate for news of survivors from other rescue areas. Perhaps the saddest sight of all was 9-year-old Roy Barrington of Toronto. His mother was lost.

In Berlin, State Secretary Ernest von Weizsaecker said: "The German sea forces could not possibly have been responsible for the sinking of the *Athenia.*"

3

THE DECLARATION of war did not put an immediate end to Europe's "War of Nerves." More than ever, there were tenseness and uncertainty. Hopeful Poland redoubled resistance, awaiting Allied help. It was help that did not come—until too late.

On September 4, British fliers tossed a few bombs on two Nazi battleships at Wilhelmshaven. They called it revenge for the *Athenia*. But little damage was done. Other British planes rained leaflets over German soil—propaganda warfare that had come to be anything but new in the past year of Europe's chronic insomnia.

The active war was between Germany and Poland. More bombs shrieked down. More death and destruction. One bomb wiped out a Girl Scout canteen. Another struck the villa of American Ambassador Biddle. Nazis seized the "holy city" of Czestochowa and isolated Polish forces in the Corridor.

Mussolini urged isolation of the war to Poland. Spain did likewise. Japan announced its decision to remain neutral so that it could take care of its own war. Russia rolled one crafty eye at Hitler and the other toward the Polish frontier.

Across the Channel, play was suspended in the English football league. The British Ryder Cup golfers postponed invasion of the United States. Sporadic raids on Nazi ships in the Kiel Canal cost a few British planes. Chamberlain's government prepared to convoy merchant ships. A London publisher announced that all author's royalties from the sale of Hitler's literary masterpiece, *Mein Kampf,* would be donated to the Red Cross. Gracie Fields began singing "Wish Me Luck," a successor to "Tipperary." The principals and guests at a London wedding all wore gas masks.

England knew she was in for a long war. Londoners were still trying to acclimate themselves to nightly blackout. Drew Middleton described it:

You meet so many interesting people in blackouts.

A gentleman down the street cuts quite a swath with the girls. He has thick black hair right down to his collar. The first time the sirens blew he won the race to shelter by a head—and what a head.

The English sense of propriety isn't wavering. A fellow near the office spent all day building a sandbag parapet. When he got through he stuck up a sign reading: "In event of air raid, please do not loiter."

How do you like this? A fellow I know is having his mouth made over. The dentist yanked four teeth last Friday. The fellow goes around to see the dentist yesterday. No dentist. He'd joined up. The fellow's mouth looks like the entrance to the Holland Tunnel.

To put it mildly, Hitler is unpopular. So signs like "Nuts to Adolf" and "'Arf a mo' (half a moment), Adolf, we are coming" are common on cars and busses.

Pubs are doing a whale of a business. Down at the "Rose and Crown" the landlord told a silent drinker he had no whisky left. "That's all right," said the silent drinker. "There's no sacrifice too heavy in wartime. Give me gin."

You ought to hear the Cockneys pronounce Polish place names. A cabbie said this morning, "Old 'Itler 'e's captured," and then sneezed. It turned out the sneeze was the name of a town.

The blackouts every night add to the general chaos. One newspaperman nearly got a load of buckshot where it would have done the most good the other night. He spent ten minutes trying to get into the wrong house. His rich Midwestern exclamations shattered the quiet of a peaceful suburb. The household mobilized and an indignant old guy in a white nightshirt, sporting a gun and cricket bat, convinced the newsman he didn't have the wrong key but the wrong house.

You could read about blackouts in London, early British attempts at blockade, and incidental bombings. But, aside from what was going on in Poland, there was comparative calm. Milo Thompson, surveying the whole situation, wrote from Copenhagen:

In one week of a European war not yet general, Germany has seized Danzig, driven across the Polish corridor to connect East Prussia with Germany proper, pushed Poland's frontier far eastward, and reached the gates of Warsaw. But so far Germany's main objective—smashing the Polish Army—has not been attained.

Adolf Hitler's seventy army divisions on the Eastern Front still have not penetrated a large area of Western Poland between Poznan (Posen) and Warsaw where the Polish Army has put up stiff resistance. A giant German pincer movement has made gains, however, on all sides of the western Polish forces.

During the first week of war, Poland's allies, France and Britain, though shrouding their movements in secrecy, have been active. French troops on the Western Front pushed into German territory between the German Siegfried and French Maginot Lines.

The British Fleet slowly drew a net to keep ships from reaching Germany and to bottle up vessels in the Baltic. British planes bombed Kiel Canal defenses and struck at Germany's pocket battleships, but it remained unclear what success attended these attacks.

Germany, carefully minimizing French efforts to divert her attention to the Rhine Front, admitted however that reinforcements had been sent to the West.

Premier Mussolini's tactics appeared to be to keep his people calm, busily at work increasing domestic production, perfecting protective measures, and looking toward Il Duce for leadership. The Italian press began an apparent effort to weaken the French-British alliance by suggesting that Britain was "ready to fight to the last Frenchman," now that she already was fighting to the last Pole. The chief Italian military activity appeared to be construction of defenses along the French frontier.

The rest of Europe looked on anxiously, particularly the little nations of southeastern Europe that clung to a neutrality which diplomats said they believed was extremely wobbly. Hungary, Rumania, Yugoslavia, Greece, Bulgaria, and Turkey kept out of the fighting, but their government spokesmen in moments of frankness disclosed the belief they might be forced to join the conflict sooner or later. Turkey was the only one to call up reserves openly, and her munitions factories, like others of southeastern Europe, were running night and day.

The belief was expressed authoritatively in the southeast that the fate of that part of Europe depends on what Soviet Russia and Italy would do. The Soviet Union, pledged to a nonaggression agreement with Germany, called up reserves and mobilized doctors, nurses, chauffeurs, and railway workers.

Heavy reinforcements were sent toward her western border. Some observers in Moscow were of the opinion that Russia did not intend to aid Germany but was going to make certain that retreating Poles or invading Germans did not penetrate Soviet territory.

The little Baltic nations pessimistically prepared for all eventualities since they could not resist any strong invader. Food rationing and hoarding of raw materials proceeded along with defense measures.

The Scandinavian nations were more optimistic about their ability to stay neutral, though they watched closely along their frontiers and coastlines. There were hourly reminders of the nearness of war in the form of military balloons that had broken from their moorings, camouflaged ships slipping into neutral ports, lost belligerent planes appearing over the borders, and frequent news of ships grounded or blown up by mines near their coasts.

Other neutral nations—Belgium, Switzerland, and the Netherlands—took protective measures consistent with the maintenance of neutrality.

The first week of war brought an unexpected wave of prosperity to Civil War-enfeebled Spain where the press, though giving prominent display to news of German victories, was prohibited from any expression of favoritism and the populace in general was not excited. A golden harvest came from thousands of foreigners who streamed from France exchanging millions of francs, pounds, and dollars for Spanish money, thereby strengthening Spanish finances. Many of these had moved into France during the Spanish Civil War and now were able to return because of reopening of the French-Spanish frontier.

Nearby Portugal found little to remind her that war had been in progress a week. The government, after formally proclaiming neutrality on September 2, issued decrees assuming extraordinary powers to regulate imports, exports, supervise food prices, and penalize hoarding. But use of the powers had not been needed yet. Like Spain, Portugal was reaping a refugee harvest of North and South Americans coming from other parts of Europe.

The warfare at sea was closest to Portugal. Accounts of the torpedoing of the British freighters *Bosnia* and *Manaar* in the Atlantic were brought to Lisbon and other harbors by survivors.

As for the activities of the belligerents themselves, the news available to the world was one-sided. Poland had wasted little time on issuing communiqués while invading armies thundered across her frontiers. Her allies, France and England, described their activities in the most terse, laconic fashion.

Only Germany was voluble and the output of her information machine had been huge. Germany was predicting at the end of the first week of her "lightning war" that the Polish campaign would be over a week hence with the destruction of the Polish Army.

4

As FAR as activities along the Western Front were concerned, there seemed little disposition by either Nazi or French forces to start active warfare. The French Maginot Line and the German

Siegfried were manned, with reinforcements coming up. The Nazis wanted to create the impression among the French that their only desire for conquest lay in the direction of Poland. France, on the other hand, was awaiting equipment.

Louis Lochner went up to the Western Front and reported how things were going there:

This afternoon I stood only twenty-five yards away from a French bunker, yet no French soldier made the slightest move to shoot at me. What is more, no French soldier shot at the generals with broad red coat lapels and red trouser stripes standing next to me.

The Rhine river separated us as I, standing next to a German bunker, calmly observed life on the French side.

A few hours later I stood beside a cannon of "greatest caliber" which, I was told, can fire at an object farther than anything hitherto known to artillery. But again I was assured, as so often in the past three days during this tour of German Siegfried fortifications, that the giant would be put into action only in case the French or English bombarded German towns.

Standing on the right bank of the upper Rhine, I saw one French soldier leisurely fishing, another riding away from his bunker on a bicycle to some point farther inland. Two other poilus were stretching themselves out lazily in the warm autumnal sunshine. They and other men on duty certainly must have seen the general, his adjutant, several colonels, lieutenant colonels, captains, and lieutenants who were guiding our party of six journalists. Yet they made no attempt to shoot. In fact, the general said on the previous day he stood atop his bunker in full uniform and for five minutes watched the enemy across the river with field glasses, but nothing happened.

Two German soldiers told me one of their comrades had received a ham from home and that he waved it at the French. They said the poilus called out: "Wish we had something like that."

The soldiers said the French then knocked some pears and apples off trees on their side and gestured that they were willing to swap some fruit for a piece of the ham. Sometimes, these German soldiers said, the Frenchmen gave the Hitler salute in fun, at other times clenched their fists in the Communist greeting. One stock phrase of theirs is "Nix la guerre" (no war) and another is "Nous voulons la paix" (we want peace).

On the river side of the French bunker opposite us I read in big white letters in German: "It is forbidden to paste advertisements here." Underneath was a cartoon of Hitler.

The German soldiers said that one day the poilus called across to them: "Has your Hermann Goering become any thinner?"

Such is the war in this sector of the West Wall.

The commanding general told us the French had fired a few desultory shots from machine guns, but that the Germans under his command had not returned a single shot. No artillery has been used by either side in this Rhine sector. That the Germans have plenty of artillery available was shown us today. We inspected one artillery position after another beginning with "heavy guns," then increasing in size the farther we came away from the frontier until the climax was reached twenty miles from the border. There we saw gigantic cannon capable, we were told, of catapulting deadly loads for incredible distances.

Here along the Rhine one encounters bunkers every fifty feet. Also, we saw many devices in this section of the West Wall that we had not observed anywhere else. For instance, there are deep canals artificially constructed so as to drown any tank or armored car that might break through the Nazi obstructions and bunker turrets. At a certain point three-inch-wide steel contraptions, looking like the ribs of an ocean liner, had been planted into the scenery in such a way that tanks and armored cars must run into them and turn a complete somersault. They were hidden so that an approaching enemy could not notice them until it was too late.

The German Army considers the Rhine Valley to be the most important strategically of all sections of Germany. Hence the fortifications here not only stud the banks of the Rhine but extend far backward. There isn't a farm in the whole Rhine Valley that hasn't some hidden bunker, observation stand, or anti-aircraft stand.

5

THE "we won't shoot if you don't shoot" philosophy was not given a chance in Poland. The Nazis were redoubling all efforts in that direction.

Hitler's hordes were crushing everything in their path. As if that were not enough, on September 17—two days after Colonel Charles A. Lindbergh issued his first isolationist plea in a radio address at Washington—Soviet forces poured over the Polish frontier all the way from Latvia to Rumania. The two newly found "friends"—Germany and Russia—were trying to do the best for themselves. In the case of Germany, she was after her spoils. Russia was laying her defenses.

Lloyd Lehrbas, who had witnessed the September 1 bombing of Warsaw, had to move along with other newsmen as the siege of the Polish capital became more acute. He sought out other trouble spots in the rapidly spreading European infection—spots where the activities of Nazi fifth columnists were having their effect.

He hurried into Bucharest and was on hand for the first big break there on September 21. He got the story and sent it out of the country by five routes on the chance that at least by one of them it would reach the outside world. The story got through:

Premier Armand Calinescu, foe of Nazism, was shot and killed today by men officially identified as Hitlerite Iron Guardists. Troops were called up at once to prevent a coup.

The Rumanian premier was friendly to Great Britain and France, and only recently had outlawed the Iron Guardists because of their terrorizing fifth-columnist activities in Rumania.

He was driving in his car on Bucharest's main street, on his way to the Royal Palace, when he was shot. His car was suddenly blocked by three other machines which converged on that of the premier, while a peasant cart blocked the road ahead. One car drew alongside. Masked men jumped out and opened fire with submachine guns. Calinescu slumped in his seat. Bullets had riddled his chest and abdomen from side to side. The shots were fired at 2:16 P.M. (1:16 A.M., New York time.)

The premier's chauffeur was killed instantly. Calinescu was rushed to University Hospital, but died en route.

Eight of the alleged assassins and accomplices have been arrested. Two who were not arrested were said to have barricaded themselves in an unoccupied mansion in Boulevard Bratinau and then to have committed suicide.

Thirty cartridge shells were found around Calinescu's car, indicating that the slayers had fired wildly before hitting the premier. The police said that six shots were found in his body.

After the slaying the assassins sped by automobile to the Bucharest radio station. There they shot the doorman in the leg and rushed past him into the building, tossing explosive rockets.

They broke into the announcer's room and covered him with their revolvers while one man shouted into the microphone:

"Premier Armand Calinescu has been shot by a group of Iron Guardists."

The wounded doorman gave the alarm and the police and troops surrounded the building.

Later that day King Carol named a new government. Wholesale execution of Iron Guardists began. Lehrbas managed to get through the details the next day:

Thousands were reported executed today in Rumania as what amounts to a military dictatorship exacted a heavy blood price from the pro-Nazi Iron Guard for the assassination of Premier Calinescu.

Reliable sources said that members of the outlawed Iron Guard had been taken from concentration camps throughout the country and shot to avenge the killing of the implacable foe of the guard. These sources also said that some women had been put to death.

It was announced officially that forty-four Iron Guardists had been executed at the Merkurea-Ciuk concentration camp, while thirty-two were shot by firing squads at Prahova. Mass executions were continuing. Reliable sources said a minimum of three Iron Guard members were being taken from each of Rumania's seventy-two administrative districts for the firing squads.

The whirlwind cleanup of pro-Nazi elements was pushed also with widespread arrests by the new government. At the head of this government was General George Argesanu, a tough disciplinarian, 56 years old, and a friend of Calinescu. Observers expected General Argesanu to follow M. Calinescu's advocacy of closer Rumanian economic co-operation with Great Britain and France.

Rumanians watched the situation nervously as Germany, who wanted Rumanian oil, and Russia, who saw former Russian territory as a part of Rumania, sped their forces further into Poland north of Rumania. Hundreds of arrests were being made throughout Rumania and one question the raiders were seeking to answer was whether it was more than a coincidence that M. Calinescu was slain while German and Russian troops were moving in the north.

Blood-spattered bodies sprawled awkwardly in one of Bucharest's main streets provided grisly evidence of the government's vengeance for yesterday's assassination. Around the roped-off, oblong area, under a dreary sky, hawkers were selling cakes and beer and cold drinks to a wide-eyed stream of Rumanians come to see an object lesson in swift Balkan punishment. A banner near by carried the words: "Such will be the fate of all assassins and traitors to the country."

All the dead had the young faces and youthful figures of college students. Perhaps somewhere in the crowd stood some of their parents or other relatives—but no one attempted to claim his dead. Seven of the dead were allegedly members of the Iron Guard.

The bodies of two others who committed suicide when troops surrounded the house in which they had taken refuge, also were carted to the scene and dumped on the asphalt avenue.

The police took the accused at eleven o'clock last night to the spot where they were charged with ambushing and killing Calinescu.

The seven prisoners, terror shining from their eyes, were stood in a line near by. A small crowd gathered on the sidewalk. Clouds obscured the moon. Only flickering street lamps lighted the strange midnight scene.

Uniformed executioners walked behind each straining figure silhouetted in the fantastic light. Then, using the assassins' own revolvers, each executioner thrust his weapon behind a man's ear and pulled the trigger.

The police quickly roped off an oblong area enclosing the nine bodies, and a neatly lettered warning to others with possible anti-government ideas was hung near by.

An official bulletin gave the names of the dead as:

Caesar Popescu, law student; Ion Moldoveanu, Polytechnical Institute student; Ion Vasimiu, designer; George Parasjiescu, law student; Marin Stanciulescu, mechanic; Pragan Popescu, law student; Lazar Lurece, chauffeur; Isaia Ovidiu, photographer, and Ion Ionescu, law student.

All through the night men, women, and children came to the scene and today the stream of humanity continued. The authorities announced the bodies would remain in the street until midnight.

Meanwhile, the body of the slain premier was carried to the Atheneum, one of Bucharest's most imposing buildings, to lie in state in the great marble rotunda after a mourning procession through the city's streets. King Carol headed the government and military officials who accompanied Calinescu's widow and son to the Atheneum. The body, draped in a Rumanian flag, was placed on a raised dais in an open coffin. There was a single spray of red flowers.

In a trembling voice, King Carol read to the Crown Council a statement in which the assassinated premier begged his son to think of the "honorable name I inherited from my father" and asked that his body be carried "in a peasant cart drawn by six oxen" to a tomb beside his father at Arges.

Officials charged that the plot was headed by Domitro Dumitrescu, a lawyer, who succeeded Cornelius Zelea Codreanu as Iron Guard leader after Codreanu was killed last December 1 in an attempted break from Rumnik-Sarat prison.

The announcement said Dumitrescu took part in a terrorist plot last January to overthrow the Rumanian Government and kill Calinescu, then Minister of Interior, who was blamed by the Iron Guard for the death of Codreanu and thirteen of his followers. Among twelve members of the organization who were said to have committed suicide after being arrested in the January outbreak was Dumitrescu's brother. Dumitrescu escaped to Czecho-Slovakia, the announcement said, after hiding guns and ammunition in the homes of associates. It said he returned secretly from the Ukraine six weeks ago to organize friends in a secret Iron Guard assassination band which reclaimed the hidden arsenal.

Dumitrescu, the announcement said, carefully planned the killing of the premier and led the shooting himself.

Although a communiqué said "no foreign complications" had been found in the plot, Rumanians nervously watched the frontiers. Troops were held to barracks throughout the country and frontier guards were strengthened.

6

WITH the assassination of Calinescu, the Iron Guardists had come close to staging a coup that would have given the Nazis immediate access to Rumania. Hitler's technique was spreading.

While the world was reacting to the Rumanian crisis, Hitler and Stalin completed their Polish conquest. Hitler announced capitulation of the country. Melvin K. Whiteleather reached Warsaw by air on September 30, the first American correspondent to view the wrecked Polish capital:

Warsaw is in ruins.

There is scarcely an undamaged building in the center of the Polish capital. The former Saxon palace on spacious Pilsudski Square in the heart of the city, which housed the Polish Foreign Office, has been shelled and burned. Other buildings in the vicinity of the square suffered equally. The city's two largest hotels are located there.

I circled twice tonight in a Junkers plane over one of those hotels. Its roof was ripped open to the sky during the siege by German armies. It was a sad sight, first in the late afternoon and then at dusk as a red moon peered over the horizon casting a glow on the Vistula River.

At least a hundred fires were burning. The largest was along the coal yard on the railway line to Berlin. From the air it looked like a highly illuminated boulevard. Smaller fires could be seen burning in all quarters of the city. Most of the buildings already had been gutted and only smoke arose from them. The railway station in Praga, Warsaw's eastern section, was burning. But two iron bridges over the Vistula, connecting Praga with Warsaw proper were intact.

Bitter fighting took place in Praga before the capital was shelled heavily, and tonight it was a trench town. Trenches zigzagged along the streets and back yards. They even were dug in front of apartment house doors so that it was possible to step from the front door into a trench.

Praga's buildings had their sides blown out and their roofs caved in, but this destruction was a bagatelle compared with what I saw when I got across the Vistula and looked down on an entire city lying under the piles of bricks, plaster, and charred debris.

A long line of bedraggled Polish soldiers, unarmed, marched westward out of the city. They had stacked their guns. The first group of thousands of Polish soldiers, who held the city until it was battered to pieces and forced to surrender September 27, left last night. The last are due to depart tomorrow night. Outside the city they were met by Germans and taken prisoner. German troops were scheduled to occupy the city on Monday. So far no important body of Germans has entered the central part of Warsaw.

The streets were practically deserted. A few hundred people milled about Pilsudski Square and half a dozen automobiles were seen in various parts of the city.

On the same day that Whiteleather saw destroyed Warsaw from the cockpit of a bullet-pocked army plane, another correspondent was examining the effect of Hitler's Polish campaign from another viewpoint. With all the information before him, Edwin Shanke, in Berlin, looked beyond the obviously quick destruction of Poland for the secret underlying Nazi military strategy.

Germany's one-month campaign against Poland was a "blitzkrieg," or lightning war, in every sense of the word.

The swiftness of the German war machine indicated the campaign was planned in this manner to permit the country's full military strength to be concentrated quickly along the Western Front.

In a drive that started September 1, and this week marked the downfall of beleaguered Warsaw and Modlin Fortress, seventy German divisions thrust nine spearheads toward Warsaw. Poland's strong Corridor Army was nipped off and the valuable industrial region of Upper Silesia was taken with a minimum of damage. The air force and armored cars played two of the most important roles in the drive.

For the first time in war history, a German military writer pointed out, "We've experienced the use of modernized armored cars on a big scale in connection with the air force and likewise developed them in a mighty measure."

Military observers behind the German lines said the motorized units clicked to a surprising degree, especially in view of the poor Polish roads which many previously believed would be a tremendous hindrance. Armored car divisions proved to be the trail blazers, informants reported, making the task of the infantry much easier because of the rapidity and deadliness with which they engaged the enemy. Hitler, the self-styled "first soldier" of Nazi Germany, decided in favor of armored cars and tanks in place of the infantry and cavalry units when the time came to weigh their respective merits. The Poles, on the other hand, clung to the importance of infantrymen and cavalrymen in the field.

Lieutenant Colonel G. Soldan, a military writer, summarized the key role of the air force:

"The air force fulfilled surprisingly fast the preconditions for all modern battle successes afoot, namely, the control of the air. It successfully delayed movements of the enemy by direct attacks or by destruction of transportation facilities, bridges, and water supplies, and prevented intended retreats."

Germany's fast-moving motorized army made new assignments necessary for the air force, other than raids, observers pointed out. Due to the speed of the advance, it was necessary for transport planes to drop gasoline, munitions, and even foodstuffs to armored cars far ahead of the main body of infantry, because of the impossibility of keeping supplies moving speedily enough by land. Without the aid of planes the armored cars would not have had anywhere near the value they did have—in fact, they might have held up advances.

Motorization also made necessary a mobile General Command Headquarters so that officers could keep in closest contact and make swift decisions.

Germany's strategy had been prepared carefully since last spring by Colonel General Walther von Brauchitsch, commander in chief of the army, General Franz Halder, chief of the army general staff, and others in conferences in which Hitler participated.

In a nutshell this strategy, according to German explanations, proposed the vast encirclement of the Province of Posen, which projected deep into Germany. German Army Corps, to accomplish this, worked from Silesia, in the south, to Pomerania in the north. This pincer movement ended in a nine-day battle that started at Kutno and gradually moved eastward into a pocket formed by a bend in the Vistula River west of Warsaw, a natural obstacle. The backbone of the Polish army was trapped and surrendered.

Coupled with a second decisive battle farther south at Radom, this was regarded by military men as a coup de grâce. Thereafter, only mopping-up activity remained.

Entrusted with the broad execution of the operations were Colonel General Karl Rudolf Gerd von Rundstedt, 64-year-old officer from Hohenzollern days, in charge of the southern army groups, and Colonel General Fedor von Bock, 58, in command of the northern forces. Von Bock, like Von Rundstedt, learned army fundamentals in the days of the Kaiser and was in charge of troops which occupied Austria in 1938.

Playing an important part in destroying the main force of Poles in the Vistula bend were the armies of General Johannes Blaskowitz and General Walter von Reichenau, two of the youngest generals directing the campaign. Both split their armies into two spearheads. Blaskowitz struck from the vicinity of Breslau in a northeasterly direction toward Kutno. One part of Reichenau's army which moved into Poland from the Oppeln area south of Breslau headed on a line just south of Lodz toward Warsaw, while the other aimed directly for Radom.

From the north, meanwhile, an army under General Gunther von Kluge headed toward Graudenz, Kulm, and Thorn, crossing the Vistula and thus cutting off the Polish Corridor Army. This performed a vital job of protecting the left wing.

Three armies of General George von Kueckler's army pressed down from East Prussia directly toward Warsaw. An army under General Siegmund Wilhelm List took little part in this vast encirclement operation but instead struck eastward toward Lemberg and Lublin to the south. Military experts said success of the operation depended upon speed—quick successive battles and close pursuit of the retreating enemy. This prevented the Poles from digging in to make a stand. Mechanized equipment, especially armored cars and tanks, accomplished this "steadiness of attack."

There was debate in military circles, however, as to whether this strategy would work against France, for instance, because of the danger that the motorized arms would advance too far ahead of the main columns and be cut off.

The complete destruction of Warsaw came one year, to the day, after "Munich,"—one year from the day Hitler and Chamberlain had signed their joint statement "as earnest of the desires of our two peoples never to go to war with one another again."

Even before the mopping up of Poland began, Hitler's propagandists were letting it be known that now Herr Hitler again had everything he wanted. With Poland and Danzig prostrate and wrecked, he was ready for peace. The Reichstag was summoned. Hitler called for a conference with the Italians; bald, unsure Mussolini also wanted hostilities to end.

But Britain had other ideas. Britain said, now that she had to fight, she would fight to the end. Hitler and what he stood for had to be wiped out. First Lord of the Admiralty Winston Churchill said:

"The war will end only when we are convinced that Hitler has had enough."

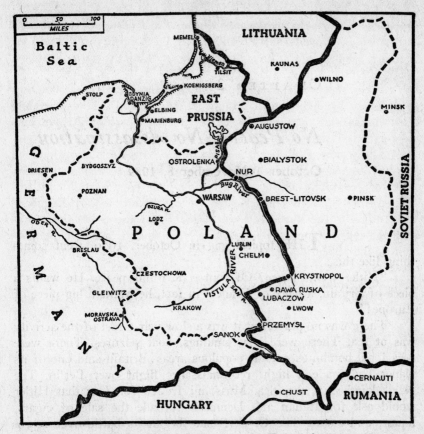

Map 3—Germany's one-month Polish blitz gave the Nazis and Russians a common frontier in another historic partition of Poland. The broken lines to the left and right of the new frontier (heavy line) show Poland's former boundaries. The Corridor, which had so irked Germany, was no more.

CHAPTER 3

No Peace—No Assassination

October 1–November 8, 1939

I

THE topical gag in October, 1939, went something like this:

"Hitler wants peace? Of course he wants peace. He wants a
piece of Britain, a piece of France; in fact, he wants a big piece of
Europe!"

There was no peace, but it was a slow war. Most of the activity
was at sea. There were boat sinkings, boat seizures. There were
occasional bombings outside populous areas. Britain said one of its
planes had made a night reconnaissance flight over Berlin. The
Nazis laughed at the idea. Mussolini fretted for fear that Hitler
would ask for Italian aid. Denmark forbade the sale of cigars,
liquor, and sugar. The U. S. Senate began its battle over repeal
of the Neutrality Act. The propaganda war continued. In London
the title of the newest song was: "We'll Hang Out the Washing
on the Siegfried Line."

Talk continued about hostilities on the Western Front, though
it was hardly an "all out" battle. In September, Louis Lochner had
told of conditions as viewed from the German side. French censorship later permitted a report from the Allied side, and on October
3, Henry C. Cassidy was one of a group of ten correspondents who
viewed the situation with the French Army:

It's a "white war" they are fighting on the Western Front.

It is a cautious campaign of men pressing steadily but carefully on their adversary. There are few wounded and fewer dead,
in striking contrast to the heavy losses of the World War. But advances into the Saar Basin vary from a few feet to several miles

and the French command considers them important both strategically and economically.

A month after the French and British declaration of war, I have just had a first-hand view of two typical operations of this warfare.

First, under artillery fire within 600 yards of the German lines, I saw French guns attack the heights two miles inside Germany controlling the road to Saarbruecken, twelve miles to the east. Columns of smoke attested to hits scored in the crest.

Again, driving a mile and a half through the Warndt Forest to the captured German town of Lauterbach, I met French troops who said they had just repulsed a German patrol.

Out of the forest on a cart came the bodies of two German soldiers as evidence of the local victory. That is the way the French are fighting the war, sparing men but using guns to clear out objectives, then holding the ground against local counterattacks.

The German reaction is slight. In reply to the French artillery attack that I saw, German guns tossed back only a few shells. The encounter lasted only a matter of minutes, with the Germans quickly withdrawing. The only fighting so far has been on German soil. German bombers have been attacking the French only as far as the border.

But the French make plain that this is a real war. The general impression from seeing them in action is that they mean to carry on the war along this line unless and until the time when the Germans may take the initiative.

The most imposing sight of all was the Maginot Line pivot from which the French are sending out attacks and maintaining defensive bases. Down a ramp, 150 feet into the earth, I walked into one of the fortresses of the line, a self-sufficient citadel with stocks to hold out for three months if necessary. Life looked comfortable there. At the heart of a maze of galleries was an electric power plant with four Diesel motors. Near it was an electrically equipped kitchen with three great stoves cooking beef stew for the troops. In the sleeping quarters, like crew quarters on a warship, the men sleep in double-deck steel bunks. They sleep in shifts.

But after seeing the subterranean works and emerging into the daylight, I could see the top of the great artillery tower at the back, with gaping casemates below it dominating the approach up the sloping hill. In the distance, knobs of adjoining fortresses could be seen.

The countryside back of the front is deserted. At a crossroads near one fort, I found a steaming lunch in the officers' mess. I picked a rose from a garden above the Maginot Line. Fields where crops have been harvested are empty. On the roads there is no evidence of troop movements. The people have moved out of the villages.

The region behind the front is organized in broad strips with troop concentrations far in the rear. Then comes a vacant area across the Maginot Line to the army which is holding the main front. Airplanes, too, are held far in the rear.

That is a lesson learned from the German campaign in Poland where advanced airbases were destroyed. I saw one mechanized division encamped in reserve but ready to reach the front in less than a day.

Even the front itself, at first glance, has the same deserted appearance as the rear. Only on close inspection do you see that the houses or border villages are crammed with men and the barns filled with both vehicles and horses, which in spite of their eclipse by mechanized cavalry are used extensively for transport.

On the actual front, the woods teem with young men living much like American youths in summer camps. Behind them are artillery batteries. Ahead of them are the advance patrols watching lest the Germans in the woods opposite try a raid.

In the Warndt Forest, I visited the French lines inside Germany within sight of a wooded ridge ahead held by the Germans. It was near there that the German patrol had just been repulsed. The previous day a German force withdrawing from a French patrol was reported by the men to have stumbled on one of their own mines, killing five or six German soldiers.

2

ON THE same day that Cassidy was reporting apathy on the Western Front there were intimations of real action out of Moscow. A corrrespondent there saw in a statement by a government newspaper the hint that Russia's next move might be toward Finland, Lithuania, and Latvia.

The Finnish-owned Aland Islands commanded the entrances of the Gulf of Bothnia and the Gulf of Finland into the Baltic, and Russia did not want to run the risk of having her Navy bottled up through lack of control of such a strategic area.

Almost simultaneously German minority groups in Rumania began to complain about their treatment at the hands of King Carol's new government—reminiscent of the work of Nazi fifth columnists in Danzig and other areas.

Hitler sent 10,000 mouth organs to his soldiers at the front. Lady Astor was discovered carrying around "doodads" in her gasmask container. Hoarders in Russia were jailed for concealing food. Bicycles replaced automobiles in Italy. A Rome club limited members to three drinks of gin, whisky, or sherry. A furniture store fire in Belgrave Square spoiled one of London's nighty blackouts. A submarine was reported off Maine. China and Japan continued their long-lasting war.

A Nazi sign on the Rhine asked the French not to fire on "your German friends." The Finns continued preparations for the 1940 Olympic Games. Britain announced she had sent 158,000 troops to France. A bronze statue of Eros, God of Love, was stored for safety in London.

On October 12, Chamberlain told the House of Commons, with finality, that the Allies could not accept Hitler's terms—recognition of the demise of Poland as a nation and a guarantee that Germany could have, unmolested, its Lebensraum in eastern Europe.

Through American correspondents in Berlin, Hitler called on Roosevelt to intervene. There was no acceptance. The Nazi chieftain announced that his war against the Allies would begin in earnest.

Two days later—on October 14—there was news out of London:

Sinking of the *Royal Oak,* one of Great Britain's twelve battleships, was announced today to a nation steeled for a German war in earnest. The sinking occurred at Scapa Flow.

It was the second major German stroke of the war against British sea power. Earlier, the Admiralty had acknowledged sinking of the aircraft carrier *Courageous* on September 17.

In disclosing the sinking of the *Royal Oak,* the Admiralty said only that "it was believed she was the victim of U-boat action."

Later in the afternoon the Admiralty said the *Royal Oak's* complement approximated 1,200 officers and men and, as far as then was known, only 396 had been saved, among them Captain W. G. Benn.

Germany also claimed the sinking of the aircraft carrier *Ark Royal,* but the American naval attaché in London reported he had visited the *Ark Royal* and found her unharmed.

The Admiralty said German reports that 86,000 tons of British warships had been sunk were incorrect. It reiterated that there was "no truth" in Nazi assertions that the battle cruiser *Hood* had been put out of commission through German-inflicted damages.

The war was on in earnest. Hitler established his Western Front headquarters at Aachen. Word went the rounds that the Nazis had developed a new torpedo that would penetrate heavy steel plates. Finland, desperate to maintain its boundaries, broke off its parley with Russia. A German-Bulgarian trade agreement was announced. Removal began of all Poles and Jews in the German-conquered territory of Poland; homeless wanderers began their sad trek. The U. S. announced its exports in the first month of the war were the biggest in eight months. The British had lost thirty-five ships, the French three, and Germany nine.

Then, on October 16, Nazi bombers which to date had been concentrating on populations—civilian and otherwise—went after the British Navy. (The *Royal Oak* had been a U-boat victim.) The story came out of London:

Scoring the first admitted bomb hit on a British warship since the war began, German bombers today damaged the cruiser *Southampton* in a spectacular attack on the vital Edinburgh and Firth of Forth area of Scotland.

The British Admiralty's first communiqué said the bombers caused thirty-five casualties on the *Southampton,* the cruiser *Edinburgh,* and the destroyer *Mohawk.*

A joint communiqué by the Air Ministry and the Admiralty said at least four of the twelve or fourteen Nazi raiders were downed by Royal Air Force fighters and anti-aircraft batteries during a fierce battle.

The first German air raiders to reach Britain, the bombers struck in dive attacks in the face of heavy fire from ship and shore batteries.

The official announcement of the attack—issued some eight hours after the fight—said the *Southampton,* which escorted King

George and Queen Elizabeth to Canada last summer, was struck a glancing blow by a bomb. Bomb splinters caused three casualties aboard the *Southampton,* seven on the 10,000-ton *Edinburgh,* and twenty-five on the 1,870-ton *Mohawk.*

Throughout the raid, trains continued to cross the high bridge between Rosyth and the south bank of the Firth, giving passengers a chilling close-up of bombs exploding huge waterspouts in the water 450 feet below.

The communiqué said the three ships were ready for the sea in spite of the raid. Terse details told of the fierceness of the air battle.

The first contact between British and German planes was off May Island at the entrance to the Firth of Forth. Two enemy planes were intercepted and driven out to sea. A few minutes later four other German planes were finished off. A member of a crew of a Scotch fishing boat told what happened to one of them:

"About three o'clock we were returning home when we saw a large black airplane traveling at high speed," he said. "It was being pursued by two British fighters and they made rings around it. They dived underneath it and then circled up again firing into the tail of the German machine which swept around in a circle, suddenly heeled over, and flopped into the sea.

"We threw ropes to the flyers clinging to a lifebuoy and when we hauled them aboard we discovered that they were all wounded. They told us another member of the crew had gone down with the plane. They were all young chaps."

3

Nazi sentiment was: "England, you asked for it and now you've got it." Germany and Estonia signed an agreement for repatriation of German minorities. Turkey made feverish military preparations after reports that the Soviet was massing troops in the Caucasus. A trade agreement between Lithuania and Russia was signed. Hitler offered "evidence" that the Poles had used poisonous gas. The thrifty Scots collected dead fish in the wake of the Nazi bombing over the Firth of Forth. French children returned to school, carrying gas masks with their books. The Germans needed 1,000,000 panes of glass to help rebuild Warsaw.

Hitler's land army on the Western Front also went into action on October 16. Stocky, clean-shaven Taylor Henry reported from Paris:

Waves of Nazi troops in field gray today launched a long-awaited attack against French positions on the northern flank of the Western Front, drove the French out of German territory at one point and although thrown back, still held a precarious foothold on French soil for the first time since the war began.

A French communiqué acknowledged that the Germans fought their way into the French village of Apach before they were thrown back by a counterattack. The fighting lasted all day and as night fell the Germans apparently still were holding the heights of Schneeberg north of Apach on western slopes that reach into France. Although the German attack covered a front of four miles, the main force of the blow was delivered at the junction of the French-German-Luxembourg frontiers on the extreme northern flank of the Western Front.

Here the French established positions during the first month of the war to prevent the Germans from driving through neutral Luxembourg territory to outflank the whole French front.

Since the French had been holding advance positions some two miles inside German territory at this point, it appeared that the attack obviously had driven the French back that distance.

The first real shock of the attack hit the French on the Schneeberg heights, which form a bastion east of Apach. Thin lines of French observation posts, guarded by land mines, were penetrated by the Germans. Before the French were able to reorganize their defenses, Nazi troops swept into French territory and occupied the first houses of Apach. Immediately, however, French artillery found the range of the advancing Germans and forced them to halt on the outskirts of the little Lorraine village.

The French reformed their lines and drove the Germans back to a position 400 yards north of Apach, which left the Nazis holding a line 100 yards inside French territory.

Today's fighting undoubtedly was the heaviest on the Western Front although no figures were available immediately on the number of men involved or the number of casualties.

And while the German forces on land, sea, and in the air were attacking Allied fronts, on October 18 Britain issued a statement over which appeared this headline: BEHIND THE WAR—A WEDDING:

A government "White Paper" hinted today that the marriage of Germany's then War Minister, Marshal Werner von Blomberg, to his stenographer on January 12, 1938, started a chain of events that precipitated the present war.

Sir Neville Henderson, in another account of his ambassadorship in Berlin, told Foreign Secretary Lord Halifax:

"In my report on the events of 1938, I drew your Lordship's attention to the far-reaching and unfortunate results of the Blomberg marriage. I am more than ever convinced of the major disaster which that minor incident in itself involved, owing to the consequent elimination from Herr Hitler's entourage of the more moderate of his advisers, such as Field Marshall von Blomberg himself, Baron von Neurath, Generals Fritsch, Beck, and others."

Von Blomberg's marriage to Erika Gruhn, a carpenter's daughter, was witnessed by both Hitler and Colonel General Hermann Wilhelm Goering.

Colonel General Werner von Fritsch, then commander in chief of the Reichswehr, was said to have acted as the spokesman for the Officers' Corps in protesting to Hitler that the marriage was socially "impossible."

The result was that Hitler assumed personal command of the armed forces and ousted von Blomberg, von Fritsch, and thirteen other high-ranking officers in a general shake-up of the socially conscious corps.

Von Fritsch was killed September 23 in the siege of Warsaw, a siege which Sir Neville now intimates might never have occurred had it not been for the von Blomberg affairs.

General Ludwig Beck resigned last October because he refused to see eye to eye with Hitler, it was reported, on the Austrian and Czecho-Slovakian occupations.

Baron Konstantin von Neurath lost control of the German foreign policy at the time of the general army reorganization and eventually was relegated to the position of "protector" of Bohemia and Moravia, in former Czecho-Slovakia.

Sir Neville's report added that, after the von Blomberg denouncement of February of last year, "Herr Hitler became more and more shut off from external influences and a law unto himself."

Hitler decided upon war without consulting any advisers, Sir Neville said, observing, "the tragedy of any dictator is that as he goes on, his entourage steadily and inexorably deteriorates. For lack of freedom of utterance he loses his services of the best men.

All opposition becomes intolerable to him. All those, therefore, bold enough to express opinions contrary to his views are shed one by one, and he is, in the end, surrounded by mere yes men. . . ."

4

LINDBERGH had just made his second isolationist speech. He suggested that Britain should not use her influence in Canada to draw the Western Hemisphere into war. U. S. Senator Rush Holt charged that Roosevelt promised aid to Britain and France long before war was declared. U. S. Senator Johnson declared it was idiotic to believe Hitler would conquer Europe and then threaten this country.

Germans generally were not getting all the food to which they had been accustomed. A new wrinkle in rationing was announced in Berlin. Owners who could not grow their own produce were required to have food cards for horses, cows, and pigs. On a muddy plain behind the Maginot Line, R.A.F. pilots relaxed by playing football. British and French troops were "holing in" for the winter. A Swiss army sergeant used carrier pigeons to send a wedding announcement.

On October 23, the Nazis seized the American steamer *City of Flint* as contraband. The U. S. was indignant. Earl Browder, secretary of the Communist party in the United States, was indicted on charges of using fraudulent passports.

For weeks the air in Washington had been thick with debate on the prime controversial subject of the times—repeal of the United States Arms Embargo. But all debate came to an end on November 4:

With members of the House and Senate participating in the ceremony, President Roosevelt today signed the administration's act repealing the U. S. Embargo and substituting a system of "cash and carry" sales to belligerent governments of Europe.

The legislation, described as the product of six weeks' fighting "to determine the best method to keep America free of war," was passed by both houses at the conclusion of a tense special session of the Congress.

Acting under the broad powers extended him, the President immediately issued an order forbidding vessels of this country to traverse a broad "combat zone" in which there appears to be danger from German submarines or British warships.

The new law, strictly regulating all dealing with belligerents in a series of safeguards against war unprecedented in the nation's history, was signed at a formal ceremony in the President's office. Stephen Early, White House press secretary, stood at the open door and waved to newspaper men in the lobby when the President affixed his signature shortly after noon.

Signing of the bill gave a signal which some government officials expected to result in the placing of $1,000,000,000 worth of war orders in this country—mostly by France and Great Britain—within the next few weeks. It was expected that Allied Powers would begin moving across the Atlantic almost immediately some 300 airplanes completed for them by American companies since the embargo went into effect soon after the war began.

Anticipating a flood of war orders, the Army and Navy, it was disclosed today, have liberalized their rules for sale of military planes and engines abroad. At the same time measures have been taken to clear all orders through a new priority committee to prevent the British, French, and other orders from interfering with American defense preparations.

The President used two pens in signing the historic document. He gave one to Senator Pittman of Nevada, chairman of the Senate Foreign Relations Committee, and the other to Representative Bloom of New York, chairman of the House Foreign Affairs Committee, who steered the legislation to passage at a special session which ended early last night.

There was much laughter during the ceremony, the President's laugh especially being heard in the lobby of the executive offices.

The ceremony marked the end of a long fight by the President, Secretary Hull, and other administration leaders to revise the nation's neutrality statute. Particularly had they sought repeal of the Arms Embargo which worked to the disadvantage of Great Britain and France in their war with Germany.

They had failed to put through their program in the regular session early this year, but the outbreak of war in Europe in September soon brought congressmen hustling back to the capital to take up the fight where it had left off when the regular session ended. It took Congress from September 21 until last night to complete the task.

In addition to lifting the embargo against exporting arms, ammunition, and implements of war to belligerents, the bill requires that shipments of arms and other materials to warring governments in Europe be paid for in cash and transported in foreign ships. Title will have to pass to the purchaser before such goods may leave American ports.

5

ALTHOUGH the Arms Embargo was repealed, a "moral embargo" remained in effect against Japan. France announced it would pay its front-line soldiers 23 cents per day. Stalin personally began to participate in the Russo-Finnish territorial controversy. Il Duce finally said that Italy was arming "for tomorrow." Ship sinkings reached a tonnage of 451,492, with 1,868 persons lost at sea. Actor Leslie Howard's jaw was fractured during a London blackout.

Came November 7—twenty-first anniversary of the first World War's false armistice. Nazi anti-aircraft guns at Hamburg shot down one of the Nazi's own planes—auspicious prelude to what happened that night. Hitler was making another speech.

It was the sixteenth anniversary of the Austrian paperhanger's unsuccessful 1923 Munich beer hall putsch. The celebration was held in historic Buergerbrau Hall—Nazi shrine. All the Nazi bigwigs were there. The beer flowed freely. Correspondent Alvin J. Steinkopf got the news:

Adolf Hitler envisaged tonight the possibility of a five-year war and declared that Germany was prepared for it. In a fifty-eight-minute speech Der Fuehrer gave as Germany's war aims security for her people and freedom to administer her spheres of influence. Only one nation can win this war, he said—Germany.

"I am told England is getting ready for a three-year war," he said. "I gave Field Marshal Goering the order to get ready for a five-year war, not because I believe it will last that long, but so we are prepared never to capitulate. The time of police dictatorship by one nation is over. The present war broke out only because England wanted it. If they say they didn't want war and they must make war to end war—why did they start this war? There will be wars so long as good things of the earth are not distributed equitably and voluntarily."

Hitler said that it was not necessary for other European nations "to share anything with us. It would have been enough to restore to us what we had been robbed of. We, too, believe the war will—must—come to an end, but each nation must limit itself to its own spheres of influence."

Hitler said the war of 1914-1918 was not won by England.

"It was won by others," he said. "The second World War—this I can solemnly assure you (here he pounded the table in front of him and was rewarded with a long demonstration)—they also will not win.

"This time England finds a different Germany opposing it. Our enemies will soon realize it. We will talk to the English in the language they surely understand. We are only sorry that France has linked her fate with Britain.

"I consider the understanding with Russia as a triumph of common sense. We have agreed not to do the favor the second time to the gentlemen of London and Paris of fighting against each other.

"So we are at the historic crossing of the roads. Germany has changed completely. Germany of 1939, 1940, 1941, and possibly 1942 isn't the same as in 1914. Today we Nazis have the power in our hands. This war will be easier than that of 1914. We are prepared economically this time. We have developed all our possibilities and resources. Neither militarily nor economically can we be defeated. Only one can be the victor and that is ourselves."

The harangue finally ended. There was "heiling" all over the hall. Hitler and his "rubber stamps" quickly left. It had been a good party. It had lasted into the early morning of November 8. And then came modern history's greatest anticlimax:

Adolf Hitler escaped possible death or injury by a few minutes today in an explosion that wrecked the famous Buergerbrau beer cellar, in Munich, after he had completed a fighting war speech.

The terrific blast brought down the ceiling of the spacious room, killing six and injuring more than sixty among the old Nazi leaders who had come together to celebrate the famous putsch in 1923 that failed.

Hitler himself, the cheers of his comrades still ringing in his ears, was safe on an armored train speeding toward Berlin at the time. The men killed were veterans of Hitler's party, who now are the aristocracy of the Nazi movement. But it was stated by authorities that none of the distinguished leaders of Nazidom was among the dead or injured.

Paul Joseph Goebbels, Propaganda Minister; Rudolph Hess, deputy party leader; Wilhelm Frick, Minister of the Interior; Julius Streicher, Robert Ley, and Sister Pia—the only woman who was among Hitler's old battlers—had attended the party's anniversary celebration. But all either had left with Hitler or departed shortly after he had stepped into his car at the conclusion of his address.

Authorities said there were clues that the blast had been arranged by "foreign agents." No reason for the suspicion that foreign agents were responsible was given, but the government at once offered a 500,000-mark (about $240,000) reward for the persons responsible—one of the largest rewards in European history.

The Associated Press was told that a "terrific charge" of some explosive had been set off either in an upper room or under the floor of the upper room. There were screams and the air was filled with dust and an acrid smell. Bodies lay under the debris and there was a great struggle as the injured strove to get free and the uninjured tried to find a way out. A great force of police immediately closed in and the region was blocked to traffic.

There was no official indication of the nature of the explosive used, nor would anyone say how such an enemy could have penetrated into the building which is the Nazi holy of holies and which is guarded by the most trusted Nazi lieutenants.

The security measures taken at once extended over the nation. The railway line over which Hitler was traveling toward Berlin was guarded every yard of the way. It also was stated that the Fuehrer slept tonight in one of the safest trains it is possible for human ingenuity to construct.

Queen Wilhelmina congratulated Hitler on his escape. Mussolini felicitated Der Fuehrer. Russia—the same. Roosevelt withheld the glad hand.

CHAPTER 4

From Finland to Montevideo

November 8–December 31, 1939

I

GERMAN aircraft made two attacks on the Shetland Islands. Air raid sirens in Paris sent the population scurrying to cover. Stricter rationing of clothes began in Germany. The British King and Queen braved a blackout to attend a movie. A British destroyer was sunk by a mine. A Norwegian tanker was torpedoed. Ten per cent of Finland's population was mobilized. Fritz Thyssen, former Hitler backer, left the Reich for an "indefinite stay."

A cat invaded a Buenos Aires police station and attacked a police dog. Mrs. Robey Harris, in Franklin, Ky., gave birth to the first girl child in the Harris family in seventy-six years.

Martial law was established in Prague after the execution of anti-Nazi student demonstrators and Nazi jailing of 1,200 others. Al Capone, one-time Chicago gangster, was released from prison. Hitler claimed control of the air. Thirteen of the Hohenzollern family were in the Nazi Army. President Roosevelt announced plans for cutting the 1940 deficit in half. American planes were delivered to the British at the Canadian border and towed across by rope. Four Spanish bullfighters balked at sailing for Venezuela, fearing magnetic mines more than bulls.

The varied activities of the Nazis—the blockading maneuvers of the Allies—often monotonous and without real action, inevitably focused attention in another direction.

Weeks previously, a correspondent in Moscow had seen in Russian actions a hint that Finland was the Soviet's next objective. Whether Stalin had taken his clue from Nazi strategy, or whether he simply was taking advantage of the European upheaval to regain lost territory, was beside the point. Russia wanted a part of Finland. She set out to get it.

On November 30, 1939, Russia formally severed relations with Finland. She charged Finnish troops had crossed to Russian soil. Finland denied it. Russia went into action.

First positive word of blitzkrieg came from Helsinki, the Finnish capital. Lynn Heinzerling, stationed there, did his best to get the story out via telephone to Copenhagen. It was sketchy, scarcely understandable. But it was recorded and relayed to the outside world just as it was heard in the Danish capital. Due to the conditions under which it was telephoned and received, it was an excellent description of the danger Heinzerling was undergoing:

Unexpected Soviet planes droned a warning of death in the skies above Helsinki early this afternoon—

[Here the telephone connection to Copenhagen was suddenly broken. It was restored in a few minutes, and Heinzerling was still dictating.]

The American legation has arranged for headquarters at Grankulla, but has not yet decided to evacuate—

[The communication again was interrupted by the crash of a bomb. "People outside are running for cover," Heinzerling said. "An air raid warning has not yet sounded, and they were caught unawares."]

Soberly thoughtful as his office received reports of Russian battling from various points, the Finnish Foreign Minister, Eljas Erkko, made the following statement to The Associated Press:

"Despite the fact that we have shown to the last a willingness to try to find a peaceful solution of the difficulties that have arisen between Finland and Russia in the face of the Soviet demands, and despite the fact we have tried all means possible to avoid any conflict on the frontier, we have been attacked today.

"As a reason for the attack, the pretext was used that we invaded Russian territory and our troops threatened Leningrad. We haven't done anything of the kind—"

[The sirens of passing ambulances drowned the conversation here, and then there was a crash as another bomb fell near by.]

"Our troops were on border duty only for possible attack against Russia and what happened today showed we have done right. Our frontier has been bombarded and Finnish territory occupied. Our capital has been twice attacked, Viborg has been attacked even more severely, and the Ensoe Hospital has been destroyed."

[Here Heinzerling interjected: "There's a big cloud of smoke outside." Then he continued with Erkko's statement]:

"We think this is the purest aggression imaginable. We believed in the nonaggression pact which was to have been in force without the right of unilateral denunciation until 1945, and we think it is still in force.

"Although the Russians denounced it, they had no right to do so, because, first, according to the treaty, conciliation should—"

[The telephone connection was broken again, this time because the time limit was up. Hours later a new call came through and Heinzerling continued with Erkko's statement]:

"I think we have shown great self-control since, from the beginning of the negotiations, Russian planes have flown over Finnish territory daily. Some days groups of from six to nine flew over the frontier, in some cases deep into the country. We have no other way than to try to defend ourselves with all the means at our disposal, but nevertheless if there is a chance of coming to an honest agreement, we are always ready to grasp it.

"I would like to send my good wishes to the people of the United States and thank them for the great sympathy they have shown in our difficult days, which has been a great consolation."

Other small countries reacted to the Russian invasion of little Finland, known over the world as one of the really happy, successful European nations in which democracy worked. Wade Werner, in Copenhagen, used all available methods of communication to obtain reaction from colleagues in other capitals:

Sweden, Norway, and Denmark tonight watched with foreboding Soviet Russia's vast war machine bring death and destruction to Finland. All three countries were profoundly shocked by the invasion.

The Scandinavian governments earnestly checked the dryness of their powder—but carefully avoided any official comment. Feelings of the public, however, were plain. Men and women crowded about Swedish newspaper offices expressing grief and indignation. Women cried when they read that Helsinki had been bombed. Typical of the outbursts of feeling was that of an unidentified Swede who jumped up during a lunch and shouted:

"It's horrible. All Europe will be drawn in before this is over."

Government officials conferred in Stockholm, Oslo, and Copenhagen. A Foreign Office spokesman in Sweden said his country was in a state of preparedness and no new measures were needed.

Many Danes felt the invasion was a personal blow because Finland was a neighbor and new dangers seemed looming for the Baltic neutrals.

Adding to Norway's fears was the extension of Russian aerial warfare along Finland's short Arctic coast to the Norwegian border.

Roosevelt denounced the Soviet invasion. The *Daily Worker* in New York maintained Russia was fighting for peace. Thomas E. Dewey opened his campaign for the U. S. presidency. Beefsteak and pork chops smugglers were operating along the Hungarian-German border. British fliers bombed Nazi warships at Helgoland. Russian parachute troops tried a large-scale landing at Vilmannstrand. Finland, staging a remarkable defense, said it was ready "to fulfill its duty unto death." Snow began to fall around Helsinki. Finland's bitter winter began to set in.

2

By December, 1939, Britain was tightening her blockade. Hostilities penetrated the 300-mile "safety belt" drawn about themselves by nations of the Western Hemisphere.

A Nazi freighter slipped into a Brazilian port early in the month. She wanted to buy British fuel, undercover. It was refused. Then before she lifted anchor, the situation changed. The freighter could have the fuel.

What the Nazis did not know was that the British had sanctioned the sale. That was something that did not become known until later. The fuel-laden freighter slipped away. The British had suspected and abetted her mission—which was to refuel Nazi sea raiders at sea.

December 13 . . . the South Atlantic rolled lazily in the early morning. War seemed far away. . . .

Then, over the horizon, a graceful craft took shape. She sliced along in the water like a giant knife. Her coloring was somber; her ease and grace spoke power. She was as long as three city blocks and as wide as a four-lane highway. She wore a complete belt of armor and she had two protective decks. Her hull was electrically welded.

Among other armament, she mounted six 11-inch guns and eight 6-inch rifles. She carried eight 19.7-inch torpedo tubes. Her powerful Diesels drove her along with almost express train speed. She could cruise at 26 knots. They said she could outrun anything she couldn't outshoot.

She was the dreaded *Admiral Graf Spee,* third and last of Germany's 10,000-ton "pocket battleships." She was vicious by reputation, hell in battle. She had sent at least nine craft to the bottom. The British had been looking for her for two months. She was cruising the South Atlantic looking for prey.

Three other craft loomed ahead. They, too, were somber in color.

There is little record as yet of what immediately happened. But there was a battle—the first really dramatic sea fight of World War II. Harold Milks, Indiana-born correspondent, got the details at Montevideo, Uruguay, a few hours later:

A fourteen-hour running sea fight between three British cruisers and the German pocket battleship *Admiral Graf Spee* ended tonight with the badly hit Nazi warship taking refuge in neutral Montevideo harbor with thirty or more of her crew killed and sixty wounded.

The British victory was not without its casualties, however, for the British admitted that one of their three cruisers, the fast 8,390-ton *Exeter,* had been put out of action after four hours of the fight.

But the other two, the 7,030-ton *Achilles* and the 6,985-ton *Ajax,* trailed the *Admiral Graf Spee* to her refuge and took up positions just outside the harbor.

The battle was fought within the Americas' neutrality belt, and much of it was within sight of the Uruguayan shore where the roar of the great guns was heard and the flashes of gunfire observed.

Uruguayan port authorities, nervous because their shore had been exposed all day to the booming 6- and 8-inch guns of the British men-of-war, and the 11-inch mouthpieces of the German, kept curious crowds at a distance as the battleship dropped anchor.

The battered warship, which had haunted South Atlantic shipping lanes since September when she sank the British merchantman *Clement,* ran afoul the *Ajax* just after dawn.

The *Graf Spee* rushed to the attack, but was momentarily repulsed by the 6-inch guns of the speedy *Ajax,* and then found herself engaged in an unequal combat with three British men-of-war instead of one. The *Exeter* and the *Achilles* came up foaming. The *Achilles'* 6-inch artillery and the *Exeter's* 8-inch guns spoke in volley after volley. The *Graf Spee* apparently found the *Exeter's* guns particularly damaging, for she turned her attention away from the rest of the pack and devoted her batteries exclusively to the *Exeter*. As a result, the *Exeter* was caused some distress, and was compelled to quit the battle.

Although the largest of the three British ships was thus forced out, the other two continued to concentrate their fire, and the German raider took to her heels.

Observers at Punta del Este lighthouse, on the Uruguayan coast, saw much of the engagement. They heard the thunderous roar of the big guns and saw the mountains of smoke that arose from the fray. Then, with the *Graf Spee's* guns still blazing, they saw her put on forced draft and flee in a southwesterly direction in search of a haven. The British pursued their prey until she brought up in Montevideo harbor.

Details of this first sea battle in the 300-mile "safety belt" that Western Hemisphere nations drew about themselves at their recent conference in Panama were radioed to shore stations by lighthouse officials at Punta del Este. South American listeners sat by their receiving sets and heard the running story.

Huge crowds along the Montevideo shore watched the German wounded brought ashore on stretchers to be taken to a military hospital.

For five days there was uncertainty as to what would become of the *Graf Spee* and surviving members of her crew. British cruisers kept a "death watch" outside the harbor. The crew of the *Graf Spee* buried thirty-six of their shipmates, killed in the battle. She hurried repairs and took on supplies from the German freighter *Tacoma,* also in the harbor. Then the Uruguayan government, on December 15, ordered the *Graf Spee* to evacuate by late the next Sunday afternoon or be interned for the duration of the war.

At 6 P.M. on Sunday, December 17, the bellicose Nazi raider weighed anchor and maneuvered uncertainly up the Rio de la Plata. Big crowds lined the shore. They almost held their breaths as the *Graf Spee* got under way. Outside, bulldogs of the British fleet waited. It looked as though the *Graf Spee* was going out to fight.

Milks, who had sent the first story on the sea battle five days before, had a "grandstand seat" for this most dramatic sea action to date. From the tower of Montevideo's tallest building, he watched the mighty Nazi raider as it ploughed seaward:

As the trim *Graf Spee* slipped between the arms of the breakwater and moved toward the open sea, there was no indication anywhere, from the snapping red Nazi flag at her staff to the curling water around her bow, that she was not headed out to challenge British sea might.

Through a telescope, her 11-inch cannon appeared powerful enough to blast a way through anything.

There had been three days of tense waiting for the *Graf Spee* to put to sea, and everyone in the observation tower expected nothing less than a sea battle.

As the *Graf Spee* slowed and finally stopped, and the rusty-hulled freighter *Tacoma* slipped out of the harbor and followed the warship's path, everyone agreed that the *Graf Spee* would take on fuel and then dash toward the sea, looking for a fight that would bring death, but also glory.

The tugboats that had been alongside the *Graf Spee* moved away. Suddenly, a plume of black smoke shot skyward amidships and a bright burst of flame was visible. Again there was a burst of smoke and flame, the sound of the first explosion rumbled like thunder and the concussion reached the tower.

Ten thousand tons of battleship steel and metal seemed to shake and list slightly. As the flames spread, the height of the black smoke increased and the *Graf Spee* settled. Within three minutes her hull was on the bottom, her superstructure still showing above the comparatively shallow water.

But it took much longer than three minutes for those of us who were watching to realize fully what had happened. The *Graf Spee* had been scuttled by its own master and crew to avoid certain death from the guns of outnumbering British fighters. It was an inglorious end to the ship that laid the keel of the battle prestige of the Third Reich's Navy.

From the high tower the scene appeared like a movie-set as flames gradually spread all over the ship above water, and the black plume of smoke became increasingly thick.

Official launches sped toward the burning battleship, but a series of fresh explosions kept the boats from approaching. As night fell, the fires appeared to spread to every part of the *Graf Spee* not already inundated.

Captain Hans Langsdorff and every member of the crew reached safety aboard other boats before the 10,000-ton war monster sank in twenty-five feet of water three miles from shore, within sight of the city.

The *Tacoma,* carrying two or three hundred members of the crew, anchored in Montevideo harbor later tonight. The remainder of the crew—about 700 men—were en route to Buenos Aires aboard tugs and launches and will surrender to the Argentine government.

Langsdorff, last to leave his ship, sent a bitter wireless message ashore from the bridge immediately before giving the order to abandon ship. He protested that Uruguay's refusal to let the *Graf Spee* remain in the harbor later than this evening "leaves me no alternative than to sink my ship near the coast and save my crew."

Authoritative German sources said Hitler himself had given the order to send the powerful German marauder to the bottom of the sea by Nazi hands, rather than have her interned or humiliated in defeat. She went to her end just as the sun dipped beneath the horizon.

3

The *Graf Spee* incident brought the European conflict closer to South America. Milks took time out a few days later to summarize the effects of the war in that part of the Western Hemisphere:

Major wars abroad mean headaches for South America's generals—and taxpayers.

The current European conflict is no exception. Already officials of the ABC nations (Argentina, Brazil, and Chile) are watching with some apprehension for wartime developments that may completely outmode their own armed forces.

Keeping pace with the world's Great Powers in the matter of national defense even in peacetime is a task that frequently strains both the ingenuity and finances of the South American republics. In times of war this task becomes harder and the generals and admirals of this continent can at best sit tight and attempt to read and understand reports of their military attachés abroad on the latest methods of armed conflict.

The start of the European war found Argentina, Brazil, and

Chile well along on a program of modernizing their armies and navies of standards built up by the Great Powers after the last World War.

Where the European fighting will leave them is a question on which South America's military leaders hazard not even a guess. None of the republics is in an economic position to attempt to keep pace with Germany, France, and Britain. How far behind the current march of armaments the European fracas leaves them will depend on the inventiveness of the Old World's warmakers.

Argentina, Number One military power in South America today, was rapidly whipping its national defense forces into what, according to continental standards, were models of efficiency, when the new war began. Its air force, trained by United States officers and equipped with up-to-date American and European warplanes, is learning fighting methods of fliers in the current war. On land, the Argentina Army has taken its first steps into motorization. On the sea, its Navy is eighth in the world, with the aid of U. S. instructors, trained in naval warfare.

Even the "keeping pace" in peacetime is costing Argentina's Army 112 billion pesos (about $30,000,000) this year. The Department of the Navy budgeted 1939 expenditures at seventy-six million pesos. Both budgets included heavy expenditures for aircraft and the Army's expenses listed the first purchases of anti-aircraft artillery.

Across the Andes, the Chilean popular front government, busy with social problems, has decreased rather than increased its defense expenses. The 1939 budget for the Army, Navy, and Air Forces totaled 389 million Chilean pesos (about $12,966,500) or 10 per cent lower than in previous years.

To the north, Brazil's military leaders look to the European war as a factor that may affect recent modernizations. Like her sister republics, Brazil has concentrated on building a modern air force. Recently her leaders invited bids on anti-aircraft equipment with a view to strengthening defense against bombing raids.

Two days after the *Graf Spee* destruction, the *Columbus*, pride of the German merchant marine, ploughed along 400 miles off Cape Henry, Virginia. She had slipped out of Vera Cruz, Mexico, in a desperate attempt to reach home port. But she failed. A British warship put into view. The crew of the *Columbus* saw her approaching and sent their ship to the bottom.

England's Navy was effective whenever it came out to fight.

CHAPTER 5

The Giant Chessboard

January 1–April 7, 1940

I

In 1938, Hitler had said all he wanted was the Sudetenland region of Czecho-Slovakia. Exactly one year later Hitler said all he wanted was Danzig and the Polish Corridor. On both occasions he got what he said he wanted. Ultimately, he also got a fight with Britain—and France.

Russia was comparatively quiet until Hitler set an example. Then Russia decided she wanted something from Poland, Estonia, Latvia, and Lithuania. She got what she wanted. A little later she also wanted something from Finland. She went after it and she also got a fight—a fight that surprised her.

While both Germany and Russia were prosecuting their fights, this obscure item appeared under the heading ANCIENT HISTORY on January 8, 1940:

Twenty-two years ago today, President Wilson stirred the world by offering a fourteen-point program to be used as a basis for settling World War I. Here they are, summarized:

1. Open covenants openly arrived at.
2. Absolute freedom of the seas, except where seas are closed to enforce international covenants.
3. Removal of trade barriers.
4. Guarantees that armaments be reduced to the lowest point consistent with domestic safety.
5. Impartial settlement of all colonial claims, with natives having an equal say with governments doing the claiming.
6. Evacuation of all Russian territory and noninterference with Red Russia's national policy.
7. Restoration to Belgium of its sovereignty.

60

8. Evacuation by Germans of all French territory and restoration to France of Alsace-Lorraine.

9. Reconstruction of Italy's frontiers to include Italians living in neighboring nations.

10. Guarantee of autonomous development to peoples of Austria-Hungary.

11. Evacuation of Rumania, Servia, and Montenegro and granting of guarantees to the Balkan states.

12. Guarantee of autonomous development for non-Turks in Turkey and opening the Dardanelles to all.

13. Erection of an independent Polish state.

14. Formation of a general association of nations to guarantee the integrity of great and small states alike.

These were the famous "Fourteen Points." History had been written about them—around them. Nations had split over them, even before the Treaty of Versailles which ended World War I. Very little of anything had ever been done about them—not even by the League of Nations. But now it was the beginning of 1940 and all of this really was "ancient history." The bigger nations of Europe were embroiled and, as was inevitable, the little countries were the first to be trampled on. There had been Poland. Now there was Finland.

Thirty-year-old Thomas F. Hawkins ploughed along with the Finnish forces on the freezing Lake Kianta battlefront. He saw most of the struggle. On January 8, 1940—the same day that the "Fourteen Points" were briefly revived—he told what was happening:

The Finns apparently held the initiative in a roving, hit-and-run war today deep in the brooding forest along both sides of the border in this wild northland.

In a heroic stand that has captured the imagination of the world in little more than a month of fighting, tiny Finland was beating off the armies of a country fifty times her size along makeshift battle lines where the white of the Arctic snow was crimson with the red of Russian blood.

This little nation was amazing even the ponderous legions of the Red Army.

The fighting raged the length of the long border between the two countries, with Russian strategy aimed at cutting Finland in two by a main thrust at the narrow central sector, known as Finland's "waist."

There have been two principal battles. Both were fought between Lake Kianta and Suomussalmi. They covered a fourteen-day period and were fought during Finland's worst winter in twenty-five years.

The Finns destroyed two of Premier Joseph Stalin's crack divisions and a third still faces annihilation.

Heavy snows and biting cold froze the engines of Stalin's war machine in the wooded hills around Lake Kianta. Impassable roads cut off supplies from the Red soldiers—and then the Finns struck. Sweeping over the snow from defense lines in the deep forests, ski-born infantrymen fell upon the cold-numbed Russians. The ghostlike Finns, clad in white garments, took a heavy toll in a hit-and-run war. Shattered remnants of the Reds' 163rd division were driven back over the Russian border in disorder by guerrilla bands of Finnish soldiers.

I saw vast quantities of supplies that had fallen to the Finns. Many of the Red Army's newest weapons were captured. Some of the big guns had never been fired—the grease in their mechanisms had been frozen by the 50-below-zero cold.

The battle also uncovered one of Russia's "secret weapons" of the war. It was a "sled tank" mounted on skis and driven by an airplane propeller. The craft was armed with machine guns and light cannon and could travel at a fast clip over the snow.

The second Finnish triumph came at Suomussalmi, on the Southern Front. After a bitter three-day encounter, the Russian 44th division was shattered, reeling back across the border. The fighting almost completely demolished the town of Suomussalmi. Victory came to the Finns when one of their patrols destroyed a bridge and kept reinforcements from reaching the Russians. Here, also, the Russians lost hundreds of trucks and tanks and uncounted numbers of guns. Cannons with hundreds of shells and shellcaps still piled beside them lined the highway, stark reminders of the ferocity of the Finnish charge.

Finnish officers said a lack of ski scouts led to the Russian rout. But the Russians apparently were learning the new type of warfare, for dozens of books on "How to Ski" were found in the shattered Russian supply trucks. The fighting also uncovered some Russian ingenuity. The Red Air Force, hampered by the lack of airports in the Arctic zone, made landing fields by flooding farms with water. The water quickly froze, providing smooth landing surfaces for planes.

The third Russian division is surrounded by the Finns at Kokkammo, south of the scene of the earlier clashes.

The Finns held the initiative in a roving, hit-and-run war, but there naturally is question as to how long their phenomenal defense can continue against the bulk of her powerful foe.

In England, 2,000,000 additional men were called to the colors. Roosevelt recommended a budget of $1,800,000,000 for national defense. Oscar, a dog in Salem, Virginia, made a hit with his master by finding lost pennies and bringing them home on his tongue. The "oldest elephant in captivity" celebrated its seventy-fourth birthday in the Boston Zoo. A Bulgarian trade delegation awaited a hearing in Moscow. British seamen and members of the *Graf Spee's* crew drank together in Buenos Aires. London restaurants were allowed to serve one-sixth of an ounce of butter with each meal. Hungarian police attempted to break up a terroristic Nazi band, which operated within its borders. King Carol said Rumanians would die to defend their boundaries.

The following gags were going the rounds in Washington:

"The Germans are putting zippers on their battleships to make scuttling easier."

"The loyal British have presented King George with a diving bell so he can review his fleet."

"The practical French are putting seed packets in boxes sent their boys on the Western Front."

Perhaps the French soldiers really did have time to plant garden seeds. There was little doing on the Western Front. There was little doing on the sea. There was little doing anywhere except in Finland. Again it was mostly a war of words, as far as Germany, Britain, and France were concerned. There probably never had been anything like it before.

Tired of listening to speeches, soured on the ranting of "statesmen," correspondents relieved the monotony by going out to see how things were going among those who invariably bear the brunt of an economic war—the ordinary, everyday people.

Hugh Wagnon, blond, thin-haired native of Kansas, looked over London:

Many of the stay-at-homes in this war are complaining of having to pay all-time high income taxes to make ends meet, what with bigger bills for groceries, gasoline (if they can get it), and a general 10 per cent jump in the cost of living.

On the home front they find that war, today's style, does not call for brass bands and whoopee. In 1914, the Tommy's attitude was: "The Kaiser is getting a bit thick, it's time to do something about him." Today's attitude toward Hitler is much the same, but Tommy is much more sophisticated. Flag-waving and pinning feathers on lapels of "slackers" are out.

The man in the street is reserved, rather shy, far from warlike in his talk. So far the Germans are still Germans; they're never referred to, as in 1914, as the "Huns." There is respectful silence when newsreels show the burials for German aviators brought down in raids on the Firth of Forth.

When British statesmen talk about the war against "Hitlerism," it's no generality even to the sophisticated Englishman. He claims he has a real grudge against Hitler.

Picture the average Englishman in peacetime: He had a cozy home with a flower garden. If he had the income, all the luxuries of the world were at his command.

When he awoke in the morning the maid brought him a piping hot cup of tea. Then he breakfasted on bacon and eggs, kippers and toast. He rode to work in a fast, comfortable train. He lunched on roast beef and Yorkshire pudding without thought of stinting. Between four and five o'clock he had tea and cakes. And then about 9 P.M. he had supper at home with the family, with time beforehand to work in the garden.

Now his wife and children have been sent to the country to live among strangers. He has to brew his own breakfast tea, fry his own bacon and eggs. Lately there has been no bacon from Denmark. For economy, the maid has had to go. The kitchen sink is piled up with dishes. The house is a mess.

He is in a surly mood by the time he starts for work. All trains are packed at rush hours; service has been curtailed to clear lines for movement of vital supplies.

His factory office looks like a place near the front line. Doors and windows are piled with sandbags. The lighting is bad. No longer has he a full range of the world's foods for lunch. He can't get his favorite tea; the government has pooled all brands. To tea drinkers like the English, the result is horrible. To get such staples as meat, sugar, and butter, his wife must now present ration cards, or soon will have to. She is limited to twelve ounces of sugar a week, four ounces of bacon, and four ounces of butter. At sunset he has to put black shades on all windows: for a fair-sized house, shades cost about $20.

The blackout has virtually stopped social life. To get to his favorite pub or club, a Briton risks his neck walking through pitch-black streets, with automobiles and buses whizzing past him lighted only by bare flickers.

The biggest worry is the family budget. Take the case of a $2,500 a year married man with one child. In peacetime he ran a ten-horsepower midget car, went to a movie with his wife about once a week, and to a stage play about six times a year. He drank about three pints of beer a week, didn't indulge in more than three bottles of whisky a year. He and his wife smoked about twenty cigarettes a day, consumed about a quarter of pound of tea and two pounds of sugar a week.

For 1940–1941 his automobile license tax alone will amount to $62.25, if he hasn't sold the car by then. Used-car lots already are full of bargains.

The dark side of the picture doesn't mean Englishmen have any intention of yielding to "Old Hitler," but many of them wonder what's around the corner.

Louis Lochner surveyed things in the Fatherland:

Life in embattled Germany presents itself to the average civilian in colors of the rainbow.

The citizen ventures out at night; then, bang, he strikes a lamp-post in a darkened street. First lesson in color: Forehead, next morning, is black and blue, and possibly green. Wisened by that experience, he buys a pocket lamp if he can find a shop that still has them, and inserts a piece of blue or red paper over the bulb so as not to throw too much light. If he cannot get a flashlight, he buys an old-fashioned barn lantern, with red, green, or blue glass.

Also, he buys a phosphorescent button for his lapel. That is to signal to fellow pedestrians: "Look out! Don't bump into me!" If he's of a fanciful mind, he buys a tomcat, a monkey, or some other little pet carved out of the phosphorescent material. If he's a cavalier, he presents his lady with a phosphorescent rose, lily, or forget-me-not.

Every morning, color life starts all over. The male of the species makes sure that he has his yellow certificate entitling him to purchase five liters (about five quarts) of gasoline per coupon. He also makes sure he takes his red bread card, his blue meat card, and his pink card for staples like rice, macaroni, lentils, etcetera, with him to present at his favorite restaurant.

The choice of dishes is made rapidly. On two days of the week, no meat is to be had. On other days no restaurant can serve more than half-a-dozen choices of main dishes.

Meanwhile, the gentleman's faithful wife has spent about half an hour putting away all signs of last night's blackout. Next she starts her daily shopping. To the red, blue, and pink cards of the sort her husband has taken, she adds a white card for marmalade and sugar, a yellow card for fats, margarine, and oil, and a brown card for soap. Not that she will be able to get all the things she wants; her tradesman may shrug and say, "Sorry, madam, but our new consignment hasn't come as yet."

When the man of the house has reached his office, he tells his secretary to go out and buy some badly needed towels. "Nothing doing," the fraulein says. "I haven't any Bezugschein." Another of his peeves! To obtain a "Bezugschein" (permit) for towels, he must convince a hard-boiled official that the old towel is absolutely unusable.

And no matter how shapely a lady's legs may be, if she has one change of stockings, officials may refuse her authorization to buy a new pair.

This writer knows of a man who asked for a Bezugschein for a business suit. The official asked if he had any other suits. "Only the one I have on today," was the answer. The man thought the official was concerned about his everyday clothes.

"Please take a seat in the anteroom," he was told.

After half an hour he was called in again. On a hall-tree were his tuxedo and his dark, Sunday suit.

"Are these yours?" he was asked.

To his affirmative reply, the official said: "Very well, here is your Bezugschein for a new suit of clothes. But you will donate these other two suits to the Winter Relief. You understand?"

Of course the man understood: These two suits were of good

wool; the certificate entitled him to a modern suit made of a fiber mixed somewhat with wool.

William McGaffin looked at conditions in France:

Mme. Jean Q. Frenchman is holding her little family together these days by long-distance methods. She not only has to write to Jean but to their children as well.

This is one of the chief effects this war has had on Madame. In other wars, she and the children were together after Papa had gone to the front. But now the children have been evacuated to the country.

Madame has many things besides letter writing, however, to occupy her. She knits for the soldiers. Frenchwomen always have been ardent knitters. But Madame has changed her prewar favorite colors of blue and pink for khaki and beige.

There are men's jobs to be filled. Madame may now be punching tickets in the subway—or even reading gas meters. And if she has time left over there are the volunteer service corps. She doesn't have to worry about money too much if she has a job or a nest egg. The government allows her 12 francs daily for herself (10 francs in the provinces) and 4 francs 50 centimes daily for each child. (The franc is worth about 2¼ cents.)

She still dresses smartly—and on a small amount. She can buy whatever she pleases in the shops, although some shops have closed through lack of business or of personnel. The principal difference she notices is that shop windows are crisscrossed with gummed paper as protection against splintering and there are big signs pointing the way to the nearest air raid shelter.

The only food restrictions Madame has to face are the closing of all butcher shops on Mondays and a ban on the sale of beef on Tuesdays. Keeping the home fires burning has become a problem. Many apartment landlords, bereft of most of their tenants, cannot afford central heating for those who remain. So Madame has resorted to electric heaters, coal fires, or to digging the old base burner out of the cellar. The landlord helps on the fuel bill by reducing the rent.

Madame still goes to the movies—unless she has seen all the shows in town. Cinemas were forced to continue showing the same pictures or to revive old ones. That is nothing, however, compared to closing time of the cabarets.

2

THE LULL in Germany portended the same fate for other small countries that was being dealt by the Russians to tiny Finland. In the winter of 1939-1940 it was Stalin's move. It appeared that other small countries would hear from Hitler soon.

Courageous Finland was a happy little democracy—the only nation that religiously paid her American World War debts. She kept her house in order. She had lived uprightly among her thousand lakes until she finally met what amounted to virtual death in her own snow.

It was a tribute to her standing among neighboring small nations that she received their aid—sometimes surreptitiously, sometimes openly—throughout her struggle. Alvin Steinkopf told about it from Copenhagen on February 13:

Men and munitions are pouring into Finland, and the most effective aid in her fight against Soviet Russia is being given by Scandinavian countries.

In spite of governmental attitudes of neutrality, citizens and officials of these neighboring nations openly assert Finland is fighting a common cause in her attempt to prevent the westward sweep of Communism.

Neutral observers estimate that more than 6,000 Swedish volunteers already are on Finnish soil in addition to several hundred Norwegians. Last Thursday, Copenhagen sources disclosed that the first company of Danish volunteers had landed in Finland.

In Norway and Denmark, recruiting is not being carried on openly, but willing volunteers experience no difficulty in learning where to apply for service under Finnish colors.

A recruiting office in Stockholm is doing a lively business openly. Many adventurers from the United States and other countries also have enlisted there along with the Swedes.

Sweden makes it easy for the officers and men in her Army to go to Finland. They are released readily for volunteer service. Some of her best officers have gone after resigning from the Swedish Army.

King Gustaf of Sweden in a speech to Parliament, which was

convened to consider vast defense expenditures, expressed sympathy
for the Finns. A similar expression of sympathy was made by King
Haakon of Norway yesterday in Oslo. The King said the government would give military training to men who wished it—presumably to prospective volunteers for Finnish service.

Up to now, military help has been on a much smaller scale than
economic aid. A central agency co-ordinating collections in Sweden
said voluntary gifts for Finland up to this afternoon totaled 8,500,-
000 kroner (about $1,991,000).

Among Swedish workers it has become customary to donate
a day's work occasionally. Swedish farmers have fallen into line—
members of one rural organization are now giving a day's supply of
milk, fifty pounds of corn for each twenty-five acres, or one egg
for each hen.

Finnish Premier Risto Ryti's appeal on January 8 for foreign
credits brought about the extension of favorable terms to Finland
by business firms in Scandinavian lands. Some goods even were
sent without any arrangements for payment.

Emotional appeals are becoming increasingly effective in the
northern countries. A Copenhagen paper published a song by a
Danish volunteer glorifying the Finns for their defense and pleading with all northern countries to join in the war.

But Russia got what she wanted from Finland. Out of Moscow
on March 13, Henry C. Cassidy sent word of the end of the
struggle:

Soviet Russia early today announced the signing of a peace
treaty with Finland which wrests, as the spoils of three and a half
months of invasion, Finland's defense bastions on Baltic and Arctic
seas and makes part of the vast territory of the U.S.S.R., the whole
fortified Karelian Isthmus, where uncounted Russian and Finnish
dead lie beneath the trampled snows.

Finland gets peace, a yearly rental of about $120,000 in return
for a thirty-year lease on her Hanko "Gibraltar" at the mouth of
the Gulf of Finland, and evacuation of the Petsamo Arctic district
by Soviet troops. She agrees:

To give up the entire Karelian Isthmus and its Soviet-pene-
trated Mannerheim Line; the shell-wrecked city of Viipuri, once
Finland's third metropolis, and the islands in its bay; all the shores
of Lake Ladoga, largest in Europe, and three towns; Hanko, naval

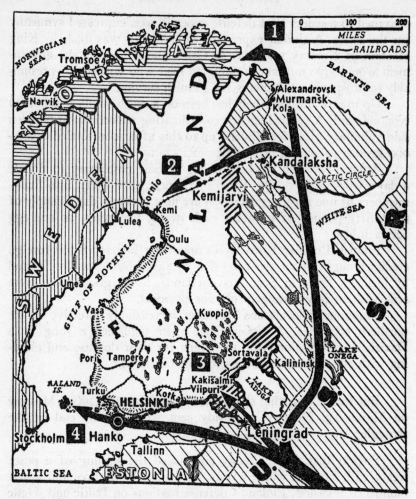

Map 4—The arrows above show what happened to Finland when she lost her war against Russia. At (1) she gave up the shaded tip of the peninsula immediately under the arrowhead and waived duties on Russian trade with Norway through Finland. The treaty provided for construction of a railway at (2) bisecting Finland above its "waist." At (3) Finland lost all the Karelian Isthmus and the shore of Lake Ladoga, along with other shaded areas, and at (4) Russia got a long lease on Finland's Hanko "Gibraltar," dominating the Gulfs of Bothnia and Finland.

base on the southwest, and the surrounding peninsula, on a thirty-year lease; part of the Sredni and Rybachi peninsulas in the far north on the Arctic Ocean; certain islands in the Gulf of Finland; a great slice of northeastern Finland, including Kuolajarvi; to build a railroad during 1940, which will link the White Sea within northern Russia to the Gulf of Bothnia, west of Finland, the railway bisecting Finland above her narrow waistline; to grant free transit for Russian goods across the Petsamo Arctic area from Russia to Norway, duty free; and to surrender the right to maintain any Finnish warships, submarines, or warplanes in its Arctic waters, with the exception of small coast guard vessels.

An exchange of papers of ratification of the treaty is scheduled to take place in Moscow. Under the pact, Finnish and Soviet troops are to begin to withdraw at 10 A.M. Friday to their new frontiers, a map of which was appended to the treaty.

The treaty was described by Moscow as one that will "create mutually stable and mutually peaceful relations." Actually, it gives Russia an uncontested clutch on the northern Baltic. Before she invaded Finland on November 30, Russia had got concessions from Estonia, Latvia, and Lithuania, but these are nothing as compared to the conditions for Finnish peace.

3

GREAT BRITAIN was criticized for failure to aid Finland. Leslie Hore-Belisha, replaced as secretary of state for war, attacked British policy in the House of Commons. David Lloyd George, prime minister during World War I, declared: "It is the old trouble —too late. Too late for Czecho-Slovakia. Too late for Poland. Certainly too late for Finland. It is always too late or too little, or both. That is the road to disaster."

So Finland came to the end of her unhappy struggle, and other small countries felt the approaching storm. Charles Foltz, Jr., wrote about the Balkans:

The "little fellows" of the Balkans look forward with no pleasure whatsoever to taking another beating.

Their tragedy-tailed peninsula, where jigsaw frontiers have changed perhaps more frequently than those in any other part of the world, may be "in for it" this spring.

A Balkan—whether he be Yugoslav, Bulgar, Rumanian, or

Greek—probably doesn't want war of any kind, but nobody ever asks him. Nobody asked him in 1914. For a few years, millions even blamed him for starting the war. Since then, most historians have agreed that if there hadn't been a shot at Sarajevo, there would have been something else to start it.

John Balkan's business throughout the last century has been to plough his fields, serve his term in the army, and not speak unless spoken to. Then he'd better say "yes, sir" or there will be trouble.

John Balkan's governments, dictators or kings, are much in the same position on an international basis. Their business is to run their governments inside as best they can and not to speak in international affairs unless spoken to. Then they'd better say "yes, sir" to the right big power. Right now they're caught in a powerful squeeze between the Germans who want to keep their Balkan back door open for supplies, and the Allies who want to close it. Russia has a finger on the pincer too and the Balkans would like very much to know which power to pal with.

Between motorized German divisions on the west, Russians on the north, and a growing Allied Army in the Near East, the Balkans sit and shiver. They'd just love to stay neutral, but they have an awful feeling they can't. Some of the Balkan governments (nobody has asked the people) might like to have a little "all-Balkan" war to change frontiers again in their own back yard. They're afraid to try it, though, for fear the war will become a free-for-all with big powers commanding.

Rumania is on the worst spot. Russia, Hungary, and Bulgaria all have territorial claims on her. The "Caroline"—Rumanian defense line—exists mainly on paper. The country, sapped by internal graft and working with a currency whose "black bourse" rate is three times lower than the official rate, would have a hard time defending herself against any neighbor.

Bulgaria, "good boy of the Balkans," has found that being good hasn't helped much. The country is the only one of the first World War's Central Powers that hasn't recovered some territory since the treaties divided territories.

Both Rumania, the "have" state, and Bulgaria, the "have-not," are almost certain to become battlegrounds if war comes to the Balkans. Balkan war lanes run that way.

John Balkan's farms are in those war lanes. He can't help that —it's the land of his forefathers. He is a little fellow in little countries. Although he'd rather stay home and till his fields, when the order comes to go, he'll go. But don't try to tell him that his love of war has turned the Balkans into Europe's powder barrel. He knows better.

4

LLOYDS listed total Allied shipping losses at 338 ships; Germany's, 34. Soldiers along the Swiss frontier installed fine furniture from Baden Casino in their dingy dugouts. All Germans of the military class of 1921 were ordered to report for duty. Bohemia-Moravia marked its first anniversary under Reich rule. Under-Secretary of State Sumner Welles was on a fact-finding tour of Europe.

William Hatfield in Carrier, Oklahoma, said he had a hen that was laying eggs branded with a "W." A 1908 municipal law which made it unlawful to "giggle" came to light in Helena, Montana. A woman in California claimed possession of the iron with which George Washington's lace cuffs and collars once were pressed.

Europe's spring snows were beginning to thaw. Hitler—scheming, plotting, rebuilding—was ready to begin again. Sporadic bombings and ship sinkings during the previous few months could scarcely be called serious war. Hitler had not wanted to run the risk of war on two fronts simultaneously. He was relieved that the Russo-Finnish campaign was out of the way. Cautious, aging Mussolini had a similar though less positive notion. Although he had had no sympathy with the Finnish debacle, he was hopeful that the Soviet now could give the Axis co-operation on supplies. He favored that.

Perhaps there is nothing more ineffective than an aging, uncertain dictator. Mussolini was the dean of the dictators. But he no longer had the nerve to go forward under his own steam. His people were not solidly behind him. Yet he couldn't stand still. That would mean he was slipping. The best Mussolini could do was to ride on Hitler's battle wagon. He still didn't want to declare war, but he did want the ride.

March 18, 1940, and historic Brenner Pass. . . .

Emperors and their armies of the past had used it to cross the Alps between Italy and the Teutonic lands. Hitler secretly left Berlin for the Pass in his special railroad car. Mussolini secretly left Rome. His destination was the same.

There at Brenner Pass, while the snow swirled down, the two dictators met. They sat and talked in Der Fuehrer's private car. The conversation lasted for two and one-half hours. No correspondents were permitted. Only intimates of the two dictators attended. But the story was pieced together from Rome and Berlin:

Adolf Hitler and Benito Mussolini held a sudden, momentous conference on their common frontier at the Brenner Pass today from which Germany emerged with these certain expectations:

1. That Italy was ready to join the European war actively on Germany's side, if and when needed, and

2. That the Rome-Berlin Axis might make another bid for support from Moscow.

The dictator powers, in their plans for remolding Europe, hoped to have Moscow's endorsement, excellently informed quarters said. Germany did not expect, however, that Russia would become a belligerent. Rather, she was looked upon as potential storehouse for raw materials.

As details of the spectacular meeting trickled through to Berlin it appeared that the two statesmen agreed that Italy would join the war on Germany's side if it should become desirable for her to abandon her present status in which she is not neutral and yet not waging war. Until such time, it was said, Italy would lose no opportunity to demonstrate to the Western Powers that she is Germany's ally economically, politically, and ideologically.

The two statesmen were understood to have agreed that an Italian-Russo rapprochement should come next, with a careful delineation of spheres of influence in the Balkans to follow. Berlin was filled with rumors that Foreign Minister von Ribbentrop might confer with Russian Premier-Foreign Commissar Molotov immediately upon his return from the Pass. He and Italian Foreign Minister Count Ciano sat in the conference with their chiefs.

So cocksure was German public opinion tonight that Britain must fight her own battles with only France aiding her, that the *Deutsche Allgemeine Zeitung* editorialized:

"Our soldiers are carrying the war to those points where the English do not want to see it. Our political leadership is preventing war at those points where the English would like to see it."

5

MUSSOLINI had been none too cheerful in recent months. That night he sang on the way back to Rome from Brenner Pass. Maybe he sang because he still had not had to declare war.

Prague Jews were ordered to give up their valuables. Two men were arrested in the Netherlands for sending weather news to the Nazis. Swiss guns fired on foreign airplanes. Chamberlain said the Allies were ready for any Nazi move. He demonstrated it by an R.A.F. attack on the Nazi air base on the Island of Sylt. French police seized thirty-three persons for distributing Communist propaganda. The much-vaunted military strength of the French had not materialized.

Two days after the Brenner Pass confab there was word out of Paris:

Premier Edouard Daladier resigned today amid criticism of France's conduct of the war against Germany. President Lebrun asked Finance Minister Paul Reynaud to form a War Cabinet.

The president called in M. Reynaud, who has been notably successful at his finance post, after M. Daladier's Radical-Socialist party had announced the retiring premier's refusal to attempt a new combination.

M. Daladier declined in conformance with parliamentary tradition. That meant he interpreted as an expression of disapproval of his conduct of the war a minority vote of confidence which the Chamber of Deputies had given him earlier in the day. Although the vote was 239 to one in his favor, there were more than 300 abstentions in the total Chamber membership of 551.

Some 300 deputies thus showed their disapproval of M. Daladier's virtually dictatorial rule. His critics have demanded a more extensive and vigorous prosecution of the war.

M. Reynaud, who parliamentary circles thought could speedily form the "action" government for which all the press has been clamoring, entered the presidential palace at 4:45 P.M. It was expected that he would have the support of both Rightists and Leftists.

Though it was none too apparent at the time, some painstaking analysts felt they could perceive what had been going on behind the scenes in France. But none of them could even guess the extent to which France was disintegrating.

6

CHAMBERLAIN'S government also was girding on the home front. France had not been the only Allied country in which there was dissatisfaction with conduct of the war. There had been months of dissatisfaction in England. Drew Middleton covered developments on April 3:

Winston Churchill, fighting heir to Great Britain's lofty traditions, became her "man of battle" tonight in a drastic shake-up of the Cabinet which made him director of all the nation's warring services.

Standing close behind the pudgy but volatile First Lord of the Admiralty in the figures emerging from Prime Minister Neville Chamberlain's third government shift of the war, are two other key men—Sir Kingsley Wood and Sir John Simon. Reporting with Churchill to Chamberlain as heads of war committees, they form a War Cabinet in fact if not in name.

Sir Kingsley, who traded his Air Ministry with Sir Samuel Hoare for the latter's post as Lord Privy Seal, will head the Home Policy Committee. He will direct and advise on social and domestic problems of wartime, including food and agriculture—vital to this importing, heavy-eating nation of 45,000,000.

To Sir John Simon, silvery haired veteran of finance, remains the staggering task of presiding over the Cabinet's Economic Policy Committee. As Chancellor of the Exchequer, he directs Great Britain's mighty offensive of pounds, shillings, and pence.

With the nation quickening to the increased tempo of aerial warfare, and with Germany's Goering declaring the Reich will strike on the West, Chamberlain bowed to public clamor to "fight the war" by making Churchill head of the vital Armed Services Committee. He remains First Lord of the Admiralty as well.

On the Services Committee will serve Oliver Stanley, the war secretary, Sir Samuel Hoare, the new air minister, their chiefs of staff, and Churchill's own First Sea Lord—Admiral Sir Dudley Pound.

Also in the Churchill committee is Leslie Burgin, minister of supply, who, although under almost continuous fire for the last six weeks, confounded prophets and remained in the Cabinet.

Thus three seasoned veterans—Sir Kingsley Wood, 59; Sir John Simon, 67; and Churchill, 65—will combine with the 71-year-old Chamberlain to lead the nation through whatever is coming. The Cabinet's only outstanding change in actual ministry assignments was the shift of Sir Samuel Hoare for Sir Kingsley Wood. Sir Kingsley, although criticized for failure to maintain a high rate of airplane production, still is regarded highly as an organizer and "driver."

In his announcement of the shake-up, Chamberlain said that his assignment of Churchill as head of the Armed Services Committee would enable him to "keep under constant review the main factors in the strategical situation and the progress of operations and to make recommendations to the War Cabinet on the general conduct of the war."

In addition, restoration of Lord Chatfield as minister of defense co-ordination, leaves Churchill almost undisputed master over the fighting services. Furthermore, he will control the work of the Ministry of Supply.

Thus Churchill's natural exuberance and daring will be checked only by the cold logic of Chamberlain, the hardware maker turned statesman. It is no secret that Churchill has desired authority of some sort over the other services since the start of the war.

He always has declared that the blackest mark on his record, the grim and bloody failure of the Gallipoli landing during the World War, might never have been made had he then had direction over Army forces as well as the Fleet.

More than any other Briton, he will have the ear of General Maurice Gustave Gamelin, the Allied Army generalissimo, in the periodic meetings of the Supreme War Council.

CHAPTER 6

Spring Lightning

April 8–May 23, 1940

I

THE giant chessboard was set up. By now Hitler knew that a general European war was certain. His other conquests had been quick ones. The problem of supplies had not been acute. For a general war, he needed to make sure of a number of supply sources. He had been getting iron ore from Sweden. The ore came to Fatherland foundries via Narvik on the Norwegian coast. British blockade could prevent a continuation. Consequently, two more small countries must be overrun. Not only would they give Hitler access to the iron ore, but they would be strategically important. The two small countries were Norway and Denmark.

Britain knew what Hitler was up to. On April 8, she announced she had mined Scandinavian waters. The Nazis, already on the move, ingenuously met the statement with one of their own:

"Icily cold, Germany watches these developments. Icily cold, Germany watches the unfolding of this drama. Icily cold, Germany reserves her own decisions to meet the situation."

In Berlin late that same night of April 8 there was denial of the quick developments. But facts were facts. Denmark's communications had been suddenly shut off—important phase of the Nazi technique of overrunning a country before word could reach the outside world.

First sketchy news came out of Stockholm. It said that Oslo, capital of Norway, had been attacked "by a mysterious naval expedition of an unknown power striking from the darkness of Skagerrak Channel—less than a month after the northern countries had thought to escape war by the Finnish-Russian peace." Within a matter of hours the whole story was developed from half a dozen sources:

78

By land and sea, Adolf Hitler's mighty army streamed today with speed and precision into Denmark and Norway, seized the capitals of Copenhagen and Oslo, brought about a new Nazi-headed government in Norway, and extended the wartime "protection" of the Third Reich to two kingdoms—3,750,000 Danes and nearly 3,000,000 Norwegians.

Denmark met the invasion with disciplined nonresistance; Norway met it with fighting which the Germans termed "local" and "slight," principally at Oslo.

After the Norwegian capital had capitulated in midafternoon, DNB, the official German news agency, made a report. It announced that the regime of Premier Johan Nygaarsvold had turned over its powers to a Cabinet headed by Major Vidkun Quisling, Norwegian Nazi leader, as premier and foreign minister. Quisling, in a radio proclamation at 8:30 P.M. called upon the people to cease resistance to the German Army and avoid "criminal destruction of property," and demanded that the Norwegian Army obey his "National Government."

Quisling said he had taken over to "protect Norway."

Earlier, the Nygaarsvold government had retreated to the lake hamlet of Hamar, north of Oslo, and half the population of the capital had fled, with the Norwegian Army drawing up a defense line between Oslo and Hamar. At least one Norwegian port, Kristiansund, on the west coast, was bombed by the German air force because, Germans said, it resisted occupation.

DNB said that only a portion of the Norwegian Government left Oslo for Hamar, and that two members later returned to Oslo and joined with other Cabinet men in forming the Quisling Government.

Germany's Fleet steamed up the northern North Sea into Norwegian ports, in position to match fury with the British Navy; mine layers infested the western coastal waters of Norway and the Danish Skagerrak.

The Reich's formidable air force took possession of strategic airports in Norway and Denmark. New Messerschmitt patrols swarmed over the west coasts of the two countries; other formations swept out over Helgoland Bight in an aerial blockade of the "protected" nations.

At the end of the day, the German command said all important military bases in Norway were in German hands; that Norwegian coastal fortifications, seized by shock troops, naval units, and planes, were ready to repel any Allied attempts to land and that powerful air force units were ready in Norway for any sort of action.

Those points in Norway listed as strongly occupied by German troops were Oslo; Narvik, the ore port; Bergen, Stavanger, Trondheim, and Kristiansund. Resistance at Oslo and Kristiansund was "broken," the command stated. It also said that new and heavy German forces are on the march, at swift tempo, without interference from the enemy.

Danish troops did not resist at all. Under protest, the Danish King and Government submitted to the invasion and told their people it was their duty to offer no resistance.

Norwegian coastal batteries offered original battle to four German warships in Oslo Fiord, and the United States Minister, Mrs. J. Borden Harriman, reported to Washington that the Norwegian Government had advised her that it was "at war with Germany." Through the morning Oslo's anti-aircraft guns roared, and several German and Norwegian planes were shot down. Two German ships also were sunk at the port of Narvik.

But by 4 P.M. Oslo had surrendered, and green-clad German troops, after a thirty-five-mile march from Moss, on the coast, were in the capital's streets and in possession of government buildings. German officials replaced the Norwegian police chief, who resigned. Withdrawals from Oslo were stopped, although there was indication of further Norwegian resistance in a Stockholm report that Norwegian soldiers had formed a defense line between Oslo and Hamar.

The German high command said the Reich had assumed "armed protection" of the two countries to prevent anticipated occupation by British and French troops and to ward off attack upon the Reich from the north.

Using armored trains, ferries, and warships, the Nazi troops moved into Denmark at dawn, while infantrymen, seamen, and air squadrons invaded Norway's coast—a vast, carefully planned operation which burst upon the world less than twenty-four hours after it had heard about the swift sowing of British mine fields.

These mines were intended to trap and halt German ore ships from Scandinavia. But it appeared today that German troop ships had been moving north even while the fields were being sown. One such ship, the *Rio De Janeiro,* was torpedoed on Monday off the south coast of Norway by a British submarine, with 350 men lost.

While the German troops marched today, Germany laid mine fields of her own off the Norwegian and Danish west coasts and in the Skagerrak to protect her operations. The net result of today's overwhelming German invasion was this:

Hitler, unless dislodged by the Allies, will, for the rest of the war, lord it directly over 80,000,000 Germans; hold sway through his occupation and administration over 14,000,000 Poles; impose his will via Baron Konstantin von Neurath, his Reich-protector, on 7,000,000 Czechs; wield a protective hand over 5,000,000 Slovaks, and guarantee to Norway and Denmark that German arms shall ensure for both northern kingdoms "immunity from international carnage."

Into this "protection," incidentally, were brought two reigning sovereigns, Christian of Denmark and Haakon of Norway; one Queen, Alexandrine of Denmark; two Crown Princes, Frederik of Denmark and Olaf of Norway, and their consorts, and twenty-two other Princes of royal blood.

To foreign correspondents, it had been obvious since late last week that events of great consequence were in the offing in northern Europe. On Saturday authorized spokesmen announced that one of the gravest week ends in the history of the war was at hand—that the northern neutrals must decide right away where they stood.

Foreign newspapermen in Berlin were not alone in their surmise that something would happen. Most foreign military missions, although invited to start Sunday night for an inspection of the Western Front, left at least one expert behind in Berlin.

In spite of all that, there were indications that Hitler did not tell Axis partner Mussolini what he intended to do. Asked if Italy had been apprised in advance, an authorized spokesman replied cryptically: "Everything went like a stroke of lightning."

Foreign Minister Joachim von Ribbentrop, exhausted after a sleepless night, appeared personally before the foreign press.

"Germany, by its action," he said, "has saved the countries and the people of Scandinavia from annihilation, and will now guarantee true neutrality in the north until the war's end."

2

NORWAY didn't give up quite as easily as Hitler had expected. There was a fight. The Swedish iron situation was a vital one, and Britain gave assistance. Her first efforts on behalf of Norway were on the sea. On April 13 her Fleet, led by the battleship *Warspite*, raided the fiord of Narvik. Seven German destroyers were sunk.

Germany landed parachutists. British troops disembarked at several points.

Blood, donated by English volunteers, was flown to Norway. London banned nudity in shows and night clubs. The U. S. warned Japan to keep hands of the Dutch East Indies.

For days the Nazis denied Britain had retaken Narvik. J. Norman Lodge, called "The Old Sarge," because he served with the A.E.F. in World War I, filed the dispatch which ended the dispute. He slipped across the Swedish border and made a first-hand report:

After a thirty-five-hour journey northward from Stockholm on a crowded, uncomfortable train, I reached the Swedish iron mining town of Kiruna, only to be told I could proceed no further.

Kiruna is about seventy miles from the Norwegian frontier by the railroad which continues on to Narvik, a matter of some eighteen miles more.

I found that all foreigners had been ordered from Swedish border areas, especially foreign journalists with or without passes. Swedish journalists apparently were permitted to cross the frontier into Norway at will, but when I protested that this was not exactly cricket, a Swedish captain said, "Neither was the invasion of Scandinavia," and ordered me to return south.

There was nothing to do except board a train for the return trip to Stockholm. But fifty miles south of Kiruna, I slipped off at Gellivare, determined to get across the border somehow. A taxi driver, unable to resist the promise of a bonus, finally agreed to take a chance on driving me the 120 miles to the frontier. By hiding on the floor of the taxi now and then I managed to reach the border a mile north of Vassijaure-Riksgransen, on the Narvik-Kiruna railway, and stepped across in midafternoon without benefit of visa.

In a storm, with snowflakes that seemed as big as marshmallows, I tramped fifteen miles or more to the outskirts of Narvik, traveling by wooded paths instead of the main road. As I attempted to enter Narvik, I was arrested by British patrols, which proved conclusively enough for me that Narvik again was in Allied hands.

The British let me loose, but my freedom was short-lived. As I started out again in the hope of visiting surrounding towns, Norwegian military authorities collared me and escorted me back to the Swedish frontier. We arrived there unmolested and I was turned over to Swedish authorities. With 250 Norwegian troops who had crossed the frontier and been interned, I was taken back to Kiruna and put aboard a train for the south. The conductor was directed to see that I didn't leave the train this time until it reached Vannas, 280 miles south of Kiruna. I didn't.

Except for Narvik, Britain did not distinguish herself in Norway. The Nazis held the edge from the outset. Britain began withdrawal from central Norway on May 2. The next day she was doing the same from Namsos.

Lodge again got into the thick of things. On May 3 he was back in Norway, at Namsos. And again he was in trouble. His story got through:

The British forces in this Namsos area are evacuating tonight. The French already have gone.

I am writing this account of the Allied departure in the smoke-filled lobby of a small Namsos hotel as I prepare to embark with the British on a destroyer which will be a part of the evacuating contingent. To make matters less comfortable, as far as I am concerned, I have had no sleep for two days and I have been under military arrest for the same length of time. A "good deed" got me into my trouble. I had slipped across the Swedish line to try and reach Namsos because I heard that things were happening here. Outside of Formofoss, I stopped an American ambulance to try to get a story on the day's bombings. They asked me to take some letters to Colonel "B," a British medical officer, and I readily agreed because I thought the letters might be an open sesame for sleeping quarters. They were—under British "protective arrest."

With me are Arthur Menken and Bonny Powell, Paramount and Fox Movietone cameramen. We arrived in Namsos Wednesday night. I had the letters with me.

As we passed a British outpost into territory occupied by the French, we became conscious of an air of suppressed excitement. French officers were rushing about issuing orders to soldiers who were hurriedly putting their gear together. Then they were getting into march formation.

For a considerable distance along the road we passed marching units, trucks, and field pieces. It was shimmering twilight and the marching groups had a ghostlike appearance as the men moved along silently.

We were plenty tired when we reached Namsos and so I presented my letters and asked for lodging. That is when I got arrested. I guess they were helping to save my life because there was every indication that the Germans were on the way. But the British didn't go out of their way to be nice about it. We were told bluntly that we were not welcome visitors and that we were to ask no questions and not to move from the vicinity of the hotel until instructions regarding us could be obtained from headquarters.

At 9:30 A.M. Thursday we heard the roar of approaching planes and immediately there followed blasts of anti-aircraft fire. These attacks lasted throughout the day, directed, we later discovered, against a ship in the harbor. It was obvious enough that something unusual was taking place, but such questions as we dared to ask went unanswered.

At intervals we shuddered under air attack. We had the feeling of being cooked in a burning prison with only the medley of sound such as war can produce to tell us what was going on.

Now our vigil of suspense appears over. We just have been informed by a British officer that troops are boarding ships and that most of the French already have left. We must choose, he says, our individual destiny as regards Namsos.

"Where," we asked, "are you proceeding?" As calmly as though he were commenting on the weather, he replied: "England."

We decided to go with the British forces, who for hours had been embarking into launches for transfer to the ships in the harbor. I am told the embarkation is taking place in the full glare of a large fire started by air bombs, and the glow is visible from where I am writing. I am informed further that the British had to leave behind large quantities of stores and heavier equipment. It also seems that the news the troops are going only now has reached the residents of Namsos, leaving them stunned and bewildered.

All the British soldiers appeared downcast over having to evacuate without getting a further chance to fight. The entire embarkation has, it seems, proceeded in excellent fashion. It is apparent that this means the end of the campaign in the Steinkjer sector, since only the Norwegians now are left to hold the Germans.

[NOTE: At this point Lodge's dispatch contained the parenthetical note that the rest was written "From the harbor."]

Behind us, as we step into a launch, is the ruined little town that caught the full fury of an air attack. Ahead of us in ships taking them to a new destination are the British Tommies who only a short time ago landed in this area. It is a strange scene—curious

product of a great war. In the haste of the departure one British
soldier was left behind. He took too long with his packing and arrived at the dock too late to catch the last launch. I was told he was
P. N. Brew, 21, a British anti-aircraft gunner, and that Norwegian
authorities started him toward the Swedish frontier. He will be interned after crossing the border.

True to the British promise, Lodge reached England, his
odyssey at an end. His two weeks of dodging in and out of Norway
had produced an unusual record of one phase of Europe's war. He
picked up his story where it had left off the night he evacuated
Namsos, adding pertinent details of the perilous voyage to safety:

The censor has my diary for the time being, but I don't need it
to remember the events of the past five days. I landed at a northern
British port yesterday with the Allied evacuation forces from
Namsos.

We put our feet on solid ground again after a crossing during
which we were attacked thirty-nine times by German planes and
lost three Allied destroyers—the British *Afridi,* the French *Bison,*
and the Polish *Grom.*

All of us—troops as well—were dead tired when we boarded
our ships at Namsos in the eerie light of burning supplies. Incendiary bombs had set fire to the water front. Our party was placed
on a French ship. It was heavily laden and improperly trimmed. We
had an anxious moment when we found her nose was stuck in the
mud. Hastily herding the troops aft and ordering full speed astern,
the ship was pulled out of the mud and we joined the homeward-
bound convoy.

But peace was not for us. Just after a breakfastless morning,
the first Heinkels appeared and cannonading began. Bombs dropped
all around the convoy ships, especially ours, which was the flagship.
One bomb, apparently a 500-pounder, fell less than fifty yards
astern—so close its splash fell on the afterdeck. Not content with
that miss, three more Heinkels dropped a series of chaplet bombs—
small incendiary missiles—which formed a perfect spray framing
the ship.

Bonny Powell, Arthur Menken, and I remained as much under
cover as we could, but still on deck. They ground out a pictorial

history, while I made notes, of which I was relieved promptly by the Admiralty when I arrived in Britain.

The bombings continued. We were paid thirty-nine visits in all with from fifteen to twenty bombs on each visit. Our ship alone fired more than one hundred 3-inch shells and several thousand rounds of machine-gun bullets. A dive-bomber laid a perfect shot on the *Bison* and British cruisers and destroyers removed the survivors and wounded. German Junkers and Heinkels finally singled out the *Afridi*. Disabled and lagging, she sank, too. As night fell, the attacks ceased.

During the first day's fighting one Heinkel, which was struck behind the cockpit, dived into the ocean and disappeared.

The French crew of our ship, which had been away from its home port for three months, carried on almost without sleep for the entire trip of five days. They were uncomplaining fellows but the most souvenir-hunting sailors afloat. Everything mysteriously disappeared, including my Finnish hunting knife.

Nearing a secret northern military zone, a French naval officer herded us together and explained that we were entering a secret area and must go below. We did—into a small detention room, where we were kept without food or water for twenty-four hours. Finally, Captain "K," who had been our custodian at Namsos, learned of our fate and personally brought us hardtack and red wine. He tried to get us turned back to the British but without success.

However, the troops transferred to a British ship and when we sailed from the prohibited area—of which maps are readily obtainable in Fleet Street—we were taken to the wardroom mess, wined and dined with provisions brought aboard that night, apologized to at every turn, and treated like ranking diplomats.

While we were hove to in the "prohibited area" services for the dead of the *Bison* and *Afridi* were held aboard the flagship. As a slight breeze flickered the candles on the altar, Abbé Parquin, spiritual adviser of the French sailors, chanted a requiem mass and sprinkled water on the sea for those whose last resting place was beneath the waves. Earlier, Protestant services were held aboard the British cruiser *York*. The sound of the low chant of the service could be heard in our detention room, and, through a minute crack we could see the flickering candles.

For the next thirty-six hours we had the run of the ship, hammocks for sleeping, and plenty of food. Arriving at a northern

British port, however, trouble appeared again in the form of entry officers. Landing permission readily was given. But how do you do it? The French, who had refused to turn us over to the British, insisted now that the British should send a gig for us. The British insisted the French were our custodians.

We fumed and waited. Finally, after waiting offshore in sight of the first green grass we had beheld in months, we were taken ashore, turned loose, and promised a dinner. The French first officer who convoyed the expedition from Namsos evidently was contrite over our treatment and told the whole story of the Allies' entry with withdrawal. He said that the British, sinking knee-deep in melting snow, were fortunate that their casualties during their short stay on the Steinkjer front were kept so small.

3

BRITAIN was criticized for withdrawing from Norway. She was fighting a long war; she could not spread her strength too thin. Norway continued to fight, but it was a losing struggle.

Occasional exchanges of fire broke the calm on the Western Front. A Nazi spy center was raided near the Rumanian royal palace. Germany denied her air force had bombed Red Cross ships. Japan reiterated her noninvolvement in the European war. Two hundred French Communists were exiled. Laborite Morrison asked Prime Minister Chamberlain to resign. Five Norse whalers put into New Orleans after a successful hunt in the Antarctic. The President of Carnegie Institute offered $1,000,000 for the capture of Adolf Hitler.

Hitler didn't even wait to mop up Norway before moving into some of the other little countries. He was staking much on the kind of blitzkrieg that had been so successful since September 1, 1939.

The next break came the night of May 7. First word of it originated, of all places, in New York. J. M. Roberts, Jr., cable news editor of The A.P., got the story from a confidential source. It was denied in Berlin. It was denied at The Hague. It was denied in Amsterdam. It was denied all along the German border. But the Roberts story stood:

Two German columns are advancing toward the Netherlands from Bremen and Düsseldorf, an authoritative source in New York said tonight, adding that they were the cause of intense military preparations and disruption of the Netherlands' international communications.

This source, kept informed from Europe in spite of rigid restrictions against communications in the area involved, was the same that advised The Associated Press a short time previously that Alexander Loudon, Dutch minister in Washington, had been ordered last Saturday to take control of Holland's interests outside the mother country in event of a clash with Germany. This latter report was confirmable in Washington within a few minutes.

The German troops were reported advancing rapidly, and this source stated flatly that they were heading "for Leeuwarden and Arnhem." This would mean that the actual German objective is believed known in Holland, since Leeuwarden is in Friesland Province, not far from the northeast coast and the Frisian Islands, which would provide jumping-off places for planes attacking England.

Holland was prepared for a last-ditch fight, the New York source said, while Germany was known to desire bases on the English Channel from which to attack England.

The same source disclosed that the possibility of bringing children of the Dutch royal family to the U. S. for safety had been discussed, but that the reply had been: "We do not run. The family stays with the people—stays to fight."

The story was true enough. Hitler was moving on Holland, Belgium, and Luxembourg. In addition to providing additional English Channel bases, access to these countries also would give him entry to France around the northern end of the Maginot Line. His pretext was that the "Low Countries" were spying on the Reich, plotting with the Allies. Germany "had to act first."

Two days later this latest phase of Der Fuehrer's "lightning" war was confirmed in Berlin. Hitler told his followers:

"The hour of the decisive battle for the future of the German nation has come. . . . The battle beginning today will decide the future of the German nation for the next thousand years."

Holland had said she was ready. Some countries had metal armaments; Holland had dykes. The dykes could be opened, the country flooded, and Hitler's progress impeded. His progress may have been impeded, but it was not stopped. Hitler's war came by the sea, air, and land. Parachutists and fifth columnists played big roles. Lochner reported on May 10:

The thunderous impact of German total war descended upon western Europe today.

Adolf Hitler pushed his tremendous armies by land and air across the frontiers of Holland and Belgium, through the tiny Grand Duchy of Luxembourg and gave these countries and his great enemies, France and England, the first real taste of hell from the air.

Superbly equipped platoons, ferried by planes or dropped by parachute, penetrated the lowland seaports and airports on the very western coastline of the Low Countries. They formed enemy islands within the carefully prepared land and floodwater lines of the little defenders, while by land the German columns beat across eastern frontiers.

Swarms of bombers smashed at airports at Brussels and Antwerp, in Belgium, and Rotterdam and Amsterdam, in Holland. Others, streaming into eastern and central France, were declared by the high command to have razed the airport at Metz, and to have bombed airdromes at Saint Omer and Vitry-Le-François.

Other planes darted straight for the heart of England, to drop bombs and engage defense fighters. One British Spitfire pursuit plane, said the high command, was shot down north of the Thames, in the vicinity of London.

With Hitler himself at secret general headquarters, "Somewhere in the West," directing operations along a fighting front that now stretches 1,200 miles from Basel on the Swiss frontier to Arctic Norway, the army tonight announced that resistance on the Luxembourg-Belgian-Netherlands frontiers had been "broken everywhere in the first attack."

Within these frontiers, the Germans smashed across Holland's "appendix" province of South Limburg, seized Dutch Maastricht and the vital Albert Canal bridges on the Belgian frontier; penetrated to the Ijssel river east of Arnhem in east central Holland; crossed the Maas river at several Dutch points, seized Malmédy, former German town in Belgium north of Luxembourg, and crossed the Belgian frontier farther south after moving through Luxembourg.

The Albert Canal is Belgium's great defense weapon, and the Maastricht bridgehead is an important key to it.

At the same time, the high command said that a British submarine had been sunk by a German U-boat near the Dutch North Sea island of Terschelling and that a destroyer had been sent to the bottom by the torpedo of a German speedboat.

An official Nazi announcement tonight said that almost one hundred "enemy" airplanes either had been shot down in aerial battles or destroyed on the ground. Seven German airplanes were reported missing in addition to two known to have made forced landings.

Hitler offered Belgium, Holland, and Luxembourg "protection" if they capitulated, but bloodshed and ruin if they resisted. He was following the familiar pattern of conquest which has given him everything he has sought thus far in Europe.

4

WHILE the Nazi attack crashed down on the Low Countries that May afternoon, a pale, broken man emerged from London's Number 10 Downing Street. His head was bowed. His face was drawn. He drove to Buckingham Palace. He spent twenty minutes with the King. Then he trudged away.

He was Neville Chamberlain. He had had a long tenure as British prime minister. Apostle of appeasement, he had been at Munich in 1938. He had coined the phrase "peace for our time." He had been responsible for British conduct of the war. The poor showing in Norway and Denmark had increased opposition to his regime. Hitler's quick invasion of Belgium, Holland, and Luxembourg had been the last straw. Chamberlain was through. He had failed.

That night the story came out:

Winston Churchill, First Lord of the Admiralty, became Great Britain's prime minister tonight, succeeding Neville Chamberlain as war surged over western Europe.

The government announced: "The Right Honorable Neville Chamberlain resigned the office of Prime Minister and First Lord of the Treasury this evening, and the Right Honorable Winston Churchill accepted his Majesty's invitation to fill the position. The Prime Minister desires that all Ministers should remain at their posts and discharge their functions with full freedom and responsibility while the necessary arrangements for the formation of a new administration are made."

One of the most popular personalities in British official life, Churchill is an old-time foe of Hitler expansion. Long before there was any recognition of the air force the Nazis had developed, Churchill, then the most voluble critic of the British Government, was crying in the House of Commons for Britain to recognize danger in Europe.

Chamberlain said his valedictory in a broadcast to the Empire just after resigning.

". . . You and I must now put all our strength behind the new government . . . And we must fight until this savage beast who has sprung out of his lair at us is finally overthrown."

He recalled the recent parliamentary crisis in which his leadership was but barely upheld after sharp and angry debate, and added that after that he had "no doubt that some new and drastic action" must be taken to restore confidence.

"By today," he went on, "it was apparent that some unity could be attained under some other Prime Minister. . . . My duty was plain. I saw his Majesty."

Churchill put new life into the British attack. Allied troops moved up to assist Holland. British warships closed in. A new British War Cabinet was named. All enemy aliens were rounded up. Doctors were urged to volunteer for Britain's Army.

Nazi dive-bombers polluted the sky over Holland and Belgium. R.A.F. planes went after them. In two days 180 Nazi planes were shot down, with a British loss of 100. Allied bombs shrieked down on German-captured areas and airdromes. The British assault was not confined to the invaded countries; bombs also rained on the German Krupp arms works at Essen.

The Germans blasted city after city in Belgium—Brussels, Alost, Renaix, Louvain, Verviers, Antwerp. Holland cities met the same fate. Bombs crashed on the center of Amsterdam, burying, killing, and mangling civilians.

Nazi parachute troops streamed down on the Low Countries. Camouflaged in Allied uniforms, they facilitated German occupation. Dutch women fought them with guns, knives, or any other weapons they could get their hands on. Dutch and Belgians dealt death to all recognizable fifth columnists. British warships bombarded the waves of parachutists as they sailed earthward.

The parachute troops were one of the prime factors in the quick capitulation of the Dutch. Used on a big scale for the first time, they landed behind Allied lines and held bridges and other transportation facilities to aid Nazi progress.

Correspondent Lynn Heinzerling, following the Hitler forces, found out about their exploits:

The pioneer parachute troops are the mystery men of the German Army, especially since they caused such havoc in Holland. They also are silent men, especially when it comes to talking about the weapons they carry on their descents from the sky.

I talked to three of a group who dropped down and held two tremendous bridges—at Moerdijk over Hollandisch Diep, and south of Dordrecht—and while they seemed fond of their jobs, they were quiet about their methods.

The parachutists seized control of the bridges from the Dutch, they said, and held them against all attacks for three days and nights until land troops reached them.

"We flew over high," said one who had received the Iron Cross for his exploit. "We jumped from a low altitude so we wouldn't be in the air so long—probably about 300 meters. There was a bad wind and some of the boys landed in the river."

The trooper, a short, freckled lad of about twenty-two, from Hanover, said they immediately dug into shallow holes around the bridge and resisted all efforts to dislodge them. Their object was to prevent the Dutch from blowing up two bridges, each about a mile long—one a railroad bridge and the other on a highway.

He and his two companions, obviously proud of their success, declined to say what weapons they used or whether they relied wholly on the light machine guns that were dropped in separate "chutes."

The Hanover boy said two British planes bombed them. Craters in the soft earth around the bridge showed where the bombs had fallen. One day, he added, three British ships came up the river with troops, but were sunk before they reached the bridge—how, was not explained.

The sky troops landed on the first day of the invasion and they boasted that by noon they had taken all bunkers occupied by the Dutch near the bridge. Artillery fire then was directed upon them.

A little distance from the Moerdijk bridge, a small group of men in civilian clothes was clustered around thirteen fresh graves marked with wooden crosses. Dutch helmets lay on each grave. Two German soldiers walked up. They took off their caps, stood silently for a minute, then walked away after one of the onlookers whispered to them. A little man with a shovel was there, too. He was not digging a new grave. He was taking home the body of his son.

5

THE LOW Countries were swept by a hurricane of aerial war. Nothing like it had ever been seen before. The Polish blitzkrieg paled by comparison. The rain of death and terror was not confined to combatants. It was total war—not only because the Nazis were throwing everything they had into it, but also because no element of population or property was spared.

France also felt the Nazi terror. Taylor Henry, covering the French Front, saw enough of it to retain a lasting impression of what can happen when modern war machines are at their efficient worst:

Fleeing crowds of (three words censored) refugees from Belgium and northeastern France are streaming toward the interior while the French Army meets the trip-hammer blows of the invading German shock forces.

I have just returned to Paris from a week's stay along the sector of the Front where the fighting is now heaviest.

As P. J. Philip, of the New York *Times,* and I were setting out early yesterday for Paris on bicycles, the only available means of transportation, a German plane dive-bombed behind us. It loosed five bombs on some railroad tracks. We were within forty yards. We threw ourselves flat against a wall amidst a shower of bricks and glass and then raced to a shelter to avoid the plane's spraying machine-gun bullets as it returned.

I pedaled back toward the hotel. Again the planes attacked. The bombs fell a block away. They were bigger bombs this time. The force of the explosion knocked me off the bicycle, ripping the back wheel to pieces. Again the plane returned to attack. Again I ducked to the cover of a wall.

A French major who slept in the hotel room next to mine the night before was among those killed. I recalled he had said to me:

Map 5—The heavy line shows how far the Germans had swept through the Low Countries when the Dutch abandoned all resistance in mid-May, 1940. Belgium, Holland, and Luxembourg, having refused Hitler's "protection," were crushed by a hurricane of land and aerial war.

"If they get one of us and the other escapes, it will be pretty nice shooting, won't it?" We were not over fifty yards apart when they got him, and I escaped with only bruises.

Screams of the wounded after the bombing were ghastly. One woman with arteries severed in both legs was holding a small baby in her arms, crooning to it. An old man hobbled around trying to stop the flow of blood spurting from the stump of his arm. A baby huddled in the corner of the station kept wailing, "Mama, mama."

Bombs destroyed the hotel that for a week had been my headquarters between trips to the front. Everything I had, including a typewriter and a steel trench helmet issued by the American embassy, was lost.

I prevailed upon a terror-stricken boy on a bicycle to repair my wheel. Philip and I started out again for Paris. As we left, a squadron of at least thirty planes was bombing and machine-gunning behind us. We saw billowing clouds of smoke rising from burning towns and villages as we pedaled seventy miles to the next halting place.

From every hill unbroken columns of refugees could be seen winding down to the main highway. Nazi planes were flying everywhere singly and in squadrons up to thirty. Time and time again we ducked from our bicycles and hopped into the ditches alongside the roads to hide.

Town criers went through villages ringing bells and warning everyone to be on the move within an hour. Methodically the peasants closed their homes, loaded their belongings onto pushcarts, in old trucks and great two-wheeled farm chariots drawn by four to eight farm horses. What was left they strapped to their backs and, with scarcely a look behind, started on the same trek that all but the very young had made in 1914.

We reached a little town on the main highway line to Paris, just before nightfall, too tired to do anything but wait for a train. It never came.

I finally left by car, driving a family of refugees and taking the place of a 76-year-old woman because there was nobody else who could drive and there were a mother and five children in the car with room for only one more. The old lady gave me a tearful smile as I left her behind.

"Take care of yourself," she said, "My husband and son were killed in the other war. I am all alone and don't matter."

The Netherlands lasted only a few days. Queen Wilhelmina fled to London. Heinzerling, who seemed to have a faculty for being on hand to witness the final destruction of blitzed cities, saw the last of Rotterdam:

Ruins in proud Rotterdam and the crumbled works of "strong points" in the Dutch defenses tell the story of the shattering impact of Germany's mechanized army and the devastation rained from the skies by the Nazi Stukas.

The Stukas, say the Germans, completed their work in seven and a half minutes, from first bomb to last. The Dutch commander had received a three-hour ultimatum. Shortly after the deadline had been reached, he capitulated. But by then the Germans, fearing that he was holding out in hope of reinforcements, already had started the bombers on their way and it was too late to stop them.

The official toll of wounded is set at 354, while unofficial casualty lists run as high as 10,000. One of the buildings ruined was the American consulate. The consul, John H. Lord, got out before the building was hit.

The 28,000-ton liner *Statendam,* one of the largest in the Dutch merchant fleet, is still smoldering in the harbor. She lay alongside Noordereiland (North Island) in the center of the Nieuwe Maas (New Meuse) River. Chances are that she may have been set afire by a Dutch shell, for it was on Noordereiland that the German positions were centered, and the Nazi forces used the *Statendam* as an effective barricade.

By no means all of the casualties were Dutch, however. German troop planes, seeking to land at an airport a few miles outside the city in the direction of The Hague, found fighting already in progress. The planes—trying emergency landings on a road nearby —were caught by crosscurrents of wind and fifteen cracked up.

In a clearing on top of the fortified hill north of here I saw 450 graves marked by wooden crosses, with trench helmets hung on them. They were about evenly divided between Dutch helmets and German. There were barbed-wire pits and shell holes on all sides. The litter of the equipment of the fallen lay on the ground around the clearing. A German officer stood at one end of the line of crosses and told a handful of correspondents:

"The Dutch Army fought bravely, and the German soldier would be the last to reflect on the honor of a soldier who had fought in such a manner."

The Grebbe fortifications extended from this hill north to Amersfoort and on to the Zuider Zee. To the north of the hill, the Dutch had many more fortifications, as well as one of the areas where they had thought that flooding the land would hold up the German advance. There, too, the Germans broke through on their great surge to the west.

"We knew all about the plan to flood the land and our technical men knew it would not stop us," the German officer said.

The Dutch seem to be taking the occupation philosophically. A few are bitter over the lack of British help—the Germans say only 700 British troops landed in Holland—but otherwise they are seeking to return to normal after an invasion that left them stunned by its speed.

Nor has the occupation appeared to have had much effect on the life of the former Kaiser Wilhelm. The 81-year-old exile is still at nearby Doorn. German authorities say he declined a British Government invitation to remove him and his family "in protection" to England, his enemy of 1914-1918.

6

Nor was life too dull for the white-haired "Exile of Doorn." The former Kaiser kept busy. He traced on his maps the sweep of Hitler's army as it smashed into France. There Hitler pounded through the historic Meuse River Valley and fought the French on the blood-steeped field at Sedan.

The gigantic struggle at Sedan found the French on guard. They had watched the tank-led Nazi columns sweep over Luxembourg in five short days. They knew Hitler wanted to trample a path of invasion toward Paris. They tried to prevent a Nazi crossing of the Meuse at Sedan.

By the night of May 14, the tide was surging back and forth. French military observers called it "the greatest battle in history." At least it was one of the most significant as far as France was concerned. The decisive battle was along France's northern defense —known as "The Little Maginot Line." That was the "soft spot" selected by the Nazis for their Paris break-through. The French said the Nazis were using 7,000 planes, thousands of tanks, and several divisions of foot soldiers along the 100-mile front. The Hitler forces had two objectives:

1. To dominate the whole French coast of the English Channel
—potential springboard for a direct assault on England.

2. To cut in two the Allied Armies before clamping down the
stranglehold that they are confident would mean death or surrender
for French, Belgian, and British forces.

This was the situation on May 20:

The blitzkrieg drive toward Paris appeared for a time today to
have veered toward the English Channel.

The German high command said that its drive to the west had
gained twenty to thirty miles on a line northward from St. Quentin,
which is eighty miles northeast of Paris. It claimed the capture of
Laon, seventy-five miles from the French capital, and a further advance to the Oise-Aisne Canal.

If successful, it was estimated that the German thrust to the
English Channel might isolate 300,000 British soldiers on the Allies'
north flank—and also attain Channel bases for an attack on England. The Channel port of Calais, presumably one of the main
German objectives, is only twenty miles from Dover.

The sudden shift in Nazi tactics came after the Allies were
reported to be massing a huge French-British-Belgian force to pinch
off the fifty-mile-deep German salient striking into the heart of
France on the Meuse River Valley front.

But the Allies could not cope with the Nazi machine. It operated like clockwork. Luxembourg fell. Then Holland. Belgium
wavered. The Allies fell back. Civilians fled Paris. The heavy rum-
bling of artillery fire could be heard in England. The terrific struggle continued. Louis Lochner, touring the lines, caught up with the
Nazi advance guard on May 23. His dispatch that night said:

I have reached the English Channel to find German forces here
and the Nazi swastika flying.

It seems almost unbelievable that I should find Germany at this
Channel. But the swastika waving from the local commander's headquarters leaves no doubt about it.

Here, as elsewhere, the roads of approach are jammed with infantry, more infantry, and still more infantry, and with artillery
even more formidable, backed by an air force equipped to the last
fine detail. All are awaiting Hitler's final command to go to Eng-

land. Everywhere one hears soldiers singing the "Engelland" song. The young men realize that such a venture would be no picnic.

"Maybe fifty of each one hundred ships will be sunk by the British," one infantryman from Saxony said to me in his quaint dialect. "But why shouldn't I be lucky and be on one of the ships that gets over? And if not—well, that just can't be helped."

Just when and if Hitler will push the button, however, nobody could predict.

Meanwhile the opposition forces have tried to restore life to normal on this sector of the front. The Belgians go about their work as usual. Cafés and restaurants are open, with Germans and Belgians mingling freely. Shops are open and goods are sold for either Belgian or German currency.

In spite of the enthusiasm for such an adventure, Hitler is not likely, however, to attempt to attack England herself until he has paved the way to his own satisfaction with a tried and trusted program of these main points:

1—Destruction of all British naval, air, and ground organization by air raiding; 2—Similar destruction of airplanes and vessels; and, 3—Combined attack by speedboats, submarines, and air bombers on British transports and warships.

Not until Der Fuehrer feels that this has been done adequately is he likely to aim a decisive blow with land forces. Continuous bombing of the Belgian Channel port of Ostend and the French ports of Dunkerque, Calais, and Dieppe is in line with this policy, the intention being to demolish docks to which British reinforcements might come and from which British and Allied troops might escape in the event of a rout.

Another thing the Germans are doing now is to try to smash enough Belgian and French airports to prevent the Continental Allies from bringing effective air aid to England in the event she needs it during any German attack on the British Isles.

The men of the armies with which I have been traveling for five days frequently ask me what has happened in the Channel. They seem to be itching to get over to England. But the German leaders are dealing first with the situation at hand and, in addition to pushing forward the right wing and mopping up, are preparing for a possible counteroffensive from the Allies.

Whatever Hitler's plans might be, the swastika was flying at the English Channel.

CHAPTER 7

Over the Arc de Triomphe —
The Swastika

May 24–June 26, 1940

I

HITLER didn't strike out immediately for England. His strategy called first for the defeat of France. He had to make sure of the safety of his English Channel occupation. The Battle of Flanders began.

General Maxime Weygand, placed in command of all Allied Armies four days before the vanguard of Hitler forces reached the Channel, was a disciple of offense. On May 19 he had replaced General Gamelin, a believer in defense. Weygand maneuvered seven divisions of the French between Amiens and Péronne. They were to battle north and meet British forces, which were striking south. This would cut the salient of mechanized Nazi forces down the Somme Valley.

The British Parliament hurried through an Emergency Powers bill giving the government dictatorial authority. The Nazi threat at the Channel brought invasion closer to England than at any time since Napoleon. The Belgian forces continued their stand although the government had moved to Paris. King Leopold was personally directing his Army.

One of Weygand's first acts was to remove fifteen French generals. The damage they had done to morale could scarcely be counted in francs or pounds or dollars. He replaced them with men who had fighting, daring ideas. One of the fifteen replacements was Colonel Charles de Gaulle.

The Allies were squarely behind Weygand, but they got trapped. The only means of rushing supplies to their forces—estimated at 750,000—was via the beleaguered Channel ports. Nazi planes pounded these ports from the air and moved in on them by land. The Nazi air force was too strong. The Nazis were more than the Allies could cope with. Their invasion of France and Belgium demonstrated new tactics. A correspondent in London made a study of what was happening:

The modern method of warfare as used by the Nazis was said today by military observers to have revolutionized tactics. It was described as a naval battle on land. The idea that artillery preparation must precede infantry advance and that supply and ammunition trains must follow the troops was said to be a thing of the past.

Under the new method employed by the German war machine, a huge armada of heavy bombers appears over the country or objective to be attacked. Carrying bombs of up to 500 pounds, these act as the long-range artillery, dive-bombing previously selected targets. Each plane has a definite target of its own.

As these planes drop their bombs and turn about, they become, on the return trip, mechanized machine-gun units, strafing anything visible on the ground. As they return, a new wave of lighter planes, armed with lighter bombs and incendiary fuses, descends like locusts, taking the part formerly delegated to cavalry.

Screening the attack, the new wave clears the way for still another squadron which attempts to take over gasoline depots and supply stations and to make contact with previously planted fifth columnists. The demoralizing of civilians and whatever defensive troops may be in the vicinity also is their aim.

With the way thus cleared, a new air force comes to protect the advance of heavy tanks. The tanks in battle arrange themselves in a fashion similar to naval warfare. The 30- to 60-ton tanks are in the middle, while lighter and faster armored cars and small tanks are on the flanks. They screen the advance of the infantry, which is moved up in buses, trucks, and whatever mobile facilities are available.

These infantry troops are never brought up unless the way is cleared, and the entire mission under the constant protection of fighter planes.

While the infantry is coming up, the parachutists—and there are several branches of parachute troops—perform previously appointed duties. Parachutists wearing five winged birds on their tunic lapels make contact with the fifth columnists, who have been protect-

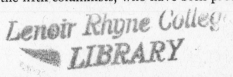

ing their descent, for subsequent maneuvers. Parachutists wearing four birds are landed beyond their objective and make a back-trek toward it, mopping up whatever they find. Three-birders grab and hold supply depots, while the two-birders seize whatever airports there may be, or lacking those, suitable landing fields. The single-bird troops are engineers who open roads so that the advancing infantry may be rushed onward.

Co-ordination of these tactics has been attained thus far. No defense against such an overpowering attack has been created.

Like clockwork, still another transport plane group appears, drops from thirty to fifty parachutists, and then lands at fields presumed to have been seized for the use of wounded soldiers. The purpose of these planes is to return the wounded to home hospitals.

2

BY May 27 the Allied situation was critical. Nazi forces lunged through the line in Flanders, almost to Ypres. They added a length to the steel wall with which they were trying to split the Allied Armies in northern France and Belgium.

The British fell back toward their last port of exit—Dunkerque. The Nazis reported the water front there in flames. Mosquitolike torpedo boats stung the Allies along the Channel coast. Other speedboats rushed Ostend harbor and sank a British destroyer. An Allied submarine was destroyed off Helder, once a Dutch naval base.

The next day came the break that spelled the beginning of the end of the Battle of Flanders. It was a development that opened wide to the Germans the route to Dunkerque. Approximately 500,-000 British troops were being trapped. Roy Porter reported from Paris on May 28:

King Leopold of the Belgians ordered his army of approximately 300,000 men to surrender to the Germans today and was promptly deposed by his own government in Paris. Prime Minister Churchill of Great Britain immediately told the House of Commons that Allied generals had been ordered to continue their campaigns.

Premier Hubert Pierlot announced, contrary to the monarch's order to lay down arms, that such Belgian forces as could be reorganized would continue their fight on the Allies' side. However, Paris announced tonight that the Belgian Army, practically in its entirety, had ceased to fight and that only minor units or new levies

Map 6—The Allied situation was critical by May 27, 1940. The Germans (shaded area) had reached the Channel (1), were closing in on Lille (2), and were repulsing Allied attacks at (3), the narrow point of their spearhead. King Leopold's surrender of his Belgian armies on May 28 set the stage for Dunkerque.

raised from among the throng of Belgian refugees in France would be at the disposal of the Belgian government.

In England, although there was a hint that the B.E.F. in Flanders might sail home, military observers believed that it would fight its way south to the French front. Some experts felt such a course, although desperate, would result in fewer casualties.

Tonight reports from Bern, Switzerland, stated that a huge Allied force, estimated at 450,000 to 600,000 men, was massing on the Aisne River for a now-or-never offensive.

Earlier, the German high command had announced a new series of smashing Nazi successes. Hitler's mechanized columns broke through strong French border fortifications on a broad front, the high command said, and captured numerous towns and villages in the giant squeeze movement on the trapped Allied Armies in Flanders.

The unconditioned surrender of the Belgians broke the back of the Allied Armies of the north and brought the Battle of Flanders to its culminating point.

By the Belgian surrender, the Allies have lost an army of at least eighteen divisions. The way to Dunkerque, the French Channel port through which supplies have been reaching hemmed-in Allied Armies, has been opened to the Nazi legions.

Authorized French military sources called the Belgian King's order "personal treason, of which the King alone must support the total responsibility." Belgian newspaper men in France echoed this charge.

"The King is dead!" they declared, "Long live Belgium!"

Throughout the French-Belgian campaign Hitler's parachute troops and panzer divisions had done an effective job of terrorizing civilian populations. Hundreds of thousands of these ordinary, every-day people—people who never wanted war anyway—took to the highways. They had no place to go. They became homeless wanderers. They were pawns in the Hitler strategy. They caused the world's most tragic traffic jam. Unwittingly, helplessly, they clogged highways and other Allied transportation arteries. Particularly was this true along the route of British retreat to Dunkerque. They made it impossible for Allied troops to remain mobile. Lochner told of the heartbreaking picture they presented:

This war has set in motion one of the most tragic migrations in history.

There is nothing more pitiable than the endless streams of human misery that I have encountered again and again in northern France and Belgium. Death and suffering are bad enough for the men in uniform. But these hundreds of thousands of old men, women, and children, and infants, plodding along as the merciless sun burns their faces or backs, had no choice about their role in this war.

So fast do armies move today that these refugees couldn't even make a sensible selection of what to take with them in their hurry. Nor did they know at the time of fleeing that they would have to keep on the move, constantly retreating from Belgium or northern France, farther and farther south.

En route to St. Pol, I found chalked on houses such remarks as: "Grocer Monsieur Chablis fled with his family to master's house St. Pol," or, "Monsieur and Madame Yvels and their children have gone to Rue de Marseille 21, St. Pol."

But when we reached St. Pol we realized that no one would find Monsieur or Madame Yvels in that town. It had been shelled in the meantime and the civilian population removed. Where Monsieur and Madame Yvels had gone nobody knew.

In the headlong flight, children became separated from parents, husbands from wives, brothers from sisters, in utter tragedy. Had I not traveled for days and days along main roads leading from Cambrai to Arras I wouldn't have believed my own eyes. Marching in one direction, and having the right of way, were German troops with complete equipment, including heavy artillery, soup kitchens, supply trucks, reserves of horses, ambulances, soldiers on foot, on bicycle, on motorcycle, and in armored cars. And plodding through the dust columns in opposite directions were hundreds of thousands of refugees. They always had to move far enough to one side to allow the German troops to pass.

Moreover, when they reached some narrow emergency bridge, they had to wait until many miles of German columns had passed. That sometimes meant hours, during which time the refugees could move neither backward nor forward.

In the villages through which refugees made this pilgrimage, especially in northern France, little help could be given them. The citizens themselves were dependent on Germany's food kitchens. Bread was given out at ten o'clock each morning at local magistrates' offices. On more than one occasion I saw women standing in line beginning at 6 A. M. because they said that by ten o'clock the queue was too long.

Here are a few individual flights of refugees: One family fled as fast as possible in the family automobile, packing it with household goods. But nowhere in northern France is gasoline now available except to the army. So the father and two sons hitched themselves like horses ahead of the auto. The mother and two daughters in their teens pushed behind. Inside were a canary cage and a 3-year-old boy.

One sturdy boy was pushing his aged mother on a wheelbarrow. She looked decidedly uncomfortable, for she sat perched on bedding, cooking utensils, and a suitcase. Sweat streamed down her son's face.

A father and mother pulled an ancient springless cart. In it lay a baby sucking away at a pacifier. Trudging behind the car were boys and girls of 8 and 10 years old. They carried a parrot in a cage suspended on walking canes.

One woman, evidently of the leisure class, walked painfully in high-heeled shoes with costly furs around her neck. Her fashionable hat was bedraggled. She didn't seem to mind the heat so much as her hurting feet.

A tall, gaunt priest had a suitcase slung over his back and fastened there with a leather strap. His right hand clutched a prayer book.

Two nuns led a bicycle by hand. In a wire basket fastened to the handlebars were two baby orphans. On the saddles of the bicycle were bedding and bread bags.

Interspersed among the thousands of pedestrians were horse-drawn vehicles—especially hay wagons. In these, whole families sat on top of their household goods amid purposeless but sentimentally cherished belongings, such as framed wedding pictures and embroidered pillow slips. Often all members of a family had gas masks flung over their backs.

One wondered how and where order would ever come to this confusion, where these fugitives would finally land, and how much of their families would ever be reunited.

3

PATRIOTS could shout, "Long live Belgium!" But Belgium was lost. That was not all. Henry C. Cassidy, assigned to the French side, covered the events of May 29:

The Allies tonight gave up as lost the Battle of Flanders and, in a great retreat, opened the flood sluices around Dunkerque to guard their last port of escape on the sea.

The bloody conflict in the north was all but over. The Germans thus were left substantially in control of France's northern industrial region and her northwest coast, across from England. The virtual collapse of the Allied cause in Flanders—when the Belgian Army's surrender ordered by King Leopold left their flanks laid open—came amid scenes of fire and flood.

While the waters rose steadily in the vast system of streams around Dunkerque, French divisions fought across the tortured landscape to hold the rear while British troops defended the main points of passage for the main forces seeking the coastline.

The Allies brought on the inundation by opening the locks southwest and northeast of Dunkerque on the great canal that flows by the city and follows the coast for many miles.

In Dunkerque the last Allied resistance was rallied under Vice-Admiral Jean Marie Abrial, 61-year-old commander of the port. The Allied navies and air forces fought together in an effort to save as much as possible from the wreckage of Flanders. The retreat was harassed by heavy German fire. Some Belgian units, refusing to lay down their arms despite their King's order to capitulate, were still fighting beside the British and French. A single French division, which had been stationed with the Belgians as the backbone of their front, tried to hold back the Nazi rush in the Nieuport-Dixmude sector, a World War battlefield on the coast northeast of Dunkerque. Suicide squads also held out on the eastern and southern sides of the Allied path to the sea.

Dunkerque, manned by French sailors, was the last stand of solid Allied positions. The rest of the battlefield was a maelstrom of free-for-all fighting, lighted up by blazing fires. Airplanes tangled in the heavy clouds hanging over the battle area. Allied dive-bombers, using the low-flying tactics they employ against submarines and warships, plunged on German tanks.

The Germans made Lille, the industrial center of northern France, and Calais, on the Straits of Dover, particular battlegrounds. But their advance was slowed by Allied sharpshooters waging guerrilla warfare in the fields and fighting in the streets of the cities.

And tonight, toward the vital city of Dunkerque, the bulk of an entrapped army of half a million was backing.

4

AFTER May 29 no chance remained for the British to stage a
come-back. They could not rejoin the main French armies south of
the Somme for a counteroffensive that such a concentration of
forces would have made possible. The only possibility of escaping
butchery was evacuation by sea from Dunkerque. Even that seemed
hopeless. The desperate flooding of sluices around Dunkerque was
not sufficient to stem the Nazi hordes. It slowed enemy land forces,
but the Stukas did not have to worry about water.

The happenings during the next two or three days amazed the
world. With hell breaking loose on land, sea, and in the sky, British
rescue ships fought their way into the harbor. Protecting warships
and R.A.F. bombers built a wall of flame between the retreating
forces and the blinding Nazi attack.

Across the Channel thousands of English families heard of the
situation at Dunkerque. Husbands, sons, brothers were being slaughtered. There was every prospect that thousands of their people were
dying without even a chance to defend themselves. That was not
the worst of it. Invasion of the British Isles themselves appeared
imminent. England had not faced such a situation in the memory
of any living man or woman.

It was the same in the streets, in the stores, and in the homes.
For the first time since the war started, there was reluctance to
discuss what was taking place. Ashy-faced citizens, most of them
awaiting word of a relative or a friend, no longer could talk about it.

Then the first rescue ships from Dunkerque began to return.
Out of them came dirty, crippled, blood-covered men. Many were
unrecognizable. Some babbled incessantly. Some were wrecks of
what they had been. And many of them needed only a shave, sleep,
and food.

A score of correspondents, awaiting the return of the rescue
ships, found out what had happened. The legend that newsmen are
hard and emotionless should have been dissipated once and for all
that day. Some of those who witnessed the Dunkerque return probably never will forget the sight of so many men returning from
the dead. But they rounded up what they saw and reported it with
restraint:

Thousands of Britain's smashed army of Flanders, staggering
with fatigue from the bloody twenty-day failure across the Chan-

nel, landed on home soil tonight. But many were lost on the narrow stretch of water that was turned into a raging strip of fire.

From crowded liners to tiny boats with only a few men aboard, a great armada brought them home, poured them onto troop trains, and went back, under the fire of German guns and bombers, for more.

Tonight the total of the British, French, and Belgians brought over the tortured Channel ferry routes of war was somewhere near 100,000. But one of them said: "Thousands more were massed at the Dunkerque wharves early this morning waiting for ships."

On the narrow station platforms along the way to London stood the anxious wives and wide-eyed children of the B.E.F., straining at the windows of the troop-filled trains. They were waiting, too, with dread, for the casualty lists that have not come.

In London, when they opened one compartment door, they found a British officer dead, his pistol beside him. On one platform a 6-year-old girl sprang into the arms of a grimy soldier. It was her brother, unheard from for six weeks. One soldier held a bottle of beer to the lips of a sailor who had both arms swathed with bandages. Many of the men limped until they saw a sympathetic eye upon them; then they straightened fiercely. Padres straight from the front and women of the auxiliary territorial services came back with the fighters.

Across the Channel the sun gleamed on the white shoreline of France and the green fields beyond. The black plume of smoke from a huge fire near Dunkerque mounted in the sky.

"It's an inferno over there; a hell made by man," said one artilleryman. "The Germans asked for a truce to bury their dead after a thirty-six-hour barrage had held up their advance. We replied: 'There's no truce.' And we gave them another seven hours of barrage."

With those who returned were many French infantrymen. There were men who told in awe of the might of the German Army and air force and of the cheapness with which life was held in the Nazi columns. Their trip across the Channel had been scarcely less punishing than the twenty days spent in ravaged Flanders.

One soldier thus described the embarkations: "When we were hit (by bombs) we swam ashore, but when the ship didn't go down we swam back to her again to take her out of the harbor. Then she turned turtle and we had to swim again. Some of us were in the water for hours before we were picked up by a British warship."

Telling of suffering continuous air attacks from the very beginning of the Flanders campaign, they all declared it was the great
swarms of German planes and the great weight of German numbers that finally sent them reeling in retreat. Hospital ships as well
as troopships, they declared, were targets for Nazi bombs.

"Our flyers are magnificent," said one, "but it's volume that
we need."

Another, telling of the Channel trip, philosophically described
his troubles with a ship that had been hit:

"I was very thankful when, after swimming seven or eight
miles, I was able to get hold of a table. Another fellow and I sat on
it until we were picked up. All of us were almost naked, and we
have had no food since yesterday and no sleep for three days. But
it's back again now to help the army.

"It's not only British troops we're bringing over," he explained,
"but French and Belgians too. The Belgians don't want to give up
fighting. If only they would give us more planes, we could tell the
Germans a different story. As it is, they have got as much as they
have given, and we have not been bombing and machine-gunning
men in the water."

The withdrawals from Flanders, which already have cost the
British three destroyers and a number of auxiliary craft, went on
tonight while those remaining on the French side were fighting a
great rear-guard action to hold Dunkerque until the retreat is
complete.

Over and over these returning men, many blood-stained and
black with powder, emphasized the need for planes and more planes.
They told of Germans attacking in waves of fifty planes time after
time, literally filling the air overhead. They accused the Nazi flyers
of mass murder of refugees, flying 200 feet off the ground and
sparing nobody.

"They mowed them down with machine-gun fire like grass
under a mower," said one.

A private who had been shot in the foot declared he wanted to
go back as soon as his wound healed, adding: "I can't forget the
way those Huns treated the refugees."

A sergeant major asserted: "Although we come back wounded,
we have given them plenty to remember us by. At times the slaughter
was wholesale. Column after column (of Germans) was mowed
down by our Bren guns. The morale of our men was superb. When
they were embarking, bombers raided the ships and one (ship's)

gun crew was put out of action. Wounded men went to take a share in feeding the guns."

One trooper carried a cloth doll as a present for his young daughter; it had been blown out of a toyshop window in a Belgian town by a bomb.

One seaman said that, when the boats of his rescue ship were sent ashore to look for the British troops, the men came out wading up to their necks in the water. Shortly afterward, German planes swooped down and the rescue work was carried out in a hail of bombs.

"On our way home, however, we got some revenge," he said. "Our gunners brought down five Dornier Flying Pencils."

Another Tommy exclaimed: "I never believed anything like the wall of fire our ships put up to screen troops was possible. Shells fell in a mathematically straight line behind our positions, while beyond the line British planes dropped bombs like hail. Jerry never had a chance to get at us."

Still another: "From a long line of British warships poured an unending stream of shells to form a barrage beyond our line, while squad after squad of bombers poured tons of explosives on German troop concentrations."

An army officer said: "Our losses in the last few days have been far less than might be expected, but the slaughter among the Germans has been incredible."

Loaded down with full equipment, shipload after shipload arrived. Police and military guards kept from the piers crowds pressing for a glimpse of loved ones. But coast dwellers got near enough to the disembarking warriors to give them a great cheer.

The soldiers were singing, shouting, and waving as they took places in trains and motorbuses. But they slumped into their seats, too tired and worn to do much of this. Typical was a heavy fellow with several days' growth of beard. He gave a tired grin and said:

"We've had a terrible time this 'ere last fortnight . . . swimming canals . . . nights without sleep . . . bombings. Fifty or more Jerry planes would sail over and drop their bombs. Just as we were getting over that, here would come fifty or so more, and so on, in relays."

All ranks said the Germans took a terrific pounding in spite of their temporary gain of territory. The Tommies said, too, that the Royal Air Force showed "marked superiority" over German flyers, man for man and plane for plane, despite its far inferior numbers.

One group reported that German planes bombed them steadily before embarkation and told of raids by bombers on their steamer after they had left port.

A veteran of the last war said that German advance was accomplished "by sheer weight of numbers."

"The British put up a barrage a mile long to stem the advance," he added. "I fought in the last war, but I have never seen anything like it. The Germans advanced right into it, disregarding danger. Their casualties must have been tremendous."

Another soldier said fleeing refugees hampered movements of the Allied troops throughout. He added: "The Germans drove tanks right over them, caring nothing for men, women, or children. It was mass murder in the first degree."

5

THE Medical Ministry appealed for nurses and more nurses. Women took over men's jobs in London subways. Roosevelt said all continents eventually might become involved in the war; he asked for billions for rearmament. Britain banned auto radios. The British battleship *Nelson* was reported sunk.

The Nazi land and air attacks continued in France. One bomber killed sixteen civilians and wounded ninety others near Lyon. Heavy German artillery and dive-bombers continued to blast the Dunkerque barricades. Nazi planes roared over the Rhone Valley and Marseille. They left death and destruction in half-a-dozen cities and towns.

While England was "holing in" for the expected Nazi assault on her own shores, Taylor Henry looked down on France from an army plane:

Seen from the air at night, the entire northern front in France looks like a flaming torch. I have just made a long night reconnaissance flight over the northern battlefields. The red glow from flaming cities and towns gave the low-hanging clouds the appearance of a late summer sunset. Far below, along the battle lines on the Somme and Aisne Rivers, flashes of artillery fire looked like matches flaring.

To the north and east there was an almost continuous line of

burning towns—Cambrai, St. Quentin, Arras, Péronne, Valenciennes
—linked by smoldering fires in the little villages between. Most of
these were fired days ago by incendiary bombs and torch-bearing
parachutists, but still the flames rise.

It was just at nightfall that the bombing squadron, of which
I was a guest, received its orders: "Attack in force against Cambrai
airport and the crossroads south of Abbeville, where important
German troop concentrations have been observed."

Tonight was dark and moonless, and only an occasional star
peeped in and out of the late spring rain clouds, hanging low over
the zone. The commander of the squadron who, only two days
before, had bombed his native village in the Ardennes, now German-occupied, loaned me flying gear—three suits of heavy cover-
alls, one heated by electricity; fur-lined boots, a crash helmet, and
thick gloves.

When we reached the darkened airport, the plane was ready.
After a quick handshake around, the five of us took our places. A
thin line of red lights flickered on the field to mark our runway. The
first pilot—I was listed as a supernumerary second pilot—gave the
huge plane the gun and we lifted into the air, circled the field, and
then headed toward the battle zone.

Below us stretched the peaceful French countryside. Heavy
dark masses marked the forests, while the rivers and highways appeared as black ribbons. Some ten minutes before the front was
reached, it was outlined by flashes of artillery fire.

Because of the clouds, we were flying low over French-held
territory, but as we neared the battle zone the plane rose to escape
the fire of anti-aircraft guns. The French pilots have nicknamed the
German 20-millimeter anti-aircraft guns "poms-poms," and that is
exactly the sound they make as the shells explode in the air.

The heaviest anti-aircraft fire was concentrated by the Germans
around St. Quentin and Péronne. It is not exactly a comfortable
feeling to be sitting in a plane while the "poms-poms" burst around.
They explode on almost every side at almost the same moment that
you see the flashes on the ground. Unless they are very close, they
give the sensation of a gigantic fireworks display.

From the air at night the battlefront running from Montmédy,
where it leaves the Maginot Line, through Stenay, Attigny, Rethel,
Neufchâteau, Anizy, La Fère, Chauny, Ham, and Amiens to Abbeville, on the English Channel, shows as a scarcely defined line. If it

were not for the Aisne and the Somme Rivers, which the line follows, it would be difficult to recognize.

Apparently heavy fighting was going on in the Amiens-Albert region, where the French seem to have driven a salient. There the flash of artillery was heavier than at any other part of the line and there we saw minute flames which the observation officer said were from machine-gun fire.

Our plane was scouting to learn the effect of the bombing of the other planes. The squadron already had bombed the Cambrai airport when we arrived over it. The southeast corner of the airport was in flames, indicating that a direct hit had been made on either gasoline tanks or stocks of incendiary bombs.

The squadron skirted the zone where British and French forces were almost cut off in Flanders. Flames could be seen raking the Channel ports, which are the only means of supply and evacuation for the two embattled armies there. As far inland as we were, it was difficult to establish the line of the seacoast, but flashes from what we believed were Allied warships indicated the fleets were supporting the Allied Armies.

Behind the German lines, fast-moving convoys were outlined as dark blurs on the roads. Only at crossroads could their movement be distinguished.

From the air, the effect of the bombs dropping was almost undistinguishable. It may have been because they were dropped from another plane, but the only noticeable effect was the blurring of an already obscure mass. Observers of the plane that dropped the bombs, however, reported direct hits.

The return flight was uneventful except for the delicate task of setting the plane down on a darkened field. Even fully loaded bombers are given only a brief flash of light as they start to settle down.

Laurent Eynac, French air minister, reported tonight, after a visit to squadrons equipped with newly arrived American bombers, that the flyers were "highly satisfied" with the American machines. He said that they are arriving in "considerable quantities" from the United States.

6

HITLER's plan was to complete destruction of the French forces in the field. For a few days, Weygand and his forces held on the Somme. They were fighting alone since the British had evacuated.

They did not last long. By June 3, Hitler was sufficiently confident to turn some of his terrorizing attention elsewhere.

Beautiful, ageless, effervescent Paris basked in the June sunshine. Along the boulevards people were enjoying their midday meals. There was an alarm, and 250 Nazi planes roared overhead. The greatest air armada ever launched up to that time was bent on wreaking more Hitler vengeance.

It took the bombers only sixty seconds to spill their cargoes of death. Two hundred and fifty-four people were killed; 652 wounded. A total of 1,050 bombs were dropped. Ninety-seven building were hit, including eight schools. Ten bombs crashed into one temporary hospital, killing two nurses. Sixty-one fires were started. American Ambassador Bullitt narrowly missed death from a bomb that fell six feet away but failed to explode.

Robert Okin was one of those who felt the first deafening impact:

Three bombs fell 150 yards from where I was lunching today (four words censored) in the brilliant sunshine of a June day.

The café trembled as though in an earthquake, and the shrill whine of bombs was plainly audible before the explosives crashed just around the corner.

One flattened a district post office into a mass of rubble. Another, apparently a small one, nearly took the corner off an apartment house. A third hit diagonally into the cellar of a bank, leaving the bank standing. For an area of a block around where each bomb struck, the streets were littered with glass and mortar. Pieces of steel girders lay crumbled in the street.

In the distance, black smoke was rising from a fire and the air was thick with dust for half an hour after the bombs were dropped.

People sat calmly at tables in the café as the bombs fell. One man called for more wine between explosions. Several army officers laid down their forks, but others continued to eat. A few people went into the basement.

Up and down some of the city's most fashionable boulevards, bombs smashed into buildings, broke the pavements, sent lampposts bouncing into streets, and jolted trees to their roots.

Several bombs landed near the house of the Duke and Duchess of Windsor. Down the street from where they live, an apartment building caved in. Next door the neighbors stared glumly through paneless windows into a hole forty feet deep, scooped magically and thunderously out of their front yard.

William J. Humphreys, another of the Paris correspondents, was taking his day off when the bombing began. Several paragraphs of his story were eliminated by the censor, but most of them got through:

The sirens across the river from where I live began wailing at 1:20 P.M. (8:20 A.M. New York time) today and the thunder of the first exploding bombs was heard ten minutes later.

My Polish maid, Anna Malarz, who used to live in Massillon, Ohio, rushed in and shut all the windows. Then she gathered together a few possessions and hurried to the air raid shelter in the basement.

Then the bombing began in earnest. For more than half an hour the bombardment kept up steadily, bombers circling around (here one word censored) suburbs. None fell nearer than a block away, however (eight words censored).

(Fourteen words censored.) Four of the wounded, none of whom was hurt seriously, were treated at (one word censored) hospital, directly across the square from where I live. Among those in the hospital was Mrs. Maurice Dalva, an American of New York City, who gave birth Sunday morning to a daughter. She was not hurt.

Before I could get dressed and get downstairs to an air raid shelter, the building shook from terrific explosions almost in the front yard. Windows in the building were shattered.

Edwin Pitt, second secretary of the American embassy, who lives next door, said that he saw stones bounce off his car. He watched the bombing from behind closed steel shutters with smoke drifting in through the air holes.

Ambulances and fire engines streamed across the bridge near my house. The bridge was not damaged although bombs fell near both ends. I could see the damage done at one factory. There were dead and wounded inside, but a fire kept rescue workers away. In one street I saw a bomb hole at least forty feet across and thirty-five feet deep.

Five hundred persons in the State Old Peoples' Home, just two blocks away, escaped injuries. At the first signal they herded into shelters. One bomb fell only twenty-five feet behind a chapel, but a park near by took the full force of the concussion away from the buildings, which were not damaged. Along one quay, windows were broken from the ground floor as far up as the seventh.

Ten minutes after the last explosion street department trucks appeared to patch up the holes. The whole neighborhood helped. The coolest man I saw was the superintendent of our apartment building, a veteran of the last war. Sitting calmly in the basement shelter, he said: "Why worry? If a bomb hits us, it hits us. This may be only the beginning."

7

THE CRADLE of Christianity—Jerusalem—was blacked out. French planes bombed Frankfort. The British estimated that 335,000 had been rescued from Dunkerque. British bombers attacked the munition works at Mannheim. The Netherlands began pumping water from flooded regions in order to plant late crops. Five were sentenced to death in France as spies. Churchill reported loss of all British military equipment in Flanders. There was talk about manufacturing synthetic rubber in the U. S. British women agreed to forego permanent waves.

All of Norway finally surrendered. King Haakon and his government fled to England. That was on June 9. The same day General Weygand told his hard-pressed troops: "The German offensive has now been launched on the whole front from the sea to Montmédy. The order remains that each one fight with no thought of retreat, staying where he has been placed, and looking straight ahead."

Weygand and his men stayed where they were placed and looked "straight ahead." But they had neither sufficient equipment nor sufficient numbers. The French had lost their stomach for war.

The government sprang the next surprise. Its action stunned the nation. Parisians stood open-mouthed and speechless when they heard the news on June 10. The French government, without ceremony, had fled Paris. France was as good as taken although Weygand and his men continued their stand. In a matter of weeks she had gone the way of so many of Europe's smaller countries.

In Italy, Mussolini finally was on the move. He heard of the imminent fall of France. The dictator's somewhat flabby face tightened in stern imitation of old-time power and determination. Now that the European war was as good as won, he could join Hitler and share the spoils. That day—hours before any declaration—

Richard G. Massock slipped through a cable that told the world what to expect. That night he sent the details from Rome:

Italy joined the war tonight on the side of the German legions which are pressing down perilously on Paris, and in Berlin it was announced that Italian troops already had entered France through the Riviera.

Notice of the plunge into hostilities, after months of teetering on the brink, was made by Premier Mussolini from the balcony of the Palazzo Venezia. In announcing his war aims, he called chiefly for recovered control of the Mediterranean and declared for preservation of peace in the Balkans and in Turkey and Egypt.

"Our will," he said, "is that Italy does not intend to bring other people into the conflict. Yugoslavia, Greece, Turkey, and Egypt will take notice of this fact."

Speaking from the balcony to Fascist Blackshirts gathered in the square below and in other squares over the kingdom, where loud-speakers were rigged up, the premier declared:

"We are descending to the battlefields against the plutocratic reactionary democracies."

Mussolini warned the Balkans and the Mediterranean nations that any breach of neutrality would spread the war to them. His pronouncement affecting Egypt and Turkey was seen as an attempt to divert them from pledges to assist the Allies. Overtures to Egypt were made by the Italian press last week but were generally rejected. The Romans also have attempted to break up the mutual assistance pact the Allies have with Turkey, a vital point in the control of the eastern Mediterranean. With Turkey favorable or acquiescent, Italy then might open up for herself the British-controlled gateway to the rewards of its conquest of Ethiopia. Similarly, at the other end of the Mediterranean, the Axis Powers hope to wrest control of Gibraltar from England.

Italy's fateful step was taken after months of hesitation to weld into actual hostilities the ends of the long-existent Axis between Berlin and Rome. Before making the announcement, Mussolini called on "combatants on land, sea, and in the air, Blackshirts of the revolution and of the legion, men and women of Italy, of the Empire and the Kingdom of Albania" to listen. He said that Italy had tried in vain for peace. He declared that "the Allies should have accepted the proposals of Hitler before the Polish campaign." He concluded:

"A great people is ready to face its destiny and mark its own history in the future. We want to break the chains that bind us in the Mediterranean. It is a struggle between young and progressive people as against the decadent people, the struggle of one century as against another century. The die is cast!"

8

CHURCHILL termed Italy's delayed entry into the war as "cowardice." Roosevelt said: "On this tenth day of June, 1940, the hand that held the dagger has struck it into the back of its neighbor." Then he urged "full speed ahead" with a dual program of helping to arm the Allies and preparing America for any eventuality.

Russia and Japan ended long-time hostilities by agreeing on boundaries. Britain bombed Italian bases in Libya. Turkey and Germany signed a trade agreement. Italian forces attacked Tunis, Malta, and Corsica. German troops reached the outskirts of Paris. Rome's blacked-out pedestrians were told to wear luminous buttons. Egypt severed relations with Italy. In a ten-minute action, British planes dropped 100 bombs per minute on Nazi forces in France, wrecking convoys, mechanized columns, and land tanks. Still Hitler ploughed forward on all fronts. His elaborate machine, seemingly impregnable, amazed all who sought the reasons for its invincibility.

Claude Jagger, AP Financial Editor in New York, pored over the facts behind Germany's impressive effort and found an answer to history's strangest "success" story:

War is fantastically costly, yet a nation internationally bankrupt and vastly deficient in natural resources is able to build and launch a war machine of such might and destructiveness as to shake the world.

How does Germany do it, in defiance of traditional economics, in seeming repudiation of all accepted canons of finance?

Only six years ago the Reich, denuded of gold and foreign balances and her credit shattered, suspended payments on all foreign debts. Dr. Schacht, then head of the Reichsbank, complained of his country's dependence on foreign raw materials, appealed to the world for a "spirit of compromise, patience, and good will." Financially and economically, the nation seemed down and out. Yet, within a few months Adolf Hitler was rapidly developing his vast and costly armament program.

Last autumn Hitler said he had spent 90,000,000,000 reichsmarks to rearm. The world was incredulous. Since the German currency was unbacked by gold and had no free world market, one could not say how much that was in dollars, but at the official rate, it would come to $36,000,000,000. What Germany currently is spending is not known, but the expenditure is enormous. British sources have placed it at $15,000,000,000 annually. Other estimates are higher.

Any consideration of what can be spent on war, economists explain, must begin by banishing peacetime standards. In 1914, economists were almost unanimous that no nation was financially able to wage war for more than a few months. Yet the direct money outlays of the first World War, exclusive of costs of loss of life, destruction of property, depreciation of capital, and loss of trade, has been calculated at the astronomical figure of 186 billion dollars, about seven times the entire amount spent by the United States government from 1789 to 1916.

Consideration of how Germany, a poor have-not nation, has been able to pay for its breath-taking adventure in conquest in this era when war rolls on wheels and plunges through the clouds and is immeasurably more expensive than in 1914-1918, must go back to the beginnings of the Nazi regime.

Hitler found some 30 per cent of German workers unemployed, factories were idle, there was lack of money to import essential materials and food supplies. In this crisis, Germans willingly acquiesced in a system of controls of industry, labor, trade, and finance such as had never before been applied in any modern industrialized nation. These controls increased until today, if you are a German, the government tells you what you may eat, what you may wear, where you must work, the hours you shall labor, what wages you may receive, what prices you shall pay for the essentials of life.

If you are a manufacturer, you are told what you shall make, what you will sell it for, and that after you have paid your taxes, profits left must be loaned to your government. If you operate a savings bank or an insurance company, you are told where you must invest the funds of your institution.

Only last month the British government asked and received similar authorization powers. Regimentation is a program of enormous detail and takes time. Hitler has a six-year start.

Germany is paying the costs not only by leveling staggering taxes and borrowing all of the people's savings the government can lay its hands on, but by severe sacrifice of the standard of living and of the creature comforts of her people. Thus, economists explain, the whole national effort is geared for war. Normal replacements and repairs to industrial plants, housing, and institutions not needed for the conduct of the war, are neglected.

Walther Funk, present head of the Reichsbank, said in April that production of consumers' goods must be restricted and businessmen must refrain from investing in replacements. Savings, he said, must be made available to the Reich through savings banks and credit institutions. How much of the total German effort is going into war, it is impossible to estimate, but an analysis of the situation at the outbreak of the war, recently made public by the U. S. Department of Commerce, said that taxes and other levies in the fiscal year 1938-1939 took 17 per cent of the national income. Currently, the percentage must be higher.

But, aside from the intensive internal organization of the Reich, she has the problem of finding ways to obtain essential materials from abroad. Of three principal industrial materials—coal, iron and petroleum—Germany is well supplied with coal. Domestic sources of cotton, wool, copper, rubber, and a host of other materials are lacking.

First, say international trade authorities, it must be remembered that Germany imported greatly more than her normal needs of many supplies in the years before the war. Also, early in the Nazi regime, all foreign trade was placed under rigid regulation. Free dealings in the world market in German currency were banished. An American exporter could get payment of German money, but it was kept in the country. The exporter could use the currency there to buy German goods, which he could then import to the U. S., sell here, and thus get dollars.

This sounds complicated, but a whole range of different kinds of German money, which one could get in varying amounts depending upon the type of transaction often enough made these deals attractive to foreign traders. For instance, the Reichsmark has an "official" exchange rate of about 40 American cents, so that in selling a $40 article in Germany one would get 100 Reichsmarks. But on certain transactions, desirable to that government, one would get 20-cent Reichsmarks, or 200 of them.

Nevertheless, the supply problem for Germany, in the minds

of most economic and military experts, remains Hitler's Achilles' heel. Of coal, he has plenty. Iron supplies have been increased by the seizure of Luxembourg; Sweden, chief ore supply base, must presumably do what she can to meet German demands, taking currency good only in Germany, spending it there for whatever supplies she can get, since she is cut off from assistance from Allied Powers.

The Reich has acquired big food and industrial supplies by her seizure of the Low Countries and Denmark, but will have a problem of feeding their peoples when the supplies are used. Oil seems the most serious problem. International oil experts say even if Germany were able to get the entire Rumanian flow, the annual output of that country, together with the Reich's own small production and what she is getting from Russia, would mean in a year only what the U. S. produces in twenty days.

Thus, the fantastic German organization and endeavor, economically and financially, seems to make a "short" war essential to German victory.

9

As FAR as a "short" war was concerned, there were times when it appeared that a short war was all that was necessary—at least as far as Hitler was concerned. On June 13, Paris was declared an open city. Hitler's forces poured through the gates. Lochner arrived with them. The veteran correspondent had been on the fighting line for days. He was dead tired. Cable communications direct to the United States had been cut. He got his story out by courier plane on June 14:

The swastika banners of Nazi Germany, unfurled by the Austrian vanguard which Adolf Hitler significantly sent as the first of his troops to occupy Paris, floated today from atop almost every prominent and historic structure in this German-captured capital of France.

It is recalled that last January 30, in a speech commemorating the seventh anniversary of the Nazi rise to power, the Fuehrer twitted the premier of France for having expressed "a pity" for Hitler's native Austria, and warned:

"Oh, Monsieur Daladier, you're going to get to know my Austrians. You're going to make their acquaintance."

Only the Austrian vanguard is here. Other divisions have passed through the city, hurrying on to battle without pause. The bulk of the Army of Occupation is not here yet, but is expected to start arriving before this is received in America. That Hitler himself is due here soon is taken for granted.

We arrived last night in this city that seems dead. I just do not recognize Paris again. Seventy per cent of its population has fled. From the Hôtel Crillon, where once President Wilson of the United States addressed French crowds, the swastika is flying. The banner also is flying from atop the Quai d'Orsay (the French Foreign Office), from the Arc de Triomphe, under which lies buried France's Unknown Soldier of the World War; from the historic City Hall, and from the Eiffel Tower. It all seems unreal, like an Arabian Nights tale come to life.

We came by way of the Clichy Gate. No Germans were visible anywhere along our drive through this section. Such few citizens as stood around at corners or gathered about radio loud-speakers, gazed at us in curiosity. They apparently had not seen any German officers before.

The familiar cries of Parisian newspaper vendors, which in normal times simply belong to Parisian life as an essential component, are missing. Along the Champs Élysées, only one café was open—all else was deadly silent.

Other avenues radiating from the Place de la Concorde, which normally are crowded with people sipping their apéritifs, were deserted. At the normally busy Place de l'Opéra, I counted exactly eleven persons, two of them policemen. Many of the city's most popular hotels were closed.

The Scribe Hôtel was requisitioned and we found clean rooms and beds there but almost no personnel to look after us. The kitchen was closed, so we had to go over to the Ritz. Here the restaurant manager tried to beg off from serving our party which included nine foreign correspondents.

From the American embassy the Stars and Stripes were displayed. Near by the swastika waved on the flagstaff on the Crillon Hôtel.

Paris was quite another city when the fountains of the Place de la Concorde were not playing, when taxi drivers were not honking, when bookstalls were not doing business as usual along the Seine, when all business life was at a standstill.

Le Bourget, the great Paris airport, was a shambles. It had been singled out especially by German bombers for destruction. Creil, too, was badly shelled and little remained.

En route, we had to cross the Oise River near Oriel on a pontoon bridge hastily constructed by German Army engineers, since the original bridge had been dynamited. Amiens had been heavily bombed. All around its priceless cathedral—the largest ecclesiastical edifice in France—everything had been blown to bits, including the bishop's residence. Block after block in the heart of the city was in ruins, and clouds of smoke still hung over whole sections of the still-smoldering city, yet the cathedral, completed in 1288, escaped unscathed.

Throughout the eighty-mile drive from Amiens to Paris, I had plenty of occasion to note evidences of the vigor with which the retreating French had fought. When the Germans started from Amiens against the so-called Weygand Line on June 5, they ran up against a system comparable in many respects to Germany's own Siegfried Line, which differs from the Maginot in that it is not linear and massed but is carried far to the rear on a stagger principle. General Weygand's plan, which the Germans themselves admit was cleverly conceived, lacked time for realization.

Those who loved Paris, which was so much more than just the fifth largest city of the world, will not wish to go over all the depressing details of June, 1940. France formally asked for an armistice on June 17. Marshal Pétain made the request. His action stunned the battle-worn poilus, who had fought day and night. The Pétain request came on the heels of French Premier Paul Reynaud's "final appeal" for "clouds of airplanes from across the Atlantic to crush the evil power that has descended over Europe."

Berlin claimed that the conquest over France had been so fast that the Nazi invaders were hard put to catch up with the fleeing enemy. But the Nazi onslaught had not ended with the fall of Paris. It surged ninety miles beyond. The mighty Maginot Line was abandoned. Hitler's legions penetrated the $500,000,000 fortifications, and found them almost empty.

Four days after Pétain asked for an armistice, Hitler met the French envoys at Compiègne Forest. It was as ironic to the French as it was satisfactory to Hitler. The meeting occurred in the same railroad car in which Foch had given defeated Germany its peace terms in 1918. Lochner covered the negotiations:

Adolf Hitler reached the highest point of his meteoric career in historic Compiègne Forest when he personally received the French

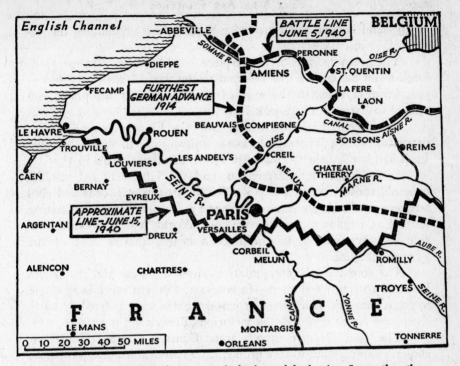

Map 7—By June 15, 1940, the Germans had advanced farther into France than they had in the first World War, and Paris, the prize they could not attain then, was in their hands. A ten-day blitzkrieg—the battle lines above indicate its sweep—had turned the French withdrawal into such a rout that on June 17 France formally asked for an armistice.

envoys and handed them armistice terms which proclaimed the defeat of France.

The meeting was a masterpiece of Hitlerean revenge, prolonged and handed to France—and to the world—with a bluntness that brought tears to the eyes of the Frenchmen who had been elected to barter for France's future.

Der Fuehrer laid the setting for the French surrender with dramatic cruelty. The scene was the railway car in which Marshal Foch had handed the Germans the Allied armistice terms in 1918.

In the lengthening afternoon shadows, Hitler entered the historic old railway car. He was flanked by his top war lords and civil advisers. He took the same seat used by Marshal Foch in dictating terms to Germany at the conclusion of World War I. Looking outside the car window, he could see a nearby marble bust of the French marshal.

The four French representatives entered the car and Hitler and his staff rose to greet them—in contrast, German officials asserted, to the manner in which the German delegates were greeted in 1918. Then, the Nazis declared, the victorious French did not rise.

The four French envoys were General Charles Huntziger, chosen as spokesman for the group; Rear Admiral Maurice Athanase Le Luc, Léon Noel, former French ambassador to Poland, and General of Aviation Jean Marie Joseph Bergeret.

Seated with Hitler at the conference table were Field Marshal Hermann Wilhelm Goering, whose Luftwaffe had blasted French resistance from the sky, and Rudolph Hess, deputy fuehrer, among others.

At a nod from Hitler, the chief of the German high command, Colonel General Wilhelm Keitel, slowly read the preamble to the armistice terms. This took about ten minutes. When it was over, Hitler stepped from the car, his face wreathed in smiles. Then the French delegates also left the car. They went to a tent near by and began a discussion by telephone with the French government at Bordeaux.

The preamble read by General Keitel first denounced the Allied peace terms in 1918 and then outlined Hitler's 1940 demands. The preamble was:

"In reliance on assurances given the German Reich by the American President Wilson and confirmed by the Allied Powers, German forces laid down their arms in November, 1918.

"Therewith was ended a war which the German people and its

government had not wanted and in which the enemy, despite tremendous superiority, did not successfully in any way conquer the German Army, Navy, or German Air Force.

"However, at the moment of the arrival of the German Armistice Commission, violation of the ceremoniously given promise began. On November 11, 1918, in this car then began the time of suffering of the German people.

"What dishonor and humiliation, what human and material suffering could be caused had its outlet here. Broken promises and perjury conspired against a people which after more than four years of heroic resistance had only one weakness—belief in the promises of democratic statesmen.

"On September 3, 1939—twenty-five years after the outbreak of the World War—England and France again declared war on Germany without any basis.

"Now the decision by arms has been reached. France has been conquered. The French government has requested the Reich government to make known to them the German conditions for an armistice.

"In the historic Compiègne Forest, designated for the reception of these conditions, this is done in order once and for all to wipe out by this act of redeeming justice the memory which for France was no glorious page in its history, but which the German nation has always felt as the deepest humiliation of all times.

"After heroic resistance, France has been defeated and broken down in a sequence of bloody battles.

"Germany, therefore, does not intend to give the armistice conditions or armistice negotiations characteristic of aspersions against an enemy so brave.

"The purposes of the German demands are:

"1. To prevent a resumption of the fight.

"2. To offer to Germany all guarantees necessary for continuance of the war against Great Britain, which Britain forces upon Germany, as well as

"3. To create preconditions for formations of a new peace whose essential contents will be reparation of the wrong done to the German Reich by force."

Thus did Hitler preface his peace offer to France with all the bitterness he felt against the Allies since the signing of the Versailles Treaty on the same spot.

After some twenty-seven hours of discussion, the French government agreed to Hitler's terms, and at 6:50 P. M. on June 22, the armistice was signed formally—by General Keitel for Germany; by General Huntziger for France. Terms were not disclosed, the German announcement saying only:

"The cessation of hostilities is not connected with the signing of the treaty. It will follow six hours after the Italian government has notified the German supreme command of the text of the Italo-French armistice treaty."

In signing the armistice, the French delegates are believed to have used the very pen used by the German plenipotentiaries in 1918. Tears came to Admiral Le Luc's eyes as he scribbled his signature on the document. General Huntziger's eyes also were moist. He disclosed the severity of the German terms with this personal declaration:

"By defeat of arms to cease the struggle in which we were engaged on the side of the Allies, France sees imposed upon it very hard conditions. France has the right to expect in the future negotiations that Germany will show a spirit that will permit the two great neighboring countries to live and work peacefully."

The faces of the French negotiators mirrored their anguish at France's fall. And their sorrow was deepened by Hitler's order that the historic railway car, long enshrined by the French as a memento of victory over Germany, was to be taken to Berlin. With it will go a monument near by bearing this legend: "Here on November 11, 1918, was frustrated the criminal arrogance of the German imperial Reich, defeated by the Free peoples which it sought to enslave."

Thus was the bitter sequel written in historic Compiègne Forest. There wasn't much left of France.

Two days later . . .

In Paris the unimpressive figure of Hitler alighted from a motor car at the Hôtel des Invalides. He wore a light-brown duster over his Nazi uniform. He stopped in the big rotunda and looked down silently on Napoleon's tomb. Then he walked over to the memorial tablet on which the French Emperor's words were inscribed:

"I desire that my ashes rest at the banks of the Seine among the French people I loved so dearly."

Hitler stood there for a long time.

Outside, was the hushed corpse of Paris. Paris was dead—most of its people gone. . . .

CHAPTER 8

Britain's Ordeal Begins

June 26–October 2, 1940

I

FRANCE was the ninth nation to succumb to Germany in a little more than two years. By now the ordinary, everyday people of Europe had experienced the full impact of modern war. The populations of all nine countries were in the same sinking boat. The only possible exceptions were the fifth columnists and bootlickers willing to sell out for a mess of Nazi pottage. Even they were not necessarily immune to the Hitler purge. Many of them got what they deserved once they had served the Nazi purpose.

The glory and the stink of war continued. The majority of the little nations were in a squeeze play between Germany and Russia.

On June 27—five days after France accepted Hitler's armistice terms—Russia moved on Rumania. The Soviet began occupation of Bessarabia. In the newest wrinkle of war, tanks were landed from planes.

Wendell Willkie got the Republican nomination for President of the U. S. He opposed Roosevelt, who was ignoring all tradition by seeking a third term.

Sporadic air raids continued between the Nazis and the British. Churchill was concerned about what was left of France's Navy. His own Navy captured the bulk of it. The battle occurred at Oran, in Algeria, on July 3. Hugh Wagnon, in London, got the details:

The British Navy has fallen with reluctant ferocity upon the Fleet of its old French ally, and in battle and by threat of battle has wrested the great bulk of it from the grasp of Germany.

This, the strangest of all naval actions in the world's history, was announced today in the House of Commons by Prime Minister Churchill in a speech that was like no other ever heard in its ancient halls.

With tears on his heavy cheeks and his voice tight with pride and sorrow, Churchill told Commons how, with "aching heart," the British government had seen to it that the French "surrender cabinet of Marshal Henri Philippe Pétain would never carry out its promise to turn its battle vessels over to Germany—which now only awaits the chance to strike a last great blow at Britain across the Channel."

This, in substance, is what he reported:

In a ten-minute action on July 3 off Oran and Mers-el-Kebir, Algeria, British guns sank a French battleship of the *Bretagne* class; damaged and grounded a battle cruiser of the *Strasbourg* class; sank or set on fire two destroyers and France's only seaplane carrier, the 10,000-ton *Commandant Teste;* torpedoed an escaping battle cruiser, probably the *Dunkerque.*

Before this happened, Churchill disclosed for the first time, a great flotilla of French warships had entered the English ports of Sheerness, Plymouth, and Portsmouth. These, now out of any possible hostile action for the duration of the war, included: Two battleships; two light cruisers; a number of submarines, including the 2,880-ton *Surcouf*, the world's largest; eight destroyers, and 200 mine sweepers and antisubmarine craft. Additional vessels of the French Fleet are understood to have reached Scottish waters.

At Alexandria, Churchill said, a French battleship, four cruisers, and a number of small ships, warned that they would not be permitted to leave the British Mediterranean base, joined British warships in fighting off an Italian air raid. In all, nearly 250 French warships—the greater part of what was the second biggest fleet in Europe—are understood to have fallen into British hands.

Churchill began his dramatic announcement with what he termed "sincere sorrow." But near the end he made it clear that the resolute action against the French Fleet should convince the world that "there is no thought here of peace."

British guns blasted the French warships at Oran, Churchill declared, only after French Admiral Gensoul had rejected a British ultimatum concerning the future of the French vessels. The formal demands made upon the French admiral proposed that the French warships join forces with the British against the Axis; that the vessels sail to a British port, or that they be immobilized at a French port in the West Indies such as Martinque. The demands were ceremoniously presented, ceremoniously declined—and then the guns roared.

A final rupture of diplomatic relations with the Pétain government was predicted as a result of the British action.

2

ITALIAN troops pushed across the Egyptian frontier—object, control of the Suez Canal. King Carol finally made his Rumanian government pro-Nazi in an attempt to save his throne. The British minister of information aimed to be startling by the announcement: "There are too many Germans in the world." Japan asked that U. S. economic pressure be lifted. The first air raid on Gibraltar was repulsed.

In Virginia a Negro butler, looking for a successor after forty-five years with a Richmond club, outlined two essentials—proper mixing of a mint julep and memorizing the farewell address of General Robert E. Lee. In Memphis, Tennessee, a woman was seen pushing along a baby carriage from which a portable radio blared forth a gangster program.

Vichy was chosen as the new French capital. Two hundred and eighty Jews and Communists were killed in Rumanian riots. Hitler influence on the new French Government began to show itself. What was left of France broke off relations with Britain. Kiteflying was banned in England.

Great Britain claimed victory in the first round of the British-Italian battle for supremacy in the Mediterranean. Haifa, in the Holy Land, was bombed by the Italians.

Britain had not forgotten that Hitler might invade England. Neither had Hitler forgotten it. He was preparing, meanwhile talking about peace on his own terms. Britain also was preparing. She scorned the Hitler brand of olive branch. England was blacked out. Already there were scattered Nazi raids over outlying sections. King George narrowly escaped one of them. The real battle began over the Straits of Dover in mid-July. A London broadcaster picked up the encounter and reported it in terms of a boxing bout:

Britons at home and safely out of bomb range today were given a blow-by-blow account of the air battle over the Straits of Dover—with a convincingly explosive overtone of bomb bursts, engine roars, and machine-gun rattling.

The eyewitness-commentator reeled out the exciting details like an American prize-fight broadcaster and his listeners cheered at the British successes; white-haired old ladies dropped their knitting and screamed with delight. Charles Gardiner, the announcer on this program, unique in the British Broadcasting Corporation, talked like this:

"They're letting bombs go now . . . A miss . . . They haven't hit a ship yet. There's one German machine coming down. One of the crew is bailing out—oh, here come the Hurricanes.

"Boy, oh, boy! Three Hurricanes are chasing three Messer-schmitts—if you could see them. . . ."

While scattered Nazi bombers raked the English skies, Milo Thompson looked in on some of the night spots:

Swing music, quips as to the danger of German bomb hits and winner-take-all sweepstakes on air raid alarms, are spicing the monotony of England under aerial siege.

I set out to survey the wartime life of Britons whom the Germans describe as "quaking" at Hitler's threats and so fearful of fifth columnists that they sometimes shoot each other.

I went into a rural pub on the exact spot that was a target of German raiders in the last war. The door opened into a dark vestibule and drawing aside the heavy blackout curtains I witnessed a strange spectacle. Instead of solemn groups huddled in gloom, I saw scores of couples whirling about the dance floor while a band played American jazz hits. Men grouped about the bars were singing vociferously.

Outside, the street scene was brilliantly, eerily lit by a parachute flare drifting to earth. Far above, I could hear the drone of planes, but still came the blare of the jazz band and the sound of stamping feet. Though none knew what might come, motorists cheerfully utilized the light of the flares to find their parked cars.

A factory worker told me that his plant near by has an electric clock system which stops the moment an air raid alarm sounds, and that the workers have sweepstakes in which they draw the minutes in an hour at sixpence (about 10 cents) each. The winner takes all as they troop to shelters.

At a London private ballroom, I found a gay "flannel dance" in progress—so called because it is permissible to attend in cricket or boating flannels.

An interesting sidelight is the education the war is giving

ears. Listening for the distinctive heterodyne beat of German motors, one becomes supersensitive to sound, and many wagers are laid on the kind of vehicle passing on a distant road or the number of planes somewhere overhead.

The slogan of the English is "Be ready, keep cheerful." They are both.

3

IN HAVANA, twenty-one American republics agreed on "close consultation" respecting the European war. General Pershing suggested the U. S. give Britain fifty old destroyers. Britain listed Axis shipping losses at 1,172,000 tons. Italy began invasion of British Somaliland. English parents got instructions on how to rear children in underground shelters.

Around the other side of the world, there was activity in the "land of the Rising Sun." Japan moved to spread her domination in "Greater East Asia." Glenn Babb, who had spent twelve years as a correspondent in the Far East, described what it was all about from his desk as cable news editor in New York on August 1:

The collapse of European Empires under the impact of Nazi conquest has opened to Japan a prospect of sudden, comparatively easy gain perhaps never before offered a fighting, expanding people.

Already some 1,000,000 square miles of rich territories, with populations totaling 85,000,000, come under the sphere of Japanese domination because of the fall of France and Holland.

Japan apparently sees little to prevent realization now of ambitions long cherished but held in check. Britain might win her war with Germany and return to the Orient as a Great Power. Russia might strike from the north and thereby halt Japan in the south. The Chinese war, already three years old, might bleed her to the point of collapse. The United States might invoke naval power to protect her own Far Eastern interests.

But Japanese leaders apparently are gambling on these things not happening. If they do not happen, there will be opened to Japanese economic domination and, perhaps outright ownership, a glamorous empire of islands and coastal regions stretching over 3,000 miles from east to west and 2,000 miles from north to south, rich in oil, rubber, and many other necessities of modern conquest.

This is the "Greater East Asia" which has replaced "East Asia" in the officially declared expansionist program of the Japanese

Government. "East Asia" was largely continental—Japan's colonies, her puppet "Empire of Manchukuo" and the eastern third of China held for her armies. She has been integrating these into a single economic bloc, using the Japanese yen for money, dominated by the powerful Japanese Navy—the world's third largest—and the Army.

Similar control is envisaged for the expanded area. As defined by Foreign Minister Yosuke Matsuoka, this already includes the possessions of two fallen European empires, French Indo-China and the Dutch East Indies. Together, these embrace over 1,000,000 square miles—seven times that of Japan proper—and a population of 85,000,000, greater than that of Japan.

But "Greater East Asia" definitely includes other places in the South Seas in addition to the East Indies. For example, there are the Philippine Islands, where the United States still is sovereign, and Britain's holdings in and around Southeastern Asia— a rich group of states and islands with the great naval base of Singapore as the center. Perhaps it points even further afield to British Burma, even to India and to the Dominions of Australia and New Zealand.

The Japanese term "Nanyo"—the South Seas—is a very elastic one and often is employed to mean all the regions mentioned. Japanese legend has it that the conquering race that came to the Islands of Nippon and there founded the "dynasty of the Sun Goddess" before the beginning of written history—660 B.C., by Japanese chronology—came from the south seas. Hence, return to "Nanyo" as conquerors would be to the Japanese a sort of historical homecoming.

Were Japan to add any considerable portion of these territories to her sphere of domination, as she proclaims her intention of doing, she would have a maritime empire rivaling in wealth and power even the British Empire.

Already, Japan has made her power felt in Indo-China and the Dutch Islands, administered by local regimes cut off from any outside help. A Japanese military mission headed by General Issaku Nishihara has taken station in Indo-China's railway centers to make sure no war supplies reach the Chinese Government of Generalissimo Chiang Kai-Shek.

The Dutch Government in the Indies has shown itself anxious to placate Japan and has little power to resist pressure from Tokyo. The Japanese Government has asked Kuniaki Koiso, one of the ablest exponents of expansion, to undertake a special mission to the Indies. His record indicates what may be expected of such a mission. He has commanded the Japanese garrison in Korea, been chief of staff in Manchukuo, until recently was overseas minister—dealing chiefly with expansionist policies—and one of his last acts in that post was formally to tender the government a document labeled "important advice on overseas policy."

Another powerful Japanese, Admiral Kichisaburo Nomura, one-time foreign minister, already is traveling in the South Seas, having reached Manila late last month.

Japan's expansionist prospects in "Nanyo" depend largely on the outcome of Hitler's campaign against Britain. If England is crushed, the great base of Singapore, chief obstacle to Japan's ambitions in the south, will become virtually impotent. Then British Hong Kong, Malaya, and possibly Burma would go the way of French and Dutch territories. These British holdings total about 310,000 square miles (Burma accounting for 260,000) and more than 20,000,000 population.

Britain's fall also would powerfully influence the fate of the Philippines. The United States, in any case, is committed to give the islands their freedom in 1946. Japanese commercial and economic inroads in the islands already have been great; there is a Japanese settlement of more than 30,000 in the Davao region; Japanese goods are replacing American in many lines.

So, add to the potential Japanese sphere of domination the Philippine Islands, 114,400 square miles, 13,000,000 population. There remains the one independent nation within the scope of "Greater East Asia"—Siam, area 200,000 square miles, population 15,000,000. Siam is tucked away between Indo-China and British Malaya, and if those go she probably would go too.

4

A Nazi broadcast said London was Germany's next air target. Almanacs showed the tides right for an invasion. Britain was bombing industrial centers in Germany. Little came out of Germany about this action because of Nazi censorship. But that did not prevent word of what was happening. The British told about it. Drew Middleton spent some time with the Royal Air Force "Somewhere in England." The date was August 6:

Long hours of methodical preparation go into every one of
the hundreds of raids on which Royal Air Force bombers have battered at the heart of industrial Germany.

Here is a description typical of any of the last thirty days
during which the R.A.F. has dropped 37,000 bombs. Objective:
the Ruhr Valley.

At noon, as orders come through specifying the target and the
number of planes to be used, the R.A.F. station goes into action.
All through the afternoon sweating men in overalls feed gas to the
heavy bombers, overhaul motors, restock the gunners' supplies, prepare the bomb racks. Pilots bend over plotting their courses—"Guns
are pretty thick there. Better go north of it." Wireless operators
check codes and signals. Gunners inspect their weapons. Then comes
dinner, a merry meal in spite of the possibility that in twelve hours,
at another meal, some places may be empty.

At 11 P.M., when the English countryside sinks into sleep, a
Whitley bomber trundles down the runway. A moment later it
noses into the air. The others follow. They fly above the airdrome
for a moment, then the motors break into a roar and the formation
heads east toward the Channel.

As the drone of engines dies, the ground crews troop off to
their billets to sleep. The raiders will keep silent until sometime
during the night when word will flash back to the command, telling
whether the bombing was successful.

What's it like?

A flight lieutenant who has flown his Whitley over Germany
two of every three nights for six weeks gives this picture:

"We know the continent as we know our pockets, from the
leaflet flights (which preceded actual bombings). It's easy going
until we reach Germany. We rendezvous and then glide toward the
target to obtain maximum surprise. When you near the target,
things heat up. It's dark, then suddenly searchlights are around you
like pillars of white. Their anti-aircraft starts to hammer. Their
blackouts are very good. So, if there's no moon, we drop flares.
Moonlit bombing is a picnic. The blackout doesn't help very much
then. We go over the target, drop our 'sticks' (dropping the bomb
load in a line across the target) and head home singly."

As returning planes pass over the coast, they give a recognition signal. The ground crews count planes as they come in. The
first plane lands and its weary crew steps out, joins in scanning the
skies and counting other planes, swearing or praying according to

their natures. Then they go silently to breakfast and bed. The ground crews work the planes over to their ground "garages."

There is silence again over the big airdrome as dawn breaks. But in five or six hours the telephone from general R.A.F. headquarters will ring briskly. Another night's work will start.

5

THEN began—on August 8—the mightiest aerial battle the world had yet known. The Nazis hurled hundreds of planes against Britain's outer defenses over the English Channel. The fighting lasted fourteen hours. Each wave of bombers was screened by fighter planes. The British downed fifty-three. It was the heaviest one-day loss sustained by the Germans thus far in the war. The British toll also was high. They acknowledged loss of sixteen planes and "several" convoy ships.

On August 11 they were still at it. It was the beginning of the Battle of Britain. Robert Bunnelle went down from London and watched the battle as it developed around Dover:

From a balcony spattered with machine-gun fire and jarred by deafening bombardment I saw a new chapter in the Battle of Britain written today in a Sabbath sky thick with airplanes and spotted with mushroom puffs from anti-aircraft shells.

Between attacks, we gathered shell fragment souvenirs. We found machine-gun bullets imbedded in the concrete a few feet from where we stood. Anti-aircraft guns thundered a nerve-racking din one hundred yards away.

The raiders screamed down—sometimes from 15,000 feet—out of the early morning sun, pouncing on coastal balloon barrages. From the ground and in the air the British gave them a hot reception. In one attack I saw four German planes bagged by British fighters and anti-aircraft shells. Another correspondent farther down the coast counted, one, and possibly two others, plummeting from great height and trailing dense smoke.

The raid began as a surprise attack on the balloons, but developed into fierce dogfights, and was followed by repeated attacks by larger and larger waves, finally attacking the town as well as the water front. The gunfire rolled like thunder. One flight of raiders was split into two parts by anti-aircraft fire, which kept one group performing aerial acrobatics while British pilots engaged the other.

Sometimes the planes were so high they looked like tiny specks of wind-blown paper. Some fought clear and streaked back toward the German-held coast of France. One of these trailed a great black plume of smoke. The battle raged so furiously it was impossible to keep accurate track of the planes that fell. A pilot of one destroyed plane drifted by parachute into the water two miles off shore.

Little files of towns folk on their way to church looked back toward the coast for glimpses of the air fight and heard the Messerschmitt fire directed at barrage balloons. Heavy anti-aircraft fire beat the raiders back from the balloons at most places. Before church services were over, new flights of raiders dived out of the sun, with machine guns and bombsights aimed at streets and buildings. Explosions shook the town and motors screamed as planes tangled overhead in a blaze of action.

An air raid warden strode past with the warning: "Better take cover, they're machine-gunning the streets. Don't say you weren't warned."

Throughout the firing, balloon barrage crews worked as calmly as carpenters filling new balloons to replace those shot down. Most church services proceeded without interruption through the din. Two churches, however, were struck by bombs and forty children in a Sunday School were showered by glass and debris.

A whole row of homes was demolished in a southwestern town during a fifteen-minute attack by 150 planes. Forty homes were smashed and 140 others damaged. Casualties there were described as "amazingly low" considering the number of bombs dropped.

Outside one damaged church the rector placed a sign: "Give thanks to God. Thanksgiving services will be held at 6:30 P.M. in the open air."

Bunnelle's ear drums took plenty of punishment during the next several days. For that matter, Bunnelle generally took plenty of punishment. Day after day, night after night, the raiders came. As yet they were making no effort to reach London. They were pounding the smaller southeast towns. Bunnelle was still with them on August 14:

War, as only a hundred or more German bombers can wage it, came back like an avalanche to Britain's new coastal defenses today. I saw a lightship literally blown out of the water and sunk, her seams ripped open; I peered from a shelter while barrage balloons plunged in flames from the sky, their clashing cables falling almost at my feet; I saw a melee of perhaps 150 raiders and defenders surge through the clouds, and in my ears all day dinned the crash of anti-aircraft and the dull thud of bombs behind me—inland.

The biggest cloud of German raiders—I counted about 100 plainly visible, with others dotting the sky up higher—roared across the coast this forenoon from France, defiantly breasting a circle of twenty-seven British fighters. The British ringed them; then, one by one, dived on them. One vast, wild jamboree of twisting, flame-spitting planes developed. Four planes, then another, then others rocketed, burning, into the sea. We could not tell which side they belonged to.

In a crazy din of anti-aircraft, machine-gun, and cannon explosions, six big Junkers screamed at the lightship, dropping two bombs apiece. They sent up geysers from the sea; others dropped on land.

A new swarm of raiders tore viciously at the barrage balloons moored from coastal barges. Some, in flames and shreds, came down—in a shower of spent machine-gun bullets, aerial cannon shells, and anti-aircraft fragments.

While other planes were getting inland and up and down the coast to other targets, a low-flying German bombed one sea front near us, killing a Home Guard soldier, wounding several civilians, and wrecking three houses. In another town a Messerschmitt machined-gunned a railway station. Shelters saved the civilians there. In a house that had not a window left the family remained at the dinner table. A newspaperman poking his head through a gaping window, apologizing at the same time for the intrusion, was told by the father of the family: "You aren't the first one. It's a bit public not having windows, but the fresh air is nice."

6

DOVER was just a prelude. On August 15, Hitler's death birds struck all the way from the north to the south of England. They dumped their lethal loads in a thundering follow-up that struck at the very outskirts of London. Correspondents stationed all over England covered the details. They rushed their information into London, where it was put together into one story:

They struck in Scotland; they struck in vital munitions areas of northeast England; they smashed at the long southern coast all the way from the Thames estuary—leading to London—to Lands End, the far western frontier of these islands.

It was an attack of such incredible fury as to make the ceaseless assaults of three days seem but mere preliminaries. Every indication was that the hour of the great test had come at last. Antiaircraft guns thundered at the planes which raided suburban Croydon and British fighters swarmed to attack them as the war moved a step closer to the heart of the Empire.

Mothers and fathers rushed into the streets of Croydon and dragged their children to shelter as the roar of the planes and the exploding bombs came from the direction of the airdrome.

Plumes of smoke rose from the field, one of Europe's most famous airports. The chatter of machine guns could be heard by persons crouching in doorways. They cheered when they saw the raiders suddenly make off toward the south with British fighters in swift pursuit.

The Royal Air Force, defending this kingdom from such a blow as never was struck before, loosed every turreted gun in its fighter force and crippled airplanes fell steadily on English soil. The Air Ministry announced tonight that ninety-one German planes were destroyed, and that nineteen British fighters were lost.

[Note: DNB, the official German news agency, reported that thirty-six British planes were destroyed and others damaged, while only four German planes were missing.]

The German strategy was simple: While German fighters took on the British Hurricane and Spitfire patrols miles above the ground, the Nazi bombers snaked across the coast in close formation. The objectives were everything that Britain has and must have to keep on fighting: shipping, ports, munitions and industrial plants, and, above all, airports.

Known to have been bombed was the great Tyneside industrial and shipbuilding area on the East Coast near Newcastle. Not alone the coasts were hit, but the heart of the country as well.

[Note: The Germans specifically reported certain of their objectives. Bombed, they said, were the great Vickers Armstrong Armament Works at Hebburn; the port of Newcastle, Dover, and other ports and shipping convoys in the Channel.]

One Associated Press correspondent on the southeast coast—

only one of the areas of heavy action—counted six waves of eighteen heavy German bombers in less than three minutes.

There were 100 casualties alone at Croydon, eight miles from the heart of London. Factories were wrecked. People were killed as they entered air raid shelters. Rescue workers dug through the debris all night. Volunteers offered blood for transfusions. A bomb smashed a double-decker bus seconds after passengers had alighted. Pubs closed down. An express train was machine-gunned, passengers killed.

Drew Middleton picked his way through wrecked London outskirts:

I entered the bombed southwestern suburbs of London by motor car this evening, just after the mass German air raids, and the first sight I saw was two dead air raid wardens, lying on the ground in their tin hats and blue overalls. One had been hit by a fragment of steel; the other didn't have a mark on him.

I found a factory burned to the ground; windows within a mile's radius were smashed. Two pubs were a tangle of bottles and bricks. Several persons were killed by a bomb that hit a railway station. Outside one wrecked house, a police constable stood guard. Inside, were the bodies of his own stepdaughter and her 7-year-old daughter. It was his own home.

Rows of houses near a children's recreation ground were damaged. Autos were burned up. Machine-gun bullets hit a score of stores and houses, chipping the walls and dislodging roof tiles. The roof of one church was damaged. Another church was wrecked and a mission hall was cut in two.

Two men at work in a garage were killed. A woman, who hurried home from the grocery when the raiders came, arrived just in time to be killed. Two men were killed in a road where a bomb made a big crater. In another place a 5-year-old girl in a shelter was wounded by a bomb splinter that penetrated the back of the shelter. A mother who threw herself over her child in the street escaped injury, but another who tried the same tactics was wounded.

One suburb alone was struck by thirty to forty bombs. Girls in a factory near where a bomb burst rushed outside. They said machine-gun bullets spattered about them in the street. Fragments of bicycles and baby carriages littered one street. Some parts of the bombed area were roped off and the public barred. One man, pointing up a street, said: "Go up and take a look there and you'll know why I hope I'm called up for the R.A.F. next week. They killed my nephew—a fine nineteen-year-old lad. He was just walking across the street to see a friend when a bomb hit the friend and wife too."

Nazi assaults persisted. Hitler said the worst was yet to come. The talk of invasion intensified. Hitler announced "total blockade" of England. He claimed unrestricted warfare on all vessels in the war zone. He said the British were violating "international rules of war conduct."

Henry Ford said he would build airplane motors for the U. S. Skilled labor shortage hindered American arms production. Explosion of a Missouri TNT plant killed five. Nelson Rockefeller became co-ordinator of commercial and cultural relations with Latin America. American listeners heard London air raid alarms over their radios. Britain received 3,000 of her order of 11,000 American planes. New Panama Canal locks were planned. The U. S. and Canada agreed on a joint Board of Defense.

In Weatherford, Oklahoma, Charles Bloomer held out a hand to determine how hard it was raining and a hailstone broke an index finger. All six children of a Boonville, Missouri, family had their tonsils removed in a mass operation. A judge in London, Kentucky, fined himself ten dollars for being late to court.

The British withdrew from Somaliland. That gave Italy her first major victory. Churchill announced an agreement to lease the U. S. Western Hemisphere bases. Nazi "Big Bertha" guns bombarded England.

On August 23, London had her first night raid. William McGaffin, who followed the war to England after experiences in France, was in the city's West End when it began:

This midnight bombing, from a moonlit sky, was the first direct attack on London since the war began, but was the third on Greater London in less than a day.

Crowds seeped in from the dark narrow streets about this area, which had been nearly deserted, as usual, on the British week end. They talked among themselves, quietly but bitterly.

The presence of helmeted soldiers carrying gas masks gave

wartime trimmings to this scene which already had all the emotion of a spectacular American fire. Tin-hatted policemen let me through the fire lines. I shouted: "American reporter." They replied: "Go ahead, boy. Tell the States about it. Best thing you can do."

I got so close that the flames flushed my face and I was wet from fire hose. Curbs flowed deep with water. Three big red fire engines like those in the U. S. plus tough little auxiliary engines jammed the streets. Firemen on tall towers were silhouetted against the red background as they fought the flames under guidance of portable telephones hooked up with the engines below.

Just as the firemen got the flames under control, a gutted brick wall began to totter, and the sirens suddenly shrieked again. The throng ran for shelter, falling over tangled pythons of fire hose, then pulled up abruptly as the police yelled: "It's just the clear signal. The raiders have passed."

I came upon a little old man watching the scene where an incendiary air bomb had wrought havoc. Bobbing his cloth-capped head, he complained querulously: "It didn't make half an explosion. It musta been one o' these 'ere incendiary bombs. I fell on the floor when I 'eard 'er come whistling down. Then I went out in the street."

Presently a woman walked past. Tragic-eyed, dressed in night clothing and a man's old greatcoat, she clutched a baby to her breast. There was silence when she passed. The men's faces reflected sober, fierce anger.

A man came pounding up the street, bawling: "Stretcher party! Stretcher party!" His cries soon brought four men carrying stretchers. One of the stretcher-bearers was immaculately clad in evening dress. In a few minutes they trudged back, their stretchers occupied. A limp arm dangled from one.

7

On September 6, 1940, while the bombing of London was nearing its height, Hitler's intrigue in the Balkans paid dividends. King Carol stepped out and Rumania and her oil went to Hitler. Robert St. John reported Carol's hasty flight into exile:

King Carol II and his red-haired friend, Elena Lupescu, usually known as "Magda," reached the Yugoslav border today a few hours after the Rumanian monarch had yielded his throne to his 18-year-old son, Mihai:

The former playboy King's last hours in his kingdom were the stormiest of his colorful reign. His armored train bore bullet marks, work of a band of pro-German Iron Guardists who waylaid the special train as it crossed the border.

An alert stationmaster saved the King and his companion from harm. The railway agent told the Guardists that the party would stop at the station, but then wired ahead for the train to speed past.

Carol's abdication was the climax of a bitter intrigue that put the King on the spot after he had tried to go along with the Nazis, even to giving Transylvania to Hungary and Dobruja to Bulgaria. That satisfied Hitler's immediate demands. Later, however, the Iron Guardists stirred up trouble again and Carol called in pro-Nazi Ion Antonescu as his dictator. Still, demands for Carol's abdication increased. He finally agreed to abdicate. But he insisted that the news be withheld until he could start his flight into exile. Then he packed hurriedly and, in fear of his life, he and Elena Lupescu slipped away on the special train.

8

THE EYES of the world remained on London. Bombings continued. The raiders did not respect historic spots. Sam Robertson of the Canadian Press told what happened on September 14. It was not Robertson's last story because he wrote many others. But the prematurely gray young Canadian with the infectious smile did not survive many more months of the war. He was lost with an Atlantic convoy. His September 14 story told what the Nazi raiders did to one of London's historic landmarks:

Buckingham Palace was turned into a suburb of Hell today when the Nazi Luftwaffe loosed its fury on the area surrounding the royal residence. Like flaming meteors of hate, seven bombs plummeted from one raider apparently bent on shattering the palace.

Two bombs which fell in the inner quadrangle shattered about 200 windows in the century-old palace, tore two craters in the courtyard, and left a great crack that might have been caused by an earthquake.

Others tore gaping craters in the grassy turf, scarred the gray-

stone walls, and ripped out several yards of the great wrought-iron
fence that surrounds the palace. One bomb sent a shower of cement
and mud from the roadway over the majestic statue of Queen Victoria, which stands in St. James's Park circle. Blobs of mud stuck
to the statue.

Fragments which tore through the lower windows of the palace
damaged two of the irreplaceable paintings that cover the wall of
the ambassadors' corridor in the south wing of the palace. Five
holes were torn in the painting of Her Royal Highness Princess
Augusta Wilhelmina of Hesse-Cassel, Duchess of Cambridge, which
was done in 1835 by C. F. Reichmann. One of them was as large
as a man's hand. A companion picture of Adolphus Frederick, Duke
of Cambridge, done by John Lucas in 1839, gave up a few particles
of paint to the concussion, but otherwise escaped damage.

When I stopped to study these paintings, I became detached
from the rest of some sixty newspaper men and women who were
being taken through the palace to see the damage. I wandered about
the deserted corridors for a quarter of an hour without seeing a soul.
Members of the Royal Household seemed to have left until the
worst of the damage is repaired.

One of the scores of doors I opened gingerly led me into a
small anteroom that was full of royal ghosts. It was used to store
a dozen paintings. Nine of them were stacked on the floor and three
were hung temporarily. Those three were full-length paintings of
the last of the German Kaisers, Wilhelm, who flung the world into
the first great war; the last of Austro-Hungary's Emperors, Franz
Joseph; and Russia's last Czar, Nicholas. It was like a visit to the
morgue. I tiptoed out. A corps of 100 workmen is repairing the
damage.

Some of the London correspondents were having their living
troubles because of the bombings. One of them was J. Norman
Lodge. He was the one who "invaded" Norway months before to
find out how the battle was going at Narvik. The continuous bombing of London was keeping him on the move. He wrote about it on
September 25:

In a city under nightly bombing, every other day is moving day
for me.

For the third time in exactly one week I am practically homeless again. This time a fire chased me out into the street. It looks like some kind of record, but I'll gladly swap it for a used bus ticket.

A week ago I came over to London from peaceful Dublin. That night one of the Reichsmarshal Goering's boys routed me out of bed with high explosives that ruined my hotel.

The next night I fooled them. I stayed in an underground restaurant. When I got back to my newly chosen home I found a crater outside the door. I got a new place.

Yesterday I was congratulating myself on being able to get some sleep, but I crowed too soon, for fire got my latest abode last night.

Maybe lightning doesn't strike twice in the same place, but this isn't lightning. I've stood machine-gun and artillery fire in Mexico and learned some things about bombs in the World War. Norway improved my military education, but all these were only the primer grades. This London stuff by comparison is like Harvard, Yale, and Oxford rolled into one piece.

But there's no use in worrying. The *Medical Journal* recently observed that there is only one chance in 80,000 of an aerial bomb striking within fifty yards of any one person.

And there's one consolation. My clothes have been so thoroughly smoked that everything I wear smells like Genuine Harris tweed.

Edward Worth, Associated Press photographer, was knocked out by a bomb. Here is his story:

I woke up on a stretcher, gingerly feeling myself. The last thing I remembered was hurling myself into the gutter next to my car. I had a lump over my left eye. I said to the bloke at one end of the stretcher: "Where you taking me?"

"Oh, just around the corner to the first-aid station," he replied.

I thought of my car and camera and plates.

"Not bloody likely you're not," I said, and jumped off the stretcher.

One bloke said to the other: "We carry that so-and-so a couple of miles and he runs out on us!"

9

MUCH-BOMBED London was not the only place where things were happening. There was the French West African capital and port of Dakar. Britain feared the strategic South Atlantic port would be seized by Hitler as a submarine base. It sought a way to prevent such a coup. The opportunity came. General Charles de Gaulle, leader of the Free French, asked for naval support to land a Free French force at the important base.

But such a move did not meet with the kind of success the British had had in taking over the bulk of the French Fleet at Oran. The British and Free French met stiff resistance. On September 25, the Allied forces had to withdraw abruptly. There had been a costly three-day battle. Official France retaliated for the British Dakar attempt with an air bombardment of the British stronghold at Gibraltar. There was connivance between official France and Hitler.

By September 29, London had been bombed for the twenty-third consecutive night. Reports were that Hitler was loading barges and other invasion craft on the French side of the English Channel. They were bombed to the bottom by vigilant R.A.F. squadrons.

Britain was bombing Nazi-held areas in France, Belgium, and Holland with regularity. She was also reaching into Germany itself to dump explosives. Occasional British planes had been spotted over Berlin since late August. These flights were irregular. Seldom more than a dozen planes participated. Small bombing ships were used. The round trip from England to Berlin was almost 1,200 miles. Hence, major space had to be reserved for fuel. Otherwise, the returning ship could never reach its British base.

What was perhaps the most disastrous raid over Berlin killed ten persons and injured thirty or more. The bombs blasted street craters ten feet wide and five feet deep. Berlin's censorship, usually generous whenever Nazi exploits were concerned, was less co-operative when British bombs fell on Berlin. At that, there was little to hide. Berlin did not suffer much in 1940.

Tom Yarbrough, in London, talked to one of the R.A.F. pilots who had flown over Berlin four times:

Asked how it feels to dump bombs on Nazi targets, the 31-year-old Irishman said:

"You get a great kick out of bombing Berlin when you think

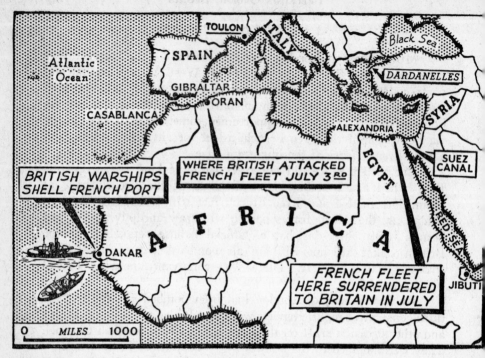

Map 8—Here is what happened when the British Navy turned on the fleet of its former French ally. Early in July, 1940, a French fleet at Alexandria had yielded to the British. But Vichy's ships at Oran refused to give up, with the result that some were sunk and others put out of action. On the other hand, the British had to abandon an abortive attempt to take Dakar on September 23 because the French there showed fight.

of all the stuff they're chucking on London. My main reaction was a feeling of satisfaction—rather of glee. Naturally, there is a feeling of tenseness until you find your target and the bomb aimer lets go."

He admitted that during the long flight to Berlin the British airmen couldn't help but envy the Germans for the short distance they fly to London from the Nazi-held Channel bases.

"On my first flight over Berlin," he continued, "I spent fifty-five minutes locating Tempelhof Airdrome. Some of the boys search a couple of hours. When you find your target you relax and feel good about a job well done. The crew members talk back and forth on the communication system and when we're over our target you can hear someone say, 'right in the center' or, 'a little to one side.'"

The pilot said it is easy to tell from a pilot's face whether he found his objective—the one he was sent after. If he has to be satisfied with an alternative he "grouses."

"The main thing is to get your primary target. When you get it, it's swell. When you hit an oil plant and see the fire you say to yourself: 'Well, it'll be a good while before they get anything out of that again.'"

CHAPTER 9

They Stood Firm

October 3–December 31, 1940

I

JAPAN joined the Axis in an alliance which, in effect, pledged Nipponese help if the U. S. joined the European struggle. On October 3, Chamberlain resigned from the Churchill Cabinet. He was succeeded by Sir John Anderson, who had directed interning of enemy aliens and the building of air raid shelters.

Mussolini was at work on the British in the Mediterranean. He was also heckling them in Albania. He had had a few minor successes. But he had not delivered any death blows. The main purpose of his adventure was to blockade British shipping and to divide their power so that Hitler's projected invasion of England would be easier.

Both dictators had been promising their people an end of the war in 1940. It was not ending that way. On October 4, they met again at Brenner Pass.

It is possible they criticized each other. Neither had accomplished his task. Apparently they decided an actual invasion of England was off at least for the time being. Perhaps Hitler was more pointed in his remarks than was his ally. Mussolini had to do more in the Mediterranean. His unenthusiastic Navy had been playing hide-and-seek with the British. Something also had to be done about the Greeks. Although Hitler couldn't actually invade England in 1940, he would keep pounding away at London. The purpose was to break down civilian morale. While he was doing that, Mussolini had to do his share elsewhere.

The two dictators came away from their latest Brenner Pass meeting to the echo of their respective high-sounding words. They were words designed to bolster the people back home. The war had to go on. England would not surrender. She had to be blasted out of the sea and off her own streets.

There was no report this time that Mussolini sang on the way back to Rome. Hitler went back to his London bombings; Mussolini to his problems in Albania and the Mediterranean.

In Canton, Ohio, bees swarmed in the living room of Mrs. Paul Foaster and she met the situation by turning on the vacuum cleaner. In Kewanee, Illinois, a drum majorette broke her own nose while twirling her baton.

London was bombed for the 200th time. Britain finally caught up with some of the Italian Navy in the Mediterranean off Sicily on October 12. There were some real fireworks. Correspondent Larry Allen watched what happened from the flagship of the Mediterranean Fleet. Back in the summer he had talked his way into regular assignment with the British Navy. Since then he had been on hand for every major naval encounter. His story on the October 12 engagement reached New York:

From the bridge of this man-of-war, I watched Britain's Fleet smash a hole in Italy's sea power, sinking three of Premier Mussolini's swift destroyers in a battle beginning before dawn and ending hours later in the glow of a rainbow stretching over the broad expanse of sea.

It was in Saturday's gray dawn that the British warships came upon the Italian craft, off the southeast coast of Sicily, and in the ensuing battle the powerful cruiser *Ajax,* hero ship of the South Atlantic victory over the Nazi pocket battleship *Admiral Graf Spee,* emerged a hero for a second time.

Single-handed, the *Ajax* shelled and sank two Italian destroyers and badly damaged a third, the *Artigliere,* which was finished off a few hours later by a torpedo that was rammed into her vitals by the cruiser *York.*

When it was all over, two Italian squadrons were racing full speed to their home bases, leaving the seas to the British.

The *Ajax,* one of a squadron of cruisers and destroyers forming a protecting screen for the Fleet in another wide sweep of the Mediterranean, was splashing through blue calm waters under starlit skies when suddenly she sighted a trio of Italian greyhounds at 2:30 A.M. The *Ajax* kept up her barrage for several minutes. Then there were terrific blasts as the magazines of two of the Italian ships blew up, and they sank. The other fled into the darkness. About a half-hour later, the *Ajax* met two other large Italian destroyers and quickly engaged them. Both turned tail and jammed on full speed. One of them, later identified as the 1,620-ton *Artigliere,* was hit. A mass of flames swept skyward from her decks.

Still a few minutes later, the *Ajax* sighted an Italian cruiser and four destroyers, but was unable to make contact with them because they steamed northward in a hurry, making direct for Sicily.

The *Ajax* then turned to the trail of the flaming *Artigliere,* and this flagship dispatched a number of cruisers to join her. British planes of the Fleet air arms, looking like silver bullets in the glow of the rising sun, shot from the decks of aircraft carriers and spotted the burning warship, then being towed by another destroyer.

A small striking force of the Fleet air arm was ordered to speed ahead and drop torpedoes around the towing ship. The latter, frightened by the approaching aircraft, slipped the tow line and headed for Sicily, leaving the blazing *Artigliere* to shift for herself.

Some of the *Artigliere's* crew stubbornly fought the flames rapidly enveloping their ship, while others hurled themselves into lifeboats. Many stripped themselves of their clothing and jumped in naked. Others who kept to their ship saw the hopelessness of their fight and waved white sheets. Then the captain of the *Artigliere* hoisted a white flag.

The cruiser *York* signaled the Italians to abandon ship. She waited until all had got their life rafts clear and then fired heavy shells into the *Artigliere.*

As the first correspondent accredited to the Mediterranean Fleet, I was standing on the port side of the flagship and watched the proceedings through field glasses.

The flaming *Artigliere,* burning in the distance, merged into a funnel-shaped mass resembling a Kansas tornado. Fully six hours after the first shells were fired into the burning ship, the *Ajax* sent a high-explosive shell into her side in a second attempt at a coup de grace. The *Artigliere* shivered, and sent up more billows of jet-black smoke. Shortly after 9 A.M. I saw a sheet of flame spout skyward. A torpedo from the *York* had touched the vessel's magazines. Then she went down in a death plunge, a rainbow band of pink, light green, and purple framing her in a semihalo. As she disappeared, her red-hot plates sizzled and sent up geysers of steam.

The rainbow disappeared almost as quickly as the *Artigliere,* and a long spiral of white smoke spreading out like a big fluffy powder puff, marked the spot where the vessel had been.

The cruiser *York*, remembering the experience of other British ships that were bombed while trying to rescue Italian seamen from the sunken Italian cruiser *Bartolomeo Colleoni* after another British victory last July, decided to avoid a repetition of that experience. So she dropped large rafts into the water, supplementing those already carrying the *Artigliere's* seamen, and Admiral Andrew Cunningham, commander in chief of the British Fleet, sent a radio signal in Italian giving the position of the survivors.

British aircraft some time later sighted three Italian cruisers and several destroyers southeast of Sicily, apparently dispatched in the hope of covering the *Artigliere*. The British flagship sent cruisers to contact them, but the Italian vessels turned about quickly. They attempted to make the British pay for their victory by showering bombs on the Fleet, but the Fascist planes, diving from rain-laden clouds, failed to hit their targets.

Pom-poms and 4-inch anti-aircraft guns beat off six heavy air attacks within a few hours. British fighter planes also scampered from the decks of aircraft carriers to engage the attackers. Their machine-gun fire downed one Italian plane shadowing the Fleet and two Italian bombers, wreathed in flames, plummeted into the sea. Still another bomber was downed by anti-aircraft guns and a fourth was seen fluttering toward land with one motor dead and part of its fuselage shot away. All the British fighters returned safely to their mother ships.

The Italians, apparently sticking to a policy of avoiding contact of their main units with the British, sent out a large force of submarines, causing attack warnings almost continuously aboard the flagship and other units of the British Fleet during the last two days of the week-long sweep through the Mediterranean.

2

MUSSOLINI gave Greece a three-hour ultimatum. To all appearances, she was little more than a spot on the map. Her army was small, her equipment meager. Mussolini thought he could ride over her and impress the world. He needed to do some impressing. Greece rejected the ultimatum. Mussolini invaded. He had to fight.

Washington's big "fish bowl" was used again. The U. S. had its first draft lottery since World War days. London parks were cleared for cabbages, onions, and other vegetables. The Nazis sequestered 63,000,000 bottles of French champagne. Submarines were sighted in the Pacific. Britain sent troops to Greece.

Two Colorado-born newsmen arrived in London to help cover the war. They were Alfred E. Wall and William W. White. They got off the boat and walked right into one of the Nazi's daily raids. They sent a joint dispatch telling about their first-day experiences:

"Jerry" may not have undermined British morale, but he put an awful dent in ours in our first day in besieged London. We watched all along the railroad route to London for bomb damage and saw but little. Then we stepped into an air raid alarm the minute we got off the train. We saw people running. The sirens were wailing. We could almost hear the German bombers overhead.

"What'll we do now?" we asked a porter.

"Well, you can go into that shelter over there," he said, pointing.

"Let's go!" we said. He lingered, so we urged: "Hurry up. Aren't you coming?"

"No," he said nonchalantly, "I'll just hang around here with your luggage."

So we stayed too. And we saw, then, that the people were running to catch a train, not to take shelter.

Nothing happened then, but plenty happened in the next twenty-four hours to curdle our nerves, while Londoners, used to it, seemed amazingly unperturbed. It's bad form to show concern over danger, we found. The blackout was a horrible ghastly experience, but it was nothing compared with the intense terror of the first bombing we underwent.

Drew Middleton and Hugh Wagnon, confrères of our London staff, remarked casually after dinner:

"It's a fine night for him."

"Him, who?" we said.

"Jerry," said Wagnon.

We had just got into our hotel room when it began . . . first the clatter of anti-aircraft guns, then the roar of planes high overhead. After a few moments of suspense, the bombs started to fall about half a mile away. A stick of bombs, each falling closer, seemed to shake you. It makes flight—anywhere—seem the only thing to do. But there was nowhere to flee. We dressed hastily and went downstairs, heading for the hotel shelter. Calm Britishers sipping drinks, reading books, looked up as we dashed in, making us feel sheepish. So we went back to bed—and awakened hours later to the soothing sound of the "all clear" signal.

Sometime, somehow, we guess maybe we'll get used to it—maybe.

3

On November 4, Roosevelt was re-elected for an unprecedented third term. He had campaigned against Wendell Willkie. Five days later "the man with the umbrella" ended his unhappy career. Neville Chamberlain died, broken in health and spirit after his "appeaser" policies had failed to bring "peace for our time."

On November 13, Russia and Germany did some more agreeing. Their earlier agreement—the amazing nonaggression pact of August, 1939—was still very much remembered. It never had seemed plausible. But now, a little more than a year after the war started, they were collaborating again. This time they agreed on a Russian sphere of interest. It lay generally between Japan's Eastern sphere and Europe and Africa, which Rome and Berlin had already allotted to themselves as a part of Hitler's fanciful "New Order" of Europe.

Just to lend color to the occasion, the British dropped a few bombs on Berlin while Nazi bigwigs were feting the Russian premier after signing the accord.

The next day Nazi bombers made a shambles of Coventry. Scarcely a street escaped the fury of the assault. Alfred E. Wall risked his life in the hail of death. He reported the attack that turned parts of the once peaceful English Midlands city into an inferno:

Coventry, chosen by the German high command for the most concentrated aerial bombardment of the Battle of Britain, emerged today from that scourge with at least 1,000 dead and wounded, not counting unknown numbers trapped in her smoking wreckage.

Berlin dispatches said the high command represented the assault as vengeance for a recent British bombardment of Munich, birthplace of Naziism. Last night it was Coventry's turn and German bombing planes, busy from dusk to dawn, smashed the heart out of this industrially important city in Britain's smoky Midlands.

Coventry, with a normal population of 190,000 now is known more for her place in Midland industry than for her legendary past. But it was streets through which Lady Godiva rode nearly 900 years ago that were churned by incendiary and high-explosive bombs last night. It was here that men strove in a thundering hell against growing piles of stone and smoking timbers to bring out the dead and injured.

Stories of heroism, of rescue workers dying in the debris they were trying to move, of first-aid workers killed while trying to save lives, of narrow escapes and sudden, wholesale death piled one on another in an overpowering array. Cases of bomb shock were reported in which victims, otherwise unscathed, were powerless to help themselves after the night of terror.

At three o'clock this afternoon the clock in the main spire of St. Michael's Cathedral struck the hour for the first time since a bomb smashed into the building last night. In Hertford Street, the statue popularly believed to represent Peeping Tom, the fellow who peeped at Lady Godiva, still stood as a reminder of this city's yesterdays. Some authorities believe the statue to be an image of St. George, England's patron saint.

The fourteenth-century brownstone cathedral, save for its 303-foot spire, was a jumble of stone and dusty mortar. Aside from the cathedral and countless homes, other damaged places included two hospitals, two churches, public baths, two clubs, a school, a hotel, four public shelters, movie theaters, the police station, the post office, and two first-aid posts.

In a dash into the burning sector this correspondent had to scramble over great piles of brick and broken stone. Fires ringed the night sky around us. The smell of explosives was in the air. Gaunt pillars of stone rose in the midst of confusion, pointing stubbornly at the sky.

The German air armada set the town alight shortly after sunset yesterday. The same opening thrust had been made before. Raiders and bombs were not new to industrial Coventry. But the twelve hours that followed were like nothing before, here or in all England.

Not until nearly daylight had the relays of planes emptied their bomb racks. They came in numbers that virtually nullified Coventry's anti-aircraft defenses. The sky flowered with flares. Amid the cannonading of Coventry's anti-aircraft batteries could be heard the rattle of rifles and machine guns in the hands of men trying to shoot down the illumination flares.

Whole blocks of dwellings and business establishments were leveled. Police and military forces from surrounding towns were brought in to help restore order. In spite of efforts to keep the townspeople from flight, traffic was in disorder. The highways were jammed much like the highways of the Low Countries must have been last May.

Many of the rescue workers had their own homes to work on. They clawed into the debris, using bare hands in lieu of tools, crying out the names of their wives, parents, or children and shouting, "We're coming—we're coming!" One young man tunneled through debris with his bare hands, although they were cut and bleeding, to drag out the body of his wife.

Coventry was like a scene out of Hades.

4

As IF Rumania's political disintegration were not enough, an earthquake killed 1,000 of her people. The Greeks routed the Italians on a 100-mile front. Mussolini retaliated the next day with a statement that he would "break Greece's neck." Hungary and Slovakia joined the Rome-Berlin-Tokyo alliance.

In Buenos Aires, three pigs flying swastikas, mysteriously set loose on elegant Florida Street, caused a mild panic and gave police a chase.

One correspondent, seeking to get away from the constant bombing of London, went over to Cahirciveen, County Kerry, to find out what the Irish were thinking about the war. He didn't go for a fight. He didn't find a fight. Tom Yarbrough was the man and he wrote a "letter" from Ireland:

It's a long, long way to Tipperary, but Cahirciveen is even farther. And this is where I got off a train one night at 6:30, out for a change from air-raided London and to find out how Ireland felt about the war.

It would be a swell place to come for a vacation. Just twenty-four hours from the harried heart of England, it has cloud-capped mountains and the sea, plenty of light to see by, and twenty-four hours of quiet every day.

John, the hotel man who meets all trains, didn't say a word. He just took my bags and started walking. I followed, more interested in the cows, dogs, two-wheeled donkey carts, and black-shawled old women in the slanting street then in John, who left me in the lobby, carried the luggage upstairs and in two minutes came down again.

"Number Nine," he said, and that was all. He didn't care about London. At least he didn't ask.

This is a pious town of 1,700 persons. To Cahirciveen the war is mostly a matter of headlines, of a tragic spectacle far removed from this simple life on an inlet of the Atlantic. But the people talk about the war occasionally with a good word for both sides. The opposite viewpoints were exemplified by two archeologists in front of a smoldering peat fire one night.

One said the crumbling walls of old English estates in Ireland were "the signs of the time, the symbols of a passing order." Then he added, paradoxically, and with a tone of despair: "British influence is stronger in Ireland today than ever. We have been conquered by them too long. The Germans would be no worse."

His companion pulled on a pipe and countered: "It's better to have a devil you know than a devil you don't know, better an old experienced imperialism than a bold, untried new one. We've come a long way since the last war, when even the little donkey carts in our town carried the British flag. At the start of this war a lot of people said neutrality for Ireland was impossible, but we have been neutral for a year already. We've come a long way!"

This was the first land that Charles Lindbergh saw when he flew to Paris in 1927. Cahirciveen still laughs about the woman who was walking along a country road when he flew over. Terrified by the sound, she looked ahead and behind, then out to sea and back to the town—but she never looked up.

The region has close ties with the United States, for, as one townsman put it: "We raise O'Connells, O'Sullivans, O'Neills, and O'Sheas for export to America." Some have made money and have come back to the green hills of home. Mountains rise in a semicircle around the arm of the sea that holds this old settlement. Misty clouds hang over them, half obscuring a gorgeous patchwork of soft purple heather and flaming yellow gorse, whitewashed cottages and stone walls that checkerboard the landscape into countless brilliant greens, flecked with sheep and cattle.

The night I arrived, two friends took me into the bay in a rowboat. At the little pier we found Danny O'Sullivan, a leather-faced farmer and fisherman, whose talk was the fastest I've ever heard.

"What's he speaking?" I asked; "Gaelic?"

"English," my friend said, "it takes time to understand him."

Kerry people accent sentences rather than words, and usually end the sentence with a rising inflection that gives it a singsong sound. And they seldom answer a question with a simple yes or no. They say "I did," or "I will," or "I have," and so on.

Cahirciveen was startled one evening with the news that a German bomber had crashed on a misty mountain across the bay. With three companions, I reached the nearest village about midnight and found the people proudly showing souvenirs—an airman's cap, a revolver, an automatic pencil, the crew's lunch kit full of heavily buttered sandwiches.

At 6:30 the next morning we found sleepy soldiers making tea in a farmer's cottage at the foot of the mountain. They advised us not to try to climb until the weather cleared, but the captain finally assigned five men to go to the wreckage with us, guided by a tall shepherd lad named Patrick O'Connell, who has cousins in New York and Indianapolis.

A twin-motored bomber had plunged into the rock near the top, bounced twice and settled in a thousand pieces. Nothing but ashes remained where the fuselage had been, but the tail and rudder were intact, with black swastikas gleaming when occasional shafts of sunlight burst through. We took sixteen pictures and came down —and found the police waiting for me. They detained me nearly five hours. They took my film and released me.

But Cahirciveen didn't tarry long over this intrusion of the war, for bigger things were at hand—the pig fair and the all-Ireland hurling championship final!

5

THE IRISH might be calm about it all, but the battlefronts were broadening. Hitler was still bombing London. The British were looking for another real fight in the Mediterranean. And the Greeks were dishing it out to the Italian bombers at Salonika. Wes Gallagher watched Mussolini's fighters fall back before the Greek Army:

For three days I have watched Italian planes rain death on this second largest Greek city, but I have not seen one military objective hit or one essential service disrupted.

Methodically enough the Greeks have been driving Mussolini's men back into Albania, all along this northern sector. The city's inhabitants have seen Italian planes crash in flames and have witnessed roof-to-roof chases between policemen and fallen Italian airmen in running gun battles.

I was in the center of this city at the top of the Aegean Sea during the first big raid when six bombs fell around my hotel and one bomb hit it squarely. Hurrying to a window, I saw a large geyser of water as the first bomb fell in the bay sixty yards from my hotel. I was showered with glass as two bombs exploded in the street forty feet away. Rushing into the hall, I encountered C. L. Sulzberger, New York *Times* correspondent. Together we started toward a stairway when a bomb struck the roof a few feet ahead. Neither of us was hurt. A few seconds later the raid was over. In the air thick with dust, we looked into rooms just three doors away from our own and found them in ruins.

Outside a fisherman lay dead a few yards from the hotel. A few fires were burning in the central business district, the section hardest hit, and firemen quickly were on the job.

Near a blazing bus and building, two wounded men lay by a wall which appeared ready to collapse. In spite of warning shouts, two boys in the uniform of the Metaxas Young Organization rushed forward and dragged them to safety.

This was the first of five raids on Friday and six on Saturday. Many casualties were reported when bombs hit a residential section, smashing small homes to bits. Greek anti-aircraft batteries brought down six attacking planes. Observers believed that this performance accounted for the Italians' caution in attacking the city yesterday when two alarms were sounded but no planes were sighted.

I saw four captured Italian airmen as they were being questioned. None looked to be more than 18 years old and all admitted having had only a few hours' flying experience.

6

ENGLAND's system of air raid protection was well established long before now. It was routine for thousands of people to spend the night in subway tunnels and other caverns, fantastically burrowed beneath the surface of the world's largest city. Drew Middleton wrote about a wizened little man with a big heart who conducted one of the labyrinthine shelters:

The dwarf, looking like a child in the half-light, came to the shelter entrance and said:

"I'm Mickey Davis; I run this shelter. Come on down."

I went down the stairs behind the tiny figure. Mickey Davis is 29, less than four feet tall. His back is humped and misshapen. He is absolute master of a shelter which nightly houses 2,500 to 3,000 people in its labyrinth of corridors and cubicles.

He is master and policeman, judge, father-confessor, and elder brother to these thousands of the East End whose homes and lives have been wrecked. He hasn't drawn any pay for it since he moved in last September 13 and found "just plain hell." Running the shelter gives him something to do since the Luftwaffe blew his "nice little optician's shop" to bits.

It was 11:30. Twenty feet underground, you could hear the rumble of bombs and the thud-thud of the anti-aircraft guns. People were wakeful and restless, chattering in the narrow brick passageways.

Mickey pulled aside the curtain at the entrance to a cubicle. "Fifty people in there," he said, flashing his light over rows of bunks, stacked three high. Two little girls, their faces whiter than their pillows, lay in the nearest. They whined fretfully in their sleep.

People were sitting on their bunks in another cubicle, gossiping. They greeted Mickey fondly.

"How is everything, Momma?" he asked an old crone.

Pathetically, the people had striven to make the cubicles homelike with what is left of their possessions. Photographs of Ginger Rogers, Deanna Durbin, and Vivien Leigh smile down in the midst of squalor. The names of London's swankest hotels—The Savoy, Dorchester, Ritz, Grosvenor House—were chalked above the entrance to the cubicles.

There were figures lying in the corridors.

"We give married folks first call on the bunks," said Mickey, "but there aren't nearly enough to go around. We need another two thousand."

A man and his wife were sleeping with their baby between them on the cold cement floor. Most single men had only one blanket. It was damp and chill. The air reeked of disinfectant and other smells. Just as though it were a country lane in Hampshire, a boy and girl stood talking and giggling.

"We've got a doctor who used to practice among these people," Mickey said. "He isolates people with skin diseases. He does what he can, gives the kids gargles, and takes care of the old and sick. He tries to disinfect the place but that's hard because we haven't got any real water supply. . . . We've only had him for a week though.

"There's no running water. We have to go outside with a bucket. Sometimes when it's hot (dangerous) outside we cut cards for it. We need running water badly. Some of these people haven't had their clothes off or had a bath in weeks.

"When I came down here first it was horrible. People were sitting up because there wasn't enough room to lie down. I got some young fellas that had been raising hell and put them to work. Work was all they needed. We got some bunks from the borough and some chemical toilets. We've been getting some stuff every week. Not much, not enough, but some."

He perched on the edge of the bunk and swung his legs. His eyes glowed with pride.

"People are pretty good down underneath. They can take a lot. If we can keep disease down, we will get through the winter all right. If we don't . . .

"There's still a lot we've got to do—but you want to see what it can be like. Come on accross the street."

There was a church across the street. In the crypt people were sleeping atop the ancient stone coffins or on the floor. There were only a few bunks. The walls exuded moisture and cold. There was constant coughing. Women moaned in their sleep, lay curled against the cold. A big man cradled a child and hummed to it.

"The mother of that kid got killed last week," Mickey said.

When a bomb fell, the old church shuddered.

We went back to Mickey's shelter. A man came up and said: "Mr. Davis, they want you in number six; some kind of a row about bunks."

"O.K.," Mickey said, and went back to his task.

7

CHRISTMAS, 1940, passed. Although London was still being bombed regularly, there was a Christmas-Day lull. But there was activity again on December 27 and 29. On both occasions at least a part of what happened was of especial interest to the correspondents. The Associated Press building, in which they worked, had been damaged for the first time on September 24. The men were driven out only temporarily. The same thing happened again on December 27.

But on December 29 it was worse. William W. White was one of those on duty. He had arrived in London only a few weeks before to help cover the war. With a fellow correspondent, he had written a story of his first experiences. By now he was acclimated to the shriek of bombs and the bark of anti-aircraft fire. It was just as well because the night of December 29 the war came close—in fact, it came right down on his head. The Associated Press building was destroyed. His dispatch cleared on the cables:

We were doing a story on planes over Eire when last night's alert sounded. Within a few minutes the first three bombs thudded on the roof above us.

"Incendiaries!" yelled a member of the staff who was standing behind my chair.

Our men donned tin hats and rushed to the roof to fight the fire. Canadian Press men, whose offices were on the third floor, joined them. Others grabbed files and books and headed for the basement shelter. From the shelter I telephoned two staff members, Alfred E. Wall and William J. Humphreys, to tell them that the building was ablaze and that we'd probably have to get out. They, in turn, advised Hugh Wagnon, acting chief of bureau, and staff members Robert Bunnelle, Tom Yarbrough, and Drew Middleton. All headed for the office. We put in three calls to the Fire Department, but they were too busy to help us, for other bigger fires were raging in the neighborhood.

"The building can't be saved," somebody yelled and we ran for it. Just as we dashed from the building, the lights in our basement shelter winked out.

We went first to the *Daily Mail* building a block away and then a block and a half more through crashing bombs to the building occupied by the British Press Association and Reuters, a British news agency. Soon we were joined by other staff members, who brought along photo equipment, a typewriter, and some clothes.

We soon set up temporary offices in the basement of the Press Association building and tried to tell our New York office that our building was burned out, but that we all were safe. The censor refused to let this information through immediately. We managed, however, to keep a running story of the raid moving, though it was necessary to telephone our account directly to Western Union.

At last the all-clear sounded and we went back to find the roof and top four floors of the five-story AP building completely burned out. Water was inches deep in the news room and basement shelter. It cascaded down staircases and dripped on soggy newspaper files. The "morgue" records of tens of thousands of news stories—of the coronation and deaths of kings, of war and happier events—were destroyed. Daylight streaked into what is left of the upper floors. There is a mass of tumbled girders, tangled wires. The floor crunches under a man's weight. Where a few hours earlier printers and typewriters had clattered, the only sound now is steam hissing from cracked radiators.

Thus at Tudor and Dorset Streets, stand the blackened ruins of the building which first was damaged on September 24, again on December 27, and reduced to a shell on December 29.

8

AT BRENNER PASS in October the two dictators had decided to bomb the British out of the seas and off their own streets. But the British wouldn't surrender. They dug themselves out of London's wreckage. They fought their fires and were ready for more. Women donned helmets and worked side by side with the men. Hitler and Mussolini had underestimated the stamina of the foe.

Late in 1940, Milo Thompson wrote about the unconquerable spirit of a people who would defend their homeland to the end:

Invasion of England may not be an immediate probability. Defense against mass daylight raids may be "right up the alley" of the boys of Britain's R.A.F. And night bombing of England may be so slow that it would take ten years for Hitler to gain victory that way.

Official and private summaries clearly support all these observations in the war today. But, lest the world should assume this means the worst is over, that London is not to lie in ruins and Britain is safe, it should be remembered that Londoners still walk hourly with tragedy. Often without warning, death spills from the skies on fair days and foul.

In a shattered flower pot beside her favorite sewing chair, my wife found a jagged 4-inch shell fragment. A gaping hole was in the ceiling above. One of our neighbors groped in an unlighted room for pajamas laid out on the bed. His fingers met the still-hot nose fragment of an anti-aircraft shell. Another neighbor found a dud lying on a sofa after passing through three rooms.

Just down the street is—or was—a doctor's mansion. A bomb, whose scream made my wife clutch my arm in the dark, chose the doctor's home—not ours. Three members of his household died in the kitchen, which had seemed the safest place. The house is a pile of jackstraw.

A woman friend of ours drives an ambulance. Sometimes she says a brief word about a particularly bad night. The other night she tried to give water to poor souls lying wounded in a dark place. She put her arm under the shoulders of a man to raise his head. There was no head.

She was still trembling from the shock as she rushed five of the wounded to a hospital. When she arrived, the hospital was gone —blown to rubble. Only two of her passengers were alive when she reached a second hospital.

A bomb-shattered bus on a principal thoroughfare yesterday was not a pretty thing. It was my bus. Had my subway train been on time, I would have been on it. The other day my wife and I were sitting in a little restaurant when the air raid sirens wailed. We went on with our meal. One does. We passed the restaurant this morning. It was just a junk pile. So were three adjoining buildings.

This is very much still the "front line" of battle. The soldiers include women and children, who help carry bodies from the "trenches" daily. We who share in the agony of London owe much to these people who refuse to be made hysterical or stampeded. Their reactions help us to control our own.

A writer in one of the morning papers said today:

"Some day there will be written the London Tales, and it will be one of the great books of the world. It will make young men say centuries hence: 'I would as soon have been living among the Londoners of 1940 as in the Athens of Pericles. It was one of those periods when the threat of death made men truly alive!'"

CHAPTER 10

The Classic Battlefields

January 1–May 10, 1941

I

AN OVERWORKED American veteran of
World War I stopped in at a London pub one blacked-out night
early in 1941 to take the "bomb cure." Then he wandered out to
find a bus to take him home. Feeling his way toward his accustomed
stop, he fell into a bomb crater. It was dark, it was deep. It was the
cold, war-torn earth to which, in 1917, he had been accustomed.
Overhead Nazi bombers were bombarding. Off to the right and off
to the left, anti-aircraft guns were clattering—hurling their loads in
a desperate defense.

The night air and the once-familiar surroundings went to the
head of the man in the crater. Memory of 1917 caught him up and
transported him back through the years. Suddenly, it was all real.
It was 1917 all over again. He began to sing. He began to shout.
He was in the front line trenches again and he defied any German
to blast him out.

His songs and his shouts attracted a passing bobby. The policeman cautiously approached the crater. It was pitch dark. He
flashed his light for a scant second. He saw the man in the bomb
hole.

"I say, my man," he asked in his polite, clipped accent. "What
are you doing down there?"

The unmistakable voice of the London cop brought the man
back to the present. His singing stopped. His mind cleared. He
passed off his lapse with a typical American wisecrack.

"What am I doing down here?" he exclaimed. "I'm waiting
for a Number Fifteen bus! What do you think?"

The bobby saw nothing unusual in the situation.

"I'm sorry, sir," he replied, "but the Number Fifteen bus doesn't run by here any more."

By 1941 the English were taking it for granted that "the Number Fifteen bus doesn't run by here any more." They didn't let it bother them. All of Hitler's roundabout offers of peace had been on his own terms. As the British saw it, that meant a less desirable sort of life for those who survived. The English would die first.

Britain's traditional strategy was blockade. It was a strategy she had employed for centuries. She was still employing it in 1941. The question was whether she could maintain her naval power in the face of the new factors of aerial power and submarine strength. Germany admittedly was superior in those respects.

At the same time, the Western Hemisphere was beginning to question its own place in the world should the Hitler ideology prevail. One of Roosevelt's first acts after his third-term re-election was to speed up U. S. aid to Britain. Aircraft factories increased production. Labor strikes, however, impeded progress. The Dies Committee, investigating subversive activities, was attracting some interest. There were scattered opinions that the U. S. should take a more active part in the war. The Army wanted an additional $3,000,-000,000 for its armament program. Fifty-three prominent individuals signed an "open letter" to Congress asking "mobilization of America for war." But there still was great sentiment against too-positive U. S. involvement.

Dog meat was legalized for human consumption in Germany. The British blasted the Italians again at Taranto. There were 20,-000,000 or so men under arms in Europe, Africa, and Asia. Britain had about 3,675,000 of them; Germany 5,000,000 to 8,000,000. The others were apportioned between other warring or near-warring nations.

2

As 1941 got under way, most of the Balkan countries were in hot water. They had oil, copper, tin, bauxite. They also had food supplies. In short, they had many things Hitler needed for a long war.

The whole Mediterranean was important to him. It was the key to supplies through the Suez Canal from the Far East. It was a symbol of British might. As long as the British had it, they had the balance of power. Hitler had been depending largely on Mussolini in that important part of the world. But Mussolini had not covered himself with glory. Hitler let him stew with his troubles as long as he could afford to do so. But when the acute need for more supplies arose, Hitler had to act. He finally went to the aid of his Axis partner.

War Analyst Mackenzie summed up the situation on January 3:

Call it any name you like, but Hitler's move in sending an air force to Italy still is in the nature of a rescue party for Mussolini.

Italy's position is so precarious because of the debacles in Egypt and Greece that Rome is in grave danger of being knocked out of the war. That would represent a disaster not only for Il Duce but for his Axis partner as well, and the Fuehrer can't afford to let it happen.

Hitler held off as long as he could, in order not to give Italian arms a black eye or to cause disquiet among the people of Italy. The fact that he finally has acted is confirmation of the seriousness of Mussolini's need. To get the full meaning of this maneuver it is necessary to recall what the Hitler-Mussolini partnership was trying to achieve.

Britain's naval supremacy in the Mediterranean has enabled her to defend her vast interests in the Middle and Near East. This sea has been determining the destinies of nations since history began and is a main arterial road for the British Empire. It was logical for the Axis partners to set about to destroy this domination.

Their strategy provided that the Fascist Army under Marshal Graziani in Libya should drive across Egypt, knock the British out on the sands of the desert, and capture the all-important Suez Canal —link with India and the Far East. That operation would also deprive England of the great naval base at Alexandria. Meantime, the much-sung Italian air force would blast Malta and other British bases. It was figured that might turn the trick. But, if necessary, the Axis Armies would drive down the Balkans, force the Dardanelles, and attack Britain on the Suez Canal from the east.

It looked like a neat set-up until somebody in Italy fumbled. A force was sent against Greece at the worst possible time of year and without adequate preparation. You know the rest. The Italians suffered a terrific beating. The British were enabled to occupy Crete, giving them a base from which they could lash out in all directions.

This victory permitted the Allies to take the initiative in Egypt and administer the heavy defeat to Graziani's army.

In short, the Axis plans for the Mediterranean have been knocked into a cocked hat, and Italy herself is rocking on her heels. So we see Hitler trying to save utter collapse.

Probably one of the first Nazi moves will be to try to keep the Romans from being thrown out of Albania by the Greeks. Loss of Albania would deprive the Axis of an invaluable base for the Balkans. This may temporarily weaken the force of the Nazi air attack on England, though probably not much. Hitler presumably isn't ready to undertake his invasion because of bad weather. He can withdraw his warplanes from Italy fast enough when he needs them over the English Channel.

On January 4, Larry Allen told what the British Fleet did to Italian combatants along the Libyan shore:

The British Fleet, ending a thunderous, four-hour bombardment of Bardia during which Italian mechanized units disappeared as though swept from the cliffs by a great broom, steamed slowly back out to sea patrol today, apparently assured that the way was cleared for the fall of that Fascist base. Bardia's batteries were silenced.

The gunboats *Terror, Ladybird,* and *Aphis,* which have been flinging shells at Bardia intermittently for six weeks, opened the predawn shelling, pounding the Italian bases for fully two hours before the battle fleet itself joined in.

Then battleships, cruisers, and destroyers, moving close to the shores in the red light of the dawning sun, turned their big guns upon long lines of Italian tanks, armored cars, and motor transport moving slowly over the desert highways.

Scores of shells exploded near the highways. The Italian batteries, which were between cliffs, spurted shells, some falling close to the British warships. But that burst of enthusiasm cost them dearly. A squadron battleship opened up all her 15-inch guns. I observed a destroyer protecting the (main) fleet during the shelling and saw huge clouds of smoke arise from the cliffs, indicating that British projectiles were falling dangerously close to the Italian batteries. Then came a mighty blast from battleships, cruisers, destroyers. The shells had found their mark. A whole section of cliff crumpled in a great avalanche. Hundreds of tons of sand and rock buried the Italian gunners.

Overhead, British planes poured bombs upon the Italians, destroying whole truckloads of infantry and wiping out tanks, armored cars, and troops in column.

For Britain's warships, it was the biggest bombardment yet in the Mediterranean war: Six hundred tons of high explosive were flung into Bardia, and after it was over the Italians were attempting a headlong flight toward Tobruk.

The next day the Greeks dealt destruction to the Italians on the Albanian coast. Daniel De Luce, reporting from "Somewhere in the Greek First Line," described the encounter:

From the half circles of rock which hide Greek machine-gun crews I watched Italian infantry platoons scale a canyon wall a mile away. They were dark little figures etched with the sparse green bushes against the gray limestone. As they climbed, each man choosing a different trail, they must have known they were as visible to Greek artillerymen as flies crawling on a windowpane.

"Look what happens now," a Greek gunner beside me said.

The Italians were no more than twenty yards from the crest of the canyon when I heard a Greek shell whine overhead. Two more shells shook the canyon walls and when the smoke arose the gunner beside me said:

"Good hits. If there are any Italians left alive, they'll finish the climb on their bellies."

This occurred a quarter of an hour ago and I am writing this in the captain's shelter under a ledge thirty yards from his advance machine-gun post and only 330 yards from the Italian outposts. At our back lies the picturesque seaside village of Khimara, the Greeks' latest acquisition. No other correspondents, foreign or Greek, have come this far with the army. A comparatively long and difficult stretch of coast stands between the Greek lines and the Italian seaside base of Valona, but the Greeks are determined to reach that objective, just as they have been determined on earlier objectives. Mile after mile up precipitous slopes soldiers carry food, water, and shells for the front-line troops. It's too steep even for donkeys to pack supplies here.

Below the ridge, unshaven and unwashed Greek infantrymen await impatiently for the order: "Empros" (advance)!

"Waiting is the hardest thing we are asked to do," the Greeks say.

The sea breeze sent clouds scudding over the peaks and only one enemy reconnaissance plane appeared. It was driven back by anti-aircraft batteries. Italian bombers have been active in this sector the past few days, but the Greeks voice contempt for efforts which they say frittered away superior air strength with aimless attacks that touch neither troops nor supply lines.

In the forty hours it took me to travel 150 miles by truck, motorcycle, and horse cart to this spot, nowhere along the way was I delayed by bomb-damaged roads or bridges. A half-dozen bridges which had been attacked by Italian airmen still were in use.

Italian shells that arch over the ridges to explode in a spray of shrapnel command far more respect from the Greek troops than an Italian strafing plane. Tonight, New Year's gifts of brandy, cookies, and chocolates are being consumed. It's almost like a party, with shellfire for music.

3

R.A.F. BOMBERS raided Wilhelmshaven for seven hours. Australia contributed air squadrons to Britain. Italian losses in Greece were estimated at 100,000. London suffered its heaviest night bombing. The Nazis claimed that no German factories had been put out of commission. Alaskan air bases were mapped by the U. S.

A Kansas pastor bought some aspirin for a headache, shoved the tablets in his pocket, and plopped the dime in change in his mouth. The London Ministry of Health issued suggested "cures" for air raid shelter snoring. In Kinston, North Carolina, police arrested a man for "operating a horse while intoxicated."

The air force sent by Hitler to help relieve Mussolini was on the job by January 10. At 12:30 P.M. that day the British aircraft carrier *Illustrious* was escorting a big eastbound convoy. Other units of the British Fleet also were along. The big Nazi bombers appeared as out of nowhere. A bugler aboard the huge carrier sounded the warning. A voice on the loud-speaker system called out: "All hands to action stations."

Larry Allen was aboard. Four days later the battered plane carrier reached a Mediterranean port. Allen told the story:

This scarred aircraft carrier, attacked for seven hours last Friday by German dive-bombers, came into a Mediterranean port under her own power today.

Forty to fifty Nazi planes, making the heaviest attack upon a single British warship of this war, flung torpedoes at the *Illustrious'* sides and 100,000 pounds of high-explosive bombs at her flight deck in an unsuccessful attempt to sink this newest of Britain's carriers. The German pilots, diving head on, plunged into a great wall of gunfire; they spattered the decks with bullets and dropped scores of bombs on the *Illustrious'* port and starboard sides. Seven hours of this violent assault ended at dark.

The German pilots dived so low that the markings could be easily seen on their big Junkers planes. They dropped bombs all around the deck. Bomb splinters flew about the bridge and the rest of the carrier like hailstones; near-misses so shook her that it seemed they would hurl her over on her side.

The attack occurred while the *Illustrious* and units of the British Mediterranean Fleet were escorting a big eastbound convoy, and after a British cruiser had sunk the 642-ton Italian destroyer *Vega*. I reached the bridge just as the first bomb struck the ship. There was a shattering blast. Almost simultaneously another crashed alongside and a blinding flash seemed to envelop the ship.

One officer put it this way: "It was the most tremendous, terrifying thing I have ever seen. It seemed like all the fires of hell had been kindled. A blast of a thousand-pound bomb is so crushing, so incredible, that there are no words to describe it."

The first bomb fell almost at the moment some British fighter planes took off to engage the Germans. Another bomb tore holes in the carrier's side. Still another crashed and fragments from a near-miss struck a gun crew at a pom-pom station. They stood up unflinchingly and pumped shells as fast as they could into the bombers.

The entire crew of the *Illustrious,* except the officers on the bridge and the crew firing the pom-poms, helped carry their wounded companions across the flight deck to medical stations. They worked under direct fire. As soon as the seriously wounded were pulled out of the wreckage their comrades dashed in to get others.

The few fighter planes which the *Illustrious* was able to get into the air before the first bombs struck, forced the Germans off temporarily, but that short respite was the only break during the whole afternoon; less than an hour later the Nazis returned. Again there was the deadly drone of bombers; again sheets of flame from all the carrier's guns until, with smoke hanging over her flight deck, she looked like a moving monster of fire. Bombs fell to port and starboard; at bow and stern. Another bomb crashed, causing casualties—including one R.A.F. officer who had come to sea, as he termed it, "just for a week's rest."

Windows in the entrance to the captain's bridge were shattered. A dive-bomber swooped just in front of the bridge on the starboard side. Its bomb threw a çolumn of water over the bridge and the force of its blast threw me down the hatchway to aviation intelligence quarters one deck below. A sheet of fire burned my face. Another German dived head on. The bomb creased the side of the carrier.

"We are hit," mumbled an officer lying beside me, his face pressed against the deck floor.

Between 2 and 7:30 P.M. there never were more than a few minutes free of the sound of projectiles crashing about the *Illustrious,* her gun crews flinging shells on and on at attacking planes in the face of machine-gun fire. Just before dusk small columns of smoke poured from the flight deck. Shell casings and bomb splinters formed a strange carpet there.

In the engine room the men kept one turbine and then another operating, and then resorted to steam pressure to keep the *Illustrious* going steadily on eastward to the nearest Mediterranean port. When that port was near the bombers dived again. Rear Admiral A. L. St. George Lyster watched the dive and shouted to his aides while shrapnel and machine-gun bullets peppered about him. On the bridge below Captain Dennis Boyd puffed his pipe and again ordered: "All hand to action stations."

Three Germans dropped torpedoes, but a moment before the captain had ordered full speed, and the torpedoes landed in the water a few feet off the stern.

During all the struggle British planes made the Germans pay. The final score in Nazi planes shot down was twelve. As soon as the *Illustrious* reached port, a small fire was extinguished in her interior, and shipwrights plugged the bomb holes, getting her ready to go to sea again.

The dead were taken out for burial at sea in the areas where they had fought. The wounded were sent to hospitals. Even in port, German and Italian planes have tried to sink the *Illustrious.* They have found her guns still firing.

4

AN ITALIAN submarine came to the surface off an island in the Aegean sea, banged away without success at a Greek policeman who was resting his feet on a shore-side seat, then dived and departed.

The R.A.F. raided Palermo, on Sicily's northern coast. Haile Selassie and his black followers engaged in guerrilla warfare against the Italians in southern Ethiopia. A Chinese-Russian pact provided for an exchange of Chinese minerals for Russian military supplies. Bulgaria, resisting Germany, looked to Russia for counsel. The Nazis beheaded a man for "attempted high treason." U. S. Secretary of War Stimson warned that this country would be invaded by air if the British Navy collapsed.

Lindbergh suggested a negotiated peace. Roosevelt personally met Britain's new U. S. ambassador, Viscount Halifax, aboard a battleship in Chesapeake Bay. Hitler declared ships of any nationality would be bombed if they carried supplies to England. Strikes blocked $60,000,000 worth of U. S. defense orders. Russia budgeted 215,400,000,000 rubles for war equipment. In addition to helping Mussolini in the Mediterranean itself, Hitler was also intimidating Bulgaria and Yugoslavia. They would give the Nazis access to Greece.

Louis Lochner, in Berlin, took a minute to answer a question many people over the world were asking: "How does Hitler, personally, get paid?" He told as much as Nazi censorship would permit on February 11:

Officially, Adolf Hitler—the biggest man in all Germany— draws no salary.

Royalties from the sale of his book *Mein Kampf* throughout the world are regarded as large, however, providing him a substantial income.

The Fuehrer has funds, raised by popular subscription, at his disposal. For instance, on the annual stamp collectors' day, a special stamp is issued and the proceeds distributed in accordance with Hitler's personal wishes. Similarly, on his birthday, a special stamp is issued with the proceeds going to his cultural fund.

Each cabinet minister, moreover, has a so-called representation fund for expenses connected with his office. Inasmuch as Hitler is both the head of the government and chief of state, this fund is believed to be considerable.

Edwin Shanke, back in New York for a holiday after months in Germany, wrote good-naturedly about life on February 28:

Life in Germany isn't a complete blackout. It has some of its brightest moments when it's blackest.

You have been to dinner or a show with a friend. At the door he says "Bolona" and you shoot back, "S.O.S." It doesn't mean that he is insulting you or that you are calling for help. It's just the Berlin way of saying "good night" since the British have been coming. "Bolona" stands for "bombenlose nacht," meaning "bombless night," and "S.O.S." is short for "schlaf ohne sirenen" or "sleep without sirens."

Then you hustle off for the underground train home. Perhaps you meet an acquaintance. The conversation is in English.

"When in Germany speak German," comes a guttural command from the other end of the car. You look up surprised. "We have enough English spies in Germany already. If you don't speak German, I'll have to call the police."

Pasted on each car window is the stern face of a steel-helmeted German soldier with his forefinger set across his lips to seal them. The caption reads: "The enemy is listening."

Or:

You take a bus on a very inky night. It just crawls along; the trip takes much longer than usual. The driver seems to be making unfamiliar turns. One passenger, peering into the night, discovers the bus is way off its route. Sure enough, the driver is one of those "wrong-way" fellows, and you've landed miles from home.

"I'm new on this run and the blackout confused me," the driver volunteers sheepishly. "Hop in; we'll try again."

Or:

Your last streetcar barely slows down at the transfer corner to pick up passengers and you have to make a running jump to catch it.

"What's the idea?" you ask the conductor.

"Oh, we're trying to beat the British raiders to the barn," he explains. "The policeman told us the alert signal already has been flashed but if we hurried we would be able to finish our run."

Getting down to work during the day is easy. It's getting home late nights that's tough. You have to outguess the British night raiders. They never come regularly and if you finish your night trick at midnight without a raid, you never know whether to start home immediately or wait on the chance the British will be coming soon. What you want to avoid is getting caught in a strange public shelter. The benches are hard and without backs and the rooms are damp and cold.

If you should happen to reach home before the British attack, you will find the house looking as though it had been taken over by a second-hand clothing dealer. Everyone is set to go the moment the warning signal sounds—just as they are down at the corner firehouse. Shoes, trousers, jackets, flashlight, valuables, a thermos bottle with a hot drink; pillows and blankets—all are laid out or draped neatly over a chair where they can be found in the dark without fumbling.

It pays to be an American and play dumb under the German rationing system. Fifteen chocolates a month is the normal ration of sweets, but there are ways of getting around clerks in candy shops. You go into the store and point to a box of candy. The clerk asks for your ration ticket, but you don't understand German. You just continue to point to the box. She tries to explain, but in very awful German you manage to tell her that you are an American visiting the country, don't know a thing about ration cards, and would like to buy a box of candy—please. She gives up in desperation just once, and emphasizes her position by holding up her finger. But tomorrow is another day and it has worked again and again.

5

ON MARCH 1, Hitler pulled his first decisive coup in the Balkans since the capitulation of Rumania. His gray-green legions poured into Bulgaria. They arrived by plane, armored car, and truck. That night mystified, terrified Bulgars doused their lights. They feared a British bombardment. The Nazi invasion was bloodless. Fifth columnists and Hitler's secret police had done an effective job.

Still the Fuehrer was not satisfied. There was Yugoslavia. She was still in his way. He went to work anew on that country. Hitler was doing all right for himself in the Balkans. Nevertheless, he may have been going just a little too far. His nonaggression pact with Russia of August, 1939, still was in effect; Stalin only recently had promised to help feed the Nazis. But Hitler's move on Bulgaria and his hankering after Yugoslavia disturbed the Soviet.

Russia denounced the Bulgarian adherence to the Axis pact.

She also had some interests in the Balkans and what the Balkans stood for. She did not want Hitler to have access to too much. Hitler kept quiet while Russia complained. DeWitt Mackenzie sized up the situation on March 7. It was a sizing-up which threw some light on the strange Russo-German "friendship." Here is the way he figured it out:

The vast interests and aspirations of Russia and Germany in the Balkans are converging—at the moment rather rapidly—toward a clash, and the focal point is the Dardanelles, connecting link between the Black Sea and the Mediterranean.

This waterway is the gateway to riches and power. A couple of days ago I suggested that if we wanted to gauge the trend in southeastern Europe we should keep an eye on the Dardanelles. Developments impel me to repeat this advice.

A recent Bolshevist note to Sofia, saying that the Soviet cannot support the Bulgarian policy of agreeing to the German military occupation, looks more like a warning to Germany than to Bulgaria. Then yesterday a mysterious German plane swooped down on the Turkish capital of Ankara with a communication from Herr Hitler for the government. Word from diplomats in Sofia is that the message was an attempt to persuade Turkey to throw over her alliance with Britain and make a new one with Germany. It is said this suggestion was made on the basis that only the Reich can protect Turkey against the historic designs of Russia.

The historic designs of Russia are like the historic designs of Germany—to get control of the Dardanelles, and let none doubt that Britain is any less concerned over the fate of this strait.

Since Peter the Great, Russia has sought control of the Dardanelles, partly for defensive reasons, to keep any enemy from sailing into the Black Sea and partly for expansion and extension of domination.

Germany's purpose has been to further her grandiose plan for a drive to the east. "Berlin to Bagdad" was one of the big German slogans in the first World War. Hitler would give his right arm to break through to the oil of Iraq and Iran, and also smash British control of the eastern Mediterranean.

Hitler and Stalin have been maneuvering against each other for domination of the Dardanelles ever since the war started. Stalin made a gain when he went into Rumania and got his troops up against the Danube. Hitler countered by occupying the rest of Rumania and now he is in Bulgaria, close to the strait.

These two leaders have been working together—up to a point. Their interests clash so violently all along the line that many believe war is inevitable sooner or later. Neither has found the time opportune. Hitler hasn't wanted Russia on his neck while he was trying to crush England. Stalin hasn't liked to tangle with the vast and efficient military machine which Hitler has stacked up against the Russian border.

One of these days, though, the Berlin-Moscow diplomatic cord will snap.

6

Germany claimed sinking of three British convoy ships. Greek women helped their soldiers by rolling down rocks on Italians' heads. Turkey mined the Dardanelles. The R.A.F. raided western Germany. The latest Nazi raid on London wrecked a night club. Rome admitted loss of additional ships. Britain said Nazi air raids had killed 24,371 of her people and injured 35,373 others through February, 1941. Italian soldiers returned to Rome with arms and legs frozen by the hard Balkan winter.

On March 11, Roosevelt signed the new Lease-Lend bill. Minutes after signing it, he ordered millions in war materials released immediately to Britain and Greece. Then he asked Congress for $7,000,000,000 to finance this country's new "Help-Britain" program. The Lease-Lend measure superseded the earlier "cash and carry" plan. It also gave the President of the United States sweeping powers in allotting Allied aid.

A survey by the Bankers Life Company disclosed that the names most frequently given children were Mary and Robert. A dispatch from Huntington, Indiana, said that eleven school girls in one grade were named Phyllis.

Yugoslavia didn't drop into the pattern of conquest Hitler had cut out for the Balkans. During March, 1940, he thought he had made sure of "co-operation" from the government of Regent Prince Paul. So, for some time things had been looking up for Der Fuehrer. But even as Prince Paul's advisers were signing away Yugoslavia in the spring of 1941, Hitler's plan blew up. The Yugoslavs themselves revolted against the Nazi influence. They set up an anti-Nazi government under young King Peter.

Again a dictator was attempting to force himself upon a people. When they rebelled, he bellowed about "mistreatment and murdering" of his fifth-columnist hordes. To him it was criminal that infuriated residents of a weaker country would attempt to protect their freedom.

The final break came on April 6. That morning Hitler issued his marching orders—not only on Yugoslavia, but on Greece as well. He blamed the British for the necessity of the attack. He said Yugoslavia had been "intriguing" with Churchill. Here is a portion of his order to the "soldiers of the Southeast Front":

"Yugoslavia for weeks has planned a general mobilization of its army in great secrecy. This is the answer to my eight-year-long effort to bring about closer co-operation and friendship with the Yugoslav people, a task which I have pursued most fastidiously.

"When British divisions were landing in Greece, just as in World War days, the Serbs thought that the time was ripe for taking advantage of the situation for new assassinations against Germany and her allies.

"Soldiers of the Southeast Front: Now your zero hour has arrived. You will now take the interests of the German Reich under your protection as your comrades did a year ago in Norway and on the West Front. You will do just as well on the Southeast Front. In doing this, your duty, you will not be less courageous than the men of those German divisions who in 1915, on the same Balkan soil, fought so victoriously. You will be humane only in those places where the enemy is humane toward you. Where the enemy confronts you with utter brutality, you will beat him back with the same weapon."

Again the telltale proof of blitzkrieg was evident that morning of April 6. All lines between Yugoslavia and the outside world were cut. Hitler was taking over before warning could reach Allied forces. Nazi bombers swarmed over Belgrade. Only the day before, Russia and Yugoslavia had signed a treaty of friendship and nonaggression. It didn't help any, as far as Yugoslavia was concerned. She didn't last long.

Yugoslavia war correspondents were unable to report in detail. They could not get through immediate eyewitness stories. They had to flee for their own lives. On April 18—only eleven days after Hitler moved on Yugoslavia—Berlin announced surrender of the

Balkan state. But thousands of tough Slav soldiers who fled to mountain fastnesses vowed they would wage guerrilla warfare to the last man.

Yugoslavia was incidental to Hitler's big plan. He was moving on to Greece where the British had come to the aid of the Greeks. Hitler went after them. Domination of Greece would put him closer to the Suez Canal. J. Reilly O'Sullivan, Oklahoma-born correspondent, was in Athens when first word of the Nazi invasion came. The Greeks were still in control and so he had no difficulty in getting his story to the outside world:

Greece's 9,000,000 peasants and workers, already at war with 40,000,000 Italians, took up the task today of fighting 80,000,000 more Germans, with the aid of ancient warriors. For two hours singing and cheering crowds swept through the streets.

Salonika received the first news of the German attack by radio while waiting in air raid shelters during an alert which sounded at 6 A.M. Hundreds rushed from the shelters as word of the new phase of the war was received, paying no attention to the burst of anti-aircraft fire overhead as the Luftwaffe made its first raid. Standing in the streets, the people watched the battle and cheered.

In Athens, at the height of such a demonstration, British soldiers were lifted to the shoulders of the paraders and carried along, singing and shouting. Marching Evzones (mountain troops), in their stiff, white kilts, were followed by half a dozen bands. The people cheered the British and American legations and jeered the German legation, which was guarded by police. All through the city, martial music blared from radios. King George II and Premier Alexander Korizis drove through the streets in an open car between lanes of shouting men, women and children.

"We will win!" the crowds shouted. The King smiled and waved.

Many carried placards which said "No!" and "They shall not pass!"

One newspaper printed two big cartoons. The first, labeled "1940," showed Mussolini, dagger in hand, approaching Greece while Hitler in the background shouted: "Good luck, Benito!" The other, labeled "1941," showed Hitler with a dagger while Mussolini stood in the background shouting: "Good luck, Adolf!"

People spoke confidently of the help the United States would send. Statements of President Roosevelt that Yugoslavia and Greece would get all help possible were headlined. Hundreds of soldiers recovering from wounds and frozen feet, received in the Albanian campaign, hobbled about the streets. One young Greek private, moving with the aid of a cane, spoke to a crowd gathered around a large handwritten poster announcing the start of the new war. "We will throw them into the sea," he cried; "the Baltic Sea!"

7

BUT THE combined Greek and British forces could not throw the Nazis "into the Baltic Sea." Already the Greeks had suffered severe losses in the long Italian campaign. The British could contribute somewhat less than 100,000 men. Hitler had 500,000. Hitler also employed shrewd strategy. His invasion of Yugoslavia separated the Yugoslav forces in the southeast from those to the north. In Greece, the British forces were overrun by Nazi forces in the east. Simultaneously, the Italians took on the Greeks to the west. The British and the Greeks never had a chance to combine. Nazi air power supplemented the land attack.

On April 21, Greece fell. Guerrilla warfare continued. The Greeks, heroic to the end, tried to carry on their "holy cause."

Days before the end it had become obvious to correspondents that they would have to evacuate if they were to get out reports on the last hours of the Greek struggle. Daniel De Luce embarked on a small fishing boat in an attempt to reach Turkey. Other correspondents tried other means. Some were missing for as long as four weeks. With De Luce were four aviators and two sailors demobilized by the Greeks. They were almost bombed out of their little craft near the island of Chios. They reached Smyrna, Turkey, on April 23. De Luce filed his story, unhampered by censorship:

To eight million Greeks the German victory in Greece is as tragic as any ever conceived by their great playwrights of classical days—Euripides, Aeschylus, and Sophocles.

To the modern Greeks, the entry of Germany into the Balkan conflict was the intervention of fates as inexorable as those depicted in the *Oresteia*. It was intervention which, the Greeks felt, snatched away at the last moment a victory won by blood and pain over the Italian legions who swept in from the north last fall. Every regimental headquarters on the Albanian front, from Khimara to Pogradec, had planned the spring offensive which was to shove the Italians back out of Albania.

"We will throw everything into it, all our men up to forty, all our guns," Greek commanders told me before Germany marched.

Thousands of wounded in base hospitals at Koritsa, Iannina, and Arta prayed for speedy recovery so they could fight in the "last battle." Twelve divisions of the finest Greek fighters—hardy mountaineers of Epirus and Peloponnesus and tough Crete islanders—were ranged along the crescent-shaped front for an all-out attack expected to sweep the Italians from Tepeleni, Berati, and Elbasani. They looked forward to the zero hour as eagerly as a champion football team anticipates the kickoff. But the offensive was stillborn.

Heartbroken generals tore up their plans when Hitler launched his men and machines across the Yugoslav frontier. Sensing the Yugoslav collapse before it occurred, the Greek commanders foresaw the impossibility of maintaining their northwestern line and they gave the order to withdraw in order. Not all obeyed. The brilliant Major Maniatakes stayed with a suicide squad in concrete blockhouses the Greeks had built beside Lake Ohrid and calmly awaited the enemy advance over a field planted with 3,000 land mines. Two nights earlier, in stockinged feet to avoid noise, he had escorted me to within 200 yards of Italian Alpini trenches and joked about the "surprise party" that awaited the Nazis.

Indomitable junior officers held Trebecina Heights while khaki battalions marched back past Balibani (where a German Stuka had been shot down early in March, weeks before official Nazi intervention), past Klisura, Premeti, and Pantalonia. All these towns had been won only a few weeks before at the point of the bayonet in fierce winter battles.

On heights overlooking Tepeleni, husky Evzones reluctantly shouldered dismantled light artillery, and with downcast eyes joined the Greek columns that marched painfully toward the rear. Koritsa and Argyrokastro, twin symbols of Greek military prowess, were abandoned without a shot in a withdrawal executed with the precision of a peacetime maneuver—but with far deeper emotion. Peasant soldiers cursed Mussolini and Hitler with all a trooper's traditional vehemence.

"If we live, will those devils send us away to slavery in Italy and Germany?" they asked.

There was no collapse of morale as in Poland and France. Commanders who could easily have fled to islands protected by the

British Fleet stayed with their troops to the end. Volunteer nurses remained at field hospitals until the last wounded man was safely moved to the rear. The devotion to duty seemed to be in inverse proportion to the growing disaster.

This was the climax of a Hellenic tragedy which also enmeshed a British Expeditionary Force of somewhere under 100,000 Australians, New Zealanders, Britons, and Scots—a climax evolved from the earlier scenes of the Balkan drama as inevitably as though one of the ancient masters had plotted it.

It has the tragic mistakes of men, the diplomatic and military miscues of Belgrade and London and Cairo, the futile and bitter strife of the Croats and the Serbs who refused to bury their antipathies even while German panzers were smashing across southern Yugoslavia to Bitolj.

As early as January, Serbian generals had talked of sending sixty divisions of the Yugoslav army of 1,250,000 toward Salonika as soon as the war started, but none ever got there. Outmoded mobilization orders were revised and the Serbs were sent north to help defend Croatia; the Croats south to fight in a Serbia for whose inhabitants they bore no affection. Harried by fifth columnists and ceaseless air raids, the Serbs waged a hopeless rear-guard fight in the retreat to Bosnia, while in the south, the Croats were overwhelmed at Bitolj.

The Greeks and the Yugoslavs hastily reorganized their lines at the pass south of Bitolj, but the strength of the German Army in the Balkans had been underestimated. There, the number of Germans in southeast Europe had been reckoned at a lower figure than that supplied by the British intelligence service operating in Greece.

Until the death of Premier John Metaxas of Greece, the Athens government desperately attempted to stave off German intervention by suppressing or ignoring German aid to the Italians in Albania and German intrigue designed to undermine the strong pro-British sentiments of the Greek Army. The now-suicide Premier Alexandros Korizis, British Foreign Secretary Anthony Eden, and King George of Greece, contracted for the British Expeditionary Force about March 2, long after the Germans had begun their great military infiltration into the Balkans.

Thereafter, as the Anzacs and Britons streamed into Piraeus and marched north, the Greek masses realized that their homeland was to be a battlefield for the Axis-British war. This they awaited with the fatalism of their ancestors. A frequent comment was: "No matter who wins, Greece will be destroyed. Why couldn't we be left alone to finish the Italians in Albania, then live in peace?"

Edward Kennedy was with the British forces in Greece. A few days after De Luce reported on the end of the Greek Army, Kennedy reached Cairo, Egypt. His story told of the defeat of the British:

When I left Piraeus, Greece, the water front there was a vista of twisted wreckage—the work of waves of German bombers.

I was a passenger on a Greek steamship crowded with Australian soldiers and refugees, and in the hold were 150 captured Germans. As we waited to cast off, Greek officials came abroad and demanded twenty of the Germans whom the Greeks had taken prisoner. Roll was called and the twenty went ashore.

Piraeus, port for Athens, had been bombed three times that day and it was likely that another bombing was imminent. The question was whether the ship would get out of the harbor before it came. The soldiers remained on deck, ready to fight off the dive-bombers. The refugees huddled below. The atmosphere was tense. Small children stood quietly beside their parents, those with food sharing it with others.

Finally, a little before midnight, our little vessel, with nearly 1,000 persons aboard, slipped out into waters thickly sown with mines by the German planes. Scarcely were we outside the harbor when they came—bombers dropping flares and then hurling explosives on shipping, docks, and warehouses. Nothing happened to our little ship, however, as we were far enough away by then and protected by a moonless night.

By noon of the next day we were in another harbor. Here the Greek crew decided it didn't want to take the ship any farther. Most of the refugees were taken to a camp on the shores, but we remained aboard. We had not gained much in getting from Piraeus to this harbor, for it was undergoing a steady bombing too, the Italians coming regularly at a high altitude in the morning and Germans taking up the work in the afternoon. In six raids while we were there only one Greek ship was sunk. It went down before our eyes in seven minutes as the life-belted crew jumped overboard. Finally we got away again and made Cairo.

Here is the way the British escaped from Greece:

Whole battalions lay concealed beneath the trees by day as the soldiers waited for boats, and German bombers searched vainly for them. By night the beaches were alive with men, the sea cluttered with boats. Every vessel that could pass muster was used, and the greater part—the British now say 48,000 out of 60,000—got away. Little material could be taken, but most of that which was left behind was destroyed. The Germans, when they reached the shore, found the woods full of wrecked vehicles, destroyed supplies.

The British came down to the sea with their rifles, packs, and machine guns, and most of them carried them away with them. In the case of bigger guns, the breeches were torn off before they were abandoned.

Many trucks were merely rolled into the sea, others pitched over cliffs so the Germans could never use them. In some cases, hand grenades were used to destroy British vehicles; others were chopped to pieces with axes or set afire with gasoline.

I will never forget the two nerve-racking days I spent falling back with the British forces before we reached Piraeus for embarkation to Egypt. Riding along in a truck with some of the British troops, I must have tumbled off my seat forty or fifty times to lie flat in ditches or to clutch the ground under the olive trees. German planes thundered just overhead and the bullets of front and rear gunners whistled in my ears. The Germans must have thrown hundreds of planes into the air to harass the British withdrawal down the mountains and across the plain of Thessaly.

The retiring columns of soldiers, like myself, were forced to jump from their vehicles numberless times and take cover as the airmen dipped and struck at the highways, but each time they were back in the trucks and moving again a moment after the danger had passed. Lacking adequate defense against the assault from the air, the soldiers could only swear fervently and find some comfort in the fact that little actual damage was done.

German fighters and dive-bombers ranged the sky over the retiring Empire forces almost unopposed. On the worst day I saw only two British planes, one of which charged into a swarm of seventeen Germans and shot one down. One British anti-aircraft battery brought down five bombers, but such batteries were all too few.

Sunday was Easter in Greece.

8

By APRIL 28, all of Greece was in the hands of the Axis. The island of Crete was the next objective. Axis control there would further facilitate air attacks on Egypt and Suez.

The U. S. Supreme Court ruled that Negroes could enjoy train accommodations just as good as those furnished whites. The Admiralty figured that a total of 1,443 merchantmen doing duty for the British had been sunk. Axis planes raided the Suez Canal Zone. Rumania confiscated all radios owned by Jews. U. S. Senator Wheeler said America was rushing down the road to war. Axis submarines, prowling in the Atlantic, sank five cargo ships.

Hitler's Balkan invasion brought the entire peninsula under his control. He controlled the land, but neither he nor Mussolini could control the sea. Here he was up against Britain's traditional, invincible strength—her Navy. His bombers concentrated their Mediterranean attack. Still His Majesty's Navy rode the waves. On a brief stop at Alexandria, Egypt, Larry Allen wrote an estimate of what he had seen:

For almost a year I have had a grandstand seat on the bridges, conning towers, and signal decks of Britain's mightiest battleships, speediest cruisers, destroyers, and aircraft carriers, watching the struggle for supremacy of what Mussolini once proudly proclaimed Mare Nostrum—Our Sea.

From the moment I became the first accredited correspondent with the Fleet I thought the British had what it took to win a sea war. Now I am convinced they have whatever is needed in courage, resourcefulness, iron determination, and skill to bombard the enemy bases, and perhaps to wipe the Italian Navy from the Mediterranean and the Nazi and Italian bombers out of the sky.

This calls for long chances, but the British are taking them. They sent warships dashing over the sea at top speed, hoping and praying to contact the Italian fleet—unaware of the enemy's naval air strength and not caring.

I saw Air Marshal Goering's hand-picked dive-bombing pilots try to scare the British Fleet out of the Mediterranean by making one of the most punishing attacks of war history on the aircraft carrier *Illustrious*. That gave me the greatest fright of my life. But her officers and men brought her into port under her own power.

Then there was our last trip to Tripoli, Italy's strongly fortified base in Northern Africa. Formations of enemy planes frequently attempted to get close enough to bomb the warships. Not a single bomb was dropped, but British fighters shot down seven planes. Tripoli unquestionably was one of the most daring attacks of the war.

Every war technician knows that a fleet usually is no match for expertly manned coastal defenses. The fact that Tripoli had a long string of 6- to 12-inch batteries, that the harbor waters were heavily mined, and that there was great danger from mass Nazi and Italian air attacks on the warships didn't deter Admiral Cunningham from his resolve to hand the Barbary Coast enemy a dose of lead it wouldn't soon forget.

From the conning tower of the heaviest armed battleship, I watched a thousand tons of high explosive and armor-piercing shells flung at Tripoli harbor in a thunderous forty-five-minute barrage so terrific I thought the minimum personal effect would be a bad case of shell shock. My half-blinded eyes were seared by great flashes from the fire of guns.

British gunners shoved shells in the long, gray barrels of the 15-inch guns with machinelike action and thought it great fun, even when two enemy shore batteries pumped 6-inchers over the turrets. Tripoli was the biggest fireworks display I have seen in my travels with the battle fleet. I shall never forget the thousands of white splinters of flame leaping skyward from anti-aircraft batteries, the long, snaky links of multi-colored tracer bullets, the "flaming onion" of anti-aircraft fire, and the yellow masses of flame gushing from battleships' guns. Nor this—twelve hours after the last 15-inch shells were fired, I touched the gun barrels. They were still hot. So was Tripoli.

9

Past the Balkans, in Asia Minor, were other countries on which Hitler had an eye. They flanked the Suez Canal. There was Syria, Iraq—Turkey. With Greece out of the way, Hitler stirred a revolt in Iraq. He also signed a new trade agreement with Turkey. In the spring of 1941 her overthrow was not essential to his plans, as long as she would remain neutral. She was doing a fairly good job of keeping clear of the war. She was pretty well prepared. She kept a watchful eye.

Earlier, Lloyd Lehrbas had spent some time in Turkey—at Istanbul. Among the reticent Orientals he had found little startling to report. One day he wandered across the Bosphorus to the ancient town of Scutari. Among the musty evidences of the glamor and the romance of the Turkey of old, he found a story. It was not about the war:

Outside an old stone building in a narrow, cobblestoned alley in Scutari is a small sign reading: "Association of Former Servants of the Harem."

Inside, a few old men provide the answer to the question asked by many newcomers to Turkey: "What has happened to the eunuchs?"

Romantic tales of old Constantinople (which today's Turks call Istanbul) invariably revolve around the mysteries of the Sultan's Harem with its veiled and pantalooned beauties reclining on downy divans or gracefully dancing to sensuous music—and always served and guarded by faithful eunuchs. The Harems were abolished by Kemal Ataturk, dynamic leader of the revolution established on the ruins of the Ottoman Empire sixteen years ago as a plank in his platform of equal rights for women. The one-time Harem beauties—who were always slaves and of non-Turkish race—have grown old as gracefully as they danced and are now respectable grandmothers.

However, few know, and fewer seem to care, about what happened to the always tall, always picturesquely garbed eunuchs who always stood about (in every picture or photograph) with folded arms, the human watchdogs of the Harem.

The Secretary of the Association of Former Servants of the Harem—a purely fraternal organization—is a sedate little old man dressed in western clothes. He answers your questions in high-pitched, querulous tones.

"There are not many servants of the Harem left," he explains as he momentarily recollects the good old days. "Most of them have died or grown too old to work. It's been a long time since the Sultan went away and closed his Harem and the youngest eunuch left now is at least fifty-five years old."

The former servants of the palace (as they prefer to be called) are scattered about the country and rarely get together. Some are still employed by conservative old Turkish families and are rarely seen by anyone. A few were given jobs in Istanbul's museums. One is a professor of literature in a girl's school.

"Yes, they're nearly all gone," the secretary concluded. "They drop in at the Association from time to time to exchange gossip over a cup of coffee, but fewer seem to come each year. In a little while they will all be gone."

Back in Istanbul few know what happened to the once-famed eunuchs and most are inclined to smile over the fact that anyone should be inquisitive of their fate.

Hitler officially occupied Athens on May 3. His Balkan Army was put through its paces along the streets of the historic old city. Buildings shook from the rumble of heavy tanks and artillery. Lochner described the scene:

Adolf Hitler's Balkan Army marched in a two-hour parade through this Greek capital today. The troops filed past Marshal Siegmund List, Hitler's Balkan commander, who stood before the royal palace surrounded by other high officers of the German and Italian Armies. Some distance away, on the classic Acropolis, the swastika fluttered in the spring breeze. As a matter of prestige, several Italian regiments also participated.

Greeks watched silently as the modern Teutonic forces thundered past. Heavy "panzers" raised a din along the streets, while overhead bombers roared over the line of march. The very foundations of structures along the line shook from the weight of the tanks and heavy artillery.

The population seemed to accept the fact of their defeat quite philosophically. They turned out to see the parade. We who saw the German Army parade in Paris couldn't help but note the difference. In Paris the parade avenues looked deserted compared to Athens' main square and streets.

Getting into Athens was no easy matter. Because of a shortage of supplies, Marshal List decided to rope off the capital, as it were, to prevent an influx of Greek soldiers and others who might quickly eat up what is left of provisions. These provisions are regarded by the Germans as sufficient until the country can recover from the shock of war and defeat, provided the capital is left to itself. Hence, only released soldiers who themselves are residents may enter the capital. We saw them by the thousands on foot from other sections of Greece, headed southward. The German high command was given orders to release them as soon as they are disarmed.

These Greek soldiers were allowed to hitchhike on German

Army vehicles motoring in the direction of Athens whenever there was room for them. They often squatted atop tanks, supply cars, or munition trailers, their faces grimy from dust and dirt.

Another order of List's was that no German officers or men could enter the capital without a permit signed by a commanding general. Moreover, it was strictly forbidden for any officer or soldier to purchase goods in Athenian shops without a certificate entitling the bearer to make a specified purchase. This again was to prevent the city from being stripped of its supplies. In short, it appears Hitler's desire is to treat the Greeks as leniently as possible in the hope of winning them over to his "New Order" in Europe.

While the famous temples of Acropolis were intact, the harbor of Piraeus is another story. There, devastation characterizes the once-busy Mediterranean port. Seventeen British ships were sunk, docks blasted, storehouses destroyed. The harbor is clogged with Stuka-sunk vessels whose funnels protrude. From a big British transport a body rises from time to time. Just how many more are incased in the ship nobody knows.

For four weeks some of the correspondents who evacuated Greece and Yugoslavia were missing. Then Robert St. John turned up. He had been in Yugoslavia when Hitler struck. With Russell Hill of the New York *Herald Tribune,* and Leigh White of Columbia Broadcasting System, he escaped in a 20-foot sardine boat. He was machine-gunned en route. He wrote from a hospital in Cairo, Egypt, early in May:

There were clean sheets on the beds when I arrived in Cairo. We hadn't seen sheets in four weeks. They were symbols of civilization. And taxis were honking in the streets. There was butter on the tables. People were laughing. People were dancing.

You should be able to sleep nights in Cairo because no planes come over. But I still can't sleep because I remember the noise of war anyway.

There is the whistling sound that makes the flesh creep when bombs come screaming down. Then there is the dull noise when they land. You can forget other noises, but not those of war.

There was the noise made by a dark-haired little Greek girl of five or six. She lay on a mattress on the floor of the whitewashed hospital in the Greek town of Argos. We lay on mattresses scattered around her. It was inky dark. She sobbed softly. She sobbed repeatedly, uttering a Greek word we could not understand. It was like a litany.

"Blimey, what's wrong with the little tyke?" asked a British soldier beside me, ignoring the wounds which were going to cost him his own life the next day.

"Why does she sob?" I asked the nurse who was doing her best to make these bomb-blasted pieces of humanity comfortable.

The nurse turned on her flashlight. Then I saw what was wrong. The child's thin little right arm was only half an arm. It ended in shreds. Shreds of torn, blackened flesh. There were no doctors in Argos to make a clean amputation.

"She cries for her mother," said the nurse and bit her lip. But the mother was dead. So was the child's father. So were the parents of other children.

Then, there was the man lying on the lawn of the emergency dressing station near the Greek coast with arms and legs blown away. There was little left except his heart, which still beat, and his lungs, which breathed. We thought he was dead. The nurse said he would be in a few minutes. No one could bother about him. The bandages must be used on those who had a chance to live. Then he started to scream. They told me he was screaming hatred at the bombers which rained death from the sky. He lay there screaming for hours. We asked a passing ambulance driver for narcotic pills. We forced them into his mangled mouth. But the screams went on.

How can anyone sleep between clean white sheets when a man lies on the grass in a Greek town screaming because he has no other way of expressing his hatred of planes that dropped suffering on quiet Greek towns? How can any one sleep when he hears the sobs of that woman in Corinth who wanted someone to give her enough morphine so that she could go to sleep forever and forget she would never be able to walk again?

Or the crying of that mother in Patras who was led to a wicker basket covered with a white cloth when she asked what had happened to her boy who had been playing near the railroad yards? Or the curses of an old man we saw digging with his cane in the rubble of what had been his home for the wife he left there when he went into the street to see why the sirens were blowing?

Then those noises which came from the thirty-car hospital train full of wounded after bombs had set it afire. Those are noises of war men don't forget. I heard those noises from Belgrade to

Mylos when undefended cities, sleeping villages and towns, were attacked by planes that flew so low that you could almost see the faces of the men behind the guns. I know what everyone else knows who has been through it. I know that the determination of the Yugoslavs, the bravery of the Greeks, and the resolution of the British, are all of no avail when they have too few planes to keep off the machines which make these horrible memories. That is the secret of war as it is being fought today.

CHAPTER 11

Hess Performs—The Kaiser Dies in Peace

May 11–June 21, 1941

I

OVER much of the world early that May, 1941, were millions of people who couldn't sleep. There had been some respite from constant raids on London, but it did not last. On May 11, the battered capital of the British Empire suffered another night bombing. It was one of the worst. One hundred thousand bombs rained on London's historic landmarks. Again the London correspondents combined to tell the story:

> Ancient symbols of Empire, including world-famed Big Ben, the stately Houses of Parliament, and hallowed Westminster Abbey, bore the frightful scars of bombs and fires tonight as an aftermath of the most devastating German raid yet loosed upon this battered capital. There also were uncounted dead and wounded.
>
> Many were killed in one hotel alone when a bomb crashed through the roof and exploded in the basement where most of 140 guests and employees had sought refuge. Just what the full cost in lives would be no one even would hazard a guess twelve hours after the fiery assault had ended.
>
> Rescue squads, weary but determined, worked throughout this Sunday bringing out the dead and injured and trying to restore order out of the devastating confusion. Many rescuers themselves became casualties when pieces of wreckage crashed upon them from damaged buildings.
>
> Big Ben, the Houses of Parliament, and Westminster Hall, which has played its part in the story of England for nearly 1,000 years, were damaged seriously.

Westminster Abbey, across the way, also was set on fire, and the British Museum was damaged. The debating chamber in the House of Commons was wrecked and will have to be rebuilt before it can be used again. In the House of Lords, Captain E. L. H. Elliott, resident superintendent, was killed at his post. Others killed included two members of the Police War Reserves and one custodian.

Bombs also smashed the roof of the famous members' lobby, already hit in previous raids and which had been shored up by elaborate scaffolding. Doors were torn off and windows smashed.

What many consider the most magnificent roof in the world— that of Westminster Hall, with its soaring arches and sweeping oak beams—was pierced by bombs, and the interior of the hall damaged. The hall was started by William Rufus in 1097. It is believed to be the largest hall in the world with a roof supported by pillars. It is 238 feet long, 68 feet wide, and 90 feet high.

Big Ben's face was blackened and scarred, and the apparatus that broadcasts chimes to the world was put out of action. But its hands went on telling the time to Londoners and it still chimed the hour.

Westminster Abbey was open to the sky, and the roof over the Lantern, the square tower at the center of the building, had fallen in. The Lantern, the absolute center of the Abbey, is where the platform and coronation chair are set for the crowning of the kings and queens of England.

Last night's raid was carried out by between 300 and 400 bombers. In the light of a full moon they swarmed over the capital, loosing hundreds of tons of high explosives and fire bombs.

British fighters, going up to battle the invaders as the anti-aircraft barrage let up to give freedom of action, shot down thirty-one. Anti-aircraft accounted for two more, bringing to 124 the number shot down over England in the last ten days.

The deanery of Westminster Abbey, one of the most perfect mediaeval houses in England, was destroyed and the dean and his wife were left with nothing but the clothing they wore. Bits of embers from London's fires carried nearly twenty miles into the country.

Now and then the rising roar of a motor told of a German plane diving low to machine-gun streets lighted by the fires. The moonlight was so bright it was possible at times to see trails of vapor

in the sky marking the paths of the hundreds of milling planes.
There was scarcely a letup from dusk until dawn.

The Germans came in seemingly endless waves, spewing explosives and incendiaries through every part of the city, blasting and
burning. Fires in business blocks burned for hours. Watcher brigades
and firemen were given scarcely a moment's respite. Five hospitals
were struck—one of them filled with children.

The bomb that crashed through the Abbey's Lantern Tower,
directly over the center of Confessors Chapel, sent swirling steel
and timbers down upon the spot where King George VI and Queen
Elizabeth were crowned amid pomp and splendor four years ago
tomorrow.

For days searchers dug through London's debris. There was
little time to count all casualties—little time for sleep or relaxation.
There were raging fires to be fought. There were tottering walls to
be razed. On one wall of a bombed, burned-out building, wrecking
crews came across a sign. It was still intact. It read:

"Anyone found damaging these premises will be prosecuted."

2

Rudolf Hess was Hitler's "shadow." He was one of the top
Nazis of the world. The numbers ran this way: Hitler, Number 1;
over-stuffed Hermann Goering, Nazi Field Marshal, Number 2;
Deputy Fuehrer Hess, Number 3. Hess was one of Hitler's very few
intimates. He was tall, dark-eyed, beetle-browed—47 years old. He
had a wife and a 3-year-old son.

Hess met Hitler on a French battlefield in 1918. He was
with Hitler in the abortive Beer Hall putsch at Munich in 1923.
They fled together. They were captured and imprisoned together.
While Hitler dictated, Hess transcribed and edited the one-time
paperhanger's best seller, *Mein Kampf*.

He was with Hitler in the railroad car in Compiègne Forest in
June, 1940, when Der Fuehrer gave the French their armistice
terms. He was one of six members of Hitler's secret war cabinet.

On April 20, 1941—While Greece was falling before the Nazi
onslaught—Hess helped Hitler celebrate his fifty-second birthday at
the German military headquarters on the Balkan Front. He told Hitler: "Trust in you is unlimited. God protect our Fuehrer!"

On May 2, 1941, he was along when Hitler addressed the Reich-stag. It had long been known that he suffered from progressive tuberculosis but he appeared to be his usual self on this Reichstag occasion.

Eight days later—the night of May 10—a Scottish farmer heard a plane roar overhead. He looked out of his cottage and saw the craft crash in flames. A parachutist landed near by. The farmer grabbed a pitchfork, hurried out, and found the parachutist lying on the ground with an injured ankle. The farmer helped the para-chutist to his thatched cottage and gave him a glass of milk. Then he reported his catch.

The modest cottage was besieged. A little later, Mrs. McLean, the farmer's mother, described the stranger who had descended so unexpectedly into their midst. She put it in a few words:

"I liked his uniform, his fur coat and shiny shoes. His clothing seemed to be all zip fasteners. Such a handsome mon, too. He had grand teeth. I asked him, 'Are you a German?' He said, 'Yes.'

"I said, 'What a life!'"

Mother McLean's comments were but a sidelight to the main story. London correspondents rounded up the salient details from several sources, among them bewildering German announcements:

Rudolf Hess, Number 3 Nazi and high in German war coun-cils, has parachuted to safety in Scotland after a fantastic, for-bidden warplane flight from the Reich, where his disappearance had been reported with the official comment that he suffered from "hallucinations."

Circumstances surrounding the 800-mile flight by Hitler's closest confidant suggested that Hess had deliberately deserted the Nazi camp. Unarmed and unresisting, he floated down to a Scot-tish farm field where a farmer armed with a pitchfork awaited him. Suffering a broken ankle, but appearing in good humor, Hess was removed to a Glasgow hospital.

An official from the British Foreign Office sped to Glasgow to interview Hess, who, in coming to England, defied Hitler's long-standing rule barring Hess from flying. Hess was quoted as saying that he had intended to land his Messerschmitt plane, but was unable to find a suitable spot and stalled it for a crash as he bailed out.

While the British statement did not specifically say that Hess had deserted, it made three observations of seeming inescapable sig-nificance:

That Hess had brought along photographs taken at varying years of his life to establish his identity if it were questioned. . . . That he had arrived in a plane which could not possibly have had enough gasoline for a return to Germany—and thus, inferentially, that his trip was clearly not a one-man offensive but a one-way flight. . . . That the Messerschmitt's guns were empty.

This most extraordinary flight was disclosed in London a few hours after Berlin had announced that Hess was missing, that he had presumably taken a forbidden plane flight and had cracked up; that he appeared to have been suffering "hallucinations" and had "left behind a confused letter."

The magnitude of Hess' determination to escape was indicated in another way, for he left behind him his wife, Ilse, whom he married in 1927, and their 3-year-old son. So fantastic was his flight that the British themselves, after thorough identification of their hostage, announced it only two days after he landed in Scotland.

The implications of the prominent Nazi's flight were cautiously avoided by Government officials. Sir Patrick Dolan, Lord Provost of Glasgow, said:

"Too much sentiment should not be displayed over the arrival of Germany's deputy fuehrer. Hess has come to this country not for love of us, but for love of his own skin. We musn't let him divert us from our effort in increasing production with a view to winning the war."

Churchill told Parliament there was "a maggot in the apple." In London, a boyhood nurse of the Nazi bigwig refused to believe Hess was insane. Other British comment was that Hess, for years a Hitler "yes" man, had finally said "no."

Hitler immediately called a meeting of all high Nazi officials to bolster morale. The Hess flight had aroused the German people as they had not been aroused before. The party leaders gave Hitler an impressive demonstration of a determined will for victory.

The British did not tell all they had learned by talking to Hess in the Glasgow hospital, but they disclosed sufficient to show that Hess was on a one-man, self-inspired mission. London correspondents, not permitted to see the prisoner, rounded up the latest information:

Rudolf Hess broke away from Germany as a hopeful missioner of peace, it became known today with the British disclosure that his unauthorized flight was aimed at a rendezvous in Scotland with his old English sports acquaintance, the Duke of Hamilton.

Well-informed British sources said this most amazing "good-will" flight of all time was undertaken in defiance of Hitler, with Hess banking on his friendship with the duke "to bring about some peace negotiations."

Hess and the duke were long acquainted and this ripened into a semblance of friendship at the 1936 Olympic Games in Berlin, where both were officials. The friendship was trustful so far as Hess was concerned, for it was disclosed that he had written a letter —presumably a peace feeler—to the duke some time ago. The duke turned the letter over to the government and on advice did not reply. What the government did about it remained a mystery, but Hess came parachuting down on a Scottish moor near the ducal estate seeking his answer.

Britons said Hess was convinced that the war must be ended this year if the interests of the German people were to be served. Doctors found him sane and healthy.

With respect to his attempt to reach the Duke of Hamilton, it was disclosed that he carried a penciled map on which he had charted his course from Germany to Scotland. Dungavel, the Scottish estate of the duke, was only fifteen miles from the place where he landed.

Officials quoted the farmer who captured the high-ranking Nazi as having reported that his first words were to inquire the way to the duke's place. The duke, on military duty, was not at his estate.

One high British source, casting aside German reflections on the mental state of the unexpected visitor, declared that Hess had a clear view of policy which he believed would help the German people. He tried to get Hitler to adopt it, but Hitler refused.

"Only when Hess saw there was no hope of Hitler adopting his policy," said the official, "did he resort to the desperate expedient of flight."

He reasoned that it would be safer for him to fly direct to Scotland than to attempt to escape to a neutral country and then try to reach the Duke of Hamilton. The Nazi Gestapo, with knowledge of his flight, would have had him killed by fifth-column operatives.

On top of everything else, there was every reason to believe that Hess wanted to talk the British into calling off the British-German hositilities and joining in a war on Russia.

3

THE Draft Board in Cheyenne, Wyoming, looked and looked for Eddie Whitten, wondering if he was evading the issue. Then they found him. He was already in the army; had forgotten to advise them of his enlistment. Swiss bees were discovered "smuggling" honey out of German-occupied Alsace. A Texan applied for a patent on a clocklike gadget which fitted over the foot of a bed and permitted the would-be sleeper to count sheep as they jumped over an illuminated fence on the face of the contrivance.

The battle in the Mediterranean intensified. Hitler poured in additional air strength. The Nazi-inspired revolt in Iraq caused the British trouble. The R.A.F. attacked Italian and German planes on Syrian airfields. Roosevelt ordered seizure of the giant liner *Normandie* and all other French vessels in U. S. ports. An Italian force of 7,000 surrendered to the British in Ethiopia. The Egyptian seamer *Zamzam* was sunk in the South Atlantic by Nazi submarines. Over 700,000 women were included in the latest British labor draft. Germany cut its weekly ration of meat by 20 per cent.

The real battle over historic, legendary Crete began on May 20. The Nazis parachuted troops on the strategic little Mediterranean base from planes and gliders. The use of glider troops marked a new, amazing method of modern Nazi warfare. But just before this began, Eddy Gilmore, in England, discovered still another phase of the war. He wrote about it from Green Hills, Hertfordshire:

Britain's biggest nudist camp has faced the fact that modern war is war in the air, and now trades stare for stare with R.A.F. pilots who conduct low-altitude reconnaissance flights over the camp.

"They seem to be over the camp a great deal," said the proprietor, his black beard streaming in the cold May wind, "but I expect they'll get used to us as we're getting used to them."

At first the nudists, who sprawled on the greensward within the woodland camp, thought of hot-footing it for the bushes whenever inquisitive flyers swooped over.

"But everything in life being relative," the proprietor philosophized, "we adjusted ourselves. Nowadays we just look up at them as they look down at us."

It didn't take the R.A.F. patrols long to spot the ten-acre park which is dedicated to the absorption of sunshine and fresh air in the altogether.

"If those pilots are as good at locating their targets across the water as they were in finding us, they will serve their country nobly," the proprietor observed.

Speaking above the hum of a Spitfire cutting dizzy circles overhead, he said the war at first had threatened to cramp nudist activities, but that affairs now were nearing normal on the shed-your-shirt circuit. The threat of invasion broke up two large camps on the coast, so this retreat—a short trip north of London—is now the chief haven for the clothesless. Twelve families live in camp throughout the week, but on week ends more than thirty devotees— principally from London—come out to sun. Here was one place in England where prices have not soared. The rates for a de luxe furnished cabin was $1.50 per day, with meals and $1.25 without.

The proprietor's wife explained that the nudists do not shun their responsibilities during air raids.

"The nights are too cold now for fire-watching in the nude," she said, "but on summer nights we'll be out with only our tin hats on."

4

ON MAY 24 came the beginning of another of the war's biggest naval engagements. H.M.S. *Hood,* the world's largest warship and pride of the British Navy, was on Atlantic convoy duty. It was sunk by the battleship *Bismark.* Three days later the *Bismark* itself went to the bottom. The sinking of the great German ship had a significant climax. The *Bismark* was finished off by air power. There was no longer any doubt about the effectiveness of the airplane, even in naval warfare. Also, the plane that dropped the fatal torpedo was American-made.

Reuters correspondent, J.R.N. Nixon, aboard a British ship, saw the sinking of both the *Hood* and the *Bismark.* His dispatch said:

I watched the "battle of giants" in which the 35,000-ton German battleship *Bismark* blasted into wreckage the symbol of British sea power—the 42,000-ton battle cruiser *Hood*—and in turn was sent to the bottom by a vengeance-bent array of British sea and air might.

Standing on the bridge of one of His Majesty's ships, I saw

the *Hood* go down only 200 or 300 yards away with her guns still firing. The end of the mighty *Hood* was an almost unbelievable nightmare. Shortly after the engagement began shells hit the 21-year-old battle cruiser. There was a bright sheet of flame and she blew up, apparently blasted by an unlucky hit in her thinly armored magazine loaded with powder. Parts of her hull were thrown hundreds of feet into the air and in a few minutes all that remained was a patch of smoke on the water and some small bits of wreckage. The battleship *Prince of Wales* was hit soon afterward by a 15-inch naval shell, but the damage was slight.

The "battle of the giants" was the climax of a chase by the *Hood* and *Prince of Wales* and their accompanying destroyers at top speed to prevent the *Bismark* from breaking out into the Atlantic to attack convoys. Pursuit began off Iceland and continued hour after hour in the eerie half-light of an Arctic night clouded with snow and sleet.

The cruisers *Suffolk* and *Norfolk,* which had been shadowing the *Bismark* since the big vessel left Bergen, Norway, kept the *Hood* and *Prince of Wales* informed of her movements. It did not get completely dark at any time that night.

We sighted the enemy at 6 A.M. on May 27 when a curtain of snow suddenly lifted from the waters between Iceland and Greenland. For some minutes our ships sped on toward the Germans to shorten the range. They, too, (the Germans), turned toward their pursuers and the world's biggest warships were thundering toward each other at a combined speed of probably more than sixty miles an hour.

The tension of waiting for the battle to begin became acute. The "open fire" order was given by signal. Almost simultaneously, orange-gold flame burst with a roar from the *Hood's* forward guns. Within three seconds puffs of black smoke shot out from the *Bismark* as she opened fire.

The *Prince of Wales's* guns then began firing. Dense clouds of yellow cordite smoke enveloped her bridge. She was to the left of the *Hood,* 200 to 300 yards away, and still surging forward on a parallel course. Fountains of water shot up in her wake—first about 100 yards behind her and then only fifty yards astern—grim evidence of the accuracy of the *Bismark's* gunners. The *Hood* thundered on and then, suddenly, she was hit. A shell, or shells, appeared to fall just forward of one of her 15-inch gun turrets and flames and heavy black smoke burst from her. The *Hood* continued to fire and still raced forward.

What happened next was a strangling, sickening sight. There was a terrific explosion and the whole of the vast ship was enveloped in a flash of flame and smoke that rose high into the air, the shape of a giant mushroom. Sections of funnels, masts, and other parts of the ship hurtled hundreds of feet and fell on our ship. The *Hood's* bow tilted vertically into the air and within three or four minutes she was gone. A destroyer was diverted to rescue work and managed to pick up three of the ship's company—two seamen and a midshipman.

All this time the *Prince of Wales* continued pouring shells at the *Bismark*. More than once spurts of water showed she was straddled. Then the *Bismark* broke off contact and slipped into a bank of snow and mist of the Arctic waters. Efforts to rejoin action with the *Bismark* were unsuccessful and the British Navy began pursuit. Units from the British Fleet and air arm sped from points as distant as Gibraltar and Newfoundland to avenge the *Hood*.

Two days later an American-built Catalina plane spotted the fleeing *Bismark* as it raced toward a French port, probably Brest or St. Nazaire. Word was flashed to the British Navy and the hunt was on again. Heavy fleet units moved in for the kill.

It was ironical that planes from the *Ark Royal* played a major part in bringing the *Bismark* to account, for the *Ark Royal* was often reported by the Germans to have been sunk. *Ark Royal* torpedo planes caught up with her on the evening of May 26 and sent two torpedoes into the giant warship. One nailed the *Bismark* amidships but the other struck astern, crippling the steering gear and causing the sea giant to flounder in uncontrollable circles. The fortunate torpedo hit also cut the greyhound speed of the *Bismark* to a walk and she was overhauled by British naval units about 400 miles from the French coast.

Her decks littered with wreckage from the pounding salvos of British warships and wallowing from bomb and torpedo hits, the *Bismark* finally slipped beneath the waves of the chilly Atlantic at 11:01 A.M. on May 27.

5

ROOSEVELT declared a state of "unlimited emergency" on May 28. In one of his usually well-modulated "fireside chats" there was deep emotion in a voice that reached one of the biggest audiences in the history of radio.

On that same day Roosevelt's National Defense Advisory Council was one year old. It was born out of the disasters to Poland, the Low Countries, and France. In organizing it, Roosevelt had said that the U. S. should arm to the hilt for any eventuality. Frank I. Weller, in Washington, surveyed American defense efforts in the past twelve months. He summed up accomplishments in this way:

1. Army expanded from 264,128 to 1,400,000, and the Navy and Marines Corps from 178,694 to 242,000.

2. Navy contracts for 629 of 3,400 authorized warships, and deliveries one year ahead of schedule.

3. All warplane deliveries increased 300 per cent; the bombers, 260 per cent; pursuits, 260; trainers, 325, and other tactical aircraft, 720.

4. Factories producing five 13-ton tanks a day and prepared for mass output of 26-tonners by midsummer in five plants.

5. Deliveries of Garand rifles boosted 360 per cent; combat vehicles, 265 per cent; field artillery, 40; anti-aircraft guns, 35; small artillery and machine guns, 1,500; powder, 1,000; and small arms and ammunition, 1,200 per cent.

6. More than 1,600 new defense plants and additions to existing factories completed or near completion.

7. Twenty billion dollars of an authorized $44,000,000,000 of defense contracts awarded with $5,000,000,000 paid out.

8. United States produced more goods and services than it, or any other country, ever did in a similar time with industrial output 11 per cent above the 1929 boom year.

9. Employment increase 2,500,000, 1,000,000 men and women trained for defense jobs, 4,000,000 now at work in defense industries, and national income stepped up by $10,000,000,000.

6

THE Nazis needed the island of Crete. They needed it as a base in the Mediterranean for air attacks against Allied Fleet operations. They needed it so that they could strike at British land and sea bases in North Africa and the Suez Canal. They didn't take long to get it.

The parachute and glider attack that began on May 20 paved the way. The British claimed capture or slaughter of every one of the first invaders. But maybe they exaggerated. Crete was bombed, ravaged, and captured. Again, it was a startling Nazi victory, an unhappy loss to the British. Daniel De Luce rounded out the details on June 1. He sent his story from Cairo, Egypt:

Picturesque Crete, legendary birthplace of Zeus, supreme god of Greek mythology, has fallen to the Axis after a savage twelve-day struggle in which fantastically attired parachute and glider troops played an unusual part.

As battle-scarred and tattered remnants of the disorganized British and Greek forces reach this Mediterranean port, I am able to report in detail the full impact of the Nazi sweep. It is a report that shows only too conclusively the helplessness of well-entrenched land forces before the Hitler air machine.

The preview of Germany's new legions of the air came with devastating fury on the island that is tied by legend with flying. For legend has it that it was on Crete that the mythical Greek, Daedalus, flew with his son, Icarus, on wings fashioned by the father with wax and feathers.

British and Greek forces, hurled southward from Greece onto Crete, hoped they would have time to re-form and add new power to their outnumbered armies. They thought that the 100 miles of water between the cave-scratched mountains of northern Crete and captive Greece formed a barrier to Hitler's panzer units. But the Nazis were not to be halted by that short gap.

Hundreds of lumbering Nazi transports darkened the sky over northern Crete. Downward floated hundreds of picked German shock troops. There were even charges that at least 1,500 of the sky troops were disguised in New Zealand battle dress. Many of them also had on camouflaged uniforms that blended with the foliage about which they landed.

And then came a sight that amazed even the tough British veterans who thought they had seen everything in Greece. Scores of slow-flying transports appeared, tugging behind them five or more glider planes, each filled with fifteen to twenty Nazi soldiers.

Sharpshooting New Zealanders and other British Imperial and Greek forces blasted hundreds of the paratroopers before they hit the ground. Others were dispatched by Cretans armed with rusty guns, knives, and even shepherds' crooks. But still they came. They landed with cynical disregard of their lives. Some fell into the sea, others tangled in the brush, and some were shot as they struggled like apes among the trees. Some broke their legs as they dropped into craggy ravines; others were blown into snowbanks on the mountain sides.

Attempts to land planes and gliders on the beaches were frequently disastrous, because all of the island's beaches were well guarded by Australian patrols which made short work of them. The British Imperials mowed down the Nazis like clay pigeons. But the tide pouring down from the clouds day and night gradually forced the defenders southward to the Mediterranean. Soon the Nazis seized the north shore and—more important—the few suitable airports on the island. After only three days, the R.A.F. was forced to give up the fight—its bases having fallen. That marked the beginning of the end of Crete.

With unchallenged control of the air, the Nazis stepped up their glider shuttle, landing fresh thousands of troops and complete supplies. Eager for the kill, they tried to slip a sea-borne invasion force across that narrow stretch of water from Greece. A British task force surprised the convoy on the night of May 21-22. In a flaming three-hour battle, at least 5,000 Nazis drowned. When the smoke of battle had lifted, an Italian destroyer, two merchantmen, and forty-odd sailing vessels, had been sent to the bottom. Most of the sailing vessels were Greek caiques or sailing boats that had been seized by the Axis for the invasion convoy. The British warships knifed through the overloaded wood sailing boats, spilling the occupants into the fire-lighted sea.

But this triumph was only fleeting. The Germans and the Italians applied a squeeze. Within a few days the Nazis—driving from the eastern part of the island—joined forces with the Italians from the west. Some fifteen thousand Allied troops—more than half of the original defenders—were evacuated through swarms of Axis dive-bombers to Egypt. The British War Office had this epitaph for the battle:

"It became clear that our naval and military forces could not penetrate indefinitely in and near Crete without more air support than could be provided from our air bases in Africa."

The Nazis pulled other tricks out of the German war bag. One soldier told of a batch of parachutists tumbling from a Nazi transport. "We opened fire on them and thought we had killed them," he said. "But when they landed we found they were dummies to attract our fire while real parachutists were coming down near by."

Fabled Crete was gone. Thunderous old Zeus and Daedalus, God of aviation, after all, had been there only in fancy. Hitler's legions were real.

On the same day that Crete fell the British entered Bagdad, mopping up the Iraq revolt. On June 4, ex-Kaiser Wilhelm died in exile at Doorn. Axis planes raided Alexandria, Egypt, killing 150 civilians and injuring 200 others. On June 14, Roosevelt froze all German and Italian assets in the U. S. Two days later, he ordered the closing of German consulates. A week after that he ordered the same for all Italian consulates.

A Cologne newspaper reported that toothaches were becoming widespread in Germany because of a shortage of dentists. It urged people to consult a dentist "only when absolutely necessary—as, for example, when the pain becomes too great or chewing is impaired seriously."

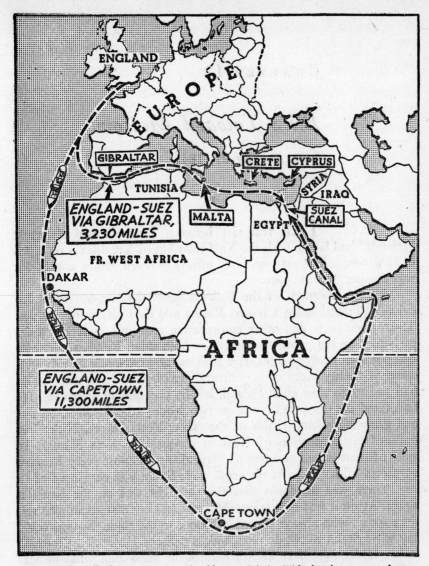

Map 9—The fall of Crete was a major blow to Britain. With that base gone, she no longer could maintain her Mediterranean life line even though Gibraltar and Malta continued to hold out. Moreover, there was always the possibility that the remainder of the French Fleet would go over to the Nazis. So Britain had to start sending her ships all the way around Africa, adding 16,000 miles to the round trip.

CHAPTER 12

Blitz Toward Moscow

June 22–July 27, 1941

I

THE real rift between Europe's two strangest "friends" had begun with the Nazi invasion of Yugoslavia on April 6. It widened. The real status of affairs between Hitler and Stalin was coming into the open.

Hitler's conquest of the Balkans made the Russian break inevitable. Traditionally, anyway, Russia and Germany were enemies. Their trade pacts and other co-operative measures in recent times perhaps were but paper maneuvers on both sides. Russia supposedly had not been ready to fight. Her political and economic system, outcome of twenty years of experiment, was untested for war. Stalin had had to go slow since Poland, but he was quietly preparing. He had faced the prospect of war on two fronts—the Japanese on one and ground-grabbing Hitler on the other. Years before, Hitler had outlined his conception of Russian conquest in *Mein Kampf*. In spite of treaties and gestures of "friendship," almost every Russian suspected Hitler still felt the same way; Stalin was convinced of it.

There was no doubt that the spotlight was on the Kremlin again. Again it was mysterious Moscow and her statesman who seldom spoke, who always played 'em close to the chest. No one could say what Stalin would do next, unless perhaps Hitler and Churchill knew. Hitler may have known because he knew that what he was doing was in opposition to what Stalin would stand for. Churchill may have known because Hess really may have tipped him off when he escaped to Scotland.

Even Moscow correspondents couldn't know too much officially. Stalin didn't talk to them—even in confidence. Some of them did know what many of the ordinary, everyday Russians were thinking because some of the Stalin subjects would loosen up and talk.

Henry Cassidy was one of the correspondents who knew about the ordinary people. He had studied them. He had talked with them. He made an estimate:

The average Russian is sure that sooner or later he will have to fight. Throughout a year and a half of general European war, the Soviet policy toward this conflict has been one of rapid but unpublicized preparation.

The Russians do not talk freely. In fact, they tell this joke about themselves which illustrates their reticence: Four men, the story goes, were riding in a train. The first one yawned. Another said, "Da" (Yes). The third said, "Da-da." The fourth immediately said: "If you don't stop talking politics, I'll report you to the NKVD (the State Police)."

Nevertheless, many Russians do discuss the war seriously in the privacy of their homes and sometimes with foreigners who have won their confidence. There are apparent reasons for their belief in the inevitability of war:

1. The government's program of constant mobilization and military reorganization means that Russia is getting ready for something.

2. Recently, Stalin abruptly abandoned the official anonymity behind which he had been guiding the Soviet Union and became himself premier, replacing Vyachislav M. Molotov, who had held that office for eleven years.

3. Even more recently, the Soviet withdrew its recognition from Yugoslavia, Belgium, and Norway. In the case of Yugoslavia, this action was taken in spite of the treaty of nonaggression and friendship signed a few hours before she was invaded by German troops. Observers saw in this withdrawal of recognition a direct slap at Hitler, although the notice itself was given to Yugoslavia.

There was a time in this war when the Russian thought he would have to fight against the Allies. That was during the Russian-Finnish war, after Russia entered into collaboration with Germany and when the British and French were reported planning to send an expeditionary force to aid the Finns. Peace with Finland and the collapse of France changed that.

The other thought that underlies the life of the average Russian is the much-vaunted "transition from Socialism to Communism." The Soviet regime acknowledged that, after twenty years of power, it has not reached its goal and that Russia has not yet achieved thoroughgoing Communism. The present Socialist system is described as "from each according to his ability, and to each according to his labor." The future Communist system is described as "from each according to his ability, to each according to his needs." To reach that goal, however, the regime first demanded an "abundance of production," and the major Soviet effort—apart from military preparedness—has been directed toward that end.

Industrial production and political isms—which often are merely vague abstractions to workers of other countries—are living realities to the Russian, who has them drummed into him daily by the press and radio, by foremen at work, by lecturers, and even by actors in the theaters.

Every Russian sees more and more signs of war every day. He sees it in the streets, where the high gray fur hats, close-fitted brown coats, and black boots of soldiers grow more prominent. He feels it particularly in his pocketbook.

The national budget for 1941 reached the record sum of 216 billion rubles—twice as much as 1938 and one-third of it earmarked for national defense. The money to pay that comes from family budgets. Official statistics place the average earnings of the Soviet worker at 227 rubles monthly. Normally the ruble is worth about 19 cents at best, though such a comparison is indefinite because many services are free in the Soviet economy. Out of that wage the Russion pays his share of the state's charges, mostly in a "turnover" tax which supplies more than half of the state income. This tax is calculated to bring in 124 billion rubles in 1941, compared to 105 billion in 1940. That means an increase in prices.

The cost of black bread, the staple Russian diet, already has increased 10 per cent. Butter and potatoes are even higher. Restrictions have been placed on amounts of food in any single purchase, but the supply has improved generally because the 1940 crop was good, the winter comparatively mild, and there were no complications like last winter's war with Finland. The prices of merchandise have gone up like those of food.

In other ways, too, the backwash of war is encroaching deeper into Russian life. The general effect is a reproduction in lesser degree of what is going on in western Europe. With nightly darkness in the west, there are periodic blackouts here in the east; with strict rations in the west, there are loose restrictions on sales in the east; with battles to the west, there are maneuvers and war conditions in the east.

Even the daily routine of Russians has been transformed by the European war. The change started last year when the 6-day, 48-hour week was put into effect, replacing the 5-day, 35-hour week. That was labeled plainly in a message to the all-union Central Council of Trade Unions as due to "war danger for our country" and intended to "raise defensive and economic power still further in the interests of the people of the U.S.S.R."

Since the change in the labor code, the Russian worker, instead of being free every sixth day, has been taking his rest on the traditional Sunday. Care has been taken, however, to see that Sunday off does not encourage an increase in the practice of religion. The Soviet constitution guarantees freedom of worship, but the Communist party doctrine is atheism, and few but elders of the pre-revolutionary generation attend church.

The press—particularly the newspaper *Godless*—has declared repeatedly that Sunday off was no reason why Russians should go to Mass. Moscow, which once was celebrated for her 454 churches, now has only twenty-five Orthodox churches and one Catholic church, two synagogues and one mosque, which still hold services.

Stalin's commandments and their effects have been accepted without question. There seems little doubt but the average Russian is sure that sooner or later he will have to fight—most likely sooner.

2

THE "average" Russian was not wrong. It came even sooner than he expected. In Berlin it was 3:20 A.M. of June 22—another famous Nazi Sunday. In New York it was six hours earlier. To Berlin correspondents it seemed that the Nazis always got up early to do their dirty work. They were accustomed to being notified at 3:20 A.M. that an "important" press conference would be held at dawn. More than one correspondent had said he didn't mind so much covering Hitler events, but he wished Der Fuehrer would change his starting time.

Like all the others, Lochner was home in bed that morning of June 22. He hurried down and got the latest news. He had already suspected what was in the offing; the night before, all communications out of Germany were cut "mysteriously" for several hours. That was the tip-off. Lochner did not wish to depend upon the slower cables. In a matter of minutes he was on the trans-Atlantic telephone to New York. He dictated the story that told of the big event of another Hitler Sunday:

Adolf Hitler declared war at dawn today on Soviet Russia.

German troops massed in East Prussia already are on the march, along with soldiers from Finland and Norway in the north and Rumania to the south.

Propaganda Minister Goebbels read the proclamation and then Foreign Minister von Ribbentrop came on the air to read a formal declaration of war against the nation with which Germany linked herself in a ten-year nonaggression pact less than two years ago.

Although the proclamation and declaration of war came with startling suddenness on an otherwise quiet Sunday morning, the break was not unexpected, since Europe has been teeming for weeks with rumors that open conflict between the two Great Powers and erstwhile "friends" was imminent.

After declaring that Russia had repeatedly violated Germany's frontier, and taken measures in Rumania, the Baltics, and elsewhere, which were aimed against the Reich, Hitler said:

"I cannot be an onlooker any more. There are 160 Russian divisions around our border. Russia organized the putsch in Yugoslavia. This was not from platonic motives and still I kept silent. It was Moscow who demanded mobilization of the Serbs."

He accused the Russians of sending planes across the common German-Russian frontier countless times and said that the moment at last had arrived when Germany could no longer overlook these developments.

"Together with the Finns, the Germans are standing from Narvik to the Carpathians," the proclamation said.

This one sentence indicated perfectly how far-reaching is the new battle front—from Narvik, in far northern Norway, to the Carpathian mountains and the Black Sea—more than 1,500 miles.

The proclamation ended:

"German people: At this very moment a marching of the German armies is taking place which has no precedent. From the rivers of the Danube to the shores of the Black Sea, German and Rumanian soldiers, under (General Ion) Antonescu, are united. The task is to safeguard Europe and thus save all. I have therefore today decided to give the fate of the German people and the Reich and of Europe again into the hands of our soldiers."

Germany had made harsh demands on Russia, especially for

the oil and wheat of the great Russian breadbasket—the Ukraine. Finland had been especially jumpy and had ordered mobilization of reserves, but there had been nothing from the censor-veiled Russian capital to indicate anything other than peace and light.

The split with Russia followed hard on the heels of a Turkish-German friendship pact and only yesterday a foreign source in London declared that the new agreement included a secret provision that Turkey would remain benevolently neutral in the event of war between the Reich and the Soviet. This could mean that Turkey, guardian of the Dardanelles, might clamp that vital strait shut, thus closing Russia's exit to the Mediterranean from the Black Sea.

German troops occupying Rumania have been concentrated on the Russian border for days. Hitler, in turn, has promised Rumania the return of Bessarabia, which she lost to Russia in a deal last year.

Hitler accused the Russians of a tremendous double cross, of having signed in bad faith the German-Russian nonaggression pact of August 23, 1939. He himself, Hitler asserted, had entered into that pact with some misgivings, but had had to do it because of Britain's policy of encircling Germany. He accused the Soviet Union —in spite of the welcome gift by Germany of half of Poland—of having tried by underhand means to cut Germany's throat. Bitterly he excoriated Russia for the Finnish and Baltic land grabs, the slicing up of Rumania. He blamed the Communist diplomats for playing England's game and stirring up the Yugoslav coup d'état.

Von Ribbentrop added to the list of charges, declaring that Russian diplomats had been guilty of espionage against Germany and that Russia long had conducted a campaign of sabotage against the Reich.

Immediately on the heels of the German declaration, Moscow issued her own. The Soviet said the U.S.S.R. and Great Britain "were in full accord on the international situation."

Suddenly, surprisingly to many, the Communists and the democracies were allied. The Nazis and the Communists, at least on the surface, had been trying to sleep in the same bed. They had failed. Their failure opened still another war front—the biggest to date.

Hitler's second fiddle—Mussolini—out of tune with real Italian sentiment, in effect said, "Me too!" He declared war on Russia the same day. Rumania likewise. The whole of Europe was becoming embroiled.

Again, Italy's role was blockade. Hitler wanted her to help prevent Soviet access to the Mediterranean through the Black Sea. Perhaps he hoped Mussolini would do a better job on this assignment than he had done on his earlier Mediterranean venture.

Hitler's new front stretched all the way from the Arctic Circle to the Black Sea—a distance comparable to that between New York and Denver. His armies now were deployed over nineteen foreign lands. Hitler was moving toward world conquest. Control of Russia would mean control of the raw materials, the industrial products, and the grain of the Ukraine in southeastern Russia. The conquest of Russia also pointed the way to easy prey in the Orient.

Hitler had stood at Napoleon's tomb. He had promoted "yes" men who flatteringly compared him to Napoleon. He was bent on outdoing Napoleon. Napoleon, too, had once marched on Moscow.

As in Poland, Norway and all the other conquered countries, Hitler tried another blitzkrieg. His plan was attack on strategic sectors. He had three major groups of troops. They all had definite objectives. There was the Northern Group that drove toward Leningrad. There was the Central Group that headed toward Moscow. There was the Southern Group that struck out for Kiev and the Ukraine.

Stalin's major forces were arrayed in three opposing groups.

The Nazi panzer troops and air force lost no time. They were rushing ahead even before Hitler's declaration disturbed the Sunday dawn. That, also, was typical Hitler strategy.

Martial law was declared throughout Russia. The weak Soviet Fleet was ordered into action. Her regular Army of 1,500,000 was in the field; 8,500,000 reserves were subject to call. Her country was thirty-five times as big as Germany, but her forces were untried in war, her real strength unknown.

The Nazis claimed capture of Brest-Litovsk, in that part of Poland which Russia had grabbed in September, 1939. The Russians bombed Warsaw, Constanta, and Leningrad. Nazi panzers pushed on into north, central, and south Russia. The Soviet acknowledged loss of 374 planes in the first three days of battle.

Hitler promised the return of religion in the event he captured Russia.

Henry Cassidy—once tipped by a Harvard vocational adviser to be a schoolteacher because he was "too bashful" to be a reporter

—was on the Russian Front. On June 26 he completed a six-day tour of one sector of the Red line:

From the Black Sea to Moscow, through regions rarely seen by foreigners, I have watched from behind the Russian lines as the Soviet provinces went to war with Germany. Mobilization was carried on without apparent hitch. The blackout was installed effectively. Trains were running promptly. Agriculture and industry appeared to be working at top pitch.

The Soviet countryside showed two striking contrasts to France of a year ago. First, there was no rush of refugees to tangle transport. Second, the people maintained complete Slavic calmness and confidence. War nerves never reached these remote districts.

The skies over Central European Russia appeared to be under absolute Soviet control. Through the Ukraine I saw no German planes, not even the scouting craft such as penetrated deep into France in the early days of the war there.

Even though there had been rumors enough abroad of the coming war, it came rather suddenly in the provinces Sunday. The radio on the night before and the provincial press that morning had not hinted of the conflict about to break. The population stiffened and listened open-mouthed to a broadcast of Foreign Commissar Molotov's speech announcing the German attack.

The outbreak of fighting brought a surge of patriotic emotion. Broadcasts of marching songs echoed through the valleys of the Caucasus after Molotov's speech. Successive broadcasts brought bursts of cheering from steadily growing crowds. Uniformed troops on leave lined up at railway stations to rejoin their regiments. Newly mobilized men marched through the streets. Army cars and trucks raced by. Houses were transformed into barracks. Blue light bulbs for blackout illumination were produced for public buildings, candles were distributed in hotel rooms, and the Russian Riviera on the Crimean Peninsula plunged into darkness.

In Russia the official news agency is called Tass. It said today: "Hitler has stretched his greedy paw toward the Soviet land. He wants to take away the land from our collective farmers. He wants to destroy our cities and take our factories and planes. He will never succeed. The Soviet people have risen to a great war for the fatherland. Our banner words are 'For the fatherland, for honor, for freedom, for Stalin.' Under this banner we will win, for ours is a righteous cause.' "

Here are two rather unusual examples of the kind of patriotism now sweeping the country. They are interesting, yet entirely different. Russian girls are clamoring for admission to the Red Army for service at the front. Simultaneously, the Moscow radio has been broadcasting "Columbia the Gem of the Ocean" and other American and Scottish patriotic songs.

To those of us who have spent much time in Moscow, the city tonight presents a strange sight. Sale of vodka, wine, and other alcoholic drinks has been prohibited, and civilians have been instructed to keep off the streets between midnight and 4 A.M. Theaters, restaurants, and other public places must close at 10:45 P.M. Russia is seriously at war.

3

IN its first breath-taking attack the Nazi blitzkrieg was effective. Its panzer troops sped ahead. Its air force raided far and wide to demoralize civilian poulation. Its heavy equipment, including fast tank corps, hurried to the Polish-Russian front. Germany's Rumanian ally to the south pushed rapidly on Bessarabia. Away up to the north, Finnish troops went into action. Additionally, Nazi planes were using Finland as a base.

Both sides suffered stupendous losses. Earlier Hitler campaigns seemed tame by comparison. The Soviet threw in men and machines to hold Hitler forces at the border. They failed. Soviet equipment was destroyed right and left. The defenders hurriedly gave way to the roughshod panzers.

Hitler's Central Group was driving along a line unmistakably the shortest distance between two points. Those two points were Berlin and Moscow. Moscow was the object of all interest because it was the Soviet capital.

Alvin J. Steinkopf got out the first eyewitness account of the Nazi drive through southern Poland. He wrote it from Lwow, where much of the action was taking place. The date was July 4:

Uncounted hundreds of Russian tanks, smashed by the German Army in this now-shattered frontier area, lie disabled in southern Poland and the western Ukraine.

Thousands of Russian prisoners, many barefoot, are marching back along roads over which hang clouds of yellow dust. I saw 4,000 of them in one vast camp in conquered territory. The Germans were putting them to work expanding the camp. Preparations were being made in this one place alone to accommodate 50,000.

A confusion of material was left behind by the Russians in southern Poland. Along every highway lie battered tanks, so many that one loses track when trying to count them. Other hundreds are in the woods on either side of roads. Seen everywhere also are Russian cannon, upset or smashed. Scores of Russian tractors cluttered the streets of towns and ditches along the highways.

All southern Poland hums with the sound of motors. On the highways are German motor columns moving eastward endlessly. In the air the Luftwaffe streaks eastward like a flock of hawks. Everywhere the story seems to be the same.

Russian prisoners and civilians declared the German Army struck with such ferocity that they were rushed off their feet. They were bombed out of half-finished fortifications. They retreated, abandoning equipment worth millions of dollars. Still, the flight was not fast enough to prevent the capture of thousands.

From a slight elevation we overlooked the camp where, at the moment, were 4,000 Russians with more arriving hourly. Hundreds were barefoot, explanation being that along the line they had traded shoes for cigarettes. Along all the roads were new graves. Steel helmets marked the resting places of German soldiers, and rifles or other equipment indicated where the Russians were buried. Every few miles the ripe wheat had been trampled by tanks and infantry. Here and there were smashed Russian bunkers.

Strangely enough, the Germans on the South Front apparently have made little use of one of their most effective weapons—the swift tank. While hundreds of Russian tanks were destroyed, the Germans said they were accounted for largely by infantry and special antitank troops. One officer told how a 92-ton Russian tank was disabled by German infantrymen who crawled up and tossed a hand grenade into the muzzle of one of its bristling cannons.

Lwow escaped with comparatively little damage. Some fires still were burning today, but there was no evidence of heavy bombardment by artillery or Stukas.

4

AT MEXICO, Missouri, a bread truck driver said a sprightly hen jumped on the bumper of his van and rode fifty miles. Near Douglas, Arizona, a man grabbed a rattlesnake and choked it to death after the reptile bit him on the finger. While housewives were giving pots and pans in the U. S. campaign for aluminum, a California patriot did his bit by donating one of his own favorite possessions—an illicit still.

In an Independence Day ceremony, Roosevelt asked the American people to pledge their lives, if need be, to maintain freedom. In Moscow, Stalin took official cognizance of the rapid Nazi strides. He told retreating forces to leave only "scorched earth" behind. Lochner, with the invading Finns, wrote about the effect of the Stalin instructions:

Five days spent with the Finnish Army have provided proof after proof that the Red Army carries out to the letter Stalin's order to destroy everything of value on retreat.

Any abandoned village or town can be spotted long before we reach it by the chimneys standing like sentinels amid scenes of desolation. Among the sights are the second-story iron stoves left in mid-air, hooked to the chimneys, when the rest of the house has burned.

No matter how small the town, it has its statue of Stalin. At first, when the Finns captured the towns, they smashed these statues. The high command, however, soon deemed it better to have them taken as trophies. At one village we saw this curious sight: From a Stalin statue the nose had been knocked off and the face disfigured, but from one arm hung a sign in Finnish: "Do not disfigure this statue—it is to be taken to the museum." Someone had put a Red Army cap on the statue's head.

At another village a church was still standing. When we entered we found it had been converted into a community movie. Along the sides were inscriptions such as, "Never shall perish the honor of the army that fought for Communism." Seats were set aside for political commissars, a colonel and a major. A religious painting which depicted Christ blessing the children hung on one wall.

One of the characteristics of all the Russian villages is a triumphal wooden arch with some Communist slogan thereon. The Finns, on capturing such localities, lose no time in tearing down the slogans, but they usually leave the red-painted arches intact.

We encountered many graves of the Finnish-Russian winter war of 1939-1940. They were collective graves, marked by red marble slabs with Soviet stars superimposed on them.

5

ALTHOUGH the Russian campaign represented a vast new front, older fronts also were active. The British advanced in northern Syria. Germany claimed sinking of eight more Allied ships —submarine victims. Ten Italian generals were captured in Ethiopia. Argentina rounded up Nazi fifth columnists. American arms moved to Egypt at the rate of a shipload a day. Washington announced the arrival of U. S. naval forces at Iceland, Trinidad, and British Guiana.

The R.A.F. pounded Germany and Nazi-occupied Europe. Volunteer American fliers helped. Tom Yarbrough visited a Yankee-manned R.A.F. Fighter Station in England and told what happened there on Independence Day:

The American Eagle Squadron of the R.A.F. celebrated this beautiful July Fourth with a roaring sweep over northern France, thus inviting Germany's newest fighters to come up and engage in battle. They did. When the dogfighting was over, the score was one Messerschmitt damaged and all Eagles safe.

I watched the beginning and the end of a large part of the day's general R.A.F. sweep from this station, but saw no Eagles. They worked from another place. But the British boys here had an even bigger day. They destroyed three Messerschmitts, probably downed another, and damaged six. I saw them take off in squadron after squadron, thundering into the dazzling blue sky, and saw them come back—all but two.

They were just taking off, a dozen at a time, at intervals of about one minute, when a small group of reporters arrived. The time was 2 P.M. sharp. The front flyer was the R.A.F.'s leading hitter, a fast-talking young South African. Two hours later he and his pals were landing again. They had guarded a fleet of bombers to Bethune and back—a more hazardous daylight job than any they did last autumn when the Germans were swarming over Britain.

While they were out the station was a dull place, but when the leader returned it came to life. His tunic was soaked with perspiration and he was as excited as a kid with a box of firecrackers. An intelligence officer pumped his arm and slapped him on the back, for he had got one and a half Nazi planes—one by himself and the other with a Polish flyer.

Somebody said: "That's your thirty-second, isn't it?" and he said he really didn't know. "I think it's somewhere around thirty," he said. The intelligence officer later declared it was his thirty-third.

We were at another squadron's hangar when the time that all were due back had passed.

"How do you stand?" I asked the leader.

"We're one short so far," he said.

That one "short" was the station commander who always told his pilots to "come on" instead of "go on." The pilots covered up their uneasiness with mock amusement at the "chief" getting shot down. An hour later he turned up with a laugh about having been "all by myself in the middle of France."

"Five Messerschmitts got on my tail," he said. "But when I faced them they all went off."

They had given him a few "squirts" and he landed safely with his aileron hanging by a thread.

Finally, without waiting any longer for the pair that was still missing—and without talking about them—the pilots drifted into their mess for late tea. Over in a corner a radio was softly playing "America, I Love You."

6

A RUSSIAN pilot made a suicide dive into a concentration of Nazi fuel cars. Stalin called for guerrilla warfare to wipe out the Nazis in occupied areas.

Successful blitzkrieg was not Hitler's only problem. He faced another—inevitable for any successful invader. It was the problem of prisoners. The Nazis handled it with characteristic efficiency. Steinkopf looked in on one of the new camps:

A week ago this prison camp for Russian prisoners was a Polish meadow. Now it is covered with 500 acres of low barracks of new lumber which shines brightly in the moonlight. A few hours ago the population was slightly more than 5,000. Now there may be thousands more because several columns of foot-weary Russians have been moving through clouds of dust in this direction on different highways.

All along the Eastern Front prison camps of this type are being organized. I sauntered through precisely-laid-out streets of the new prison town. Blue-eyed, broad-faced Slavs gazed with silent curiosity, not sure whether to hide or to come up and ask for cigarettes. Under these circumstances I met 18-year-old Achmed Agalam, of Uzbekistan, one of the Soviet republics. He wanted to know whether I was an Englishman, because he had studied English for two years.

Each barrack is a low structure accommodating about sixty men. To save on lumber in this region, where it is scarce, each of the head-high buildings is put up over an excavation of about two feet. Prisoners put them together under the direction of Germans who don't know a word of Russian. They knock a building together in a few hours.

Prisoners are coming so fast that the administrators have difficulty in recording them. So they are registered first by numbers. The number is traced in indelible pencil in figures two inches high on the skin of the prisoner's chest. When asked to identify himself, the prisoner opens his shirt. The sergeant then knows immediately whether he came today or yesterday and whether it's his turn to work in the field kitchens.

The kitchens are set up almost entirely of captured Russian equipment. The ration today was a liter (1.05 quarts) of stew made of barley and potatoes and possibly a suspicion of meat. The first day it took three hours to serve the meal. Now it is finished in an hour because the camp director has systematized things. A Russian in each barrack has been made mess chief of his building. He has a numbered placard, and when his number is called in all languages he comes forward with a large can. He gets the food for his group.

Drainage, sanitation, and water supply are chief problems in choosing prison camp sites. At the camp I inspected six wells had been sunk in two days. The side-hill situation helps drainage. All around are machine gunners on platforms built fifteen feet up in the trees. They watch every move in the camp and could make short work of any break for the wheat and flax fields surrounding it.

Germans say prisoners of various types should be segregated, that just a few days' experience has shown it to be a wise policy. Ukranians would fight Laplanders, they say, and Mongolians can't get along with Russians. A special section of the camp has been set aside for Jews. Jews have proved of unusual value in the camp administration because they are the linguists of east Europe, and it is usually possible to find someone among them who understands any obscure dialect.

7

BY JULY 21 the Nazis had shortened the distance to Moscow on the Central Front. Shock troops with flame throwers and hand grenades reached Polotsk—340 miles from the Soviet capital. Tens of thousands of Russians were killed or wounded. The Nazis claimed the slaughter was in retaliation for Russian raids on Bucharest and Helsinki.

That same day Moscow suffered her first Nazi bombing. The raid lasted five and one-half hours. Two hundred bombers participated. Civilians were killed. The Nazi raiders swooped over Moscow again the next night with greater force. Henry Cassidy was among the thousands who dodged the bombs:

Scores of persons were killed and wounded and several houses, a hospital, and a school were heavily damaged last night by a wave of Nazi bombers which attacked this Soviet capital for the second evening in succession.

At least fifteen German planes were shot down as ground batteries lifted a terrific barrage, and Soviet pursuit fighters tangled with the Germans in dogfights over the Kremlin.

The capital was under alarm from 10:10 P.M. yesterday (3:10 P.M. in New York) to 3:30 A.M. today. When the raiding was all over I saw a big bomb crater in Mokovaya Street in front of the U. S. embassy. The Kremlin and other public centers were not touched, but many private dwellings were destroyed. From sunset to dawn I watched a squad of Russian Home Guards toss incendiary bombs off the roofs and put out fires.

The raid over, life surged back in the early morning as though it were noon, when thousands normally take their midday stroll.

One of the incendiary bombs landed on the roof of my apartment house, but we threw it into the courtyard. It is lying out there today—a harmless-looking, burned-out metal tube about a foot long. There are many others in the streets.

8

Moscow was the tenth European capital to be bombed. Most bombed and damaged was London. The others: Warsaw, Brussels, Amsterdam, Paris, Belgrade, Helsinki, Bucharest, and Berlin.

The bombed condition of most of the European capitals was

due to Hitler and his Luftwaffe. Mussolini's contribution had been negligible. There were rumors of impaired vigor, even of illness. Mussolini moved to do something about it. He figured an exhibition of horseback riding would be convincing. On July 27 he arranged a show for members of the foreign press. Richard G. Massock was there and cabled the story:

Benito Mussolini, 57 years old on Monday, galloped and jumped his chestnut mare before a gallery of international newspaper men today and called on them to answer this: "Do I look sick, weak, tired?"

Mussolini arranged the show for forty-five members of the foreign press on the grounds of his Villa Torlonia estate after he had been asked about his daily routine, now that the nation is at war.

The correspondents went there in two bus loads, and Il Duce was ready for them a few minute after 8 A.M. Cavalry troopers were warming up two horses before the Greek-columned portico of the century-old villa when they walked up the graveled drive. Then they were conducted to a great circular riding lot like a vast circus ring, with brush fence and timber hurdles in the center.

The sixteen German correspondents were stationed in first position at the fence around the ring; then the nine Americans; finally those from other countries. Only one request was made: that the reporters refrain from smoking in front of Mussolini.

Il Duce rode into the lot on Tiene, his Hanover-bred mare. Without effort he began putting her over the jumps. Troopers thundered after him. He wore a white military cap, undershirt with tails out, gray breeches, and riding boots. A white belt encircled his waist. His riding master, Console Ridolfi, stood by, astride another horse.

Mussolini took a dozen jumps in ten minutes of going. Once he galloped the mare up to a hurdle with cries of "Eh, eh, eh!"

Another time, when two photographers approached dangerously near a hedge which he was about to take, he waved them away with shouts: "Via! Via!" (Away! away!)

After ten minutes the Duce rode up to the German correspondents and asked his question in their language: "Bin ich krank? Schwach? Muede?"

Then he took a couple of parting hurdles, patted his horse on the neck, saluted the newspapermen with uplifted arm, and thundered back to his house.

The correspondents had breakfast there. Since no coffee is available to the public in these times in Italy, there was none at Mussolini's board. There was, however, orange juice, hot chocolate, iced tea, whisky and gin.

C H A P T E R   13

Spreading Inferno—The New European Order

July 28–September 10, 1941

I

THE British were getting more help from the U. S. by late July, 1941. Ferrying American bombers via Canada had developed into an essential delivery line of war. From Montreal, D'Arcy O'Donnell, correspondent for the Canadian Press, described what was being done:

> By day and night a steady stream of U. S. bombers are flown across the North Atlantic to battle-scarred Britain by a group of young ferry pilots who consider the trips "just routine" jobs.
>
> For the last year or so, the pilots, 65 to 70 per cent of them Americans, have been delivering the bombers in good and sometimes in bad weather conditions and have lost only one plane so far. This was the craft that carried Sir Frederick Banting of Toronto to his death in Newfoundland last December.
>
> Four pilots, allowed by Atfero, the Atlantic Ferry Organization, to tell their experiences, said there was not a single instance of a ferry crew getting a glimpse of the enemy either in the sky or on the water. Among the men, whose names were withheld, was a 28-year-old Texan who once operated an air line service in Arkansas.
>
> "If the enemy should ever try to intercept us," he said, "there are usually lots of nice fluffy clouds over the ocean to disappear into. Nothing bothers me in the least, and the only time I was the least bit worried was when making low approaches during bad weather."
>
> Another of the men had fifteen years' flying service with the

Imperial Airways and British Empire Air services before taking the ferry job. A third man, a young Canadian from a northern Ontario town, had about 2,000 hours' flying time to his credit before accepting his present assignment. He, too, finds the Atlantic trips pretty much routine although quite different from the jaunts he used to take over the northern Ontario bush country.

The fourth pilot, a native of England, flew for an oil company before the war and later was a member of the Air Transport Auxiliary.

The men said that sometimes they fly in groups and sometimes singly, but all prefer to fly singly because "we feel we have more room to ourselves." Most navigators on the aircraft are civilians, but the British Empire training plan supplies some navigators for one trip only.

An executive of the ferry service said that when a plane lands in England some additions have to be made before it goes into service. Some of the additions are secrets, but others are made in England simply for convenience—Hudson aircraft carry flotation bags, and an automatic rubber dingy, life jackets, rations, and flashlights. The bags, he said, would keep an aircraft afloat indefinitely.

The machines all set out for a definite airport in Britain, but where they actually land is decided by the aircraft control in England.

The executive also said that "we are and have been right along in a position to handle at least three times as many planes as have been supplied to us." Some are calling the Atlantic ferry service a bottleneck in the delivery system, he said, but "we have delivered everything that was slung at us and we did it through an Atlantic winter, which was never done before."

Pay in the service is $500 per trip for captain pilots and $400 for first officers, with a minimum of two trips per month. U. S. papers have recently announced a substantial increase for American pilots.

Australians, South Africans, New Zealanders, Rhodesians, French, Norwegians, Poles, Dutchmen, Americans, and Canadians are employed, but most of them are commercial flyers from the U. S.

2

AMERICAN-MADE British bombers dropped explosives on the Nazi naval base at Kiel. Harry Hopkins visited Moscow as the personal envoy of President Roosevelt. Manila, in the Philippines, staged a practice evacuation. A Soviet submarine sank a Nazi munitions ship. Berlin claimed bombing of Moscow war plants. Eight thousand pro-Russian Jews were slain in Rumania. Roosevelt and Churchill met at sea to discuss U. S. aid and their conception of the world of the future.

Returning empty-handed from a prospecting expedition, a Perth, Australia, miner stubbed his toe on a rock, had the offending piece assayed, and found it contained $875 worth of gold.

The war was spreading toward the Orient. Ambitious Japan was an increasing threat. She was trying to sneak control of rich British territory while Britain was busy elsewhere. She didn't like the British. The British didn't like her. She didn't like the U. S.— and vice versa. There were trade as well as territorial troubles.

The British guarded the Thailand border against Japanese invasion. They expected trouble. Relman Morin, who had been in the Orient since before the latest difficulties began, made a tortuous journey from Singapore to Saigon. He found out what was going on. Saigon is in French Indo-China. His story came from there:

The British have placed thousands of their finest troops, mainly tough Australian and the pick of the best Indian regiments, on the Malaya-Thailand border in expectation of a showdown with the Japanese. They are fully equipped with tanks, heavy artillery, and other methods of modern warfare.

These things I have just seen after covering the entire area outside Singapore, traveling by train, bicycle, and finally by oxcart between Thailand and Indo-China. The frontier is still closed in spite of the cessation of hostilities. No newspapermen had been there since a Dutch correspondent was killed in the border warfare last November.

Everywhere along the border were British forces, including a new contingent of 150 R.A.F. pilots and crews who arrived recently. Moreover, the British are preparing room for additional thousands of Australian infantrymen. All these preparations are the result of the British belief in Singapore that Japan is exerting and will continue to exert pressure on Thailand for naval and air bases.

The atmosphere in Bangkok is one of extreme uncertainty. Some sections of the Thai government seem to regret having accepted the Japanese mediation of the dispute with Indo-China, and feel that it is impossible to refuse whatever proposals Japan may make. Well-informed sources in Bangkok assert flatly that Japan is demanding bases in Thailand and access to vital raw materials. In the meantime, the Thai armies are pouring into the new border zones. At least three long and heavily laden troop trains leave Bangkok daily and I passed long double lines of cavalry near the border. Whether this means that Thailand may fight to prevent Japan from entering Indo-China, nobody professes to know.

Crossing the new boundary of Indo-China, I stayed overnight with a lone French immigration official who lives in Cambodia in a bamboo hut. Later I stayed with other French families. The French can take it. These people were living in bare unfurnished houses on deserted land, but they were optimistic. All realize, of course, the impossibility of opposing Japan prematurely. They feel, though, that should the democracies let Indo-China down, salvation will come later through their own efforts.

On my trip I passed large detachments of the Japanese Army en route to Cambodia, purring along in new American-made trucks, carrying heavy artillery and full supplies of gasoline. The soldiers seemed exceptionally young.

3

Germany's long battlefront gave Britain new opportunity to assume offensive on the Western Front. She tried to take some of the Nazi pressure off Russia by opening up again against Hitler at home. On August 4, the R.A.F. dropped explosives in the heart of the Nazi capital. They left fires seen from the air eighty miles away. The next night more British planes streaked across the Channel. They plastered Nazi-held French coastal bases. The exploding projectiles lit up the Channel on the English side.

While the R.A.F. pounded away, Lochner followed the Finnish Army on the Russian Front. He told about the fighting in that area:

During five days spent with the Finnish Army I have had occasion to work my way to the foremost lines of the front—to within fifty yards of the Russians. I discovered that unless you can duck quickly, jump alertly, and crawl easily on your stomach, you're not likely to qualify as a Finnish soldier.

Staff officers have their tiny headquarters in dugouts with camouflaged canvas covers. After giving us an insight into the military situation, a colonel ordered a lieutenant to take us forward to the outermost sentinels. These lads know the forest as nobody else does.

We had hardly left the colonel's dugout when artillery fire began on both sides. Numerous shot-off trees indicated that shells often hit about where we were. So our guide motioned to us to jump, always throwing ourselves on our stomachs when we reached a new position.

"Be careful of mines," was his cheering admonition. "Stick close to the path I make. I know where the mines are."

Soon we came to a river, with the Russian town of Toulos about two miles away. The Russians were still holding one section of this town. As we lay behind the last trees, the Finnish artillery resumed fire. One shell hit a house some distance away.

"Now is our chance to cross the river," our escort said. "The Russians will be so mad that they'll fire at our artillery position."

We ran to an improvised bridge, made by throwing boards across huge logs which filled the river at this point. We got into the forest on the opposite shore without incident. On we walked, crouching most of the time, until we reached a tiny tent containing field-telephone equipment and maps. A first lieutenant was reporting to artillery headquarters on where the Finnish shells had struck at Toulos. A few moments later violent artillery fire was resumed on both sides. The noise was terrific. But we were more interested in the sharp reports of rifles we heard ahead of us.

"Be especially careful from now on," our guide cautioned. "Don't talk. Crouch or crawl and always take cover behind a tree."

After about 200 yards ahead we detected what seemed to be huge mushrooms at intervals of several feet. Occasionally some mushroom would come to life and the next moment there would be a sharp rifle report. The mushrooms, it developed, were the helmets of Finnish outposts lying in "fox holes" ready for action should they see Russians move along the Soviet lines scarcely fifty yards away.

Needless to say I, too, wore a helmet. Out at the front, it doesn't pay to expose one's cranium, especially if it is a bald one.

The Russian uniform of a rather muddy brown is admittedly better suited to this landscape than either Finland's bluish gray or Germany's field gray. The rifles of individual Russian soldiers are so good that any Finn is happy when he can capture one. Russian munitions are said to be more than sufficient.

Another general gave a graphic description of how a Russian unit had been encircled on a wooded hill measuring about 75 by 100 yards.

"It took us five days to take that hill," he said, "and there wasn't one Russian alive to tell the story. We used rifles, machine guns, howitzers, even the heaviest artillery, so that the Russians must have realized the hopelessness of their position. Yet they stuck it out until their last man had been killed. You put a common Russian soldier anywhere and tell him he must stay there and he'll stick, come what may."

I put this question to three Finnish generals: "Are there any signs whatever of Russian morale breaking down?" In every case the spontaneous reply was: "None whatever."

4

FOR SIX days running, Japan bombed the Chinese capital of Chungking. The toll was the heaviest since June when 700 suffocated in an air raid shelter.

The Nazis pounded on toward Moscow along the Central Sector. Smolensk was directly in line. Alvin J. Steinkopf was the first American correspondent to reach there. He got his story out on August 11:

I walked through the ashes of Smolensk today on a tour conducted by German military authorities.

The ruins of this once-proud city are still in the battle zone. In the east the fighting was close enough for me to hear the boom of cannon a few kilometers away. German soldiers swarmed everywhere, and overhead German bombers roared.

Past rows of fire-blackened chimneys, past ruined heaps of factories, banks, and stores, past shattered walls, past the shells of homes—for that is all there is left of this historic city—rumbled military trucks feeding the endless demands of war.

Only 20,000 persons of the normal population of 160,000 remain. Frightened and resourceless, the people seek shelter at the base of chimneys and under bits of roof and, with familiar landmarks gone, guide their movements by distinguishing features of the debris. Standing in the expanse of devastation, I was told by a German officer that fully 90 per cent of the city had been destroyed and that most of the destruction had been wrought by the Russians under orders of Premier Joseph Stalin for a "scorched earth in the face of the enemy."

Minsk and Vitebsk appeared desolate enough, but not so utterly devastated as Smolensk. In between the larger cities were hundreds of straw-thatched villages that seemed almost untouched. Between them stretched miles of golden, gleaming fields where peasants were still gathering the harvest. The crops were too green to burn when the Germans came. Many of the workers were women, barefoot, bronzed, and sturdy, carrying on oblivious of the war about them. Here and there, however, were the blackened remains of a village.

The Germans in Smolensk are occupied with their own affairs, with little time to pay attention to the native population. One wonders what the winter will bring when the bitter winds sweep around these bare chimneys. There may be enough grain to feed most of the rural population, but what will the people of the towns do? An effort is being made by civilian organizations now springing up to relieve what is sure to be agonizing distress. One of their problems will be the ragged children who today played in the streets without realizing what is to come, or indeed what has already come.

I found the German commander of Smolensk eating a thick soup from a dirty tablescloth spread in what once was the directors' room of a savings bank. He is managing an important part of the front, and besides is directing the clearing away of debris so military traffic can go through. The time he can give to the problems of the civilian population is limited. He has appointed a Russian lawyer, who secretly had been an anti-Communist, as burgomaster.

Germans ostentatiously pointed to the old ornate white and gold Orthodox church standing almost undamaged on the hill and said that yesterday the first public mass in twenty-one years was celebrated there. A stonemason read the mass. He was a priest under the Czar, but yesterday laid aside his trowel and resumed his robes. A big sign in Russian, still on the front of the church, describes it as an antireligious museum.

4

Eddy Gilmore had written about many phases of the war—from nudists to night raids. He found still another in London in mid-August.

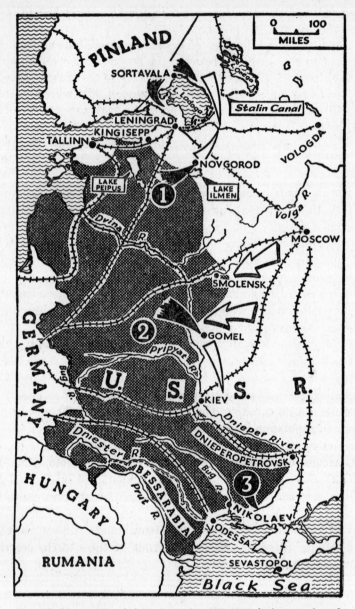

Map 10—Germany invaded Russia on June 22, 1941, had swept through
the shaded area above by August 20. The Finns help the Nazis strike at
Leningrad and Novgorod in the northern sector (1). In the center (2) the
Germans claimed crushing defeats for the Reds, and Odessa was besieged in the south (3). Black wedges show German thrusts; lighter
wedges, their apparent purposes; arrows, Russian counterattacks.

It's going to be a merrie, merrie winter for ye butchers of olde England, those thirstie despots of ye cutting blocke.

Ever since the rigors of rationing set in, the butchers (known here as meat purveyors) have been a group apart, men not catering but catered to for favors. Discovering early in the war that the best way to get a choice joint was to present the butchers with a present, customers have poured favors on them to the extent that some butchers are cracking under the strain.

With Lord Woolton announcing that rationing is to continue, there are grave shakings of heads in many quarters, at Horsham in Sussex for one. There is a butcher there who, before the war, was a model husband, coming home early in the evening and leading a quiet, almost repressed life. With rationing came the revolution. Someone discovered he had a hidden taste for drink. The word spread. Seeking a choice roast for the week end, a housewife presented the butcher with a bottle. Result, choice roast. It happened again and again.

The butcher didn't violate rationing, he just gave the best cuts to givers of the best presents. All was perfectly logical, but hard on the butcher's constitution. As housewives market early and husbands market late, he got it coming and going, his shop often the site of gay scenes with the cleaver-brandishing butcher in a merry mood, full of friendship, song, and good will toward all.

"His wife can't understand the change," a customer explained. "There must be butchers' wives all over England in the same fix."

The housewife's husband, going the bottle-bearers one better, takes the butcher home in his car.

"After he gets tired of that," said the householder, "I suppose we'll have him for a week-end guest. He certainly goes at a fast pace."

5

TRIPOLI, Bengazi, and Bardia were battered by an R.A.F. sweep over North Africa. The Nazis raided the Suez Canal, killing civilians. Nazi torpedo boats sank a 6,000-ton British ship in the Channel. Britain agreed to buy half the Egyptian cotton crop. The Australian cabinet considered the Pacific crisis. Two Japanese tankers loaded U. S. oil in California.

A New York hotel opened a "Terrier Terrace" with cod-liver oil as the appetizer on a menu catering exclusively to dogs. A Soviet communiqué paid tribute to two army cooks who not only got hot meals to the front on time, but took time out to shoot four Nazi parachutists who landed near their kitchen.

The R.A.F. redoubled its attacks on French Channel ports, attempting to reach the German battleship *Gneisenau* at Brest.

The U. S. National Debt passed $50,000,000,000—climbing at the rate of $277.50 per second. Gasoline shortage in the eastern U. S. became more acute. Two days of rioting preceded British entry into Bagdad, with 240 killed. The Nazis claimed an advance halfway across the Russian Ukraine. Moscow said "tens of thousands" of Nazi corpses had been left in the field. An American gunner with the R.A.F. dropped milk bottles on Berlin. Seventy-five persons were killed in a Nazi concentration camp. A Nazi spokesman said Germany felt the enemy should wage "a more humane war."

Roosevelt agreed to transfer fifty overage destroyers to Great Britain in consideration of the leasing to the U. S. of British naval and air bases in the North and South Atlantic.

Out of the Churchill-Roosevelt meeting at sea came the Atlantic Charter—a statement of common principles. It outlined eight points on which the two statemen based hope for a better world of the future:

1. Their countries seek no aggrandisement, territorial or other.

2. They desire to see no territorial changes that do not accord with the freely expressed wishes of the peoples concerned.

3. They respect the right of all peoples to choose the form of government under which they will live; and they wish to see sovereign rights and self-government restored to those who have been forcibly deprived of them.

4. They will endeavor, with due respect for their existing obligations, to further enjoyment by all states, great or small, victor or vanquished, of access, on equal terms, to the trade and to the raw materials of the world which are needed for their economic prosperity.

5. They desire to bring about the fullest collaboration between all nations in the economic field, with the object of securing for all improved labor standards, economic advancement, and social security.

6. After the final destruction of Nazi tyranny, they hope to see established a peace that will afford to all nations the means of dwelling in safety within their own boundaries, and that will afford

assurance that all men in all lands shall live out their lives in freedom from fear and want.

7. Such a peace should enable all men to traverse the high seas and oceans without hindrance.

8. They believe all of the nations of the world, for realistic as well as spiritual reasons, must come to the abandonment of the use of force. Since no future peace can be maintained if land, sea, or air armaments continue to be employed by nations that threaten or may threaten, aggression outside of their frontiers, they believe, pending the establishment of a wider and permanent system of general security, that the disarmament of such nations is essential. They will likewise aid and encourage all other practicable measures that will lighten for peace-loving peoples the crushing burden of armament.

Thus did the heads of the two great English-speaking nations address free men over the world. It was a message of hope to France above all—an embittered, tragically broken France, but withal a France which within a few days—on August 27—produced fresh evidence of opposition to Nazi conquest. This latest anti-Nazi act was another attempt at assassination. A smoking pistol in the hand of young Paul Colette seriously wounded the renegade Pierre Laval, who was trying to raise a volunteer army to fight with Germany against the Russians. Marcel Deat, a Laval follower, also was wounded.

6

IN THE meantime, there was activity on the Atlantic. Tom Horgan, twenty years a ship news reporter in Boston, was with the U. S. Neutrality patrol. He finally got through the first eye-witness report of convoy operations. It came from "A Recently Occupied United States Outpost." At the request of the Navy Department, the location of the outpost was not divulged at the time. The story arrived in New York in late August:

One of the most important naval operations since the first World War was completed today when a sizeable convoy was brought safely to its destination here.

Full wartime precautions were enforced throughout the zigzag voyage, which was conducted under secret orders. Ships moving in the darkness did not even show their running lights. Radios were silenced to prevent betrayal of the whereabouts of the large number of vessels.

Throughout the daylight hours, planes patrolled a wide area around the convoy. As the turn of each aircraft came for launching, officers ran out upon the flight deck of the carrier like members of football team taking the field. But they were not trying to impress the spectators; they were merely intent upon speeding the important business in hand. Some of the planes leaped from the precipice at the edge of the deck. Others hurtled from catapults. The take-offs were only seconds apart, and Navy planes landed with similar rapidity to report on their observations.

It was learned that the Navy has developed a new secret carrier landing technique believed to be superior to that of any other nation.

There were only two aerial mishaps throughout the voyage, two planes being forced down by mechanical failures. Their crews were rescued and the planes salvaged.

Gun crews remained at their stations throughout the voyage. To impress the crew of the carrier with the importance of alertness, a chart was posted showing the reported positions of sinkings, the supposed areas in which submarines might be operating, and other hazards. The convoy received another incentive for vigilance when it traversed an area dotted with flotsam, including an unoccupied life raft, bales of cotton or wool, timbers, and the drifting body of a man with a black beard.

Gray, sleek destroyers, like watchdogs, guarded the outskirts of the convoy. No blubber-hunter from a New England fishing village ever kept a sharper watch. Not a whale nor a porpoise, nor a scrap of wreckage went unreported. Amusement swept through the convoy when one ship signaled that it wished to slow down in order to shake off a whale that had been impaled on its bow.

7

CONVOYS of men and supplies assumed more and more importance. Blockade took its toll on both sides. Activities in the Middle East showed the effects of the blockade. British forces there were fighting a desert war. Sometimes their troubles seemed a long way off. But what they were trying to accomplish was all-important. Edward Kennedy was with "The Army of the Nile." In the desert, he did not always have quick access to communications systems.

But he got through another story on August 30. It reviewed his long experience with the hard-pressed British desert forces:

I have been with the British and Allied Middle East forces for a year now—with them in victory in the western desert, in defeat in Greece, in victory again in Syria.

Especially in the early days, the story was always the same—outnumbered and short of equipment, but always brave and confident. One British detachment in the desert marched out with wooden tanks and wooden cannon, intending only to distract enemy fire while the real thrust was made elsewhere. But the ruse worked so well that several thousand Italians surrendered.

The Army of the Nile up to the present has performed successfully its one big task—holding this vital gateway between East and West. Still, it has been perhaps greater in defeat than in victory. The British Army is probably the best retreating army in the world—and that's no joke. Almost any army can be good when it's going ahead, but it takes the kind of courage this army has to withdraw as well as it did from the death trap that was Greece in the face of any enemy force several times as powerful.

I doubt whether correspondents anywhere else have been permitted to see as much front-line action at close range as those with this Army of the Nile. Last winter we swept across the desert with the British and Australian force which smashed the Italians in Egypt and then took Cyrenaica. We went through fire with the first troops which entered Bardia, Tobruk, Derna, and Bengasi.

Later, while most of us were in Greece, that desert campaign largely was undone when the Germans arrived in Libya and retook everything up to the Egyptian frontier except Tobruk. But the drive removed the threat of imminent invasion of the Nile Valley, routed General Graziani's army of 200,000, and did much to discredit Italy as a fighting power.

Then we accompanied the expedition to Greece. We had barely reached the front-line region when the withdrawal began. The first action we saw in Greece was the incessant Stuka attack on army trucks moving back from the Mt. Olympus line, bombing roads and bridges to hold them up.

Soon we were a hundred miles back on the Thermopylae Line, where a second attempt was made to hold Hitler's panzer divisions. Fifty planes attacked our camp one morning, bombing and machine-gunning for an hour and a half as we lay in the mud of a riverbank.

For the rest of the day—black Sunday we called it—we were kept jumping into the nearest ditch for shelter as bombers came over in twos, a new pair every ten minutes. Then came the evacuation from Greece with the army. We spent some time in Crete but left before the parachute invasion.

In Syria we switched from sector to sector in small parties, getting together for the triumphal entries into Damascus and Beirut.

We have been shelled, bombed, dive-bombed on land and sea, machine-gunned from the air. None of these is particularly pleasant, but machine-gunning from the air is unquestionably the most disagreeable, especially when you see the plane that failed to get you turn around for another try.

One of our number met death—Ralph Barnes of the New York *Herald Tribune*—who was killed in an airplane crash. Two other correspondents were wounded in Cyrenaica. Two more were captured in Syria but later released. While the British Army has given correspondents wide facilities for seeing what's going on, the censorship here has been extremely rigid.

When the campaign opened in the desert, there were eight of us, but now there are several times that number. I am the only American who has been with the Nile Army continuously since the show started.

The western desert is not a bad place, as deserts go, except during sand storms. You get attached to it after a while. Its daytime heat is not unbearable and the nights are cool. Its sunsets are the most beautiful I have ever seen. And there's good swimming along the coast. For one period I lived with a group of Australian correspondents in a cave outside Tobruk. Its entrance was a little hole on the desert floor just big enough for a man to slip down. Inside, we had plenty of room for camp beds, tables, and benches. The walls had been plastered in some ancient day, and bore inscriptions in an alphabet we never before had seen.

The episode that has impressed me most had nothing to do with the war. One day, just before sunset, we came upon a group of Bedouins with their little flock—stunted sheep that graze on the desert's sparse camel's thorn. The group seemed sad about something until a Bedouin rode up on a donkey carrying a young lamb, whereupon there was great excitement. I asked what had happened and was told that the head of the family had just found a lamb that had been lost. I had seen a parable re-enacted: There is more rejoicing over the return of a lost lamb than over all the others that never strayed.

8

There were strategists who said the Middle East would assume increasing importance. In the meantime, the Russians had the worst of all the war. They fought stubbornly. They rolled down boulders on the Nazi invaders. They wrecked railway trains to impede progress. They waged guerrilla warfare. They divided into small groups and fought through the swamps and forests of White Russia. Their air force sprayed bombs and machine-gun fire on German troops, tanks, and trucks. They called up reserves. They threatened that, for every tortured Red, the Nazis would pay with 1,000 heads. Their women put on uniforms and fought and fell with their men. All along the long line they stood and paid with their lives. Still the Nazis flooded into Russia.

By early fall, 1941, the Reds were in a desperate position. Their censorship did not make it easier to see any chance for their survival. The Nazis claimed the end was in sight. Already they had captured an area of the Soviet equal to that portion of the U. S. east of a line drawn from Michigan to Alabama. They said the capture of Moscow was only a matter of time. The Nazi attitude was this:

"There will not be any Soviet Union at the end of this war and there will not be any Bolshevist regime which created the Union of Soviet States."

The second year of the war was nearing an end. Not including the loss of life in Yugoslavia, Rumania, Hungary, Finland, Belgium, Norway, or Iraq, the casualties were estimated at around 7,000,000 dead, wounded, imprisoned, and missing. The German share was about 750,000; Russia, 1,250,000; Britain, 140,000. Those 7,000,-000 represented the obvious casualties. There were others—millions of them. There were the homeless, hopeless civilians in all overrun European countries—the ordinary, everyday people who had been bombed into desperation and set adrift. Most of them had no place to go—no prospects for the future. They had little or nothing to keep them alive except—in some cases—faint hope. As the second year drew toward a close, a comparative few who had more hope than others were on the move. A trainload of them were bound for a hoped-for haven. Wes Gallagher was aboard the train with them:

Outside the sun beats down in muggy waves, but inside the six stinking railroad cars, fear—like a blanket of dark cobwebs—lies over the lives of 267 passengers.

Fear that visas may expire before a destination can be reached. Fear that each new border check might bring a gruff order to get off the train and turn back. Fear that scanty funds may not last until a safe place is reached in the New World. Fear that an outbreak of war in a new theater will·slam the gates to freedom at the last moment. Fears by the hundreds— by the thousands. . . .

For this is a sooty, slow, uncomfortable refugee train bringing people from the hates of Central Europe to the seaports of Spain and Portugal where they hope to embark for the U. S. or South America. Not all are Jews. There is a sprinkling of Czechs, Belgians, Netherlanders, and French who finally obtained exit permits.

There is an American, too, a young dark-haired girl who sits by herself and alternates between moods of forced gaiety and silent tears. She is engaged to a young Austrian doctor who is a refugee in a neutral country. At the last border station she clung desperately to his coat sleeve until it was wrinkled and damp.

"I'll be along soon," he said, trying to be cheerful.

But it was obvious neither believed it. He can't obtain the necessary visas to cross the countries separating him from Lisbon.

A matronly German woman tries to divert the American girl's attention with offers of chocolates and a stream of small talk frequently interspersed with laughter. Or perhaps she is trying to forget her own plight. Her son has been in New York for five years. Her husband was refused permission to leave at the last moment and she is traveling alone to a South American country where she hopes to stay until she can reach the U. S.

"It may take years," she says.

Slowly the train drags along, stopping for hours at isolated stations. No one is allowed to leave the station even for a short walk. Sometimes one can not even get off the train. There are no sleepers. Pullmans are almost a forgotten luxury. The night passes in an endless succession of shudderings as cars are switched, muffled conversations as misfortunes are swapped, and brief restless dozings in the dim compartments crowded to the doors. Always the crushing, invisible net of fear is there.

Shortly after dawn tension increases as the train approaches a new border. Papers—-those scores of papers that refugees must carry—are nervously checked for the one hundredth time to make certain everything is there. Police stroll through picking up passports. The passengers are herded off the train with their luggage, through a series of wooden gates, past long lines of officials who, in tired bored voices, ask scores of questions. Suitcases and trunks are unpacked, poked, probed, and repacked.

In the midst of the confusion an anguished cry is heard. It is from a little middle-aged Czech woman, dressed in black cotton. Somewhere a careless official has failed to fill in her visa properly. Now the customs men say she must wait until a telegraphic check can be made.

"It will not take long," one says. "We may hear in a few days." This brings fresh cries. She is on her way to the U. S. and her visa expires within three weeks. She has waited three years to get a quota number and a delay may mean another wait of months or years. The officials, hardened by months of dealing with refugees, shrug.

"It is the war," they say, "not us."

She is led protesting from the room. None of her friends interfere. They are afraid. The officials might stop them too. At last it is over. Baggage is placed on the train again. It crosses the border and the process is repeated at the next stop.

Here, too, there is a casualty. A fat little man who said he was a professor of economics from an occupied country is approached by two plain clothesmen. This time the action is swift.

"You are Herr ——," they say.

He nods and his shoulders sag under the cheap blue serge suit.

"Come with us. A telegram has come. You must stay here awhile."

He starts to say something, then stops and walks away with the plain clothesmen on either side. His fellow passengers have seen the incident but they keep their eyes averted. They are afraid. He may nod and it would not be good to be considered a friend of the little professor. He is not seen again.

This time the luggage inspection lasts for hours because three inspectors must handle hundreds of pieces. Trains leave without their passengers and refugees frantically try to find transportation. If they stay too long in this country, their visas will expire and that means jail. Police keep the group together and finally arrangements are made for them to proceed in a hot, dusty, half-freight, half-passenger train with wooden seats. The Americans are allowed to shift for themselves and wait for faster trains.

As the refugee train pulls away, the plump woman who tried to comfort the American girl, leans out and cries in a voice meant to be hearty but is cracked with fear:

"I'll see you in Lisbon—I hope—soon."

9

WHILE that and other refugee trains belched along with their cargoes of human freight, Adolf Hitler surveyed the accomplishments of his European inferno. By intimidation, coercion, whiplash, wholesale slaughter, he ruled most of Europe. His holdings included a piece of Russia bigger than Germany herself had been on September 1, 1939. Flush with success, he was talking more than ever about his "New European Order." Lochner attempted to tell what was embraced by the rather nebulous phrase which seemed to mean more to the "idealistic" Nazi chieftain than to anyone else. He wirelessed his story from Berlin on September 2:

Everywhere in Germany one hears talk about the New European Order, but although the average person's first impulse is to think of a New Order in political terms, almost nothing has been disclosed officially concerning that aspect.

Concerning economic implications, a more or less definite picture emerges, but whether economic, political, or otherwise, one word is applicable to the proposed new order. That word is Regimentation.

A short time ago the wife of a German diplomat whose last post had been as minister to one of the Baltic states, said to me: "We're leaving soon for Paris where my husband is to help set up the New European Order."

When I asked her just what he was to do and what she meant by New Order, she became vague and replied: "He's to help in the economic section of the Paris embassy."

This attitude is not isolated; yet it's hard to pin anybody down on just what is meant. Especially in the highest places, references are vague. I've spent hours looking through Hitler's utterances to find a definition, but without avail. Specialists in government departments tried to assist me but they couldn't put a finger on a concrete definition either.

GERMANY

- SEPTEMBER 1, 1939
- SEPTEMBER 1, 1940
- SEPTEMBER 1, 1941

Map 11—Even as the dread Russain winter neared, the total of Hitler's conquests in two years looked like this on September 1, 1941. Starting with "Munich," Germany had grabbed all of Czecho-Slovakia except the small part shown above as Slovakia. Poland was next on the Nazi timetable and the various shadings show Nazi acquisitions thereafter.

In his speech to the German people, explaining the war on Yugoslavia and Greece, Hitler merely said: "I've tried to get Yugoslavia to join the group of Powers that is determined in the future to build up the European continent in peace and quiet by co-operative effort and in accordance with the principle of having due regard for the justifiable interests of all."

Foreign Minister von Ribbentrop, explaining the purpose of the tri-power pact among Germany, Italy, and Japan, said vaguely: "The task of the pact is to secure the New Order under the joint leadership of Germany and Italy that is developing in the sections of Europe now at war."

Economics Minister Funk, however, speaking at the Vienna convention of the Southeast Europe Society, said somewhat more concretely: "The principle of the order championed by Germany is opposed to extreme autarchy which must necessarily lead to the impoverishment of every national economy as it is opposed to exaggerated international division of labor, which fails sufficiently to take into account the political and economic necessities of various peoples. Neither are the economically weaker to be violated nor is world domination to be striven for."

Funk saw the German Reichsmark, however, as Europe's dominant currency.

"The Reichsmark is stable and will remain so. Already today it is the dominating foreign exchange in Europe and on the conclusion of peace will also obtain international rating."

He made it clear that Germany, as leader of the New European Order, won't return to the gold standard.

[Note: Some economists say that, if Germany dominates Europe with a barter policy in the future, it would be serious for the U. S., which controls much of the world's gold, because the gold would be useless in European commerce.]

The most complete and concrete explanation of what Germany means by the New European Order that I have yet encountered is an editorial in the *National Zeitung* of Essen dated July 14. This daily enjoys the special protection of Hermann Goering, who, as dictator of Germany's four-year plan for self-sufficiency, has more concrete ideas about the question than anybody else. Assuming that the *National Zeitung* reflects his views, the following passages from the editorial are illuminating:

"The Europe of the future won't be an area similar to the U. S. In other words, there won't be any mechanical equalization of its (Europe's) highly differentiated forms of states. Most certainly Germany won't organize this vast space in accordance with Anglo-Saxon methods, as a pasture whereon a few favored plutocrats will have exclusive pasture rights. . . .

"Even the idea of a general customs and monetary union has been rejected by the Reich's economics minister as impracticable. Although Europe will be an economic 'grossraum' (vast area), it will nevertheless remain a many-limbed organism with each area pursuing its own way of life. . . .

"Individual countries are to be bound together not so much by mechanical reshuffling of frontiers as by their acceptance and readiness to strive for realization of certain cardinal principles of economic leadership."

National Zeitung then gives certain illustrations of what it means by "cardinal principles." These include:

"The right to work. Government responsibility for seeing to it that industry is fully occupied on organic bases of indigenous raw materials and labor power. Readiness of each to purchase from the other and not merely to enter the world market as a capitalistic seller. Ensuring of fair prices to farmers and industrial producers and adequate wages for workers. Removal of financial dictatorship in its multifarious forms. Basing of monetary exchange on national capacity for work and rejection of gold as a mechanical yardstick for exchange."

After reading up on virtually everything available, I have about concluded that, in addition to the above, the following constitutes part and parcel of Hitler's conception of a New European Order.

1. Germany would be the dominant power, with Italy running only a weak second. It is significant that in all German discussions of the New Order Italy is hardly mentioned. According to the Suedost *Echo:* "Europe . . . can exist only by virtue of greater Germany's might."

2. The Jew would be considered the pariah of European society, restricted to ghettoes when entire elimination isn't possible. Already France has adopted anti-Semitic laws comparable to Germany's and in all countries that joined the Axis the Reich's measures against Jewry have been copied almost verbatim.

3. England would not be permitted to have any say whatever on the Continent. Throughout the present war German commentators have harped on England as "raumfremd" (not native) to Eu-

rope. Phrases like "Britain must cease sticking her nose into European affairs" are bandied about in the daily press.

4. Europe's press would be regimented. Reich's Press Chief Otto Dietrich, addressing a group of foreign correspondents said: "Reform of the press is also a point on the program for the New Order in Europe."

5. Compulsory military and labor service in all probability would be prevalent throughout Europe, but with Germany determining what arms would be allotted to non-Germans.

6. Europe, as seen through German eyes, would emerge as a social paradise. That is, not only would the German passion for organization pervade every hour of the German's working time, but even his pauses during work and his daily recreation.

All those who obeyed the rules would share the benefits, while offenders against authority would find themselves cut off from the New Order's benefits.

In Greenwood, Mississippi, little Willie Page saw a bright object glittering in the street, picked it up, pounded it against the curb, and lost a finger because it happened to be a dynamite cap.

CHAPTER 14

Napoleon Weather

September 11–December 6, 1941

I

ON THE night of September 11, 1941, Americans tuned 45,000,000 radio sets on Franklin D. Roosevelt. In newspaper offices his words bounced off the teletypes. One week earlier, the first "incident" involving an American warship in the North Atlantic had occurred. A belligerent submarine and the destroyer *Greer* engaged in a shooting exchange. The *Greer* was on the way to the new U. S. post at Iceland. There had been question as to which craft opened fire first. But that was incidental to the importance of the Roosevelt statement on September 11. Here is the story of what Roosevelt told the world:

President Roosevelt firmly warned the Axis tonight that "no matter what it takes, no matter what it costs," German and Italian warships will be sunk on sight if they enter areas vital to American defense.

At the same time, the chief executive offered the protection of the U. S. Navy to any merchant vessel "of any flag" plying these waters. And, he asserted:

"No act of violence or intimidation will keep us from maintaining intact two bulwarks of defense: First, our line of supply of material to the enemies of Hitler, and, second, the freedom of our shipping on the high seas."

The President spoke from the diplomatic reception room on the ground floor of the White House. He spoke slowly, clearly, and quietly, raising his voice only occasionally to emphasize such phrases as, when striking at foes of his foreign policy, he said that, in spite of "what any American obstructionist organization may prefer to believe," the German submarine did strike first in its skirmish last week with the *Greer*.

And he chose to emphasize a statement that "we have sought no shooting war with Hitler," and "do not seek it now," but:

"Neither do we want peace so much that we are willing to pay for it by permitting him to attack our naval and merchant ships while they are on legitimate business."

Stephen Early, presidential secretary, had said that the speech would leave no questions unanswered. One, however, did remain. That was a definition of what areas of the sea were considered vital to American defense. Obviously they were intended to include the North Atlantic as far as the American outpost in Iceland, and a little beyond. How much beyond was the question. Obviously, too, they would include the areas of approach to the nation's outposts in Bermuda, in the Caribbean, and in the Panama Canal area.

Roosevelt called his action purely a defensive one: "Let this warning be clear. From now on if German or Italian vessels of war enter the waters, the protection of which is necessary for American defense, they do so at their own peril. The order which I have given as commander in chief of the U. S. Army and Navy are to carry out that policy—at once."

Before making this historic announcement, the chief executive recounted, one after another, attacks upon American ships that led to his statement of policy—the *Greer,* the *Robin Moor,* the *Steel Seafarer,* the *Sessa.* And to these, he added an incident at sea which had not hitherto been known to the public.

"In July, 1941," he said, "an American battleship in South American waters was followed by a submarine which for a long time sought to maneuver itself into a position of attack. The periscope of the submarine was clearly seen. No British or American submarines were within hundreds of miles of this spot at the time, so the nationality of the submarine is clear."

These incidents, taken collectively, the President said, could only be regarded as part of a general Nazi design "to abolish the freedom of the seas, and to acquire absolute control and domination of the seas for themselves." With that control in their hands, he said, the next stop would be "domination of the U. S. and the Western Hemisphere by force."

Senator McCarran termed the Roosevelt statement an "unauthorized declaration of war." He was a Democrat from Nevada. Senator Gillette said it was "a declaration of war so far as it can

be made by the executive branch alone." He was a Democrat from
Iowa. Chairman Connally of the Senate Foreign Relations Committee said it was "an eloquent and clear exposition of the Historical
and traditional policy of the U. S. with regard to freedom of the
seas." He was a Democrat from Texas. Majority Leader Barkley
said that Roosevelt had "laid down before the American people the
problem that faces them and the method by which he proposes to
deal with it." He was a Democrat from Kentucky.

Senator Nye said: "Clearly, we are going to have convoys irrespective of law and irrespective of President Roosevelt's own
promises and assurances. This means definitely that we are nearer
to a shooting war by presidential proclamation." He was a Republican from North Dakota.

The U. S. had not declared war. Only the Congress could declare war. But more and more the whole upheaval was becoming a
struggle for supplies—billions in supplies. Roosevelt was determined
to help with them.

The R.A.F. attacked a German convoy off the Dutch coast.
Nazi planes bombed a munitions dump at Tobruk, Libya. Secretary
of the Interior Harold Ickes said the Eastern U. S. gas shortage
was real. The rationing of auto tires was discussed. The British
lost eight convoy boats in an Atlantic battle with Nazi submarines
and aircraft.

The decision of Roosevelt to "shoot first" did not improve
U. S. relations with Germany. Nor did it improve relations with
Japan—equally strained. By now trade between Japan and the
U. S. had ceased. The U. S. was obviously supplying materials to
China—Japan's immediate enemy. Roosevelt's order to "shoot first"
was directed as much against Japan as it was against Germany.

The Japanese military wanted its share of world conquest.
It wanted an end to the white man's day of empire in the Orient. It
wanted a "New Order in East Asia," just as Hitler wanted a "New
Order in Europe."

Shortly after the Roosevelt "shoot first" dictum, Glenn Babb
again rounded out the whole picture of Japan's imperialistic orgy.
He wrote from his cable desk in New York, where all news of the
Far East streamed across his desk:

Historians of the twenty-first century, surveying the tragic
years of the middle twentieth, may debate among themselves whether

the second World War should be dated from September 18, 1931, or from September 1, 1939.

This is the tenth anniversary of what the Japanese call the Mukden incident, which opened their conquest of Manchuria and constituted the first major blow struck by a Great Power at the world order established after the conflict of 1914-1918. It set in train a sequence of events that crushed liberal rule in Japan, destroyed the fabric of Pacific area stability woven at Washington ten years before, led to the destruction of the League of Nations, showed the way to Mussolini in Ethiopia and to Hitler in Austria, Czecho-Slovakia, and Poland, and finally brought nearly all the world to war.

The significance of the Mukden incident was that it marked the seizure of power in Japan by the military. These ten years have brought Japanese conquests rivaling those of Hitler.

An empire of 90,000,000 in 1931, Nippon now exercises some degree of control over the lives of some 250,000,000 persons, an eighth of the world's population. Manchuria, Inner Mongolia, Northern and Central China, parts of Southern China and French Indo-China have been overrun. The arms of Japan have carried her rule from the Arctic Circle nearly to the Equator and westward to the mountain ramparts of Western China.

But this has been achieved at a terrific cost in enmity. China, unconquered, fights on. A powerful Russian army is poised on Japan's northern flank. The Netherlands East Indies and the Philippines are being armed against her. Britain has concentrated air, land, and naval forces in the Orient.

Most frightening of all to the Japanese is the pace at which the United States is arming and producing arms for her friends and Japan's enemies, her stiffening attitude toward Tokyo's expansionist policies, her determination to give all possible aid to China and Russia and to keep the sea lanes open for delivery of such aid in spite of all opposition. Japan cries out that she is being encircled.

So much has happened since the Mukden incident that few remember just what it was. The full truth may never be known—Japanese and Chinese accounts are completely at variance; and there were no other witnesses. But the Japanese version is that their infantrymen were conducting night maneuvers along the tracks of the Japanese-owned South Manchuria railway on the outskirts of Mukden. At 10:30 P.M. they heard an explosion on the right of way. Hastening to the scene, they found that a section of rail and two or three sleepers had been blown up. There was a Chinese army barracks in the neighborhood and three Chinese were seen near the scene of the explosion. They were killed. For several days a twisted piece of rail and the shattered sleepers were on exhibition at Japanese headquarters in Mukden to convince the skeptical.

But the non-Japanese world remained skeptical; few neutral investigators were convinced. The Chinese asserted the whole affair had been manufactured by the Kwantung Army, Japan's garrison in Manchuria. At any rate, the incident touched off what the Japanese admitted was a carefully worked out operations plan for seizing control of the key points of Manchuria. The Kwantung Army, under the command of General Shigeru Honjo, without awaiting orders from Tokyo, went into action. By dawn Mukden was in Japanese hands, its large Chinese garrison either dead, captured or scattered. Changchun (now Hsinking, capital of Manchukuo) was quickly captured. Other cities fell. The commander of the Japanese Army in Korea, General Senjuro Hsyashi, also without waiting orders from Tokyo, had a brigade moving into Manchuria within a few hours of the Mukden blast.

From that beginning, the Japanese Army moved to the conquest of Manchuria, a land of 34,000,000 inhabitants. Tsitsihar fell in November, Harbin the next February, the province of Jehol in March, 1933. The former boy emperor of China, Pu Yi, was taken from retirement in Tientsin and eventually made Emperor Kang Ten of Manchukuo, the puppet empire set up in what had been Chinese Manchuria.

From Manchuria the Japanese moved into North China, where, on July 7, 1937, again during night maneuvers by the Japanese Army, occurred another "incident" at Marco Polo Bridge near Peiping, beginning the war with China which now is in its fifth year.

During these years Japan developed the new technique of conquest—the development of provocation, swift movement to "protect" Japanese subjects or interests, the establishment of puppet regimes—which flowered into the vast program for "establishment of peace and order in East Asia," and the "greater East Asia co-prosperity sphere" which this tenth anniversary finds under anxious view in Tokyo.

When the Kwantung Army struck at Mukden, China fell back on the machinery of collective security so painfully but frailly built up by the victors of 1918. She appealed to the League of Nations.

The League, after eighteen months of futile debate and investigation, could do no more than vote censure of Japan, which thereupon withdrew from the whole Geneva scheme of things. This failure was the League's death blow.

The U. S., standing apart, also tried in vain to stem the Japanese tide. Washington refused to recognize the results of conquest by force. Efforts to present a joint American-British front to Japan failed.

Historians of the future may be able to trace the later policy of Italy and Germany in defying the dominant powers to the earlier example set by Japan. At least she showed the dictators, later to be her allies, the ease with which the League of Nations and the scheme of collective security could be flouted.

When Honjo set his Kwantung Army in motion, Ethiopia was just one of Mussolini's dreams and Hitler was still more than a year away from power. Nine years later Japan, Germany, and Italy, bound together by their common defiance of the Versailles world order, and together masters of most of the old world, were to become full-fledged allies with a program for setting up a new order for Europe, Africa, and Asia.

The Mukden incident was as much the culmination of a revolutionary movement in Japan as it was a blow at China and the existing world order. Japan of the 1930's really was a revolutionary state much as were Germany and Italy. At Mukden, the army was revolting against the most liberal government in Japan's history, a civilian leadership which for a decade had followed a policy of peaceful co-operation with the Atlantic Powers and the League of Nations.

For most of the ten years before Mukden, Japan's cabinets had been formed by the Minseito party. They had signed the Washington and London naval treaties, accepted the nine-power treaty of renunciation respecting China, had withdrawn from Siberia, and abandoned Japan's hold on Shantung. But the Army and Navy both had fought the naval treaties bitterly; the army especially had struggled against the policy of promoting peaceful trade with China. The Mukden incident was an outburst of long pent-up, embittered forces. It ended the era of comparatively liberal civilian rule. The Army rode roughshod over the cabinet's efforts to curb its march through Manchuria.

By December the Minseito government had had enough. It fell and was replaced by a nonparty cabinet in which fire-eating General

Map 12—Japan started her "Greater East Asia" drive in 1931 by taking Manchukuo. Thence advancing, she grabbed Hainan Island and wrested control of Indo-China from the acquiescent Vichy government. Then, to bar British and American interference, she set up a defensive triangle, based partly on islands the Japanese had taken from Germany after World War I and cutting through the Philippines and other U. S. possessions.

Sadao Araki was war minister and guiding force. Japan's experiment in modern parliamentary government and international co-operation was at an end. A decade of ever-increasing American-Japanese estrangement began.

2

THAT was Japan for the present. Hitler was still ploughing ahead in Russia. He was trying to keep his schedule up to the Napoleon schedule of many years before. He saw the dread winter approaching. He was trying to outstrip it. He didn't want to get caught as Napoleon had got caught. The British still hounded him. They lured his planes away from the Russian front to defend Berlin and the Nazi war factories in western Europe. On September 12, someone dug back into history. Hitler was not doing as well as Napoleon had done:

One hundred and twenty-nine years ago today Napoleon's conquering legions marched into Russia-abandoned Moscow and occupied the Kremlin.

The Little Corporal's timetable from the day he invaded Russia on June 24, 1812, until he got to the capital was eighty-three days.

Today, eighty-five days after striking out along the same path followed by Napoleon, Hitler's modernized war machine still is some 200 miles from Moscow.

Although Hitler's blitzkrieg had been effective at the frontier, there was still a lot of retreating space in Russia. The more he penetrated, the harder the Russians fought. Although he was still confident of the outcome, he had his troubles. Henry Cassidy was with the Red Army at the Central Front—on the direct line to Moscow. He witnessed a valiant stand—a real hand-to-hand slugging match. He described the Russian activities on September 22:

In the primitive forests, fields, and swamps of middle western Russia, the Red Army has thrown the Germans back on their heels, advanced six to thirty miles, and stabilized the entire central sector of this front.

The war there appeared to have settled down to the World War type of trench warfare amid seas of mud and devastated towns.

Red Army forces still held the initiative and were advancing at some points. The only signs of activity in these sectors from the German lines were small air sorties, sporadic artillery fire, and a single local infantry counterattack. A lull descended at some points, while the Russians attacked at others.

In this kind of fight the Soviet commanders are confident that Red Army artillery can prove a dominant and decisive weapon. I heard the earth-shaking rumble of its barrages, saw pock-marked fields where its blasts drove the Germans back. The Red air force appeared to have superiority. I saw their bombers return without a loss from a raid on Smolensk airport. Only one was scarred by German anti-aircraft shells.

In the gigantic struggle by land and air, the Russian line, now straightened by a series of pincer movements against German salients, ran within seven and a half miles of Smolensk at advanced points. The road to Moscow appeared barred by an immense force of tough, seasoned fighting men, well equipped and well supplied. Driving to the front, I went down the Moscow-Smolensk-Minsk highway where truck columns rolled endlessly to and from the front.

German planes swept down on Vyazma in a daylight raid the next morning. Nine planes scattered bombs in midtown, killing and wounding many civilians. The windows of my room were shattered. The Germans withdrew quickly from this hit-and-run sortie when Russian fighters and ground batteries went into action.

Driving out of the city I saw the wreckage of a German Junker-88 bomber. It was one of the first raiders and made a forced landing after its two motors were crippled by Soviet fighters. Through pine and birch forests I went over a dirt road, now converted by rains into a mass of mud, in the direction of Yartsevo.

There the armies of Marshal Semyon Timoshenko attacked on a sixty-mile front for ten days beginning September 1. This assault rolled back forces commanded by German Field Marshal General Fedor von Bock, inflicting heavy losses on ten of his divisions. It nipped off the German salient northeast of Smolensk while the Red Army also recaptured Yelnya and threw back eight German divisions southeast of the city.

The front in the wild country northeast of Smolensk now is relatively quiet. At one divisional headquarters near Yartsevo, which is in Soviet hands, Russian guns pumped shells into the German lines three to four miles away. Nearby, in the direction of Dukhovschina, I visited a division headquarters. Running the gauntlet across a field within sight of the German lines, I went to a battery which sent shells screaming into the Nazi positions.

At night, no man's land is illuminated by weird white light from star shells sent up by the Germans as a precaution against attack.

Yelnya, which the Germans abandoned after a Russian counter-attack virtually encircled the city, was in ruins. A church was one of the few buildings unscarred. The Germans locked the few hundred remaining residents in a church before applying the torch to the town.

Only bricks and charred wood remained of the village of Usha-kovo, six miles north of Yelnya, where the Russians started their counterattack by charging German trenches and capturing a hill dominating the region. The devastation resembled that left in France in the World War.

In London, Drew Middleton asked workers in famed East End what they thought about their Russian Allies:

The bobbie said, "They'll be talkin' about Roosia, in the pub; seems as though that's all they ever talk about these days."

It wasn't much of a pub. Bomb blasts had knocked out the windows and cracked the mirror in back of the bar. The air was heavy with cheap tobacco and the smell of stale beer. Even so, you could catch the sickeningly sweet smell of decay that covers the East End on heavy, foggy nights. It comes from bodies buried under ruins. You never mention it. The men you might mention it to may be the husbands, fathers, or sons of those bodies. If you keep your pipe lit and don't think about it, it isn't bad.

They were talking about Russia, just as the bobbie said. Two dock workers, an infantryman on leave from an old and famous regiment, an A.R.P. warden off duty, a quiet kid in army uniform with the white band on his cap that signifies officers' training unit, and a man who looked like a small shopkeeper. He was the kid's father. He and the infantryman were arguing about Russia. The soldier kept saying: "The Reds have them stopped, by God! They kept their eyes open, they did. Knew what was comin', they did."

The shopkeeper said: "It's just luck for us so far. When 'Itler gets really going they'll hand the Bolshies a 'iding, you wait and see."

His son interposed diffidently. "I don't know, Pa," he said. "The Russians are doing what everyone else wanted to do to the Jerries—let them come through and then hit them in the rear. The French wanted to do it, but they couldn't pull it off."

One of the dock workers said heavily: "I don't know about all this strategical stuff, but I ain't going to believe no one about Russia no more. Thought they was great, I did, until I kept readin' and hearin' from the nobs in Whitehall that they weren't no good, that they didn't have no church, and that they starved folk for the fun of it."

He paused as though he expected an argument, then continued:

" 'Eard as how they'd fall apart if anyone touched 'em. Well, they ain't fallin' apart and there ain't no signs they will. Looks as though they've shown some of these War Office toffs how to fight Jerry."

I asked the dock worker if there was a feeling of sympathy for the Russians.

"I hope to see my wife again, there is," he replied. "Why shouldn't there be? They're people like us. They're fighting bloody well. I ain't never been a Commie, but damned if I don't think we all oughta be after seeing what they can do."

He told me there were only a few Communists in his borough of Stepney.

"There's a lot who thinks things are all wrong but not many really in the party. Probably be a hell of a lot of them if this keeps up"—he gestured around the ruined bar—"and the Russians keep fightin'."

3

ARGENTINA foiled a pro-Nazi revolt. German and Russian troops fought in the streets of Leningrad. A British-United States-Russian war supply conference met in Moscow. The Nazis were working 1,500,000 prisoners on Fatherland farms. The Netherlands East Indies ordered $24,000,000 worth of U. S. fighter planes.

A series of Nazi executions began in German-occupied countries, including Czecho-Slovakia where an attempt was made to restore the nation's independence. A French woman who aided fallen R.A.F. fliers fared badly. Twenty Belgian "Communists" were shot for attacking a Nazi transport. Two Frenchmen were shot for possessing arms. Twelve residents of Bordeaux were killed as Red plot-

ters. Three hundred Serbian rebels were wiped out. Twenty-four
Czechs, including three generals, were shot. Likewise 106 more
Czechs. Likewise 4 in the Netherlands. Likewise 42 in Yugoslavia.
Likewise 56 more in France. Likewise 266 in Croatia. Likewise 113
more in Yugoslavia. Likewise the Mayor of Prague. Likewise, like-
wise—and likewise.

In Moscow, baseball fans were sorry because the Yanks beat
the Dodgers in the 1941 World Series. In Berlin, two Germans were
sentenced to death for listening to foreign broadcasts.

Cassidy, on the Red front, wrote about pistol-toting Russian
women:

Wearing uniforms, packing pistols—and ready to use them—
women form an integral part of the Red Army and have taken
their posts by thousands along the battlefront.

They do not fight unless they have to, but work as nurses,
waitresses, stenographers, telephone operators, and military clerks.
If their stations are attacked, however, they can and do shoot.

An example of the militarized Soviet women is Natalia, 22-
year-old-buxon blonde senior nurse and doctor's assistant. She goes
about her duties at a dressing station, four miles from no man's
land, with a pistol slapping her hip.

"I haven't had any fighting experience because the Germans
never got this far," she said. "But if they do—" and she patted her
pistol holster—"I'm a crack shot."

With Natalia, forty-two other women work in the medical unit,
dressing wounds, operating if necessary, and helping carry men to
the hospital.

At divisional headquarters, two or three miles from the front
lines, girls wearing white aprons over khaki uniforms and black
boots, wait on table as nonchalantly as though serving in a Moscow
restaurant. Civilian women also are seen in the front line areas.
Bundled in shawls and layers of heavy clothing, they go on working
in fields and villages within sound of the artillery.

Troops riding to the front and men driving tractors close
behind the lines often have their wives at their sides.

The more the Russians resisted, the more strength Hitler
hurled toward Moscow. The fury of his assault on the three main
sectors brought him closer to the Soviet capital. The Central Sec-

tor—straightest line between Germany and Moscow—moved fastest. Still, the Russians fought. By October 1, the coming of winter
faced Hitler. Cassidy described conditions:

Russian roads, one of the factors aiding the Red Army in its
fight against the Germans, already have started clutching at enemy
wheels and tractor treads to slow down the German panzer divisions.

Under sodden autumn skies and intermittent rains the dirt
tracks that wind across vast expanses of Western Russia have become ribbons of sticky mire. It is good going when you average
six or seven miles an hour in a day's driving.

Our truck transport rolls steadily down the main cobblestone
highways toward the front, while light four-wheel American and
six-wheel Russian trucks plow through the mud on the side roads.
Tractors taken from collective farms and road crews recruited from
army units tug any bogged-down cars over washed-out bridges and
through swampy hollows. Columns of as many as thirty trucks at a
time carry cargoes along the roads while wiry, sure-footed little
horses plod across the slippery fields.

4

BUT HITLER'S fanatical "I'm-bigger-than-Napoleon" complex
could not conceive of failure. Neither rain nor snow nor sleet could
stop him. Nature could not stop him. The Russians and Nature
combined could not stop him. He would reach Moscow in spite of
hell or high water. On October 2, he told his troops: "Today is the
beginning of the last decisive battle of this year."

He threw more reinforcements along all fronts. Nazi planes
went into action in the Ukraine, attempting to destroy the Russian
supply line. Planes, flame throwers, tanks, heavy artillery, blasted
the Central Sector.

Russians were crushed into the mud and snow. Their bodies
formed a tragic roadway over which the Nazi avalanche advanced.
Nazis, themselves falling by the thousands, lay with their enemy
dead. Prisoners, in such numbers that they became a serious problem
both of advance and retreat, shivered in the muck of early Russian
winter. Some of them lay down and died.

By October 20, Hitler's Central Sector was within fifty miles
of Moscow. The Soviet capital appeared doomed. Some departments

of the government hurriedly moved to Kuibyshev, 500 miles east. Embassy staffs also fled to Kuibyshev. Correspondents were forced to accompany them. The only capital dispatches came from official Russian news agencies.

Stalin remained in Moscow. He proclaimed a state of siege. Moscow might be captured, or Moscow might withstand Hitler's attack, but correspondents could not be there to see whatever did happen. Cassidy managed to get out a story as soon as he reached Kuibyshev:

With Premier Stalin's government holding the fort behind the red-towered walls of the Kremlin, in spite of the grave danger hanging over Moscow, the Soviet Union is pursuing relentlessly the course of the war against Germany.

I have seen unmistakable evidences of Russian determination to carry on the struggle, come what may. The constant shuffle of reserves and civilians, high morale, unbroken communications, and adequate food supplies, all indicate preparations for a long war. The reserves moved west to enter the lines, while eastward, out of the danger zone, rolled women, children, the aged, and all other persons not participating actively in defense. Railway communication continued to function, but more slowly under the greatly increased volume of traffic as thousands of persons and huge amounts of factory machines and other equipment were being transported.

Russian planes also plied the air steadily without evidence of unusually effective interference by the German air force. Myriads of cities and towns behind the lines bustled with the influx of new life. The military situation at the approaches of Moscow was acknowledged to be dangerous, with bitter fighting raging in the direction of Mozhaisk, west of Moscow, and other sectors near the capital.

On the Southern Front also, where the Germans were pushing with Italian, Rumanian, and Hungarian support, in the direction of Taganrog after the Russians evacuated Odessa, the Soviet position appeared serious.

The third major point of peril was Leningrad, where the Germans and Finns hammered at the approaches of Russia's second city. But deep within the Soviet Union, life surged forward at a quickened pace and Russians said they remained confident of the outcome. In one town I visited, a restaurant produced soup, fresh eggs, veal, rice, and tea, for a large party on short notice.

Stalin deluged his reserve strength over the Central Front. Moscow radio described the scene:

The battle now is raging in cold, gray fog which envelops everything. Hour by hour the battle grows in intensity. Time after time Red Army units have repulsed furious assaults and have been holding fortified positions and launching counterattacks.

The battleground in the past few hours has been covered with a thick blanket of snow. Roads watered by recent rains are hard with ice.

While Russia struggled for her life, Japan had not been idle. She thrust her hand into the grab bag and finished her overrunning of French Indo-China. Frank L. Martin, Jr., wrote of the bold move in a dispatch from Saigon on October 21:

Muscling in on Indo-China, Japan's biggest land grab is virtually complete—say, 90 per cent.

Nominally, the French have retained sovereignty. There is a governor general in the colony, apparently directing all of the normal functions. But he is like a man with a gun at his back.

A powerful Japanese force, estimated at 50,000, is stationed at Indo-China points that are within 600 miles of the big American base at Manila and the same distance from Britain's fortress of Singapore.

"And, son," as a French official phrased it, "we have become chief clerks for the Japanese. Nothing more."

This, of course, was not in the agreement signed previously between Vichy and Tokyo. French political integrity was to be respected. Japanese troops were to come only for "protection" of Indo-China. Even at that time, most Frenchmen thought the deal was a blind. Now they know it. Japan's 50,000 soldiers make up a force larger than all the French men, women, and children in the colony.

Japan explained the move was to bring the colony into Tokyo's Greater East Asia economic scheme. But observers, noting that the Jap forces were in positions for quick thrusts against British and American holdings in the Pacific, had their own ideas of what was behind the action.

5

HITLER's pressure on Vichy had helped Japan take Indo-China. As for Hitler himself, he needed more Mussolini aid against the Russians. But Mussolini was fortifying elsewhere. He was barracking troops along his long coastlines. He thought there might be a British invasion of Italy.

Mussolini's people were not happy. There had been sharp restrictions on food and clothing. Il Duce relaxed regulations briefly. For the first time in months, shoes and coats could be bought. He appealed to stomachs by promising Christmas pastries made with real honey, sugar, nuts, chocolate, fruit and ground almonds.

The British Fleet was busy in the Mediterranean. War vessels bombarded German positions near Tobruk. Larry Allen reported on October 22:

A long line of British warships stood off the bleak Libyan coast early today and pumped tons of high explosives into German artillery positions east of besieged Tobruk in a spectacular reminder that a major British land offensive may begin soon in the desert.

Not a Nazi gun spoke, nor did an Axis plane appear during and after the fifteen-minute bombardment. While the operation primarily aided in relieving pressure on the surrounding British at Tobruk, it was also reminiscent of naval activity which last winter preceded and aided General Sir Archibald Wavell's drive against the Italians from Egypt as far west as Bengasi.

The shadowy sea monsters maneuvered close to shore shortly after midnight. Weather favored the onslaught. Rain clouds drifted overhead. Gunners and officers were tense and impatient for action. I watched from the bridge of one of the ships.

British planes took off and dropped flares on the objective. As these brilliant torches floated near the earth, the big guns let go one after another. Suddenly the guns of the ship I was on spoke. A blinding sheet of flame swept back over the bridge. The shells swished shoreward and exploded in the area where Nazi long-range guns have been pumping 8-inch shells into Tobruk. On both sides, as far as the eye could see, the Fleet's guns lit the dark, choppy sea.

Perhaps the German guns feared that an answer would disclose more accurately their own emplacements. At any rate, no land batteries went into action, although the warships were within easy range.

British officers were confident that the bombardment had seriously damaged, if not destroyed, the German desert artillery.

6

On October 30, the U. S. destroyer *Reuben James* went to the bottom off Iceland. She was victim of a Nazi submarine. Forty-four of her crew were saved; seventy-six missing. Previous American losses totaled ten merchant vessels. A London newspaper said the U. S. was "on the last mile to war"; American isolationists said the same thing. Both sources probably were thinking more about U. S.-German difficulties than anything else. Colonel Knox, Secretary of the Navy, said war with Japan seemed inevitable.

In Sumter, South Carolina, the 13-year-old daughter of the chief of police made a better record on the pistol range than any of her pop's cops. A Perry, New York, judge asked a habitual offender why he got drunk every week end and received the disarming reply: "It's my hobby." In Lahore, India, a 95-year-old Hindu celebrated his sixteenth matrimonial venture by taking an 18-year-old bride.

Hitler was having his troubles on the home front. He also had them more than ever in Russia. Lochner reported on the home front:

Adolph Hitler served notice tonight that Germany would smash any attempts at revolt against Nazi rule in occupied countries. He said the Reich's enemies "no longer are faced with the memory of a Germany with kid gloves, but a National Socialistic Germany with a hard fist."

Claiming that the Germans had been "very courteous and very proper" toward the civilian populations in the overrun countries, he added:

"Perhaps sometimes we are too proper, too obliging. If anyone thinks he can resist a garrison or perhaps shake it through a cowardly murder, then we will hit as hard as we did at some in the years when our opponents thought they could terrorize us."

On the same subject, Robert Bunnelle reported from London:

The "hostage terror" sweeping nine Axis-occupied countries in
Europe has caused the death of more than 100,000 persons and
the disappearance and imprisonment of countless other thousands.
That was the report made today by the Inter-Allied Information
Committee. It said: "No occupied country is free of the hostage
terror. In seven out of the nine countries thousands of innocent
men and women have died, and in all of them thousands live daily
under the shadow of death."

The Nazi troubles on the Russian front, more than ever, were
the Russians and Russian winter. Noland Norgaard reported for
the Reds' side:

Snow, such as has helped bind the Germans to fixed positions
on most other parts of the 2,000-mile front, has caught up with the
Nazis also in the Crimea and has bogged them down worse than
ever before the gates of Moscow.
Moscow radio proclaimed that "Napoleon weather" has arrived. It said German soldiers had been frozen to death, their tanks
and heavy artillery imprisoned in ice and snow.

And from Steinkopf, reporting the German side of the Russian front that same day:

Bullets whistled through the snow, aviators flew blindly
through blizzards, and guns blazed away at tanks attempting to
charge through the snowy murk of the Russian-German front today. Fighting continued with the greatest intensity in the Central
Sector. One Nazi aviator said snow so reduced visibility that he
was obliged to approach his targets flying blind. All along the line,
German accounts emphasized bad weather.

Back in Berlin, Hitler demanded that civilians donate their own
clothing for his men in Russia. He did the same in German-occupied countries. Women had to give up fur coats, or anything warm
they happened to possess.
Communiqués from the Russian front continued. Correspon-

dents were eventually permitted again to witness the frozen, bloody conflict. Their dispatches came through with surprising regularity. But, everything considered, there was a lull in the European war. As far as the Russian-German conflict was concerned, relentless, inexorable winter had set in. As far as the British were concerned, in the words of Churchill himself, they were waiting "until the great American shipbuilding promised for 1942 comes into service."

7

ALTHOUGH a waiting war had developed in Europe, the situation was different in the U. S. and the Far East. Japan saw the U. S. making its Orient defenses stronger and stronger. In the Philippines, a new command had been created in July, 1941. It was called "The United States Forces in the Far East." It was under the command of Lieutenant General (later General) Douglas MacArthur.

The new command embraced a completed string of military, naval, and air bases reaching from Dutch Harbor in the Aleutian Islands, through Hawaii and on to Panama. The smaller Pacific islands of Midway, Wake, Johnston, Palmyra, Guam, and Samoa were also involved.

By mid-November, Japan was engaged in conversations at Washington. The original Nipponese negotiator was Admiral Kichisaburo Nomura. He had been on the scene for months. Then there was word that Saburo Kurusu would assist him. Kurusu was the "super diplomat" who had signed the Japanese agreement with Germany and Italy in Berlin months before.

The Washington conversations were billed as an attempt to find solution to the fundamental differences between Japanese Far East ambitions and the Roosevelt-enunciated policy of opposition to territorial conquest, and aid to China, the Allies, and "all governments in exile."

The Kurusu visit was to be a "last chance" attempt to avert war. As Kurusu left Tokyo, the Japanese Diet convened in extraordinary session. Correspondent Max Hill was in Tokyo. He was a former New York City editor. He had been in the Far East for more than two years—since it had seemed that Japan would eventually become very much of a trouble spot. He told what was happening in the Tokyo Diet in mid-November:

The destiny of the Pacific stood at a crisis today.

Japan stated her demands for understanding with the U. S. and on their satisfaction may depend peace or war. Before a grave and hushed Diet, the Nipponese premier, General Hideki Tojo, outlined the minimum requirements:

"1. Third Powers to refrain from obstructing successful conclusion of the China affair which Japan has in view.

"2. Countries surrounding our Empire will not only refrain from presenting a direct military menace but nullify such measures of hostile character as economic blockade and restore economic relations with Japan.

"3. Utmost efforts will be exerted to prevent extension of the European war and spread of disturbances in East Asia."

Tojo charged specifically that the U. S., Britain, China, and the Netherlands Indies were responsible for what he called the "military encirclement" of Japan which had risen as a major barrier to Far Eastern amity. And, he asserted: "The economic blockade resorted to by nonbelligerent powers constitutes a measure little less hostile than carrying on armed warfare."

Tojo spoke after Foreign Minister Shigenori Togo had declared that little time was left for negotiations to satisfy the Japanese terms.

"There is, naturally," he said, "a limit to our conciliatory attitude."

Togo expounded Japan's foreign policy in detail, declaring it aims "at establishment of peace in East Asia based on justice, thereby contributing toward promotion of the general welfare of mankind." He recalled Japan's mediation between Thailand and French Indo-China—including the basing there of Japanese troops —and deplored "malicious propaganda representing Japan as harboring aggressive designs toward these regions."

When Japanese troops entered the southern part of the French colony last summer, he complained, "Great Britain and the U. S. choose to regard it as a menace to their territories and froze Japan's assets in their countries, which constituted a measure tantamount to rupturing economic relations. As a result, he said, Britain's dominions and colonies, the Netherlands Indies and China's Chungking government, followed suit, raising an "increasingly tense" situation deeply affecting "the very existence of our Empire."

Togo said he could not divulge details of the long negotiations with Washington, but said he regarded an amicable outcome as "not impossible" provided the U. S. was "as genuinely solicitous for world peace" as Japan and "understands Japan's natural requirements" in East Asia.

He said he believed the U. S. must realize that "there is no necessity of spending much time on negotiations hereafter," and concluded:

"Should an occasion arise such as might menace the very existence of the Empire or compromise the prestige of Japan as a Great Power, it goes without saying that Japan must face it with a firm and resolute attitude. . . ."

Togo and Tojo had spoken.

Sleek, bland, unctuous Saburo Kurusu did not seem to be dripping with too much Oriental wisdom or philosophy when he arrived in New York en route to Washington. A reporter met him at La Guardia airport in New York on November 15. It wasn't much of an interview, through no fault of the interviewer:

Japan's special envoy to Washington said today that there were "very few irreconcilable" issues between this country and Japan.

He arrived by plane from San Francisco and left an hour later for Washington to confer with American leaders on relations between the two nations. Asked what he considered to be the outlook for peace, the smiling envoy said: "A single man's effort is too small in the present situation. We must all pull together."

Newsmen questioned Kurusu as he sat in a swivel chair at La Guardia airport.

"I tell you, all good diplomats should work for peace. I am no exception. It is for you to judge if I am a good diplomat or not."

Then a reporter asked: "Does that mean that if you are not a good diplomat, it will mean war?"

"I don't know. I'll try to do all I can," he said.

He was asked for comment on revision of the Neutrality Act and also upon President Roosevelt's withdrawal of U. S. Marines from China.

"I want to comment on neither," he said. "The President himself didn't want to comment."

In reply to questions as to the feeling of Japanese people about the possibility of war, he said, without amplifying: "They feel just as your people feel, I suppose."

The Washington conversation seesawed for the next few weeks. There was hope; there was gloom. The wheels of diplomacy made their rounds. The ways of statesmen—long observed but seldom contemporaneously understood—both mystified and misled.

The interests of many people, the heads of all nations, were turned toward Washington. There were many who hoped for war between the U. S. and Japan. Generally, they were the Allied countries, the Nazi-overrun countries and the interventionists everywhere. They felt a U. S. war on Japan inevitably would precipitate a U. S. war on Hitler. There were many who hoped against a war between the U. S. and Japan—or, for that matter, a war between the U. S. and any other nation. They were the isolationists, and, perhaps, some millions of the ordinary, everyday people in America who just didn't like the idea of war anyway.

8

AND there were a few who didn't even know there was a war, and didn't even care. Well across the world—east of Suez—was Iraq. She was a little country three times the size of New York state. She was the Arab kingdom that was formed after World War I out of the Turkish vilayets of Mosul, Bagdad, and Basra. She had already had her troubles in World War II, and she would probably have more. In Iraq was the fabled city of Bagdad. In Bagdad was one person at least who didn't know and didn't care. Edward Kennedy, looking for a story since the slackening of British-Nazi hostilities, found out about him:

In a big yellow palace on the banks of the Tigris lives a little boy who is a king but doesn't know it—who is in the midst of a spreading inferno of World War and doesn't know it.

He is His Majesty, Feisal II, descendant of the prophet and King of Iraq. He is six years old and the world's youngest monarch. A visitor recently asked the Queen whether her son realized he was King.

"Ask him," she replied.

"How many kings can you name?" inquired the visitor of the boy.

Feisal reeled off the names of a half-dozen living monarchs but did not include himself.

A close friend of the royal family who spends much time at the palace said: "Little Feisal sees his pictures on stamps, money, and almost eveywhere else. As he walks through the garden he is saluted by the royal guard. If he drives through the city he is cheered. He accepts all these things as natural and does not yet seem to realize that he is King."

The boy King is bright, cheerful and sweet-tempered. He learns rapidly and forgets nothing. While not especially robust, his health is good. He has a whole wing of the palace, air-conditioned and furnished by a leading London firm. Well-wishers send him so many toys that they flood the palace and he gives many of them away to other children. He has a dog and a pair of ponies.

He has an English nurse, Miss Dora Borland, and an English governess, Miss Betty Sulman. He lunches with his mother and other members of the royal family, has a nap, goes out to play in the palace garden in the afternoon. Then supper and an early bedtime.

He speaks Arabic and English equally well and never mixes the two. The Queen supplements Miss Sulman's lessons with some of her own, mainly about the Koran.

Feisal became king almost three years ago after his father, King Ghazi, was killed when he ran his automobile into a lamppost while driving home early one morning. He has no close companions of his own age, but occasionally there is a party at the palace attended by about twenty-five children. It is at these parties little Feisal gives away his toys.

CHAPTER 15

"Now That the Issue is Joined..."

December 7–December 10, 1941

I

WASHINGTON was not a unique American city on the morning of December 7, 1941. It was Sunday and, as in any city, people were apt to sleep late, get up and go to church, or lounge around with their coffee, their newspaper, and their radio. The broad streets were relatively quiet, the entrances to most public buildings uncluttered. Week-end visitors did their usual rubbernecking. Although no such official announcement was made, the chances were that some of the diplomats were among the later sleepers. They had had a busy week.

Since mid-November, the conversations with Admiral Nomura and super diplomat Kurusu, the Japanese emissaries, had continued without let-up. Secretary of State Cordell Hull had given them a statement of the only basis on which he felt a settlement of difficulties could be negotiated. The terms called for Japanese abandonment of her "New Order in Asia," the relinquishment of territory taken from China, and a promise to live up to earlier treaty agreements. Although Japan had not agreed to the provisions, at least as far as the public knew, there appeared some hope of peaceful settlement.

Sunday morning, December 7, moved along. Came noon. Came one o'clock. A State Department staff was on duty. The telephone jingled. Tokyo's two emissaries were seeking another appointment. It was granted. The two envoys were twenty minutes late.

By the time they reached the State Department, however, it did not make much difference to Secretary of State Hull if they were late. In those few minutes something had begun at Pearl Harbor, in Hawaii, that seemed too staggering to be true. Hull knew about it.

The envoys were asked to wait. Richard L. Turner, rounding up that day's developments in Washington, described their demeanor:

Gone was the blithe, breezy aplomb that had characterized their numerous previous visits to the Department. There was a tight-lipped, almost embarrassed smile for newsmen, and an absolute refusal to answer questions. Kurusu paced the diplomatic reception room. Nomura sat stolidly upon a leather divan; only a frequently tapping foot betrayed his perturbation.

Finally they were admitted to the Secretary's office. To him Nomura handed Japan's reply to this country's formula for peace in the Pacific. Gravely, Hull read it. Then the Secretary of State turned toward the Japanese ambassador and in a "tone of the greatest indignation," as the Department later described it, told him he had never seen a document so "crowded with infamous falsehoods and distortions." Wordlessly the Japanese left.

Correspondents got the gist of the news in Washington as soon that afternoon as the government would permit. It was flashed to the world at 2:22 P.M., Eastern Standard Time:

PEARL HARBOR BOMBED BY JAPANESE

To Americans generally, until that Sunday afternoon, December 7, 1941, Hawaii meant hula dancers, ukuleles and pineapples. It was famed in song and story—a vacation utopia, only slightly larger than the state of Connecticut. But to the U. S. Army, Navy, and Air Force, it was a major outpost. Situated along the southern shore of the island of Oahu, a few miles from Honolulu, it was the chief U. S. base in the North Pacific. Its harbor could accommodate the entire U. S. Fleet. It was studded with protective guns, sinewed with the most modern machinery for any kind of war.

Anxious correspondents in Honolulu rolled out that Sunday to cover the story. They had been there for months in anticipation of big news. But it is always heartbreaking to a correspondent to have the story in his lap and not be able to get it out. Honolulu correspondents were in that fix. The government immediately cut communications. Not a line could be transmitted. Correspondents fought with cable and wireless officials. They were helpless. Radio did its part. At least one National Broadcasting Company representative got through a few words. Then, suddenly, he was off the air.

The Hawaiian forces had been taken unawares. Shocked to attention, they relayed what they knew to Washington. The government could not permit immediate release of all it found out. The information would have been valuable to the Japanese. There were also whispers of laxity on the part of the military at Pearl Harbor. These had to be sifted, evaluated, judged. Washington that Sunday gave out only guarded word.

It was quick, stringent censorship. But the story began to jell. Even before it jelled, one or two staggering facts became obvious:

The attack had started at about 8:10 A.M., Hawaiian Time (1:40 P.M., Eastern Standard Time). At virtually the moment the two Japanese envoys were telephoning the State Department for another appointment, their planes were bombing Pearl Harbor—her barracks, her air forces, her anchored U. S. Fleet. That was not all. Pearl Harbor was roughly 3,500 nautical miles from Japan. Even while the two envoys had continued their talks of peace during the past several days, their stealthy forces were sneaking up on the island.

It was another of those Sundays. The Japanese blitzkrieg bore a Hitler imprint. The U. S. had observed Hitler tactics in European countries over a period of more than two years. Now the U. S. itself was victim. Japan moved first and declared war later.

In Washington, Richard L. Turner and his colleagues developed all available information:

Japan declared war on the U. S. today.

In an attack without parallel in the Far East, Nipponese planes appeared without warning over Hawaii just after dawn on an otherwise quiet Sunday morning and bombed U. S. air and naval forces at Pearl Harbor.

Deadly explosives were also dropped on famed, romantic Honolulu, Hickam Field, nearby, and at other strategic U. S. strongholds in the Pacific.

This shocked nation immediately girded for the struggle ahead. President Roosevelt prepared a message for Congress asking a declaration of war. Although complete details were lacking, a brief broadcast from Honolulu reported that some 350 soldiers were killed at Hickam Field alone, with numerous casualties at other points of attack.

Virtually all details were given out by the White House. Officials expressed confidence that the nation would understand the advisability of withholding, at this time, any information that would be of benefit to the enemy. The White House also acknowledged that Manila, in the Philippines, and the American-owned naval base at Guam, likewise had been attacked.

The attack on Pearl Harbor and Hickam Field, sprawling army airport near Honolulu, was a perfect pattern of blitzkrieg. Fleecy clouds brushed over towering Diamond Head a few minutes before eight o'clock. Most of Honolulu was still asleep.

Suddenly the morning quiet was broken by the roar of planes and the chatter of machine guns. Seconds later, houses trembled from the thunder of heavy explosions. Most of those who were up and about thought the Army and Navy were having extra-heavy target practice. But a flash from Honolulu's radio stations ended that. The city and military posts were being attacked.

Observers on the streets counted more than 150 planes with the Rising Sun emblem on their sides. The planes headed straight for Pearl Harbor and Hickam Field. Tons of high explosives were dropped on the two bases. Towering flames leaped up and great coils of thick black smoke clouded the sky. U. S. planes roared aloft to battle the attackers and anti-aircraft fire was thrown up by defenders.

There were no casualty details from official Washington, but the White House hinted that military losses were heavy. At least seven civilians were killed and many others injured in Honolulu. Several others were injured when an enemy plane machine-gunned the streets of a town near Honolulu. Persons who could see the base at Pearl Harbor said one ship was lying on her side and four others ablaze.

President Roosevelt, without waiting for Japan's formal declaration of war, ordered the Army and Navy to carry out previously prepared secret plans to defend the islands. Governor Joseph Poindexter gave the Army control of the islands. Schools were turned into hospitals and civilians mobilized to help in first aid.

An exciting picture of the attack came by broadcast direct from Honolulu. M. A. Mulroney, on behalf of the National Broadcasting Company, said that the battleship *Oklahoma* had been set afire and two others attacked. He made his broadcast from the roof of a Honolulu building. His report said:

"We have witnessed this morning a severe bombing of Pearl Harbor by army planes, undoubtedly Japanese. The city of Honolulu has also been attacked and considerable damage done. One of the bombs dropped within fifty feet of our (station KGU) tower. It is a real war. Honoluluans have been advised to keep in their homes and away from the Army and Navy. There has been severe fighting in the air and on the sea. We have no statement as to how much damage has been done, but it has been a very severe attack. The Army and Navy, it appears, now have the air and sea under control—"

At this point the broadcast was shut off.

There was little word on Guam or Manila after the announcement that both had been attacked. However, dispatches from the Philippines reported that Lieutenant General Douglas MacArthur had placed his command on the alert.

Simultaneously, Japan threw her war machine into gear elsewhere in the southwest Pacific. Japanese bombers blasted at the great British naval base at Singapore, while some 300 miles to the north, in Malaya, near the Thailand border, Japanese naval units landed invasion troops on the beaches.

In other surprise moves, Japanese troops surrounded the International Settlement at Shanghai and seized the U. S. Gunboat *Wake*. The British colony of Hong Kong awakened under the same sun to the crunch of Japanese bombs.

Washington took on a wartime atmosphere. War Secretary Henry Stimson ordered all military personnel to mobilize. Steel-helmeted guards patrolled the War Department and other important centers. President Roosevelt's message to the Congress, asking for a declaration of war, will be delivered tomorrow. He made public the text of a personal message he sent only yesterday to the Emperor of Japan in an effort to enlist his aid on the side of peace.

2

TWENTY minutes after the official Japanese declaration of war —only a few hours after the attack on Pearl Harbor—a Japanese university professor went on the air in Tokyo with a broadcast on "Good Morals." Within sight of an angry crowd of 2,000, the Japanese consulate in New Orleans attempted to burn books and official papers. In Mexico City, Japanese Minister Yoshiaki Murua said he was confident his country would defeat the U. S.—"because Japan never has lost a war."

Senator Burton K. Wheeler, a leader of the bloc opposing the Roosevelt foreign policy, said: "The only thing to do now is to lick hell out of them." Roosevelt authorized arrest of Japanese nationals regarded as "dangerous to the peace and security of the United States," and a nation-wide roundup began.

On December 8, Roosevelt told the Congress that Sunday, December 7, 1941, was "a day that will live in infamy." This country formally declared war on Japan. But even before the formal declaration by the U. S., there were developments in London. Robert Bunnelle sent details:

Britain sprang proudly today to the aid of her kinsmen and ancient friends, declaring war upon Japan even before the U. S. itself had taken formal action.

Winston Churchill rose before an impressively united and cheering Parliament to make good the pledge that he had solemnly delivered a month ago—the pledge that an outbreak of Japanese-American hostilities would put the British instantly at the side of the U. S.

He had spoken during the night with President Roosevelt over transatlantic telephone, he said, to arrange "the time of our respective declarations," and, he went on:

"The President told me he would, this morning, send a message to Congress, which, as is well known, can alone make a declaration of war on behalf of the U. S.

"I then answered him that we would follow immediately. However, it soon appeared that British territory on Malaya had also been the object of Japanese attack, and later on it was announced from Tokyo that the Japanese high command—a curious form, not the imperial Japanese Government, but the Japanese high command —had declared that a state of war existed between them and Great Britain and the U. S.

"That being so, there was no need to wait for the declaration of Congress. In any case, American time is nearly six hours behind ours. The cabinet, which met at 12:30 today, therefore authorized an immediate declaration of war upon Japan. Instructions to this effect were sent to His Majesty's ambassador in Tokyo."

Thus he told the story of the joining again of two great nations that, together, have never lost a war. And he informed the world that Britain was ready and moving without loss of time.

"Now that the issue is joined, and in the most direct manner," he went on, "it only remains for two great democracies to face their task with whatever strength God may give them. We may hold ourselves very fortunate, and I think we may rate our affairs not wholly ill-guided, that we were not attacked alone by Japan in our period of weakness after Dunkerque."

Recalling that China and the Dutch East Indies had instantly entered the mighty Allied alliance, he nevertheless proclaimed that a great struggle was ahead.

"It is of the highest importance," he told Parliament, "that there should be no underrating of the gravity of the new dangers we have to meet, either here or in the U. S. We have at least four fifths of the population of the world on our side. We are responsible for their safety and for their future. In the past we have had a light which flickered. In the present we have a light which flames. In the future there will be a light which shines over all the land and seas."

Other Allied countries followed suit. Russia remained out of it. She was busy holding off Hitler along her Western Front. Nicaragua followed up her declaration by jailing the country's entire Japanese population: Gusudi Yakata and Juan Hissi.

In Germany, Hitler kept a promise. The Nazi agreement with Japan guaranteed aid if Japan should go to war with a Western Power. Germany announced she was at war with the U. S. Italy did the same. The White House said:

"Obviously, it was the German hope that if the U. S. and Japan could be pushed into war it might put an end to the lend-lease program."

In less than a week, thirty-five nations, representing one half of the world's population, were at war. And this did not include the nations Hitler had already overrun.

3

UNTIL now this narrative has been concerned mainly with events—not with the correspondents who reported them. Its purpose has not been to make heroes of the men whose stories have been reproduced. They would not wish it. Reporting is their job, just as the dangerous job of handling a bomber is the routine of a bomber pilot.

But there is one thing inevitable about war—and war correspondents. Whenever countries declare war on each other, the status of foreign correspondents in those countries immediately changes. They become subject to imprisonment, internment, or whatever descriptive term is preferred, based on the treatment accorded by the enemy nation.

At the time Germany declared war on the U. S., Lochner and his colleagues in Berlin still filed material by teletype to a relay bureau in Bern, Switzerland, whence it was relayed to this country. The following dispatch, sent from Bern, describes what happened to correspondents in Berlin on December 10:

American press correspondents in Berlin left their offices for their homes at 12:40 P.M. today, presumably under house arrest.

Lanky Angus Thuermer, of The Associated Press staff in Berlin, answered an automatic printer query from here at 12:37 with a laconic: "Hurry up. We leave for the jug."

Asked who would fill in at the Berlin end of the wire, Thuermer messaged back: "Rudy (Rudolph Josten, German employee of the staff) will fill in. Lochner and I have to leave for home now. The others already have gone. See you."

Bern wanted to know if they would be interned. Thuermer answered: "We don't know. All American correspondents have been asked to leave for their homes in Berlin. Bye-bye, old man."

There the connection was broken, but was restored again at 1:05. Then Josten filed a brief story that quoted the German Foreign Office as saying: "American journalists no longer exist for you."

That ended American correspondents' dispatches out of Germany. The same thing was happening in Rome and Tokyo.

Many correspondents had been able to leave before the declaration of war. But some could not get out in advance. There were fifteen of these. They were quickly interned. They were to be held for the duration, or until the warring countries could make arrangement to "exchange" correspondents much as, on occasions, they exchanged wounded and disabled soldiers. Those interned as a consequence of the U. S. entry into the war were:

In Germany: Louis P. Lochner, with his wife and daughter; Angus M. Thuermer, Alvin J. Steinkopf, Edwin Shanke, and Ernest G. Fischer.

In Italy: Richard G. Massock.

In Japan and Japanese-occupied territory: Max Hill, Joseph Dynan, Relman Morin, Morris J. Harris, James D. White and his wife, Vaughn F. Meisling, R. P. Cronin and his wife, and Russell Brines and his wife.

Godfrey H. P. Anderson was captured in Libya and inasmuch as he was a British subject he became a prisoner of war.

A few of those listed as in Japanese-occupied territory were not interned on December 10. But they met the same fate as Japan overran Eastern territories.

Later, some of the correspondents obtained their freedom. As this is written, nine still remain in the custody of the enemy. Their bylines will be missed, but others took their places on the new firing fronts of the world.

4

CENSORSHIP out of the Philippines was not as stringent as that out of Hawaii. Comparatively little damage was done to Manila on the first day, in spite of Japanese claims. Clark Lee cabled from Manila on December 8:

One day of war at Manila has made tough, determined soldiers out of a good many American youngsters who only yesterday were just kids in soldiers' uniforms.

I spent the night with a group of them on anti-aircraft duty guarding Manila Bay. Their detachment shot down the first Japanese plane felled in the Clark Field battle and later downed four others, plus one badly hit and probably unable to return to its carrier.

They were dog-tired from day-long duty, but quickly sprang to man their guns when they heard the sound of Japanese bombers approaching at 2:25 this morning in a softly moonlit sky. They withheld their fire because they did not sight the planes.

In the drawling accent of a southwestern state they said: "Yesterday we'd a let fly anywhere at the sky."

Yesterday they were so green that when fifty-four Japanese bombers came over at 10,000 feet with the sunlight painting their silvered wings they remarked to one another: "My, ain't they purty?"

A few minutes later they suddenly became soldiers, instead of kids. They didn't hit any of the heavy, multi-motored raiders, but they did answer to their own satisfaction the question of whether the Japanese can fly airplanes and bomb accurately.

"Sure, they can bomb," a sergeant said. "If they can't hit a fish in a barrel from 10,000 feet, they can come close to it."

While the last bombs were still exploding, Japanese fighter planes, obviously from carriers, dived and strafed planes on the ground and the gun positions as well. The guns went into action, getting "five for sure and probably one more." Two American pursuit planes pitched into the battle and downed one each.

Japan may not have done much damage at Manila the first day, but she kept trying. Russell Brines sent an account of what happened on December 10:

Japanese four-motored bombers smashed at military objectives and ships moored in the harbor today in a prolonged assault on the Manila area that started huge fires at Cavite naval base and sent columns of smoke spiraling up from Nichols air depot.

American interceptor planes and Japanese dive-bombers fought a brisk battle over Nichols Field. I watched the attack from a house one and one half miles from Nichols. Hundreds of other persons along the beach front huddled against fences and beneath trees during the four separate afternoon attacks. From where I stood I could see flames roaring high in the air at the end of the raid. Smoke also rose from a smaller fire at Cavite an hour after the assault.

After first circling the city in two formations of twenty-seven planes each, the Japanese returned seaward, then split up for the assaults. High in the clouds above the bay at least six bombers pealed off from the main units and roared swiftly down toward Nichols. The blasts shook my house. The attack stirred alive a gigantic hornet's nest of American interceptors, which had droned over the air base throughout the morning, went into action. After their sweep onto the field the bombers climbed high and split up again. Individual dogfights developed.

The fighting could be seen through scattered clouds directly over my head. Anti-aircraft guns cracked throughout the city and the machine guns of the combatant planes rattled. The fight lasted at least fifteen minutes. One plane emitted a light stream of smoke from its motors and disappeared inland. Some witnesses reported that it had glided toward McKinley Field, after which a high burst of smoke was seen. Another slanted seaward beyond Cavite, straightened near the water, then disappeared over the horizon. The fight ended when the fast bombers climbed high and headed seaward with the Americans following.

Meanwhile, smoke began spiraling up from Nichols Field. This attack started about 12:40 and ended at 1 P.M. Heavy gunfire ceased momentarily then burst out again at planes hidden in the clouds of Cavite. As a second wave of bombers came on, smoke rings of anti-aircraft shells puffed out far below them. The planes dropped forty bombs at merchant vessels, sending up high waterspouts. Columns of dirt and smoke also shot into the air, and flames roared up from an oil-tank fire. Several bombs fell into the water off Cavite.

A third flight of nine bombers attacked soon after the second assault. Flying in close V formations, they appeared over Cavite, apparently safe from anti-aircraft shells bursting below them. The attackers dropped a cluster of bombs, sending up two new smoke plumes, swung toward the merchantmen and dropped another salvo, then bombed the Fort McKinley area and sped back out to sea.

This attack was followed by a fourth in which eight planes in close formation dropped thirty bombs.

5

BY DECEMBER 12, the U. S. eased up on censorship from Hawaii. The White House announced dead and injured in the Hawaiian Islands alone totaled around 3,000. Correspondents' eye-witness stories began to come through. Eugene Burns gave an account of some of the things he saw and heard that never-to-be-for-gotten Sunday in Honolulu:

Oahu Island's defenders rose to magnificent heights of valor in the face of six vicious raids on this Pacific outpost last Sunday. The sudden stab has left them fighting mad.

Fifty to 100 enemy planes participated in the thrust at the Pearl Harbor naval base, the Hickam Field army base and the Kaneohe naval air base.

Martin Vitousek, 17 years old, and his father perhaps were the first to see the enemy attack. They were aloft in their own plane.

"Suddenly we were in the thick of a black-painted mass of planes," Martin said. "They rocketed from the sky everywhere and I saw on the wingtips the Rising Sun of Japan. When the first bomb hit, my heart almost went out of me. Then all hell broke loose. I saw three enemy planes shot down."

Ventura Mathias, a garbage department inspector, boarded a warship in Pearl Harbor to complain about illegal dumping of garbage a few seconds before the Japanese launched Sunday's attack against the naval base.

"I had just got aboard," he said, "when I saw about fifty planes flying about 100 feet high. All of a sudden there was havoc all around. I got away—fast."

I raced up nearby Tantalus Mountain, elevation 1,350 feet, from where Pearl Harbor and Hickam Field were plainly visible, and saw three black plumes rising from Hickam Field and Pearl Harbor and blue patches of sky flecked with white bursts of anti-aircraft fire. A Japanese sat on a concrete guardrail on the peak, smoking complacently. Pearl Harbor was almost blacked out by heavy smoke and high overhead bombers roared amid intense anti-aircraft fire.

On the way to my office I saw one bomb explode less than 100 feet from a hardware store. Near by, another bomb killed a man. One direct hit on an automobile killed its four occupants instantly.

There have been no new air raids against the Hawaiian Islands since Sunday night.

Purely by chance, Tom Yarbrough also saw something of what happened in Honolulu. He was en route by steamer across the Pacific to a new assignment in Egypt after a vacation in the U. S. His story also came through on December 12:

Our ship eased into the sunny Honolulu harbor from San Francisco Sunday morning at the height of the first Japanese air raid.

They sure picked a swell day for it. Thinking it was nothing more serious than a big-scale war game, we enjoyed the show immensely. Scores of passengers, crowding the deck, remarked that it was mighty fine of the U. S. Navy, timing it so nicely with our arrival.

A whistling bomb plunketed into the water about a hundred yards from our vessel and an American automobile dealer bound for Tientsin, shouted: "Boy, what if it had been a real one!"

A half-hour later we got the full impact of the sad reality. The ship's officer herded us into the lounge and told us this was the real thing, and no fooling. The bombing spectacle we had been watching—fire, the flash of guns, the ear-splitting crack of anti-aircraft guns—was the opening stroke of the war on Oahu. The officer who announced the news was perspiring and his hands were trembling. He took a deep breath and then he said:

"It seems there's a state of undeclared war between Honolulu and the U. S."

Everybody wondered what he meant by "Honolulu" fighting the U. S. His slip of the tongue was cleared up soon, however, and we learned the truth. He told us to disembark in groups of twelve. The list grew to seventeen as a house was wrecked, and a short time later to forty-nine.

The first blow of the war struck with stunning surprise. This probably caused the people to be more excited than those I'd seen and heard in England many times in the past two years, but there was no sign of panic. Automobiles and trucks and fire engines, with screaming sirens, sped through the clean palm-lined streets without slowing down for intersections in spite of the many civilians who were ignoring "take shelter" warnings.

As our group walked toward the hotel, a bomb whistled down alarmingly close and a chorus of anti-aircraft guns roared. We ducked under a big palm tree—something new in air raid shelters. A grinning soldier across the street called out: "It looks like the real McCoy!"

A boy on a bicycle came down the street with a load of newspaper extras. The banner lines were four inches high: "War! Oahu Bombed by Japanese Planes."

The excitement wore off Monday. Thousands of Christmas shoppers mingled with Army guardsmen. The stores closed at 4:30 P.M., allowing employees and customers alike to start home before darkness.

Details of the audacious raid developed with startling swiftness. The first fatality was a 10-year-old Portuguese girl. Thereafter the toll mounted, with six, then eight, and then with a carful killed, of twenty.

Another of Eugene Burns's dispatches arrived from Honolulu a few days later:

Honoluluans are mixing smiles with grimness in reciting incidents growing out of the December 7 bombing.

Eleven prominent lawyers compared earnings for three days after martial law was declared. The highest earnings for any one of the eleven was $1.75 received for notarizing.

A woman called police for an escort to gather in her washing after a blackout. In the midst of the December 7 tension a woman telephoned police about a barking dog that was "disturbing her sleep." A jittery guard raised his bayoneted rifle and challenged: "Halt and advance."

At City Hall, the Red Cross kitchen served Hawaiian food and Hawaiians flocked there, bringing their relatives. The menu was changed to corned beef. The Hawaiians melted away. More than 150 taxicabs answered the hurry-up call for duty rushing sailors to Pearl Harbor on December 7.

The night of December 7 a house almost at the top of Honolulu's surrounding hills blazed with lights amid the blackout. Neighbors yelled to put out the lights. The people in the house asked: "What for?" Neighbors said: "We have been attacked by the Japs." The response was: "We have been moving all day and didn't notice anything wrong."

The lightest note was the federal internal revenue announcement: "The fourth and final payment of federal income taxes for 1940 are due. Don't forget payments during the war tension."

A Paul Revere motorcyclist, "feeling dandy," roared up and down the streets at 4 A.M. on December 8 arousing residents and yelling: "Wake up, everybody. Wake up, war's on!" A woman put a phosphorescent substance on her dog's tail so she could follow it on its nightly walk.

6

Taunton, England, sent greetings to Taunton, Massachussetts. Japan announced occupation of Guam. Japanese troops and parachutists gained a foothold at Vigan, in the Philippines. Hunger deaths in Athens, Greece, were estimated at 800 daily. Japan described her aims as "peace and security." More than 2,000 enemy aliens were arrested in the U. S. Five persons were jailed in Los Angeles for making disloyal utterances.

The U. S. seized the brand-new French liner *Normandie,* one of the world's largest boats, at her New York pier.

Allied bombers sank four Japanese troopships off Luzon. U. S. Marines repelled two Nipponese air attacks on Wake Island. Australia began mobilization of men between 18 and 25. The Russians claimed the Nazis had lost 6,000,000 men. The Nazis claimed the Russians had lost 6,000,000 men. Nobody believed either.

Dispatch followed dispatch as correspondents' stories came through with more regularity. In one of the daily communiqués from MacArthur's headquarters Clark Lee found a story. The statement recounted the first major clash of U. S. air forces with a Japanese convoy off the Philippines on December 9. One sentence provided the basis for what Lee found out and wrote:

Captain Colin P. Kelly, Jr., 26-year-old West Point graduate, was skipper of a big bomber that carried a crew of six. He was just another officer in the unit when his group took off to battle Japanese forces approaching the Island of Luzon on December 9. It was his first "crack" at the Japs.

Kelly's ship, like all the others, lifted smoothly from the runway and headed over the Pacific. Light, fleecy clouds flecked the sky. The planes sped straight for an appointed rendezvous where the Japanese force had been sighted. Suddenly, in the distant horizon, a major Jap force loomed. There were battleships and cruisers, all guarding transport ships heavily loaded with Japanese troops.

Kelly singled out a big Japanese battleship—the *Haruna*—and laid his plans. The Jap fleet was blasting up a steady blanket of anti-aircraft fire. The young captain took a course straight for the enemy battle wagon. Jap planes roared toward him, trying to spoil Kelly's aim. But Kelly kept his ship on line. Three bombs smashed squarely on the battleship, leaving it a helpless hulk.

Then Kelly turned his big plane homeward. The job was done. He and his crew had scored on the first Japanese battleship since Pearl Harbor. Then, within minutes of the airport, Kelly's plane was sighted by two Jap fighters. They plummeted from a low-flying cloud bank and poured out a deadly fire.

Kelly's plane staggered, then righted itself as the young captain worked the controls. Apparently it had escaped a mortal hit. But seconds later, flames laced from the motors. There was time only for split-second decision. Kelly made it. He ordered his six-man crew to bail out.

The crew parachuted to safety. But not Kelly. As the last man leaped, a terriffic explosion shattered the big bomber.

The Florida-born youth with an Irish smile and a disposition that went with it, had been only five years out of West Point. He never knew what his superiors had to say about him because he stayed with his ship to the fiery end. The official communiqué of the day's fighting said:

"General MacArthur announced with great sorrow the death of Captain Colin P. Kelly, Jr., who distinguished himself by scoring three direct hits on the Japanese capital battleship *Haruna*, leaving her in flames and in distress."

Thus was the Number 1 hero of this new war born.

CHAPTER 16

Our Tragic December

December 11–December 31, 1941

I

TWO of the first sea casualties in the Pacific were the British battleships *Prince of Wales* and *Repulse*.

Cecil Brown, 33-year-old Columbia Broadcasting System correspondent, was aboard the *Repulse*. He witnessed the battle from the bridge of that vessel. The *Prince of Wales* was in full view only half a mile away.

Aerial torpedoes, dropped by Nipponese fliers "with suicidal abandon," sent both ships to the bottom without the explosion of either. This probably accounted for the survival of more than 2,000 of the 3,000 aboard. Here is a summary of Cecil Brown's story. It was given out by CBS to correspondents in New York on December 12:

Nine Japanese bombers approach the *Repulse* at 10,000 feet. Anti-aircraft guns scream constantly. One bomb hits the water, another hits the catapult deck, penetrating the ship and exploding below. Fires rage below.

All gun crews remain cool, wisecracking. Japs drop three bombs. Destroyers at varying distances set up full barrages.

The *Prince of Wales* seems to be hit. We are twisting and snaking violently to avoid torpedoes. The Japs are coming in low one by one in single waves. They are easy to spot. The guns are deafening.

The officer beside me yells: "Here comes a tin fish!" A Jap torpedo-bomber is heading directly for us, 200 yards high. He's less than 500 yards distant. The torpedo drops, and he banks sharply, and his whole side is exposed to our guns. But instead of gliding

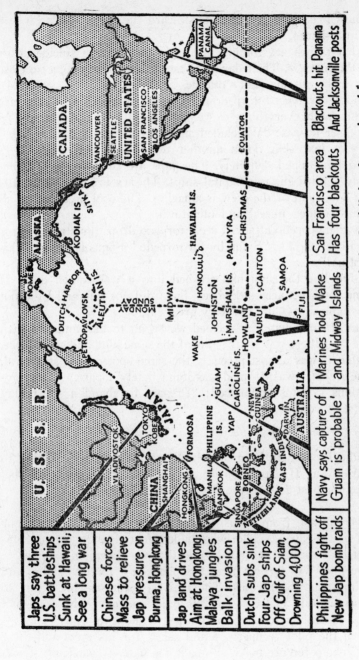

| Japs say three U.S. battleships Sunk at Hawaii; See a long war | Chinese forces Mass to relieve Jap pressure on Burma, Hongkong | Jap land drives Aim at Hongkong; Malaya jungles Balk invasion | Dutch subs sink Four Jap ships Off Gulf of Siam, Drowning 4,000 | Philippines fight off New Jap bomb raids | Navy says capture of Guam is 'probable' | Marines hold Wake and Midway Islands | San Francisco area Has four blackouts | Blackouts hit Panama And Jacksonville posts |

Map 13—The U. S.-Japanese war had moved this far in a week after Pearl Harbor. Long and careful preparation by Tokyo lay behind the speedy and furious drives the Japs had launched against the United States, Great Britain, and the Netherlands, timed with the sneak attack on Hawaii.

287

away, he's making a graceful dip toward the water. He's hit and bursts into flames.

Other planes are coming in low in an amazing suicide effort to sink the *Repulse*. Their daring is astonishing. They come so close you can make out the pilot's outline.

Another wave of torpedo-bombers is approaching. They are being met with everything we've got except our 14-inchers. The signal officer flashes: "We eluded all torpedoes this second attack."

We've just shot down another torpedo-bomber. The *Wales* seems to be stopped definitely. The Japs are throwing everything recklessly against the two capital ships. There's fire aboard us. It's not out. The calm of the crew is amazing. The cool precision of all hands has seemed unreal and unnatural.

Another torpedo attack. I see a torpedo drop. It's streaking for us. A watcher shouts: "Stand by for torpedo." Someone says: "This one's got us!"

It felt like the ship had crashed into a well-rooted dock. It threw me four feet across the deck, but I did not fall, and I did not feel any explosion—just this very great jar.

Almost immediately it seemed we began to list, and less than a minute later there was another jar of the same kind and same force, except that it was almost precisely the same spot on the starboard. That the *Repulse* was doomed was immediately apparent. The communications systems announced: "Prepare to abandon ship! May God be with you!"

Radio broadcasting, unborn in World War I, was helping to tell World War II. Tom Yarbrough got one of the most unusual stories of the first days of the Pacific war in Manila:

A broadcast from Kausi Island today related a picturesque story of how a Japanese pilot who made a forced landing in a primitive islet near there was stoned to death by a Hawaiian woman.

The pilot was thrown from his plane in a forced landing and for a time was unconscious. The natives—cautious, but ready to help a stranger in distress—hid his guns and gave him food and drink for several days. They had not heard about the war.

Then the pilot recuperated and asked for his guns and "war papers." The reference to "war" made the natives suspicious. Lacking communication with the other islands, the natives sent men in a boat twenty miles to Kauai Island to report the arrival of the queer guest who spoke strangely of "war."

The pilot, meanwhile, struck up a friendship with a Hawaiian-born Japanese, bribed the Japanese to get his guns back, and then began asking questions about the men who had left by boat.

The suspicious Hawaiian family with whom the pilot was staying took the situation in hand. The husband and wife lured the pilot and the Hawaiian-born Japanese into the woods.

The Hawaiian-born Japanese, realizing his predicament, fired a shotgun charge into his own stomach. The husband went after the pilot and the pilot shot him. In spite of his wounds, the husband banged the pilot's head against a stone wall and his wife finished the job.

2

THE QUESTION as to official laxity of Pearl Harbor on December 7 required an answer. Secretary of the Navy Knox flew to Honolulu. On December 15, correspondents heard him describe Pearl Harbor as a story of heroism and treachery, of official lack of alertness against a surprise attack, and heavy naval losses. Richard L. Turner got the Knox story:

The United States, officially listing its losses at Pearl Harbor as a battleship and five other vessels, hurled a challenge to the Japanese today by declaring its main Fleet was ploughing the high seas and wanting only to come to blows with the enemy.

The treacherous Japanese attack on the Hawaiian naval base failed, Secretary of the Navy Knox said, to achieve its prime purpose—to "knock out the United States before the war began." The Fleet's wounds were grievous, he acknowledged, giving them as:

Lost: The battleship *Arizona,* the destroyers *Cassin, Downes,* and *Shaw,* the target ship *Utah,* and the mine layer *Oglala.* Damaged: The battleship *Oklahoma* and a number of other vessels. Dead: 2,638 men and 91 officers. Wounded: 636 men and 20 officers.

Knox conceded that "the United States services were not on the alert against the surprise air attack," and announced that President Roosevelt would make a formal investigation. After telling of the losses, he said:

"The entire balance of the Pacific Fleet with its aircraft carriers, its heavy cruisers, its light cruisers, its destroyers and submarines are uninjured and are all at sea seeking contact with the enemy."

Knox unfolded an amazing story of Japanese use of fifth columnists and submarines—some of them tiny two-man craft—as well as from 150 to 300 airplanes in the surprise attack. The secretary also told how the American forces rallied and fought heroically after the first bitter blow. Once the attack began, the defense was conducted "skillfully and bravely," he said. Less than four minutes after the initial alarm, guns of the Fleet were in action. And seconds later the first Japanese plane was downed.

Proudly he cited many instances of heroism, including that of a dying captain of a battleship whose stomach was laid open by shrapnel fire but who continued to direct his men from a bridge which had become a blazing inferno. He mentioned, too, an officer who leaped from a hospital bed to take his post of action and a bluejacket who single-handedly kept a 5-inch anti-aircraft gun firing after his ten battery mates were shot down in a strafing attack. Then there was the case of the sailor who acted as a human mount for a machine gun. Carrying the gun, for which no mount was immediately available, he shot the weapon from his arms, staggering under the concussion of the rapid fire.

Knox declared there was no truth in a rumor that the Navy had been warned an attack might be imminent. He estimated the Japanese preparations for the raid must have required a minimum of from three to four weeks—a period while active peace negotiations were under way.

Two days later, the ranking officers of the Hawaiian area were removed from their commands. Admiral Husband E. Kimmel, Commander in Chief of the Pacific Fleet, was ordered replaced by Rear Admiral Chester W. Nimitz, Chief of the Bureau of Navigation. Lieutenant General Walter C. Short was relieved of command of the Hawaiian department by Lieutenant General Delos C. Emmons. Major General Frederick L. Martin, in command of the Hawaiian air forces, was ordered relieved by Brigadier General C. L. Tinker.

The tragic saga of Pearl Harbor and its December 7 blitzkrieg was over. "Remember Pearl Harbor!" became a slogan that meant something.

3

JAPAN's strategy from the start was to try to break the blockade that had been closing around her. She wanted to break it on
land as well as sea. The troops she had already sneaked into Thailand
began to advance toward the Burma Road. The name of that road
had been used frequently in 1941, and before. Still, comparatively
few people really knew much about it. There was a story. Daniel De
Luce took time out to write it:

The world's most fantastic highway—Burma Road—is as much
a part of China's war effort as are the battles fought by Chinese
Generalissimo Chiang Kai-Shek's tattered armies.

All China united with blood, sweat, and suffering to carve
through towering mountains a supply line that connects the capital
at Chungking with Burma and the outside world. More than 200,-
000 Chinese men, women, and even children did the job. Scores died
at the task, but the labor continued. They virtually clawed the road
out of the rocks with their very fingernails.

The road was born of military emergency. Japanese invasion
forces had grabbed China's coastline and ports, then settled back to
throttle China into submission. There was only a rude trail from
Chungking to Burma. It was the ancient "silk trail" used by Marco
Polo more than six centuries ago. Little had been done to improve
the trail and only crude vehicles could use it.

Generalissimo Chiang's idea was that, with the road completed, war supplies could flow into Chungking from friendly nations. He appealed to the nation. It was a staggering project to con-
template. The major task was that of connecting the terminus of
the Rangoon railway at Lashio with Kunming, capital of the Chinese province of Yunnan. Between Lashio and Kunming, lay 700
miles of the most difficult terrain in the world, mountainous and
forbidding.

The Chinese had no modern road-building machinery. The
work was done by hand, with hoes and hammers. Huge cylindrical
boulders pulled by water oxen served as steam rollers to smooth the
roadbed. No dynamite could be used for excavating because the explosive was too precious to spare from the battlefields. Instead,
primitive tools ground away through solid granite until the roadbed took shape. Earth and stone were removed by Chinese pack-
baskets. A 200-foot, hand-built suspension bridge—an engineering

feat almost without parallel—spanned the mad, treacherous Salween river, 2,800 feet above sea level.

Observers estimated that nine feet of roadway were built by every man, woman, or child who labored on the vast task. Many of the workers suffered from goiter due to the lack of iodine in the mountain salt.

Finally, the first trucks rolled over the new road. From Lashio ten-wheeled American lease-lend trucks with Chinese drivers began moving supplies to the embattled Chinese Army.

Such is Burma Road, completed in 1939 by 200,000 desperate people. The Chinese won the battle against nature so that their country would have a better chance to win her battle over the most deadly of all her foes—the Japanese.

4

UNTIL Pearl Harbor, the spotlight had been on Hitler and Europe. It had been there so long that many, perhaps, had been giving scant attention to the Far East. It was difficult to visualize the vast distances of the Pacific, or the problems they presented.

The immediate object of the Pacific war was control of many small, strategic islands and a few great military bases. One week after Pearl Harbor, Clarke Beach, in Washington, clarified the geography of the Pacific:

The curtain rose a week ago on the long-awaited, historic tragedy of the Pacific war. The stage is the surface of the world's largest ocean, and upon it untold numbers of men will die fighting for the possession of a few great bases and thousands of small islands.

The clashing fleets will pivot upon these specks of land, because of the vastness of the watery arena and the limited radius on which warships can operate. The islands also are the nesting places for warplanes. Naval strategists agree that no major fleet engagement should take place more than 2,000 to 3,000 miles from repair docks, into which crippled vessels can limp after battle. Yet it is 6,000 miles between Alaska and New Zealand; 8,000 miles between San Francisco and Singapore.

The U. S. Pacific mainland bases are at San Diego and Seattle. Its outlying bases are at Sitka, Kodiak, Anchorage, and Dutch

Harbor, in Alaska; in Hawaii; in the Philippines, and on a dozen or so islands as far south as Samoa.

The home bases of the enemy are at Yokosuka, Maizuru, Kure, and Sasebo; his outposts are at Formosa, Bonin, Camranh Bay in Indo-China, and, it is believed, on many of the mandated islands, which lie between Hawaii and the Philippines.

To the south are the bases of this country's Allies in New Zealand, Australia, and in the Netherlands East Indies. At the extreme west is Britain's mighty island base of Singapore, almost touching the southern tip of the Malay Peninsula.

Outside of Japan and the United States mainland, the only major repair bases on the Pacific are at Pearl Harbor, Hawaii, and Singapore. There the largest capital ships can be docked and put in order. Some of the other bases have repair facilities, but their capacity is limited.

Pearl Harbor is at the apex of the United States' inner defense line in the Pacific, which runs from the Aleutian Islands to Hawaii to Samoa to Panama. Within this "area of predominance," the American forces are reasonably free to operate. Being 2,400 miles from San Francisco, Pearl Harbor is a constant menace to any force seeking to make raids on the West Coast or the Panama Canal.

The Japanese started the encirclement of the Philippines when they seized Hainan Island and the Spratly Islands in 1939 and Camranh Bay last July. Manila, on Luzon Island, is the stronghold of the commonwealth and it is believed capable of withstanding a long siege and a frontal attack.

If the Philippines can be held, they might in time become the key to offensive operations against the Japanese. Only 2,000 miles from Tokyo, Manila lies much nearer to the enemy capital than either Hawaii or Singapore. Bases on the island provide fields from which to launch air attacks against Formosa, which is 600 miles from Manila; against Camranh Bay, or against the sea lanes which Japanese ships must use for communication with Indo-China, or for an expedition against Singapore or the East Indies.

There was opposition to fortifying Guam, and the first money for improvements was not provided until June, 1940, when Congress voted $277,000 for the establishment there of an "aviation and submarine listening post." In March of this year it provided $12,800,-000 for defense aviation facilities at Samoa and harbor improvements at Guam.

The importance of the small islands in Pacific warfare has grown with the development of the airplane. At the war's start, naval air bases were being constructed on Midway, Wake, Johnston, and Palmyra Islands. From these outposts, U. S. planes could patrol a front of more than 4,000 miles west of Hawaii, between Unalaska and Samoa.

Midway lies 1,134 miles northwest of Hawaii, and Wake is a little less than halfway from Midway to Guam. Palmyra, 960 miles south of Hawaii, is on the route to Samoa. In the Samoan group, at Pago Pago, on Tutuila Island, this country has had a minor naval station since 1900. It is now of great importance as a southern terminus for patrol squadrons.

Hawaii is the home station of the Fleet, and the most intensively fortified area under the American flag. Believing that the defensive weakness of Oahu was the proximity of outlying islands in the Hawaiian group, the Army and Navy lately pushed work on fortifications of those islands.

North of Hawaii, 1,990 miles, lies Dutch Harbor, southernmost Alaskan base. The airplane also made necessary the chain of bases on that rocky, fog-shrouded peninsula. Alaska's location gives it easy access to Asia by plane, which means not only that this country can use it in operations against Japan, but also that, if occupied by the enemy, it would be a menace to the United States.

The Army has been developing two primary air bases in Alaska, at Fairbanks and Anchorage. The Navy also is building air bases there.

The Great Circle route between Japan and the United States passes just south of the Aleutian Islands, on which the air distance is about 1,500 miles shorter than by way of Hawaii.

The United States has no defense outposts in the South Pacific to protect the Panama Canal or to establish blockade patrols off the western coast of South America, although some authorities for years have advocated such bases. The danger of the Japanese occupying and fortifying one or more of the islands there is seen in the fact that eight islands were within 150 to 200 miles of the Canal. The Galapagos Islands, often spoken of as desirable outposts, are 850 miles off the Ecuadorian coast.

In the South Pacific are numerous island groups controlled by the Free French such as the Society Islands, the Leeward Islands, and Tahiti; and those, presumably, will be available to the United States as bases in case of naval activity or convoys in that area.

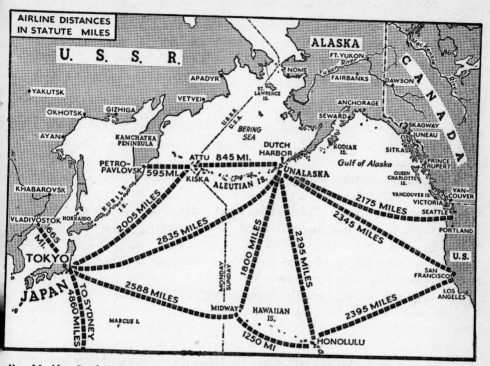

AIRLINE DISTANCES IN STATUTE MILES

U. S. S. R.

YAKUTSK

OKHOTSK

AYAN

KHABAROVSK

VLADIVOSTOK · HOKKAIDO

TOKYO

JAPAN

MARCUS I.

GIZHIGA

KAMCHATKA PENINSULA

PETRO-PAVLOVSK

KURILE IS.

665 MI.

TO SYDNEY 4860 MILES

APADYR

VETVEI

ST. LAWRENCE IS.

BERING SEA

ATTU 845 MI.

595 MI.

KISKA · ALEUTIAN IS.

2005 MILES

2835 MILES

2588 MILES

1800 MILES

MONDAY SUNDAY

MIDWAY

1250 MI

ALASKA

FT. YUKON

NOME

Yukon River

FAIRBANKS

ANCHORAGE

SEWARD

DUTCH HARBOR

UNALASKA

KODIAK IS.

Gulf of Alaska

2295 MILES

HAWAIIAN IS.

HONOLULU

DAWSON

SKAGWAY

JUNEAU

SITKA

PRINCE RUPERT

QUEEN CHARLOTTE IS.

VANCOUVER IS.

VICTORIA

SEATTLE

PORTLAND

U.S.

SAN FRANCISCO

LOS ANGELES

2175 MILES

2345 MILES

2395 MILES

CANADA

Mackenzie River

Map 14—After Pearl Harbor, Pacific distances took on more importance. For, in bombing Hawaii, the Japanese had moved nearly 4,000 miles east from Tokyo—and 4,000 miles east of Tokyo comes dangerously close to the U. S. at several points. This map shows strategic points and mileages in the Pacific.

One of the most serious menaces to the United States Navy in the Central and Western Pacific are the Japanese mandated islands—a group of about 1,400 islands stretching for nearly 3,000 miles diagonally across the route between the Philippines and Hawaii.

Japan quietly took over these ocean specks during the World War when they were held by Germany, which had purchased them from Spain. Japan held them later under a mandate from the League of Nations. From various evidence, including reports from the few persons who have been permitted to visit there, observers have concluded that Japan has established armed bases on many of them, contrary to treaty. Submarines, small craft, and airplanes operating from them could harry United States shipping on the route to Manila.

Mopping up all these little island bases one at a time is entirely practicable, military experts have said, but sailing into that hornets' nest would give the Navy a long, arduous job.

5

THE RUSSIANS still stood off Hitler in the drear winter before the gates of Moscow. Some of Hitler's freezing troops were wearing women's coats to keep them warm. In the Mediterranean, the British engaged Italy's ships and Hitler's dive-bombers. Larry Allen landed in the hospital. For weeks there were no details.

Hitler displaced Field Marshal von Brauchitsch—"heart disease," he said. He took over personal command. Roosevelt made 61-year-old Lieutenant General Douglas MacArthur, defender of the Philippines, a full-fledged general. It was a rank held only by one other American field commander in wartime—General Pershing, leader of the A.E.F. in World War I.

In Berlin, the radio was broadcasting gloomy winter poems. One of them went:

After a year of sweat and toil
No green blooms on my tree.
From the sky and from the soil
Grief has come to me.
How happy I was a year ago—
Dark looks the future—full of woe. . . .

On tiny, valiant Wake Island, bombed U. S. Marines were asked by radio if there was anything they wanted. The reply came back: "Yes, send us some more Japs." They got them. So did Hong Kong. So did Manila. The Japanese came in suicide squads, by bombers, by parachute, by two-man submarine. They were on the offensive. They made the most of it.

Throughout the Pacific there was no relief. Christmas, 1941, approached. Still the Japanese pounded. Still U. S. forces on all the islands fought their losing fight. The only relief came from the Libyan desert. There an Allied Army battled the Nazis. Preston Grover, with the British, got the story. It was about a pig—and what happened when a Scottish sergeant chased it:

This little pig didn't stay home—and thereby hangs a tale of fantastic events in the desert and how a band of indignant Scotsmen garnered a fortune in food and supplies and captured nearly 200 German prisoners.

A Scottish Black Watch sergeant was doing a bit of quiet foraging in an abandoned German camp far behind the desert front when he saw and went after the porker. Barely had the chase begun when bullets whizzed around his head. He saw some Germans and fired back. Then out of the desert appeared a British major and two captains—prisoners of the Germans, who broke away when the shooting began. They returned to camp and spread the word.

A battalion of Scotsmen went out today to mop up the outfit. They were shot up pretty badly recently by just such a band of Germans. This time the sergeant was accompanied by an armored car, trucks full of soldiers, machine-gun cars, and everything necessary for an effective cleanup. They beat the brush in two wadis (gullies) without any luck. But in the third things began to happen.

"That's the place where I found 'em," said the Black Watch sergeant.

A small band of Germans was discovered behind sand dunes along the Mediterranean shore. Machine guns blazed at them. They returned a few shots and then began surrendering. Germans bobbed from behind other dunes until ninety had appeared. A roving South African journalist surprised nine Germans hiding in a cave. They surrendered—although he was armed only with a camera.

Upward of 200 Germans were captured before the roundup ended. Then the Scots stumbled on the treasure trove of supplies in trucks, in caves, under tents, and spread out on the ground—everything from pistols to food and portable typewriters. There were cases of fruit in tins, wine and champagne and chocolate. Everybody participated. The scope of German conquests was measured in part by Norwegian fish, Yugoslav sausages, and French sauces. There was a surprise package of American tinned foods—probably from supplies captured in Flanders.

The final casualty score was two Germans wounded, not a Scotsman scratched. What happened to the pig still isn't quite clear.

6

THE WAKE ISLAND base was not an important U. S. possession. It was small. It was isolated. It was but a dot little more than halfway across the Pacific. Nor was the island itself important. What it and its handful of defending Marines stood for in the last hours was important. It finally came to its end on Christmas Eve. It didn't fall. It was killed, man by man. It was perhaps the one place on the map where no correspondent had been permitted to go. There were no eyewitnesses to its finish. Sterling F. Green pieced the story together in Washington:

In communiqué after communiqué the Navy has issued the familiar four-word report: "Wake continues to resist." The line was missing today in the Navy's sixteenth communiqué of a sixteen-day-old war. That meant that the Japanese at last had taken it.

Wake was just a few hundred acres of brush-clad upland on the three isles that together made up the "kingdom" for which less than 400 tired, sweat-stained Marines fought under the direction of Major James Devereux.

Up to today, they had fought off fourteen aerial assaults in sixteen days of war; they had brought down hostile planes and had sent to the bottom at least two Jap warships. They had had to fight without help and in full knowledge that help would not come. It would have been foolhardy, Navy sources pointed out, to divert war vessels to the relief of tiny Wake, Midway, or even Guam, when it was evident that these outposts were merely diversions in the main Japanese assaults on the Philippines and Malaya.

Besides the Marines, only construction workers were on Wake. They were there to complete a $7,000,000 seaplane base intended to supplement the clipper base which had been in service for several years as a stopping point on Pan-American Airways' trans-Pacific route.

Day after day, the brief summation—"Wake continues to resist"—has thrilled Americans who knew the apparent hopelessness of the fight. Here in Washington, where we study communiqués and wish they could do more, we have watched eagerly for that dramatic daily line. But now the line is missing.

Tom Yarbrough got additional details about Wake from district naval headquarters at Pearl Harbor. The Navy report contained two illuminating sentences. The first said: "During the closing days of the siege the defenders had only two and finally only one plane; these were patched together between flights." The other quoted the last words heard by radio after the Japanese finally landed and all hope was gone. They were gallant understatement. They were: "The issue is in doubt."

7

WAKE ISLAND was just the beginning. At Hong Kong, on December 24, Canadian and Indian troops fought off Japanese air and land forces. The Japs were trying to destroy huge gasoline stores. There were heavy casualties.

Simultaneously, Jap invaders were closing in on the Philippines. Sharp fighting persisted in northern Luzon. Strong forces landed at Santo Tomas, 125 miles from Manila. A full-fledged Jap offensive pushed toward the capital.

Jap troops also landed on the isle of oil-rich Borneo, 600 miles from Singapore. They raided the Kuala Lumpur area only 180 miles north of Britain's most important Far Eastern stronghold.

Christmas day came. Before blacked-out homes on the Kentish coast, English children sang carols. From German-occupied France, long-range artillery sent shells screaming across the Dover Straits. In Libya, the British recaptured the strategic port of Bengasi. It also was a holiday in Japan—but not Christmas. The pagan Japanese celebrated the fifteenth anniversary of the accession of Emperor Hirohito. British forces in Hong Kong had the worst Christmas of all. Communications went dead, but not before first word of what happened there was relayed west:

Map 15—When this map was drawn on December 22, 1941, the long tentacles of Japanese conquest were lashing in full fury. Based on Formosa, they already were striking mortal blows at Britain's Hong Kong and had made landing places for the many thousands of Japanese soldiers pouring into the Philippines. It was the hour of doom for Manila.

After weeks of bitter fighting, Hong Kong fell to the Japanese today—Christmas.

The capitulation of the century-old British bastion admittedly was a great strategic triumph for the invaders. There were few details of Hong Kong's last hours under the Union Jack, but there was certainty of these important gains to the Japanese:

1. An important refueling, supply, and repair base halfway between Japan and the coveted riches of British Malaya and the Netherlands East Indies.

2. Elimination of Britain's foothold on the China coast, which would have served eventually as an Allied springboard for an attempt to oust the Japanese from the Canton River area and thus open a new supply route to the Chungking regime.

3. Absolute domination of the mouth of the Canton River, and thus security from the rear if the Japanese decided to start a new thrust northward against the Chinese.

4. Valuable additional facilities for dispatching more landing forces to the Philippines. Manila is only 600 miles from Hong Kong.

There were about 1,000 American civilians in Hong Kong when the British flag was hauled down. U. S. Government officials were safe.

In the Philippines, the Japs pushed past Luzon. They concentrated on the Lingayen Gulf, headed toward Manila only 110 miles away. Clark Lee had left Manila on December 21 to visit the Lingayen front. He was gone for four days. Then, on Christmas night, he returned and wrote a story:

The Japanese Army rushing toward Manila from the Lingayen Gulf area is an ill-uniformed, untrained mass of youngsters between 15 and 18 years old, equipped with small-caliber guns and driven by desperate determination to advance.

Hundreds of them already have died under the fire of American and Filipino artillery, machine guns, and rifles, but up until tonight had been only partly checked. U. S. forces, holding the Lingayen area, have rallied and are putting up a determined defense.

I have spent four days in and around the fighting front, including a two-day hike over mountain trails after the Japanese cut the main road southward, forcing me to burn my automobile.

The Lingayen battle started last Monday at 2 A.M. with an artillery duel between Japanese warships and American shore guns. At the same time a force estimated at 500, advancing southward from Vigan, clashed with American armored car units at San Fernando in La Union province. The Japanese, who were riding bicycles, were apparently unaware of the presence of Americans in the vicinity. The fight continued until after dawn when almost every Japanese was wiped out, although many climbed trees and continued firing until they themselves were shot down like birds.

At sundown Sunday there were a few Jap transports and warships along the east coast of Lingayen Gulf, but by dawn Monday fifty-six ships, most of them small transports of about 1,500 tons each, plus a few destroyers and cruisers, were anchored along the west coast from Baguen to Damortis. The ships were in a line extending twenty-five miles and were anchored about three quarters of a mile offshore.

The gulf coast in this area is sandy and shallow with mountains four or five miles back from the shoreline. The American artillery immediately opened fire and sank several transports. One gunner named Johnny Jones laid two shells from a 75-mm. gun into a transport right at the waterline, causing it to sink slowly. Low-flying Japanese planes bombed and gunned the American positions scattered at strategic points along shore.

About 7 A.M. the Japanese troops started coming ashore in small flat-bottomed motorboats with curved bows. Many were sunk. In spite of American fire, they swarmed on the beaches and advanced toward the American positions, splitting up in twos, tandem-fashion. They carried .25-caliber rifles and about a quarter of them had .25-caliber submachine guns.

Unless they strike a vital spot, these .25 bullets will not kill a man. I have talked to many who have been wounded three and four times and still were walking about. One Filipino member of an armored car unit was hit in the head and in the back, but was not critically wounded.

As the Japanese kept landing in ever-larger numbers, the Americans drew back strategically. I met American officers Monday night at a point overlooking Lingayen Gulf. They had just set fire to gasoline stores to prevent them from falling into Japanese hands. The officers said that, prior to the landing, the Japs had bombed and strafed the shore for days. They told of one flier in a Messerschmitt who flew low, waved at them, and did a few acrobatics. They thought something was up. Sure enough, they said, "this morning he came back with planes of every description, and today we have been shot at and bombed by every kind of plane and gun."

The defenders had to leave clothing and food, but saved their guns and ammunition. Part of the Japanese forces turned toward Pozorrubio and Binalonan on the main highway to Manila.

Clark Lee didn't tell much about what had happened to him during his four-day trip. About all he mentioned was loss of his automobile. But there was drama in what he had experienced and what he had seen. Russell Brines wrote the complete story:

Big, genial Clark Lee was a mass of mud when he got back to Manila last night. Four days earlier when he departed for the Lingayen battlefront, he was dressed in immaculate white. When he returned he wore a borrowed khaki shirt and denim trousers. He had no socks. Ditches had served him as air raid shelters after repeated Japanese air attacks on his car. He looked every inch a dramatic story, and he had one—a story of personal experiences to top that of any newspaperman in the Philippines in this war.

Japanese bombs were a constant overtone in his recital. Dozens of times en route to the front, he and two friends had to leap from their car in the middle of the road and dive for cover. On their way back, the party found themselves in the midst of a skirmish between several truckloads of Filipino soldiers and a squad of assailants hidden in the darkness across a mountain canyon. Bullets splattered overhead as Lee tried to drive through. They finally got to the end of a dirt road and set fire to their car in order to keep it out of the hands of the Japanese.

Then they struck off on a series of narrow trails into wild, "indescribably beautiful" country. But Japanese bombers, which seemed to be aiming at every living creature, sent them in hiding again.

"I jumped behind a rock, seeking shelter from the shrapnel— and found myself suspended over the edge of a 200-foot precipice," said Lee. "But it was all right because I had a good hold on the rock."

Unable to stay on roads, they followed the mountain trails that whole day and toward dusk reached a small village. The village headman took one look at the strange visitors, disappeared, then returned in what he apparently considered the proper dress, in spite of the heat. He was attired in three silk shirts and a coat, above the waist. Below, he wore only a native loincloth.

Lee and his friends spent that night in the headman's house, a thatched, two-story structure set on stilts. The windows in their room were closed tightly and there was no light. The headman explained that even in such a remote region blackouts were enforced.

The next morning the headman supplied a guide who took them on a trail that led along the brink of a mountain, where the agility of a mountain goat came in handy. At dusk the party reached a small lowland town where, after showing their credentials to the suspicious police, they were allowed to catch a ride. Suddenly there was a shattering explosion. A car just ahead was blown up by a land mine.

By now Lee and his mates were sure they had exhausted their allotment of close shaves. They finally hopped an Army truck that took them to a main railway center, and there they boarded a train for Manila. Ordinarily this is a pleasant trip through the rice paddies. But their train was halted six times by low-circling Japanese bombers. Once they sat in on a bitter duel between an anti-aircraft battery and a formation of twenty-seven Japanese bombers.

Finally safe in Manila, Lee learned that fifteen minutes after he had boarded the train the station was smashed with twenty-one dead and many wounded.

8

GENERAL DOUGLAS MACARTHUR was in the field personally. He charted strategy and sought to relieve defense handicaps. The Japs came closer and closer to Manila. In an attempt to save the city from destruction, MacArthur proclaimed it an "open city" the afternoon of December 26. But Japan paid no attention to a convention of war normally accepted by all civilized countries.

Ray P. Cronin, Jr., described the Philippine capital the night of December 27:

A large area of Manila's ancient walled city was in flames tonight with a devastating rain of death. The Japanese air force was answering General Douglas MacArthur's proclamation that this capital was an open city.

And while waves of glistening bombers methodically flew

over the stricken city, reports reached here that Japanese troops, advancing more than thirty miles, had driven down the corridor south toward Manila. Baguio, the commonwealth's summer capital, was still in American hands up to this morning, and was being defended by American regulars guarding roads both north and south into the mountains from Lingayen Gulf.

Fire and bombs ruined many of Manila's most ancient religious institutions, but by sundown the flames appeared to have been confined to an area of about six blocks. The dead among Manila's 600,000-odd inhabitants were estimated at about fifty, with scores wounded—most of them by a direct hit on the roof of the treasury building.

From atop the Manila Hotel on the bay front, I watched squadron after squadron of twin-engined bombers attack the undefended city in a leisurely raid which lasted three hours and seventeen minutes. All their targets were in a half-mile radius around the hotel, where several hundred Americans and Britons were sheltered.

For the first two and a half hours the Japanese attacked the harbors and piers. They came in circling waves in groups of nine, then nine more, another nine, then eight and finally seven, picking one target after another and going back to it if they missed the first time. After several attempts, they scored direct hits on two freighters of 3,000 tons each and they sank within an hour. The planes then attacked the piers themselves, doing heavy damage and sinking four Philippine Government Coast Guard cutters.

Besides the churches and treasury, bombs fell squarely on other government buildings. One college building was hit in the walled city. Bombs also dropped close to a hospital. A church was smashed by one direct hit.

This afternoon's attack was the longest and heaviest in Manila's three weeks of war. So numerous were the swarms of raiders that the populace began to feel that the Japanese had turned loose most of their air power upon the city.

Intramuros—the walled Spanish city where much of the important civilian damage was done—is only a mile in length and half a mile in width, but it is the historical, artistic, ecclesiastical, and architectural center of the metropolis. Many residents rushed into the streets with their own individual anti-aircraft guns—rifles and pistols—and opened fire. If anger could have killed, there would have been many dead Japanese.

The Allies estimated average Nipponese shipping losses at one vessel a day. Jap forces advanced in Malaya. The British raided Japanese-held bases in Thailand. Russians reported that Germany had executed ninety of her own men and 100 Italians for refusing to fight. Nazi fifth columnists were arriving along the Turkish border—for a "rest cure." Two American freighters were torpedoed in the Pacific. Britain suffered her hardest Nazi bombing in weeks. The Jap Navy claimed sixteen enemy submarines sunk in six days. More than 1,000 Italians and 600 Japs were interned at Fort Missoula, Montana.

The Japs began mopping up Manila. They continued to bomb the ancient city. They expected capitulation by early 1942.

On December 30 they also began hammering at MacArthur headquarters on Bataan Peninsula in the entrance to Manila Harbor. Seventeen Americans were killed and eighty wounded in the first attack.

The U. S.-Japanese war was only twenty-four days old. In that time Japan had taken Guam, Wake Island, and Hong Kong. She had Manila at her mercy. She was strong in Thailand and Indo-China. She had overrun a third of Malaya. She was bombing Singapore, moving steadily on this greatest of all British fortifications in the Far East. Singapore was under martial law.

The U. S. had suffered severe losses, beginning with the surprise attack on Pearl Harbor. Japan still had the offensive. MacArthur and his forces were beleaguered on Bataan.

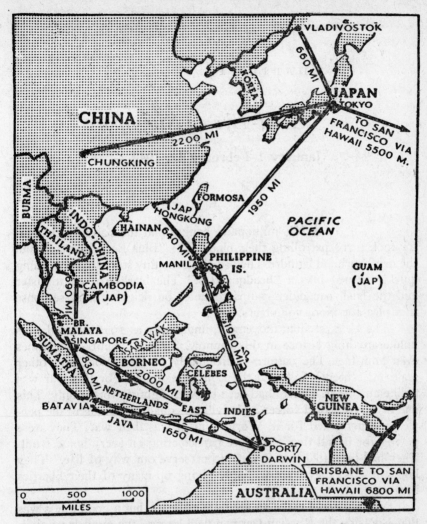

Map 16—On December 30, 1941, General MacArthur called for retaliatory measures against the Japanese for their bombing of Manila. Above are shown possible routes for such retaliation. But already the Japs had taken Guam and Wake Islands, had Manila at their mercy, and were bombing Singapore.

CHAPTER 17

"*Good-Bye to Singapore*"

January 1–February 13, 1942

I

THE millionaire banker and the $20-a-week jani-
tor took turns patrolling their block. The "Blue Book" matron and
the neighborhood laundress helped clean the tiny store that was being
quickly turned into a "headquarters." The black-frocked minister
and the Irish bartender compared notes on neighborhood response
to a plea for more volunteers. . . .

The U. S. civilian movement, under way as 1942 dawned, was
unlike anything before in this country. Strange, ironic—sometimes
even amusing. The pattern—particularly in New York and other
seaboard centers—followed the London example. For this war was
unlike any other. Others had been between fighting forces only. This
one involved armed forces and civilians equally. Although "the people" had not asked for it, World War II was their war. They were
paying for it and they also were participating on every home front.
They had been told that it was "to preserve our way of life." They
hoped it was; they were willingly giving up many of their liberties
because of it.

Nobody could make an accurate estimate, but a good guess was
that—outside the Russian-German field losses—the number of civilian casualties over the world to date represented nearly one half of
all casualties.

The development of large civilian defense organizations was
not an overnight affair. It had been growing, slowly, surely. Propaganda as to war possibility started it. Declaration of war accelerated
it. Reverses on both oceans clinched it. At the beginning of 1942
there were 3,516,600 men and women volunteers enrolled in various
services of the Office of Civilian Defense, as compared with a November, 1941, total of 949,508.

In Rochester, New York, Norman W. Fuehrer, American-born began the New Year with legal promise of a new name after complaining that he was tired of being called "Der Fuehrer." Fifteen persons who accepted an invitation to dinner in Chicago were weighed before they ate; they had pledged contributions to the Red Cross for each pound they gained. In McComb, Mississippi, a child was named Victory Pearl Harbor Moore.

New automobiles were ruled out for the ordinary, everyday people for the duration. Sugar was rationed. Washington suggested curtailment of women's girdles and other rubberized goods. The gasoline situation in the East was acute. The list of restrictions was long and getting longer.

Churchill was in Washington. On January 1, he and Roosevelt and Russia's Litvinoff, together with representatives of twenty-three other nations, pledged no separate peace and full resources against the Axis. Their joint statement was headed, "Declaration by United Nations."

The next day the Japs officially occupied Manila and the Cavite naval base.

Roosevelt's message to Congress set a production goal for 1942 of 60,000 airplanes, 45,000 tanks, 20,000 anti-aircraft guns, and 8,000,000 tons of shipping. He said: "As our power and resources are fully mobilized, we shall carry the attack against the enemy— we shall hit him and hit him again wherever we can reach him."

Joe Louis, world's heavyweight boxing champion, entered the army as a private.

With the fall of Manila, came a brief lull in the Philippines. Attention was focused again on the Mediterranean. Back on December 16 reports had arrived that Larry Allen was injured in action aboard a British ship. There were no details even after word came that he was in an Alexandria hospital. By January 10 he was out again. His story finally came through on the heels of a British announcement that the cruiser *Galatea* had been sunk. Allen's story described the sinking and his escape. Although he had been with the Fleet for well over a year, he couldn't swim:

The British light cruiser *Galatea,* struck by three torpedoes from an Axis submarine, flopped over like a stabbed turtle and went down within three minutes off Egypt in the inky darkness just after midnight the morning of December 16.

The torpedoes smashed in swift succession against the *Galatea's* port side, tearing into her interior with loud blasts and spurting flame. On the dying cruiser's quarter-deck I clung tenaciously to the starboard rail until the list of the ship flung me into the cold, choppy sea. Then I battled through thick, oily scum for forty-five minutes before being rescued.

We had been dive-bombed for more than seven hours on December 14 while patrolling with a squadron of cruisers and destroyers off Libya, but the *Galatea* successfully beat off those attacks and headed eastward. At midnight on December 15 the cruiser's announcer system warned: "First-degree readiness heavy armament." Gunners thus were ordered to stand by for expected action.

A marine sentry aroused me from a nap in the captain's cabin, and I ran to the commander's cabin and informed the Reuters naval correspondent, Alexander Massy Anderson. Adjusting lifebelts, we stepped out into the inky blackness of the quarter-deck and hurried toward the bridge.

We had barely started when the first torpedo smashed into the port side with a burst of flame. The time was 12:02 A.M. Torpedoes seemed to chase us along the deck, for the second crashed amidships with a blinding flash, and the third struck forward, just under a 6-inch gun turret.

As the warship dipped quickly and deeply into the sea on the port side, I caught hold of the starboard deck rail, dropped my tin helmet and bomb antiflash gear, and unscrewed the nozzle on the hose hung around my neck. I blew into it with all the breath I could summon, inflating it just as the cruiser flopped completely over.

The sharp heeling over of the ship flung me into the sea. Hundreds of officers and seamen plunged into the water with me. Anderson had reached the starboard railing a little to the right of me when the cruiser was hurled over. I heard him shout to an officer as I slid into the sea. I never saw him again.

I could not swim and was fearful lest the pressure of a deep submersion might collapse the old lifebelt which I had retrieved after the bombing of the *Illustrious,* just one year ago today (January 10). As I slipped under the water, the cruiser disappeared with a tremendous suction, leaving a huge lake of oil on the sea. There was one muffled blast as she took her death plunge.

I swallowed large quantities of oily scum and water before I bobbed to the surface. The water all around was dotted with the heads of hundreds of sailors. Several sailors had succeeded in getting off a small motorboat. Trying to splash toward it, I went under again. My lungs felt as if they were bursting, but I came up and a sailor helped me aboard the boat.

But a score of others had the same idea. The boat's stern section rapidly filled with water as the weight of more and more men pushed it down. Finally the motorboat tipped over, hurling us all back into the sea. I managed to reach the boat and pulled myself into the front cockpit again. Then the boat sank.

With a lone sailor, I hung to the very tip of the bow until it slipped beneath the waves. I even hung on until it pulled me under and I got another large dose of oil and water. From beneath the waves a pair of hands reached up and pawed at my shoulders, then slipped away. I collided with a small floating spar. I succeeded in tucking it under my left arm, still carefully holding up the lifebelt with my right.

I joined with scores of others in crying for help, hoping in the pitch darkness to attract the attention of the destroyers. No one had a flashlight, so it was difficult for the rescue ships to find us. At that moment I saw a huge black silhouette of a destroyer about seventy-five yards ahead.

"Help, I'm drowning!" gasped a sailor near me.

"Keep going," I called weakly. "Look, there's a boat ahead."

He swam toward the destroyer. I tried to, but couldn't get closer. The waves seemed to carry me farther away as I screamed for help. A big wave swamped me again with a mouthful of oil. Then, as if miraculously, another wave pushed me almost under the propellers of the destroyer *Griffin*. I called for help until my throat felt burned out. Suddenly a long, oily rope was flung over the side. I grasped it, but there was no strength left in my hands.

"Hang on!" an officer on the ship shouted. "We'll pull you up."

"Can't," I called as the rope slipped from my fingers.

"Try to get a little forward," the officer shouted. "We are putting over a rope ladder."

Somehow I managed to reach the ladder, but so spent that I couldn't pull myself up. At that moment a life raft drifted against the destroyer's side. It banged my head against the warship and I cried out time and again: "Stop it! You're killing me!"

Sailors on the raft grasped the rope ladder and clambered safely up while I fought desperately to keep from drowning. Several stepped on my head, pushing me down into the water. Only half conscious, I hooked my right arm through one rung of the ladder and again called for help.

A young British sailor aboard the raft saved my life. He passed a thick, heavy rope under my arms, tied it, and flung the end to the quarter-deck. Three sailors slowly pulled me out of the oily mass and flopped me on the deck like a limp fish, completely covered with scum.

"This fellow's an American," I dimly heard someone say as they read the words, "American naval correspondent" on the sleeve of my coat while pressing the water from my lungs.

They cut off all my clothes and carried me to the mess deck below, where nearly 100 other survivors were getting medical attention. The ship's doctor gave me a countershock injection and for the next ten hours, while the Navy searched the sea for the submarine which torpedoed the *Galatea*, I lay on a mass of greasy rags and oil-soaked clothes. I recuperated in a hospital.

2

ON the day after the arrival of Allen's story, came new word from the Far East. Japan was staging still another conquest. She moved on the Netherlands East Indies. The vast region covered 790,000 square miles, with 70,000,000 inhabitants. The fertile territory stretched 3,000 miles across the southern end of the China Sea. The naval gates to Singapore were at one end and Australia at the other.

Japan's big objectives were oil, rubber, tin, coal, and iron. World markets were closed to her. The Dutch East Indies and Malaya had what she needed—including tea, coffee, tobacco, rice, beans, and other foods.

The U. S. Pacific Fleet was having a tough time finding the Jap Navy.

The Nazis torpedoed an American ship off the Atlantic coast. It marked the start of an Axis submarine offensive in U. S. waters. On January 16, a War Production Board was formed under Donald M. Nelson. The Battle of Bataan raged. MacArthur and his forces were encircled in southern Luzon. They had to withdraw toward Corregidor Fortress. Japanese dive-bombers, artillery, and shock troops pounded. Death was threatened to all foes in Manila. Clark Lee remained with the U. S. forces. He wrote plenty about death and destruction. He also wrote about MacArthur and his men:

With shot and shell, but also with song, the fighting Yanks of Bataan Peninsula sound their defiance to the attacking Japanese.

To a variety of tunes the soldiers are singing a poem entitled "Dive Low, Dive-Bombers," written by Corporal Dumot F. Wade, who comes from Coronado, Cal.

Wade is one of the men in a crack anti-aircraft unit I saw in action two days ago and his poem tells the story of the spirit of these warriors:

DIVE LOW, DIVE BOMBERS

I looked straight up and what did I see?
Six dive-bombers diving at me!
If my eyes listened to my feet
My eyes would still be running—in retreat.

But I lit the fuse on a three-inch shell,
And our guns were quickly giving them hell.
Six silver planes came sailing by,
And we blasted two right out of the sky.

This is our warning to the Rising Sun:
It won't be long till we have the war won.
Dive low, dive-bombers, and give us a chance:
Dive low, dive-bombers, in your dying dance.

Here are other notes in a war correspondent's notebook:

A Sunday morning snapshot: A tin-hatted private of the hard-boiled Fourth Marines leaning his head against a machine-gun barrel and carefully reading the Bible.

The ground forces on Bataan Peninsula are composed of thousands of soldiers whose name is Joe. That's because the Americans call the Filipinos "Joe"—and the Filipinos respond in kind by calling all the Americans "Joe."

Many meals start with quinine. That's to combat the malarial mosquitoes infesting the midlands.

The Bataan Peninsula, in which the American and Filipino forces and the Japanese armies have settled down to positional warfare, is a sparsely settled, little-cultivated region of fantastically shaped trees and nearly impenetrable jungle undergrowth. Many of the trees are thirty to fifty feet in circumference and, though they tower 300 feet, there is foliage only near the top. Parasitic creepers as thick as a man's body extend from the ground to the foliage. Soldiers of both sides climb the vines and hide in the treetops for sniping and observation.

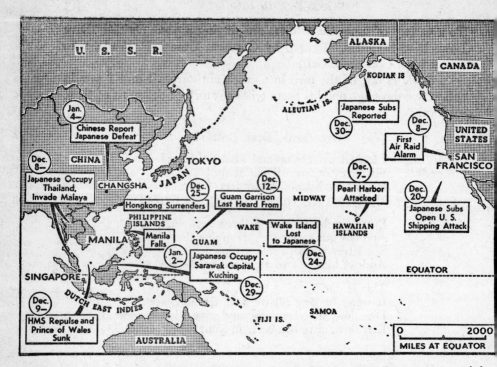

Map 17—The Japanese tide was rolling high a month after Pearl Harbor. Hong Kong was gone and the U. S. counted as lost Guam, Wake, and Manila, capital of the Philippines.

314

U. S. airmen on Bataan called the Japanese the "Nips," the "Japanzers," "Mr. Moto," and "Charlie." They referred to Emperor Hirohito as "Jeeps the Jap." On January 22, Clark Lee again reported from his assignment "With the U. S. Forces at Bataan":

American troops fought their third large-scale ground engagement of the war early today, turning back a strong Japanese night attack with heavy losses to the enemy. At dawn I saw the ground in front of American barbed wire covered with dead and wounded Japanese, while the American lines remained intact.

In one attack seventeen dive-bombers simultaneously swarmed down on us. It came at 3 A.M. when Japanese, estimated at not less than 1,000, who had crept through the underbrush toward the American protective wire, opened fire with rifles, submachine guns and grenades, supplemented by the usual tossing of firecrackers.

American light and heavy artillery replied immediately, plastering no man's land with shells, while infantrymen jumped to their firing positions manning machine guns and rifles. The defenders located the advancing enemy by tracer bullets and by the light of exploding shells. Only a handful of Japanese penetrated as far as the American positions, where they were quickly disposed of.

As the front quieted down, except for occasional American artillery fire, the officer commanding this sector of General Mac-Arthur's defense described the current fighting as "a combination of the positional fighting of the World War and old-time American-Indian warfare. There are occasional frontal attacks along definite lines, supplemented by infiltration of snipers."

Day after day, the Japanese are trying every form of trickery, but the Americans refuse to be fooled. Take, for example, the Jap attempt to pass American sentries by dressing soldiers in American or Filipino uniforms. The Americans discovered an infallible way to detect them, due to the inability of the Japanese to pronounce the letter L, which they say as R. They simply pick a password with numerous L's such Lollapalooza. Sentries challenge approaching figures and if the first two syllables of lollapalooza, for instance, should come back as "rorra" they open fire without waiting to hear the remainder.

The Japanese also have resorted to one of the oldest tricks of Oriental warfare—the setting off of firecrackers throughout the night along the front. The idea is to frighten and confuse the enemy

—but the Americans and Filipinos have refused either to be frightened or confused.

3

THE JAPANESE invasion of the Netherlands East Indies had begun on January 11. Some of the details were out. But one of the most dramatic incidents did not reach its climax for several days. Here is what happened: That night of January 11 a Dutch submarine had her periscope trained on four Jap troopships in the Gulf of Siam. Immediately upon receipt of word that the war had started, the submarine fired her torpedoes. The four ships went to the bottom. About 4,000 Japs were aboard. A little later the submarine struck a mine. She sank. Only one member of the crew survived. He was quartermaster C. de Wolf. He told the story:

It's still hard to believe that I survived that experience in which all my mates lost their lives. The night it happened we were cruising on the surface to investigate a light on the horizon. There were six of us in the conning tower, our captain, myself, and four other officers.

Suddenly a blast seemed to lift the sub and all six of us were hurled into the water. Stunned but uninjured, I began to swim around looking for the others. The captain had vanished, but the other four officers were still with me and able to swim. We started swimming according to emergency directions we had received from our captain.

All of us were driven on by the frightening knowledge that the water was infested by sharks. We rid ourselves of clothes. After twelve hours, three of the men sank below the waves. The other officer and I could give them no assistance because we ourselves were desperately tired. A few hours later, he too was swallowed up by the sea.

I had now been in the water eighteen hours and no land was in sight. My arms ached and I was desperately drowsy, but somehow —one can't explain such things—I kept going. I swam throughout the night and the next day. Apparently the sharks were busy elsewhere. Finally, I saw land. As I got close to the shore—my strength was practically gone—a wave threw me onto the rocky beach, cutting me in the back. I had been in the water thirty-five hours as far as I could figure.

For several hours I must have lain half-conscious, but eventually I was able to stumble forward. After much painful walking, I sighted a number of natives. They gave me an old shirt to wear and led me to a native proa—canoe. The owner of this fragile craft took me to a small settlement, but the end of my trouble was still far away.

After getting something to eat, I felt a little stronger and asked some natives to take me to a European settlement. They consented and we started afoot. I had no shoes and soon my feet began to bleed so badly that I had to sit down every few steps.

We finally reached a small clearing in the jungle where I lay down for about half an hour. I apparently dozed off because when I struggled to my feet I was astonished to see that my guides made no effort to get up with me. They sat motionless, with expressionless faces. One of them jerked his thumb over his shoulder and I was startled to see the gleaming barrel of a gun and its bayonet pointing straight at me from out of the jungle wall. Fortunately the man holding the gun was an Australian. Semiconscious, I was transported from there to a Singapore hospital.

But Jap submarines also had been busy those first days of the Netherlands war. They were in the Straits of Malacca, along the Malaya Peninsula. The object was to cut the British supply line between Singapore and India. Apparently they were succeeding. They were also in the Indian Ocean where they were attacking British shipping which was being forced to take a roundabout but less exposed route west of Sumatra. This time the report of what happened came from Frank Noel, who was covering the war by camera. He was a native of Dalhart, Indiana, and was aboard an Allied ship. The date was January 14, but much happened to him before his story came through from Padang, Sumatra:

Suffering from thirst and the blistering of a tropical sun, twenty-eight of us out of a ship's company of seventy-seven, have arrived here after a Japanese submarine sank our India-bound ship and spilled us into the sea five days ago.

Our ship apparently was the first victim of Japanese submarines operating in the Indian Ocean. She was attacked by torpedo and shellfire about midnight January 14 some 270 miles off the west coast of this Dutch Indies Island. The shelling finished off an attack begun when a torpedo scored a direct hit on the vessel's engine room, killing five and injuring four of the crew.

Although I suffered leg injuries, I got overside in a lifeboat with some of my photographic equipment—most of it and all my personal belongings are at the bottom of the sea. The submarine cruised on the surface for half an hour within 100 yards of our four lifeboats, but made no attempt to shell or machine-gun us. Then it fired five shells into the crippled ship and she sank by the stern.

Two of the lifeboats reached shore in the Batoe Island group, off the Sumatran coast north of here, yesterday. The others have not been sighted yet, but are believed to be in the Siberut Island area off the coast. For the first two days all four boats had remained within hailing distance of each other, but high winds and a rough sea separated them. The sun broiled us and we suffered from thirst. It's good to have my feet on solid ground again, but I wish I had all of that equipment that is now at the bottom of the Indian Ocean.

4

A 500-MILE British penetration into Libya was checked by Axis forces under General Rommel. In Rio de Janeiro, a Pan-American conference of twenty-one Western Hemisphere nations lined up against the Axis on January 21. The agreement came after Argentina and Chile agreed to break off diplomatic relations with Germany, Italy, and Japan. Foreign Minister Aranha of Brazil said: "America is for Americans and must be defended." A Cuban delegate replied: "No, señor, America is not for Americans; America is for humanity." Thirty-five Jap ships were reported sunk or damaged in a four-day naval battle in Macassar Straits.

On January 26 the first of a 1942 American Expeditionary Force landed in Northern Ireland—without fanfare. Perhaps it was one of the things Roosevelt and Churchill had discussed earlier in the month. First public intimation that an A.E.F. had been sent across the Atlantic came with release of the story. Rice Yahner had followed the Army from camp to camp in this country. He also made the crossing to Ireland. His story said:

Several thousand steel-helmeted Yanks—"All pepped up and rarin' to go"—landed here safely today as the vanguard of U. S. troops dispatched to Europe in the second World War.

Escorted by the U. S. and British Navies, their commander, Major General Russell P. Hartle, stepped ashore to the strains of "The Star-Spangled Banner" and waves of cheers from those lining the dock. After the general, came First-Class Private Milburn Henke, of Hutchinson, Minnesota, whose German-born father's parting words were: "Give 'em hell." Most of the huskies were from the Midwest, seasoned regulars and drafted men. Women nurses also were in the convoy.

The American troops marched down the gangplank and formed ranks under the stock-taking gaze of British, Irish, and American officials.

"Your safe arrival marks a new stage in the World War, and a gloomy portent for Hitler," said Sir Archibald Sinclair, British air minister, who welcomed them. "Your welcome arrival here today reveals part of one great plan to smash the dictator powers wherever they may be found. Its significance will not be lost on General Tojo."

General Hartle said: "It's a pleasure to be here."

5

ON JANUARY 30, Roosevelt observed his sixtieth birthday; Hitler celebrated the ninth anniversary of his accession to power.

Hell had broken loose at Singapore. The Japs were set on quick domination. The British had sent troops—but not enough. Day after day, Jap bombers swarmed over Burma, Malaya, Singapore. They scored direct hits. Buddhist monasteries were destroyed. Civilians were killed. The suicidal Nipponese roared across Johore State, defying death with abandon in a quick attempt to overrun Singapore.

No one could say how many were killed. No one could break through British censorship sufficiently to get out the whole truth. In face of overpowering opposition, Britain preferred to say that its position was "developing favorably." But this struggle for control of Malaya was a hell of certain death—no question about it. Jap landing parties infested a thirty-mile western coastal belt. They swarmed ashore in barges and small boats. They were machine-gunned and bombed. Still they came, like thousands of ants piling over each other into a molasses pot.

They were only sixty miles from Singapore. Forty miles. . . . Twenty miles. . . . Ten miles. . . . And then—February 9—the Japs were at Singapore.

C. Yates McDaniel had been the first correspondent to reach

Singapore a year before. He had followed the British and Australian defenders. He had led a dangerous life behind the retreating front lines. He had lain flat to escape machine-gunning. His auto had been bombed minutes after he took refuge in the doorway of a burning building. By February 9, he was the only correspondent left. Singapore was about to fall. That night the Japs began their siege. It continued into the next day. McDaniel reported:

From dawn to dusk the Japanese invaders, greatly strengthened by new landings from across Johore Strait, beat with rising fury today at the British defenders, who are falling back from the outer ring of Singapore's defenses under merciless enemy assaults by air and land.

In their hours of near-disaster Imperial forces fought bitterly and stubbornly, making the invaders pay dearly for every inch of ground. Anti-aircraft batteries manned their guns unflinchingly, but still the swarms of heavy bombers and dive-bombers came.

Sir Shenton Thomas, Singapore's governor, declared: "We are all in the hands of God, from whom we can get comfort in our anxieties and strength to play the man and help one another in all the ordeals that are to come."

The enemy's troops were believed to be 100,000 strong on the island itself and immediately across the Strait, and with his overwhelming air superiority he was steadily extending the area of his conquest.

During the early morning hours fires glowed along the northern island, and later in the day gray clouds and black pillars of smoke obscured the forward battle areas. The enemy's landings were made in steel vessels. At one point they were only five miles from the city. The outnumbered Imperial forces—British, Australian, Indian— were making a great and gallant stand, but although they were cutting the invaders down in enormous numbers, the pressure never slackened.

I looked down on Singapore in the late afternoon and saw a scene of striking contrasts. To the north, columns of black smoke billowed skyward from burning oil tanks, providing a somber backdrop for the stage on which the grim drama is reaching its climax. The opposing guns ceased their pounding for a moment, but Japanese dive-bombers darting in and out of the drifting clouds of smoke, were delivering their last loads of the day before darkness called them back to their bases. Near the center of the stage, clouds of light-gray smoke arose from rubber plants, pineapple canneries and factories to which the owners had applied the torch to prevent the enemy from using them.

To the south was an unnatural calm. In the distance, wisps of smoke spiraled slowly over fishing villages on the small Netherlands Indies Islands that dot the straits between Malaya and Sumatra. Inside Singapore Harbor, steamers, Chinese junks, Malay fishing craft, and sampans rode at anchor, just as they had when I first looked over the water front a year ago.

Along main roads in the foreground, motor cars, trolleys, and rickshaws were carrying people home after the day's work. In front of the famous Raffles Hotel cars were depositing patrons of the daily tea dance, and outside a movie house people were queueing up in front of the box office to see Joel McCrea and Ellen Drew in *Reaching for the Sun*.

One touch of unreality was provided by a letter that Eric Davis, director of the Malayan Broadcasting Corporation, received from a gramophone corporation. It informed him that "Record No. DB is unavailable for broadcast without special permission of Messrs. Walt Disney, Mickey Mouse, Incorporated."

6

THE *Normandie* was ravaged by fire at her New York pier while she was being converted into a troop ship. Hundreds of workmen were aboard. As firemen poured tons of water into her flaming hold, the giant ship turned on her side like a dying leviathan. Before the fire was out, stunned Americans would have given odds that it was sabotage. They never changed their opinion.

Then, on the morning of February 11, an unusual dispatch arrived in New York. It was from Singapore. Its first words seemed strange. They said: "Definitely last." Correspondents normally did not send such slugs with their stories. They usually expected to follow one dispatch with another. But this one was different. The dispatch was from McDaniel. It read almost like a letter:

The sky over Singapore is black with the smoke of a dozen huge fires this morning as I write my last message from this once beautiful, prosperous, and peaceful city.

The roar and crash of cannonade and bursting bombs, shaking my typewriter and my hands, which are wet with nervous perspiration, tell me without need of an official communiqué that the war that started nine weeks ago 400 miles away is in the outskirts of this shaken bastion of Empire.

I am sure there is a bright tropic sun shining somewhere overhead, but in my many-windowed room it is too dark to work without electric lights.

Over the low rise where the battle is raging I can see relay after relay of Japanese planes circling, then going into murderous dives on our soldiers who are fighting back in a hell over which there is no protective screen of our own fighters. But the Japanese are not completely alone in the skies this morning, for I just saw two "wild beasts"—obsolete biplanes with an operating speed of about 100 miles an hour—fly low over the Japanese positions and unload bomb burdens with a resounding crash. British fighter pilots were still taking on the enemy against overwhelming odds.

It makes me ashamed of myself, sitting here with my heart beating faster than their old motors, when I think what chance those lads have of getting back in their antiquated machines. If ever brave men earned undying glory, those R.A.F. pilots have done so this tragic morning.

There are many other brave men in Singapore today. Not far away are anti-aircraft batteries in open spaces—they must be to have a clear field of fire.

Please overlook the break in continuity, but a packet of bombs just landed so close I had to drop to the floor to avoid the blast.

But those gun crews keep on fighting, their batteries peppering smoke into the sky every time Japanese planes come near—that is almost constantly.

The all-clear has just sounded—what a joke!

From the window I can see three Japanese planes flying low not a mile away.

A few minutes ago I heard a tragic two-way telephone conversation.

Eric Davis, director of the Malayan Broadcasting Corporation, asked Governor Sir Shenton Thomas for permission to destroy the outlying broadcasting station. The governor demurred saying the situation was not too bad, and refused to issue a direct order. Davis telephoned the station in question, instructing the staff to keep on the air but to stand by for urgent orders. We tuned in on its wave length. In the middle of a broadcast in Malayan, urging the people of Singapore to stand firm, the station went dead.

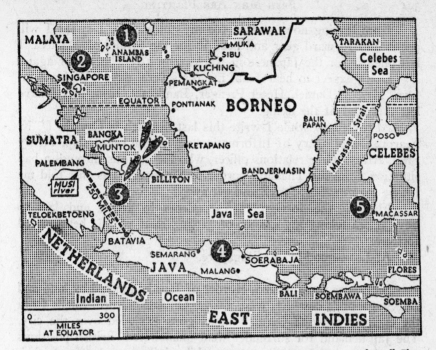

Map 18—Singapore's fall (2) was announced February 15, 1942. Nor was that all. The Dutch acknowledged Japanese occupation of Anambas Island (1), the invaders were trying to gain a foothold around (3), and Tokyo said its forces had landed in Java (4). Meanwhile, American bombers had struck at enemy shipping near Macassar (5).

I am leaving now, and as for my automobile, I swear I will put it into forward gear and head it for the Straits of Malacca. I left one car for the Japanese in Nanking in 1937, but never again.

Don't expect to hear from me for several days but please inform Mrs. McDaniel, Hotel Preager, Bandoeng, Java, that I have left this land of the dying.

At my elbow while I write this last dispatch is Captain D. K. Fearon, the Ministry of Information adviser on censorship. Henry Steel, Army public relations officer, who has seen us through a bad situation from the Thailand border to Singapore, has just told me I have ten minutes to pack and get away.

First of the foreign correspondents to arrive and last to leave, I am taking my chance of getting clear of this beleaguered fortress.

And so—good-bye to Singapore.

Singapore was doomed. Hordes of Japs hammered by land and air. Singapore's outskirts were ablaze. Oil fires burned. Shells from the enemy's 5.9-inch German-model guns exploded over the city. The Jap demand for surrender went unanswered. British positions continued to bombard the enemy while civilians and officials fled. The Ministry of Information and the staff of the Malayan Broadcasting Corporation left by boat while bombs fell into the harbor.

McDaniel boarded an overloaded harbor vessel after writing that "last" dispatch. The best he could get was deck space among the terrified passengers. But the little steamer was unable to get under way. She remained there throughout that first day and the next. McDaniel sent one more dispatch the next afternoon. It said:

"Lying offshore, we were bombed incessantly until sundown yesterday and throughout today. We were dive-bombed half-a-dozen times, but we are still afloat and may get away tonight."

Then nothing more was heard from Singapore.

CHAPTER 18

The Heroes of Bataan

February 14–March 24, 1942

I

WHILE Singapore was choking under the grip of the Japanese, one phase of the war in the Far East was at its height. Even before Pearl Harbor, a group of volunteer American and British fliers were fighting for China along the Burma Road. They operated from an advanced Burmese base. Their project was to keep Burma Road open so that supplies could flow to the Chinese.

Daniel De Luce, who had had war assignments all the way from London to Turkey and Greece, was with them. He rode in one of the bombers on a two-hour raid on the Japanese at Moulmein and Martaban. He sent the first eyewitness account of action over the Burmese jungle:

Young bomber crews and fighter pilots from the British Empire and the U. S. have been sent into action together as aerial artillery and cavalry with wings to help hold the jungle front where the spectacular battle for Burma is under way. I rode with them today in a Blenheim bomber and witnessed a typical daylight attack, escorted by British Hurricanes and American Tomahawks.

This morning this same squadron attacked the Japanese headquarters at Paan on the bank of the Salween river north of Moulmein and Martaban, starting three fires.

This afternoon it was expected that Paan would be raided again, but just before the squadron took off from the shimmering heat and dust of a converted Burmese paddy field, instructions came to relieve Japanese pressure farther down the river. We were not informed of the reason, but I could guess. Eleven days ago I had squatted near Dogra Indian machine gunners who were staving off persistent Japanese attempts to ferry troops from Moulmein across the broad lower reaches of the Salween to Martaban.

Now I am right behind the elbow of the South African captain-pilot, who bears a boyish resemblance to Doctor Dafoe of Dionne quintuplets fame. The Blenheim, paint peeling from its radial engine cowling and propeller shaft, dark with rust like a tramp steamer, bumps thrice and then shoots upward into the climb while the motor four feet from my right ear creates a blizzard of sound. We are in shirt sleeves and khaki shorts, and the sweat trickles down our necks and under our leather helmets.

Our flying escort appears—six Tomahawks with the white-spiked sun of the Chinese air force on their wings, keeping V formation, and passing about 200 feet over us—on time to a second for the rendezvous. I am not sure which of the American volunteers are up this afternoon, but they probably include Squadron Leader Bob Neale, of Seattle; Gil Bright, of Reading, Pennsylvania; H. M. Geselbracht, of Glendale, California, and Bob Little of Spokane.

Soon we are over Moulmein proper, cruising slowly and methodically, with public buildings, squares, churches, and temples about a quarter mile below—so near we can pick out the broken windows and the empty carts at the curbs. There is not a sign of life—not even a stray dog.

The river jetties·are almost deserted. Only three craft of rowboat size are tied up there. The enemy is known to have plenty of machine guns here and our Blenheim isn't too difficult a target from the warehouse roofs.

Suddenly there is a thudding noise like someone kicking the bottom of the fuselage. We peel off to the left in a dive that makes me gasp as one does on the first drop of a roller coaster. We commence to strafe. The pilot saw them all the time, but I had been too busy rubbernecking at the town to notice four broad-beamed boats lying in an estuary inlet, waiting possibly to take another force of enemy infantry to the far (Martaban) shore. They had fired on us.

We are diving head on. Faint red flames hit the water and then rise up the side on one of the boats. Our bullets are scoring as the pilot lifts the Blenheim's nose. Then he banks, and the rear gunner unlooses his turret guns. There is another roller-coaster drop. Tiny balls of fire strike another motionless schooner. We are hardly aware now that the enemy is firing back from the ground. Even tracer bullets are hard to see in the daylight.

We zigzag down the estuary, almost level with its banks. From the cockpit blister, I look back at Moulmein where a block-wide cloud of yellow smoke is rising to the right and a whitish cloud to the left, where a factory is located. Spurts of flame are discernible.

On the Martaban shore, dark-clad figures race for cover. We skim over the pancakelike mud. Now, if ever, is the opportunity for fighters to catch us. But we are still covered by Hurricanes and Tomahawks.

We are homeward bound, flying into the sun with another chapter of death in the afternoon completed for the Blenheim's logbook. The observer turns his head toward the pilot and grins.

2

THROUGH the murk of the English Channel the long-refuged German battleships *Scharnhorst, Prinz Eugen,* and *Gneisenau* slipped out of Nazi-occupied Brest. They were getting away from the constant threat of British bombers to reach a safe Nazi base. The R.A.F. and the British Navy engaged them in the greatest battle off the Dover coast since the fall of France. Even British shore guns opened up. But the mighty German ships got away.

MacArthur was holding out on Bataan. Against overwhelming odds, his men fought on. They hoped for reinforcements. They heard of Washington's plan for thousands of planes in 1943. One soldier expressed the mass opinion: "Sixty thousand planes in 1943? We don't want 60,000 then; just give us any number from six to sixty—now! Then you'll see fireworks on Bataan."

But the bombing of Bataan continued. Jap snipers strapped themselves in tall trees and took pot shots. Infiltration of Nipponese gunners and fifth columnists did their dirty work. Bataan needed men and supplies. Clark Lee tried a little different reportorial technique on February 15:

Dear Boss: Please hire Johnny Weismuller for this assignment. I am getting too old to play Tarzan.

Time Magazine's correspondent Mel Jacoby and I were sitting on Corregidor dock this afternoon waiting to ride in one of the inshore naval patrol boats commanded by Lieutenant Ted Raymond of Amesbury, Massachusetts. I was perched atop a piling, swinging my feet and trying to chew a mule steak sandwich. It was a nice calm afternoon. We were enjoying the sunshine and kidding a sailor who had tried to jump from the dock to a boat at least fifty feet away during a recent attack. He was so excited, he took off without considering the distance.

All of us reporters have had plenty of excitement in this war. We've dodged shells, developed the knack of diving gracefully into foxholes, tramped over mountains, ridden tanks, climbed trees, bounced over the ocean in tiny patrol boats, and inhaled tons of dust. We've buried our noses in concrete trenches during bombings, have been scared stiff a dozen times a week.

This afternoon, Jacoby and I were setting out to see some more Bataan fighting. But before we could get to the war, it sneaked up on us. There was a distant thump of cannon, a scream of descending shells, and nearby bursts shattering the peaceful afternoon. Then I wasn't on the piling any more, but in the water of Manila Bay, twenty feet below. So was Coxswain Harold Hershberger, Brooklyn, who had been standing next to me. Jacoby and others on the dock dived under a flat car and made their way to a nearby bombproof shelter.

Swimming with tin hat, canteen, army shoes, and camera isn't so difficult when you have falling shells to urge you on. Hershberger and I figured that the Japanese artillery on the south shore of Manila Bay was concentrating on the Corregidor dock area. The next shell confirmed our guess, so we paddled further under the pier and clung to the concrete pilings. A number of high-explosive shells hit the pier above our heads. Then the Japanese gradually lifted their range. Most shells fell harmlessly into the water throwing up thirty-foot columns of spray fringed with smaller sprays from shrapnel.

When the Jap guns shifted to other targets, we swam around to the other side of the pier. Then we climbed over barbed wire and made our way to a place of safety by easy stages. We hit the dirt when shells came near, but neither of us was hurt except for scratches and small cuts.

The trouble with this war is that it's all front and no rear. Here we are surrounded and the boys have to fight with what was here before war began and eat what already was stored here.

P. S.—If Weismuller is not available, how about sending Superman together with a few planes, ships, and soldiers?

Clark Lee wrote lightly to break the strain of the constant terror that stalked Bataan. MacArthur's men joked and fought and hoped and died.

3

Singapore formally surrendered on February 15. After 123 years, Britain had lost her stronghold in South Asia. McDaniel had been the last correspondent to leave. When last heard from, he was trying to get away aboard a small steamer in Singapore Harbor. He turned up in Batavia on February 20. He had been missing for a week. He told what had happened to Singapore—and to himself:

Seven and a half days after we left Singapore's flaming waterfront, we—fifty-five men and a plucky Chinese girl—reached safety at Batavia.

I escaped from doomed Singapore, February 13, aboard the last vessel to leave the battered and burning fortress, and reached Batavia during an air raid alarm this morning. In my seven-and-one-half day journey I abandoned a bombed ship, was cast up on an uninhabited island, made my way through a storm in a small launch to Sumatra, crossed that island's mountain wilds by truck, rail, pony cart, and completed 1,200 roundabout miles safely through the Indian Ocean aboard a destroyer.

From the salt-water-soaked pulp that is left of my journal, I shall attempt to piece together my story, which, in a larger sense, is the story of the last days of Singapore—of the few who succeeded in escaping and the many more who failed.

Early on the morning we left, we were looking at the peaceful scene of little islands when two Japanese light bombers circled and glided toward us. The old ship shuddered when the bombs exploded, just astern. A few minutes later two more planes came over, at not more than 500 feet. This time they didn't miss. The decks seemed to bounce up to meet us as we flopped on our faces. I found a gaping hole through the forward hold. Ten minutes later there was another ear-splitting crash, followed by the hiss of escaping steam. The ship listed and began settling. The engineer emerged from the boiler room and assured us that the boilers wouldn't explode, because he had opened the valves.

The officers gave no order to abandon ship, but within ten minutes a lifeboat was lowered. Before it hit the water fifteen sailors tumbled in and pulled away, too terrified to heed the officers' shouts to come back.

After having looked over the damage, the captain ordered the other two lifeboats overside. Miss Lim, the only woman passenger, got into one. Some of us remained on board, hoping that at least one of the leaky boats would reach the nearest islands, five miles away, and return before we had to swim for it. The captain said he believed that we might have another two hours, but the fire in the coal bunker was spreading and the list was getting worse.

Propped against a coil of rope, I tried to continue my journal, but I was forced to drop the job twice to answer the call of "All hands to fight fire."

We got the fire under control, but Japanese planes came over again and again. One was so low that I saw a bomb swinging on the wing rack; but the pilot didn't drop it. I helped to hoist the life rafts overboard, but the rotten bamboo lashings broke and the rusty tanks sank.

We were about ready to swim for it when one of our lifeboats returned. Thirty-six of us, including the captain and all but one officer, climbed in. Six men volunteered to remain aboard to wait for the next trip, as our boat was leaking badly and we were crammed in like sardines. After an hour of bailing, rowing and sailing, we touched on a coral reef. We waded ashore on the little island of Bangka. Japanese planes knew exactly where we were, and we knew there was little hope of our being rescued. Wet sand, mosquitoes and ants didn't help our situation.

Early February 14, as we were breakfasting on a cigarette, a tin of muddy water—which neither tasted nor smelled like tea—and one small biscuit, the lookout reported launches approaching our ship, which was barely afloat. Some were sure that it was a rescue party, but Captain Henry Steele, formerly attached to the public relations office at Singapore, and I, feared that it was a Japanese patrol. Our skipper said he would surrender if it was the enemy. Steele and I, in a quick huddle, decided that we'd make a break for the jungle in the center of the island. We weren't going to get caught by the Japanese after all we'd been through. But the launches belonged to a rubber planter on a nearby island, who said he would try to rescue us at nightfall. Our hopes were dimmed soon afterward as Japanese planes appeared and flew up and down the beach. They circled away; then we heard bombs exploding. They then circled over us again, and there were more bombs. This process continued for two hours. We were not the targets, but two ships that were sheltering at an island near us were. Toward noon a formation of seven bombers circled over our stricken ship. We saw two bursts forward. The old pride of the Yangtze reared by the stern. Our captain turned away and took off his cap. It was the first and only emotion he displayed.

Our first officer and the doctor put out in a launch to see whether the other ships needed help. We waited, knowing that if we didn't get away that night we probably never would, for we could hear planes over the area. After sundown, the first officer reported that he had taken six badly wounded women from the ships, on which casualties were heavy. All hands were ordered to the beach. We waited an hour, knee-deep in water, while the officers decided on how to get us out to the launches, for the tide was out and even our lifeboats could not approach within a half-mile. Finally we were ordered to make our way as best we could, and the next forty-five minutes were the worst I ever experienced. I clambered over coral rocks and slipped into holes. All around, men were pushing ahead through the darkness, swearing each time they fell and shouting in an effort to keep together. Then I plunged off a rock into the water.

I carried on, swimming, until I was hoisted into a lifeboat full of exhausted men. Somehow, with one oar and with everyone shouting orders, we managed to reach the launch.

Fifty-five men and the one Chinese girl, exhausted and soaked, their legs bleeding from coral cuts, boarded a launch that should have carried only fifteen. Others gave up and turned back to the island to wait until we could send help.

If the night on the island had been miserable, the one aboard the launch was indescribable. Waves rolled over the deck where we were sprawled, wet and shivering; but we were still hoping to make Sumatra before dawn brought Japanese bombers. Behind us chugged a smaller launch, on which our skipper and doctor were working over the wounded men. Daybreak found us approaching the mouth of a river, up which we worked until late afternoon. No one was quite certain where we were, except somewhere in Sumatra.

Late that afternoon we got a big thrill when, rounding a bend, we saw the White Ensign (the British naval flag) flying over warships anchored at a wharf. Ashore, we found members of the Malayan command staff. We had seen them last in Singapore three days before. They had left ahead of us and had got through un-scathed.

Early the morning of February 16 we resumed our slow jour-ney upriver. By noon we had reached the motor roadhead, hungry and cramped. But we soon were cheered by the warm hospitality of the Netherland military and civilians, who fed us and provided a truck for the 400-mile drive across Sumatra.

I sat all night beside the driver, talking and giving him ciga-rettes to keep him awake, while the rest of our party slept. Every few miles local guards halted us, but courteously waved us on. They were taking no chances on a surprise approach by an enemy patrol. Dawn found us on top a volcanic range that forms the backbone of Sumatra. Monkeys in nearby trees howled their morning hymn to the sun. One official en route had tried to halt us for fear our truck would break down and we would fall prey to tigers; but only one black panther and one civet cat crossed the road, and the truck didn't break down.

At midafternoon we reached the northwest of Sumatra. The hotels were full of refugees from Malaya and the south of Su-matra, but a good Netherlands lady took us in and gave us food. Officials held little hope of our getting out, but the next morning came news that there was a slim chance of leaving by warship if we pushed immediately on. No taxi was available, so we hired pony carts and drove to the railway station during a beating of tom-toms used to sound air raid alarms. Half an hour later we arrived at the port. Effects of a bombing were visible everywhere. Later in the afternoon we saw the most beautiful sight I expect ever to see—a British destroyer, hull down on the horizon steaming full speed toward the harbor.

4

A GREAT naval battle began off Java on February 27. It lasted four days. The U. S. cruiser *Houston* and the destroyer *Pope* were sunk. So were other Allied ships. The Japs lost eight, sunk or dam-aged. The War Production Board decreed cuffless trousers and no two-pants suits. The Allies, more and more, were being referred to as the "United Nations." There was no slackening of the Japa-nese pace. While the battle off Java proceeded, Daniel De Luce was an eyewitness to what was happening in Burma. He filed his dis-patch from Toungoo:

Sitting on the stone rail of a tiny Buddhist pagoda in the center of burning Toungoo, I am writing this by the light of flames devouring eight blocks of Burmese stores and homes.

An Indian soldier, standing guard against looters with a rifle slung over his shoulder, tells me that 350 Burmese and 40 Indian civilians, including a railroad stationmaster, were killed in the raid.

The raiders encountered no fighter opposition when they came over the city and swooped low in a cloudless sky to bomb at will. But as they arrived, they found big, ten-wheel American trucks a mass of ruins. Chinese drivers had soaked them with gasoline and set them afire rather than permit them to fall into Jap hands. Vehicles worth at least $450,000 must have suffered this fate.

The damage here is a fiery climax to the total air war which the Japanese have visited upon the main Burmese road to China between Rangoon and Mandalay. At the old fortress of Mandalay, King Thibaw's red and gold wooden palace stands in grounds pitted by bombs. Pyanmana, to the south, has become a ghostlike tomb since enemy planes wrecked the railroad station and the bazaar. Two hundred were killed in that assault. At another point a little wayside shop was razed and nineteen persons killed.

Along the route from Rangoon to Mandalay I encountered a sight as pathetic as anything I witnessed in Europe. Thousands of Indian peasants, an oxcart migration, were escaping the Pegu district. With pleading, upturned faces and dark hands uplifted in a gesture of prayer, they told me about the bandits who had robbed and killed them along the way. For more than a mile this swarming, dusty caravan of refugees—wooden axles screeching, babies wailing, shepherds shouting at flocks wandering among the big-wheeled carts—covers the highway like a blanket of sad humanity.

There are 4,000 souls here—but they are only a fraction of the 1,250,000 Indians in Burma, most of whom now seek the safety of their homeland. Correspondents en route to the front in American "jeeps" must wait half an hour to clear a narrow driveway through them. In halting English, lean, tired guides with homemade spears and swords, and only bits of gray cotton cloth around their loins, call out for help.

"Sahib, we have no money, little food and water. We must keep moving without rest. If any of us strays, the bad men with long knives attack and rob and kill. Won't His Majesty's government protect us, Sahib?"

In the countryside, where there no longer are police, looting obviously is rampant, and the Indian laborers, who were always hated by the Burmese national extremists, are now the undefended victims of whatever bands care to ambush them during their plod northward. They can go but a few miles a day, yet they have 400 miles to Mandalay and then 250 more difficult miles westward to the Indian border. Babies have been born on this migration since last week. Their mothers ride in straw piles on the carts. It is the dry season. Village wells are nearly empty and even the oxen's tongues hang out during the searing afternoon heat in the thick dust that rises from the shuffling hooves.

A father carrying his small, naked son on his shoulder and trudging behind a cart crowded with young and old, waves good-bye and he, too, pleads: "Ask help for us, sahib."

5

WHAT DE LUCE had witnessed was a prelude to the fall of Rangoon, capital of Burma. Things were also going badly in the Netherlands East Indies. The 650-mile-long idyllic island of Java was next in the ruthless route of Jap conquest. Java, the tourists' delight, was running red with blood. She had oil, tin, and rubber for the Mikado's war machine; rice and quinine for Japan's under-nourished subjects. Jap shock troops stormed at Java's capital— Batavia. Others fanned eastward toward the Dutch naval base of Surabaya.

Dispatches told of a gallant but losing attempt by the dogged Dutch and British forces to stem the tide. War correspondents, hard put to stay out of the Japs' hands, were falling back with the defenders. They had a difficult time getting their stories to the outside world. On March 2 , Witt Hancock took one long, desperate chance and put in a telephone call direct to his New York headquarters. He was connected with Cable Editor James Long, who had been trying to reach Hancock for several days. Long did his best to get Hancock's news, hampered by a bad connection and interruptions by the censor:

The telephone shrilled and I was told it was Hancock calling from Bandung, military headquarters of the United Nations in Java. One of my colleagues here in New York quickly cut in the recording

machine (to take a transcription of the conversation) and I picked
up the receiver.

After a brief pause, the operator gave the usual notice that
the call was subject to censorship and that no questions could be
asked from this end. She then completed the connection and Hancock
began his story.

He described how a taxicab army similar to the one that turned
back the Germans at the gates of Paris in World War I was streaming from Bandung to give battle to Jap forces only thirty miles away.
He described Bandung as a city on the slopes of volcanic mountains
and reported that the fighting was taking place on the flat coastal
plains of northern Java. He also told how Jap vessels were coming
and going "in a stream" through the Java Sea, indicating that
Tojo's Fleet was in the waters around Java.

"The Dutch and Allies are making the Japs pay a high price
for every foot of ground," he said.

I broke in to ask if fresh Jap naval forces had appeared off
the northern coast of Java. The line immediately went dead, and
the operator said the call had been cut by the censor. However, she
advised that the call be held. Within a few seconds Hancock—apparently after a brief bit of caution from the censor—came on again.
He merely repeated his previous statement—that the Japs were
constantly on the go in the Java Sea. He indicated that the news
he had given us was all he could put out at the time.

I then asked him if he was permitted to acknowledge receipt
of a recent cable from General Manager Cooper advising him to
use his own judgment on when and how to get out of Java. He
acknowledged receipt of the cable and said he was thinking about
leaving, although he had no definite plans. He said that Army officials had made plans to evacuate foreign newsmen by several means,
but that he had not decided when he would leave.

"Good luck, and keep your fingers crossed."

Those were Hancock's last words on the call.

That call from Hancock on March 2 was the last word received
from him. It may even have been the last dispatch of his career.
The Japs overran Java. A British public relations officer who arrived in Australia more than a month later said arrangements had
been made for all newsmen to leave Java on March 3. But he had
no word as to whether Hancock had left, or if he had, whether he
had arrived safely at some Pacific port.

Yates McDaniel, who had reached Java after his escape from Singapore, had better luck than Hancock. As at Singapore, he succeeded in getting away by boat. This time he landed at Perth, Australia. The date was March 7. He had no word of Hancock, but he reported:

I have reached friendly and still peaceful Australia, twelve days after leaving then-threatened and now-occupied Batavia as a deck passenger aboard a 40-year-old Dutch freighter with ninety American, British, and Dutch refugees. Also aboard our ancient vessel when we left was probably the last cargo of tin from the East Indies and a load of cattle, sheep, pigs, and fowl.

The 2,300-ton ship brought us unscathed into a little Australian port after tossing and pitching 2,000 miles through turbulent waters of the Indian Ocean. All her human and metal cargo was intact, but there remained only two forlorn cows out of our original livestock —for we had eaten the others.

As our convoy steamed south into the Straits of Sunda, the British cruiser *Exeter,* which helped drive the German pocket battleship *Admiral Graf Spee* to suicide off Montevideo, cut across our path leading a vessel Batavia-bound. The sun rose the next morning over Java Head, behind clouds settling over Krakatoa volcano. It was an awe-inspiring sight but few passengers were able to enjoy nature's wonders. Our little ship—which had never been outside the placid waters of the Java Sea—was wallowing sickeningly in troughs and deep swells of the Indian Ocean.

Stricken mothers, many of whom left the Indies without word of their husbands who were marooned at Borneo, Malaya, and Sumatra, were helped with babies' bottles, diapers, and general nursemaid tasks by men volunteers. All of us took turns at serving food on deck, for the gloomy hold reeked with odors accumulated from four decades of cattle-carrying.

One day I did what I wanted to do a fortnight before, while awaiting rescue after my ship had been bombed and sunk during my escape from Singapore. That was to read the Book of Job. That night I was forced into the unwelcome role of Job's comforter among the Dutch women, worried about what the Japanese would do to their husbands serving with the Java home guards.

Perth was almost an American city when I arrived late last night. Around a lamppost near the railway station a uniformed quartet was singing "Down by the Old Mill Stream," "Sweetheart of Sigma Chi," and other American favorites.

6

Two days later—on March 9—the Japs officially occupied Java. Bali, isle of romance and beautiful maidens, quickly followed, along with Borneo, land of elephants, tigers, headhunters, and maharajas. Gargoyle-shaped Celebes felt the fire of the Rising Sun. Onward and eastward across all of the gangling Dutch East Indies the Japs swept without a pause until Timor was also theirs. Rangoon also fell. The Japs began mopping up in Burma. They had virtual control of southeastern Asia.

Perhaps there was one cheerful note in World War II at this critical stage. Far to the northwest, thousands of miles from the stricken Dutch East Indies and the "scorched earth" of Burma, the Russians were still holding the Germans. They were methodically regaining territory that the Nazis had taken before the hard winter set in. Eddy Gilmore wrote about some vodka drinking he did with Russian soldiers in their snow-covered dugouts many feet below the surface of the earth:

These Russians are cheerful people. Although this war is "business" to them, for a people who appeared doomed only a few months ago, they are remarkable to observe. They find a way to hand out hospitality even from a hole in the ground. I was with the Red Army on one front today and I want to tell you what happened.

"Come into our quarters," said Senior Lieutenant Anatoly Pavlovich Bayarinov above the scream of a blizzard, "and see how we live down here."

Our party followed him into a hole. He led the way through a narrow boarded tunnel under tons of snow. We entered a small pine-boarded room to shake off the snow and then were led down a dormitory flanked on either side by neat beds. The room was warm and clean. Soldiers were playing pool and checkers, and in one corner a radio played soft music. The regimental commander marched in as the soldiers spread a table with fish, bread, and vodka.

"Good morning," the commander said slowly, in English. "I once worked in an English factory. I speak some English."

Toasts followed—first to Premier Joseph Stalin, Prime Minister Churchill, and President Roosevelt, then others to the U. S.

RUSSIA

FORMER
BOUNDARIES

0   50   100   150
MILES

Lake Ladoga

LENINGRAD

NOVGOROD

STARAYA RUSSA

KALININ

Volga R.

GORKI

RZHEV

SYCHEVKA

MOSCOW

VYAZMA

VITEBSK

SMOLENSK

RYAZAN

White

TULA

Line of
Farthest
German
Advance

Russian

OREL

S.S.R.

GOMEL

KURSK

Don R.

KIEV

KHARKOV

BERDICHEV

Dnieper R.

Ukrainian

STALINO

S.S.R.

DNIEPER-
OPETROVSK

ROSTOV

TAGANROG

MELITOPOL

BESSARABIA

ODESSA

Sea of
Azov

KERCH

CRIMEA

TUAPSE

GALATI

SEVASTAPOL

FEODOSIYA

Black Sea

Map 19—Hitler miscalculated in expecting the fall of Leningrad and Moscow before the onset of the winter of 1941. His advancing armies rolled on to the high tide of their invasion and then began a withdrawal—actually a rout at some points. By March 9 they had yielded the shaded area to the defending Russians. The Reds were harassing an encircled German army at (1) and another Red force drove toward (2), while Hitler set up headquarters at Kiev (3).

338

forces, the Red Army, the regimental commander, the junior officer, and the visitors. The Russians toast with vodka. It is bad form not to toss a whole glass off at once.

The soldiers put themselves out to be entertaining. Two muscular privates danced to the music of an accordion. Three others put on a dramatic skit showing a guerrilla dealing with a German officer and a traitor. A big gunner danced in a homemade gypsy costume, and then eight singers joined in the rousing chorus of a Red Army song.

The party ended in a hearty round of good-byes. As we walked slowly away in the last rays of daylight we turned back for a farewell look, but the shelter was so well camouflaged that it seemed to have disappeared.

7

THE conquest of Java, Malay, and most of Burma, gave the Japs a good portion of the area they had "earmarked" for their "New Order in Asia." They had taken one of the world's richest empires. They had done it all in a little more than three months. They were confident. They were moving on toward Australia. They had had phenomenal success while the U. S. was still on the defensive.

But the Japs had still one unfinished job in the Pacific. It was one they had been working on since Pearl Harbor. It was one that had already cost them thousands of men—was costing them thousands more. It was one that they had been unable to finish despite overwhelming power. It was Bataan.

The story of little Wake Island had been the odyssey of a few U. S. Marines against the might of the combined Jap Navy and air force. The story of Bataan—of MacArthur and his men—was the odyssey of a hundred Wake Islands rolled into one.

Many tales of heroism had come from Bataan. There was the one about America's Number 1 one-man army—Captain Arthur W. Wermuth, of Chicago—who singlehanded had killed 116 Japs and captured many more; another about the five men who escaped death behind the lines by lying "dead" among Jap forces for twenty-eight hours, and about Joe Smith and the Davis brothers of Carlsbad, New Mexico, who shot down Jap planes without any sights on their anti-aircraft gun.

Clark Lee had reported the story of Bataan day by day, almost death by death. The *Infantry Journal* described his dispatches as "the best this war has produced on any front." There had been such a variation of Bataan bylines that one of his colleagues in New York wrote a review:

The history books will tell it all carefully one day—all complete with dates that the children will perhaps learn; all smoothly integrated, as they say, by men who will then have plenty of the cozy leisure of peace to look at it with scholastic calm.

This does not tell it that way; this tells the story of Bataan, of death and laughter, of a cause of splendid hopelessness, as Clark Lee told it whenever and wherever he could write it from the front.

This is really a history of fragments, written in the red and often terrible haze of battle. It is a story of Americans and of Filipinos, of whom it could be said—with reference to a celebrated martial phrase: They didn't want to live forever.

Here is Lee, writing on January 16, eleven days after the big enemy push got started, from his post with the 60th U. S. Coast Artillery on Bataan:

"The sun has been up less than forty minutes when the radiophone in the dugout beneath us crackles: 'Flash, flash. Six planes flying from the China Sea just above the lower layer of clouds.'

"This battery has set a world anti-aircraft record for the number of planes downed per number of rounds fired—it has shot down twelve and is after its thirteenth. In front of us three Japanese planes go into a 45-degree dive and we hear a series of heavy 'whoops' as the bombs hit. One plane is diving straight at us now, too close for the big guns. Captain Abston grabs the interbattery phone. 'Machine guns open fire,' he orders. 'Take over!'

"But everybody is too interested to think of safety. . . .

"The Japanese give us time for an uninterrupted breakfast, but immediately after they are back again. The big guns crack and the shells scream skyward. Some pray audibly: 'Get him, knock him down!' The first shell bursts within fifty yards of the Jap plane and the pilot does not tarry to do more observing.

"These anti-aircraftmen actually pray for enemy planes to come, partly because of the fun of shooting them down, mostly because every plane destroyed is one less to harass the U. S. ground forces of the Far East. They realize that, until the arrival of American airplanes, anti-aircraft is the sole means of defense against air attack. . . .

"As I leave the post the gunners extract a promise to revisit them 'when something's really popping.' In farewell they call out 'Keep 'em flying' and I reply with the anti-aircraft gunner's slogan : 'Keep 'em falling.' They grin. 'We sure will.'

Bataan Front, January 29:

"A little inconvenience like the lack of airplanes hasn't stopped the flying men of the U. S. Army from fighting the Japanese. They have seized rifles, machine guns, and grenades. . . . Many pilots, bombardiers, mechanics, and machine gunners, have volunteered with other branches and are now making a grand showing in the mountains and jungles. . . .

"A few American planes still roam the skies, engaged in guerrilla warfare in the air. . . .

Bataan Front, February 3:

"In the most spectacular battle yet fought in Luzon, American naval, land, and air units early today smashed a strong Japanese attempt to land from the China Sea on the American left flank. Many Japanese landing boats were sunk under a storm of American machine-gun and artillery fire and aerial bombing. Details of the Navy's participation cannot now be disclosed, but the Navy was very much in the midst of the action.

Bataan Front, February 5:

"The fighting was typical of the bitter warfare waged in the jungle area of Bataan, where ground is contested inch by inch, and where men must kill or be killed. . . .

"This morning, Captain C. A. Crome, a husky South Carolinian with his arm in a sling, shouted in his foghorn voice: 'Surrender, you ———'s, we've got you surrounded.'

"The answer came back in perfect English: 'Nerts to you, Joe.'

"So Captain Crome ordered the tanks into action. . . .

"General MacArthur's troops fanned out, with Americans on the flanks and Filipinos in the center, and began their creepingly slow advance. The Japanese, meanwhile, dug frantically into foxholes two feet wide and four feet deep. Others climbed trees, lashed themselves to the limbs, and began sniping. They were so well concealed that even when killed their bodies could not immediately be located.

"Some days our troops were able to advance only three to five yards through underbrush that was so thick it was impossible to see an arm's length ahead. In these stages of the fighting tanks couldn't be used because the roads were covered by Japanese land mines and antitank guns.

Bataan Front, February 14:

"The 57th Philippine Scouts are living up to the stoic traditions of their profession, none more valiantly than Corporal Pablo Bayangas, who died bravely on the field of battle. . . .

"Late in the afternoon he heard the bushes rustling and saw a large group of Japanese crawling through the brush a short distance away. Corporal Bayangas readied his automatic rifle . . . emptied his magazine, killing thirteen Japanese with twenty shots. But . . . a Japanese officer crawled up from the other side of the tree as Bayangas was reloading. . . . The Jap officer fired a pistol bullet into the corporal's head.

"Second Lieutenant Alexander Nininger, Jr., of Lake Worth, Florida, also died surrounded by the bodies of his enemies. He led an antisniper volunteer group into the woods, but became separated from his men and died fighting. . . .

"Private Bayani reported to his superior officer: 'I met eight Japs in the woods and shot them, sir.' 'How many shots?' Surprised, Private Bayani answered: 'Why, eight shots, sir!' "

Even that was only a part of the story of Bataan. There was more. By the middle of March the battle had reached a stalemate. Lee got away to Australia. He wrote some more about Bataan from there:

In spite of all that has been written about the courageous defenders of Bataan Peninsula, there are still many tales of individual heroism that have never been told.

There is, for instance, the story of a black night when Captain Arthur Wermuth, the American officer whose legendary exploits caused him to be known as "the one-man army," was pussyfooting along behind the Japanese lines on a scouting mission. He suddenly bumped into about twenty shadowy figures, the first of whom raised a finger to his lips and murmured a warning, "S-s-s-h-h-h!" Wermuth, realizing he had run into a Japanese patrol, made a similar gesture, and replied, "S-s-s-s-h-h-h!"

Then he drew a firing pin from a grenade, pressed the missile into the hand of the Japanese, closed the man's fingers, and tiptoed away into the darkness with another admonishing "S-s-s-s-h-h-h!"

The Japanese opened his fingers a moment or two later, released the firing mechanism, and. . . .

Then there is the story of the Filipino scout who fell in behind a Japanese scouting party of eleven men marching along a trail in single file, one night near Davao. The Filipino drew out his bolo, lopped off the head of the nearest man, and then cut the whole column down one by one from behind.

It was also at Davao that an American sergeant named May, of the 31st U. S. Infantry, made a lone stand against a Japanese warship attempting to cover a landing party. Equipped with a .50-caliber machine gun mounted on a truck, May mowed down boatload after boatload of Japanese as they came ashore. The warship finally shot the truck out from under him, but he came back with another and went to work again. It was estimated that he accounted for at least 250 Japanese. He is understood to be fighting somewhere in the Philippines still.

I have been trying to recall when I had my biggest scare during the campaign in Luzon. Frankly, I was scared every time there was a loud explosion near by—and that was often. I was probably lucky to get out with nothing more serious than a broken hand, suffered while diving into a foxhole to escape a strafing plane, and a few small scars—the result of being blown off a dock at Corregidor by a shell.

A stick of six bombs, which exploded about fifty yards away while I was visiting some marine buddies in the trench at Corregidor, also left me with one deaf ear—but it was bad before that. During the first frantic days in Manila after the war started there was considerable indiscriminate shooting in the streets, and Russell Brines, also of The Associated Press, and I had a narrow escape when a sentry fired a shot through the door of an automobile in which we were riding.

While on Corregidor I couldn't decide which was worse—being bombed or shelled. I was vaguely disturbed that I couldn't get used to either and spoke to General MacArthur about it.

His reply was comforting: "No soldier ever born isn't terrified of either bombing or shelling. The test of a real soldier is one who'll cling to his foxhole or trench and shiver and shake during the shelling, but who'll stick there without yielding to his natural impulse to run, and when the enemy attacks will jump to his rifle or machine gun and open fire."

8

ON MARCH 17 the whole world was startled. MacArthur had left Bataan—days before. Immediate fear was that Bataan finally must have fallen. But it hadn't. Roosevelt had ordered MacArthur to Australia to become supreme commander of Army, Navy, and Air Forces for the United Nations in the Southwest Pacific.

It was a dramatic "escape" from Bataan. MacArthur went by a small boat to an unnamed island and made the remainder of the perilious trip by plane. With him were his wife, small son, and members of his staff. Lieutenant General Jonathan M. Wainwright remained in charge of American forces on Bataan.

McDaniel, in Australia, got the story of MacArthur's trip on March 24:

The full story of General Douglas MacArthur's hazardous voyage from the Philippines was told today.

Colonel Legrand Diller told newspapermen that MacArthur's perilous race against time, darkness, and Japanese warplanes and warships was vindication of the general's long fight for recognition of motor torpedo boats. Some advisers, Diller said, urged MacArthur to use a submarine to make his way to Australia, but the general and Navy Lieutenant John D. Bulkeley, commander of six "PT" boats that reached the Philippines shortly before the war, pinned their faith on the speedy craft. Strong opposition was based on fear that the attempt was too desperate.

This was Diller's story:

The sun dropped into the China Sea out past Corregidor on March 11, when, in the deepening darkness, the forms of torpedo boats moved slowly through the mine fields toward the entrance of Manila Bay. Bulkeley, who had won the Distinguished Service Cross for his work in the Philippines—the sinking of a 5,000-ton Japanese ship—was at the wheel of the leading craft as the little convoy started the hazardous trip, which, some advisers had warned, was a "fantastic venture." But the general said: "We go with the full of the moon. We go during the Ides of March."

It seemed strange after living in blackouts for three months to see automatic lighthouses operating. Along the shore (Japanese) signal lights were seen, flashing the warning of the approach of (what were presumed to be) enemy aircraft. The roar of the PT boats was confusing, even to the Japanese.

Just before the departure of the MacArthur convoy, we received word of the presence of enemy warships in these waters, but we roared into the night. The boats pounded terrifically through heavy seas. The general was unable to stand on his feet. Everyone was soaked. Many of the party were violently seasick.

The boats kept well together until early in the morning when, still before dawn, they separated one by one in the darkness. When the rendezvous was reached early on March 12 one boat only was there at the designated hour. The other boats pressed on individually in dangerous daylight, open prey for enemy surface ships and planes.

As the general's boat approached one of the islands in the rendezvous group, another that had arrived earlier was so convinced the approaching craft was the enemy that it cleared its deck for action, and "only by the merest chance identified the general's boat in time to avoid opening fire with .50-caliber guns." One of the boats had to be abandoned, to continue the voyage later.

At the first rendezvous, where a submarine had arrived, many urged a transfer, but MacArthur and Bulkeley had faith in the speedboats. The party members, therefore, were distributed among three boats, two of which pressed on in the night of the second day, while the third, a late arival, left afterward.

During the second night all three boats sighted Japanese destroyers, but all slipped through by altering their courses and increasing their speed, thanks to the courage and skill of the navigators. The two leading boats reached the second rendezvous at daybreak, but the third did not arrive until noon.

The party assembled inland, awaiting airplanes from Australia, but the planes did not come that night or the next. Every moment party members feared some information of the desperate voyage would reach the enemy, whose planes were based only a half-hour's flight away.

Three nights and days were spent on the island rendezvous without enemy attacks materializing or rescue planes arriving. Finally, word came that the planes were en route. Three were expected, but only two came, so it was decided to place the entire party in two planes, leaving behind baggage, arms, and equipment.

With little more than the clothes they wore, the party stowed away in the two B-17's, and took off about midnight of March 16. They flew through the night, but daylight found the planes still over

Japanese-infested areas. Gunners and observers manned their stations, searching the skies for enemy fighters.

The big bombers landed finally at Darwin, just after an air raid alarm had sounded in the northern Australian port. A hurried transfer was made there, the party had a quick bite to eat, and was off again southward.

MacArthur had "escaped" to Australia "to a greater task." The scene of the main Pacific conflict had shifted—the Japs were after Australia.

In Santa Barbara, California, Chinese Tom Moon Gungs, celebrated his eightieth birthday by offering this advice: "If you would be happy three hours—get drunk. If you would be happy three days —kill a pig and eat it. If you would be happy three months—get married. If you would be happy all your life—become a gardener."

CHAPTER 19

The Surging Pacific

March 25–May 14, 1942

I

BY THE time the Japs moved toward Australia in March, 1942, the all-out war effort in the U. S. was beginning to show results. Production, plagued by bottlenecks and labor drags, was slowly gaining momentum. On the other hand, there were advantages for the Axis. Hitler had the resources of most of Europe. He was working war prisoners and populations of overrun countries like chain-gang convicts. Japan's quick conquests had deprived the United Nations of raw materials long controlled by the British. It had also weakened Allied blockade.

Japan wanted to hurry her drive on Australia so she could sew up control before the U. S. could get adequate supplies to MacArthur. Her immediate object was the island of New Guinea. Troop landings were made on the northeast coast. Heavy bombers attacked Port Moresby, principal city on the part-Dutch, part-Australian island, 300 miles from the mainland. They harried U. S. convoys.

The U. S. and Canada sped work on an Alaskan highway. American airmen raided Wake and Marcus Islands. There was action on the Russian Front. There was action in Burma, in China, off Australia, and in the Atlantic, where Nazi submarines were sinking U. S. vessels almost within sight of American shores. There also was action in the Mediterranean, particularly around Malta, most bombed of all the British bases. The island guarded one of the narrowest parts of the Mediterranean. It already had had more than 2,000 raids—and still they came. Preston Grover was in the thick of it. Aboard a British cruiser, he accompanied a convoy seeking to reach the fortress. He saw the British rout a strong Italian force. He reported from Alexandria, Egypt, on March 25:

We feinted and bluffed, dodged in and out of smoke screens, fired our guns—although it was sometimes like shooting peas at a barn—took time out for tea in the midst of battle, and got our convoy safely to Malta.

After it was all over the captain of the cruiser which I was aboard added this statement to his brief report: "Our admiral has fought one of the most brilliant actions against superior forces ever successfully brought off."

I saw the battle with another American correspondent, Richard Mowrer of the Chicago *Daily News*. The battle occurred Sunday afternoon and ended only after dark when the Italian Fleet withdrew, puzzled, whipped, and wounded. In the Italian Fleet were one battleship of the Littorio class with 15-inch guns, two 8-inch cruisers of the Trento class, four 6-inch cruisers of the Condottieri class, and a screen of destroyers. Against them we had a 6-inch cruiser, anti-aircraft cruisers whose heaviest guns were 5.25-inch, and sixteen destroyers. There wasn't a single gun in our squadron that could make more than a minor dent in the Italian battleship. It was like throwing nails at a rampaging elephant. Yet at the end of the battle every British ship was afloat.

The convoy started from Alexandria March 20. We carried munitions and other supplies. The squadron was commanded by Rear Admiral Philip C. Vian.

Through March 20 and until after dusk of March 21, we bucked along through increasingly heavy seas, undetected by enemy reconnaissance planes. Then tough luck. At dusk on March 21, five German transport planes, escorted by a Messerschmitt-110, spotted us as they passed on the way from the Libyan front to Crete. They were beyond the range of our guns, and so they got away to report the location of our convoy. That meant not only that the following day we would be attacked by dive-bombers, but that the Italian Fleet would have time to put to sea and intercept us somewhere between Greece and Malta. Both happened.

The raid began with torpedo-bombers swinging in from all sides. One narrowly missed a destroyer, which turned in time to dodge it. Throughout the forenoon they kept coming in, but were repeatedly forced to drop their loads from a high level or from a great distance. Twice more around noon we were attacked by high- and low-level bombers. Then at 2:25 P.M., there came word from a neighboring cruiser: "Four suspicious vessels to the starboard." We were then south of the toe of Italy. With my field glasses, I looked to the starboard. There on the horizon was the Italian Fleet.

Without a moment's delay, four cargo vessels were sent in the opposite direction, accompanied by part of our squadron, and the rest of us headed for the enemy. We had a tremendous task to perform. It was six hours until darkness would permit the convoy to steal away to Malta. During those six hours our squadron had to hold off a vastly superior force, for already we could make out the battleship racing through the waves straight toward us.

Our strategy was similar to that by which the cruisers *Ajax*, *Exeter*, and *Achilles* harassed the German pocket battleship *Admiral Graf Spee* to defeat off Montevideo, Uruguay. Every ship in our squadron began making a smoke screen as we charged the Italian Fleet. The battleship's long-range guns began kicking up spouts of water to the right and left long before we were close enough to open fire. Finally within range, we swung sharply to the left and began firing broadsides. They were small shots for so big a target, but we kept pouring them in.

As the Italian guns began getting our range, we abruptly doubled back, hiding behind the smoke screen we had created. From time to time we dashed through the smoke to fire a few salvos, then ducked back again. After an hour and a half of this, the Italian Fleet withdrew temporarily, afraid to break through the screen and risk the danger of our torpedoes.

But the respite was not for long. We headed back to rejoin the convoy and give it added protection from the air-bombing, which had been incessant during the naval battle. We had just reached the convoy when the enemy showed up from another quarter and we went after him again, employing the same tactics. He had every advantage of air reconnaissance and aid from dive-bombers. But again we bluffed him off long enough for the convoy to get outside the range of his 15-inchers.

At this time British custom could not be ignored. One man from each station was sent to the kitchen to bring a pot of tea. A Briton with a spot of tea under his belt is a better fighting man. The men gulped their hot tea and stood back to their jobs.

We had fought off the enemy now through more than three blistering hours. His huge shells had whistled across us, splashed into the water in front of us and beside us. One 15-inch shell, hitting squarely, would almost have cut one of our ships in two. So far none had. But with a little more than two hours to go before darkness closed in, the Italian Fleet pressed forward.

Again we sent the convoy scampering away while we turned on the enemy. This time he appeared determined not to be stopped by the screen of smoke, and he came in to 10,000 yards. For battleships, that is almost point-blank range, and his shells smashed close to us every time we dived in and out of the smoke to have a go at him.

Once, as we broke out, the battleship and three cruisers were bearing straight down upon us. Instantly they let go a salvo of 15-inch shells, which raised house-high geysers beside us. We loosed a quick series of salvos and ducked back into the smoke, turning sharply to the right to outmaneuver his aim. It was perfect timing. Three huge spouts of water leaped up as 15-inchers hit exactly where we would have been had we not turned. Two more such salvos further traced the course the enemy assumed we were following.

By now the enemy was within easy range of the convoy, which was shielded by a thin wall of smoke, and the admiral ordered the Fleet to close in with a torpedo attack. The destroyers led off with fast sorties out of the smoke. One was struck by a shell. A companion destroyer threw a protective smoke belt about it, fired its own span of torperdoes, and ducked. Still another destroyer dashed almost under the nose of the battleship and came back to report that at least one of our torpedoes had scored. The cruisers followed, firing and lashing out with more torpedoes.

It was too much for the Italians. They pulled away as dusk was closing in. They had hit only one of our destroyers and landed a shell in a cruiser. Under cover of darkness our cruiser headed for Alexandria, and the convoy, shielded by units of the Fleet, raced to Malta during the early daylight hours.

2

THE Navy announced loss of the aircraft tender *Langley,* the destroyer *Peary,* and the tanker *Pecos,* off Australia. U. S. flying fortresses went into action in India. The War Production Board asked women to save materials by eliminating frills from their dresses and undies. Pierre Laval, pro-Nazi adherent, was restored to power in Vichy, France. Americans wore lapel buttons of General MacArthur. Store windows featured his picture. Posters warned "Loose Lips May Sink Ships," "Button Up Your Lips," and "Hitler is Listening."

By April 18, a Federal Grand Jury was getting ready to investigate the magazine *Social Justice,* founded by the Reverend Charles E. Coughlin, on charges of sedition. As a birthday present, Hitler received an old globe map on which neither America nor the Western Hemisphere was included. In St. Louis, Missouri, postal officials opened a window an hour and a half early so that 11-year-old Charlie Thompson could buy a U. S. war bond on Der Fuehrer's birthday and still get to school on time.

The British Board of Trade figured 1,000,000 yards of cloth could be saved annually by chopping two inches off shirttails. An Orlando, Florida, policeman asked an offending motorist how he should be listed and got the answer: "Poor." The policeman said: "No, I mean what's your name," and the motorist replied: "That's it, 'P-o-o-r,' and I'll be poorer still after I pay the fine."

But beneath many of the little items attracting attention on April 18, there was somber concern. This war was coming closer home. There was little about it to cheer Americans. There had not even been a really compelling war song—no "Long Way to Tipperary," no "Pack Up Your Troubles," no "Over There," or "Keep the Home Fires Burning." Then, on that same April 18, something finally happened to kindle spirits. First details came off the Tokyo radio because all correspondents in Japan were interned:

The long-awaited bombing of Tokyo—first installment of revenge for Pearl Harbor—got under way at noon today.

The Japanese high command announced that hostile planes swept in from several directions, and bombed Tokyo, Yokohama, Nagoya, an airplane center, and Kobe, a large industrial city. The raiders over Tokyo bore the insignia of the United States Air Force.

The sudden, terrifying attack caused quick air raid alarms throughout three of the four main islands of Japan—a distance of more than 1,000 miles.

Thus Japan, by her own account, experienced for the first time in her history the destruction and terror of air assault which she has visited on scores of cities, from Manchuria to India, these last ten years.

The raid appears to have been the most daring of the war. It came less than twenty-four hours after Secretary of War Stimson in Washington said the American Army was "getting pretty near to the stage of being ready for an offensive." Tokyo could not say whence the raiders came. Chungking said they did not come from China. The Tokyo broadcast said:

"Enemy bombers appeared over Tokyo for the first time in the current war, inflicting damage on schools and hospitals. The raid occurred shortly past noon on Saturday (Tokyo Time). Invading planes failed to cause any damage on military establishments, although casualties in the schools and hospitals were as yet unknown. This inhuman attack on these cultural establishments and on residential districts is causing widespread indignation among the populace."

There were no other details. Washington withheld information, but a few of its orators held forth in patriotic tones. There was not even a word as to who led the raid, or where it originated. Military officials did not wish to disclose anything that might be of value to the enemy.

Nevertheless, the exploit aroused public imagination. This was real American stuff. This was what they wanted. This was what they needed. People talked about it in subways, on trains and busses. It was the subject of excited speculation. Americans wanted to know where the planes came from, how they could reach Japan, thousands of miles away from any U. S. air base. Later, Washington correspondents supplied a part of the answer:

President Roosevelt disclosed to a thrilled nation today that the historic bombing of Tokyo by United States Army planes on April 18 had been led by Brigadier General James H. (Jimmy) Doolittle.

The disclosure came in a surprise White House ceremony in which the President made speed king Jimmy a hero by awarding the Congressional Medal of Honor. So closely had the leader's identity been hidden that only two others besides the President knew that a new war hero was to be named. The honor paid the 45-year-old slim, bashful, peacetime flier came even as a surprise to Mrs. Doolittle, who had been summoned from Los Angeles for the ceremony.

But once the ceremony was over, General Doolittle told in graphic words a tingling story of the smash against Nippon. He spared no glory for the seventy-nine officers and enlisted men who flew with him and he paid tribute to the entire Air Force in disclosing that a call for volunteers for the flight had brought many

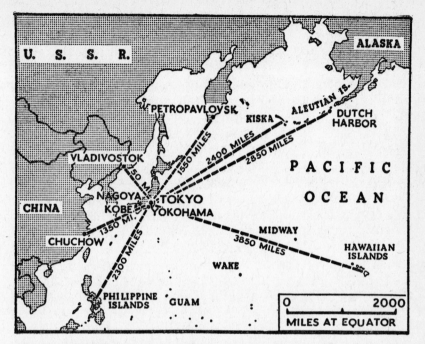

Map 20—U. S. bombers struck terror into the Japanese when they raided Tokyo, April 18, 1942. Tokyo could not figure out where the raiders were based—and that was almost as disconcerting as the raid itself. The map above indicates possible bases, with distances.

times the number of men who could be taken on the hazardous trip.

To each of the seventy-nine who accompanied Doolittle went the nation's praise—and the Army's Distinguished Service Cross medal.

The full fury of the attack on the Island Empire—as well as the surprise with which it hit—was unfolded by Doolittle's story of the bombing. Roaring over the Japanese coast at treetop level, the planes hit their targets with "practically every bomb" dropped, he said. One group of bombers plastered a navy yard with fire and explosive bombs, and left in flames a new cruiser or battleship under construction. Others—flying so low that anti-aircraft guns could not be used against them—started great fires at an aircraft factory near Nagoya, and turned a big oil tank farm into blinding flames.

Here is Doolittle's full account in his own words:

"The success of the recent air raid on Japan exceeded our most optimistic expectations. Each plane was assigned specific targets and the bombardiers carried out their expert duties with remarkable precision. Since the raid was made in fair weather in the middle of the day and from a low altitude, no trouble whatever was experienced in finding the exact targets designated.

"Apparently there was no advance warning of the raid, as we experienced little hostile reaction. Not more than thirty Japanese pursuit planes were observed during the flight and these were completely ineffective. Several we know were shot down, possibly more. Incidentally, the pilots of these planes seemed somewhat inexperienced, evidently not up to the standard of those encountered in active theaters.

"We approached our objectives just over the housetops, but bombed at 1,500 feet. The target for one plane was a portion of the navy yard south of Tokyo, in reaching which we had passed over what apparently was a flying school, as there were a number of planes in the air. One salvo made a direct hit on a new cruiser or battleship under construction. They left it in flames.

"After releasing our bombs we dived again to the treetops and went to the coast at that altitude to avoid anti-aircraft fire. Along the coast line we observed several squadrons of destroyers and some cruisers and battleships. About twenty-five or thirty miles to sea the rear gunners reported seeing columns of smoke rising thousands of feet in the air.

"One of our bombardiers strewed bombs along a quarter of a mile of aircraft factory near Nagoya. Another illuminated a tank farm. However, flying at such low altitudes made it very difficult to observe the result following the impact of the bombs. We could see the strike, but our field of vision was greatly restricted by the speed of the plane and the low altitude at which we were flying. Even so, one of our party observed a ball game in progress. The players and spectators did not start their run for cover until just as the field passed out of sight.

"Pilots, bombardiers, and all members of the crew performed their duties with great calmness and remarkable precision. It appeared to us that practically every bomb reached the target for which it was intended. We would like to have tarried and watched the later developments of fire and explosion, but even so we were fortunate to receive a fairly detailed report from the excited Japanese radio broadcasts. It took them several hours to calm down to deception and accusation."

Neither Doolittle nor anybody else disclosed the base from which the fliers took off for Tokyo. However, President Roosevelt jokingly borrowed from the fictional Tibetan retreat created by James Hilton in his novel, *Lost Horizon,* in describing origin of the flight. He said the airmen took off from "Shangri-La." Both the Japs and the Germans took seriously the Roosevelt joke. Berlin's radio said: "Doolittle carried out his air attack from the air base Shangri-La which was not otherwise described by Roosevelt."

But, irrespective of how the Japs or the Germans reacted, the Doolittle disclosure thrilled Americans. There had been nothing like it for arousing patriotic fervor.

3

To FILL the gaps caused by men workers who had gone to war, a Miami dairy advertised for women to take milk routes. Two cautious motorists lugged their spare tire into a Hope, Arkansas, theater rather than take a chance on having it stolen while they were seeing the movie. At Fort Devens, Massachusetts, cavalrymen were requested to remove their spurs before going onto the camp's dancing floor. At Turtle Creek, Pennsylvania, Private George Wong was given a special furlough so he could go home and unscramble his laundry business. A Philadelphia ordnance plant began giving each employee two vitamin pills daily to step up production.

British hit-and-run fighters—called "Commandos"—attacked Boulogne in their fifth raid of the war. It was a type of warfare that had had its origin among the Boers in South Africa years before. Hitler inveighed against the Russian winter and reiterated his "life and death power" over all Germanic peoples. Propaganda Minister Joseph Goebbels began a "politeness campaign" in Berlin, offering prizes of radio sets and theater tickets for the forty winners.

On April 26, the seriousness of the war was brought closer to Americans everywhere. Already there had been several drafts. The last registration had been of men normally above draft age—36 to 44 inclusive. That brought realization of war close. But what happened on April 26 carried the war into virtually every home. It was another registration—this time of men between 45 and 65. Its purpose was to determine national man power. It showed 13,000,000 men in this older age range alone. It meant that almost every father, brother, son—even grandfather himself—might now be on call.

The consciousness of war came home with even more emphatic impact only two days later. On April 28, the President of the United States delivered another report to the nation. Perhaps more Americans than ever before sat with their radios that night. Roosevelt disclosed that an A.E.F. of thousands had already crossed the oceans. He disclosed a program of higher taxes, stabilization of wages, billions in war bonds, personal sacrifice all along the line, stringent rationing. He listed a seven-point program of "general principles" which might avoid inflation and help to win the war:

1. We must, through heavier taxes, keep personal and corporate profits at a low reasonable rate.
2. We must fix ceilings on prices and rents.
3. We must stabilize wages.
4. We must stabilize farm prices.
5. We must put more billions into war bonds.
6. We must ration all essential commodities that are scarce.
7. We must discourage installment buying, and encourage paying off debts and mortgages.

He said: "The blunt fact is that every single person in the United States is going to be affected."

Here are highlights of his speech:

"American warships are now in combat in the North and South Atlantic, in the Arctic, in the Mediterranean, and in the North and

South Pacific. American troops have taken stations in South America, Greenland, Iceland, the British Isles, the Near East, the Middle East, the Far East, the continent of Australia, and many islands of the Pacific. . . .

"Russian forces have destroyed and are destroying more armed power of our enemies—troops, planes, tanks, and guns—than all the other United Nations put together. . . .

"The United Nations will take measures, if necessary, to prevent the use of French territory in any part of the world for military purposes by the Axis powers. . . .

"Our planes are helping the defense of French colonies today, and soon American flying fortresses will be fighting for the liberation of the darkened continent of Europe. . . .

"In the German and Italian peoples themselves there is a growing conviction that the cause of Nazism and Fascism is hopeless. . . .

"The news in Burma tonight is not good. The Japanese may cut the Burma Road: but—no matter what advances the Japanese may make, ways will be found to deliver airplanes and munitions of war to the armies of Generalissimo Chiang Kai-Shek. . . .

"For every advance that the Japanese have made since they started their frenzied career of conquest, they have had to pay a very heavy toll in warships, in transports, in planes, and in men. . . .

"We are now spending, solely for war purposes, the sum of about $100,000,000 every day in the week. Before this war is over, that almost unbelievable rate of expenditure will be doubled. But the spending of these tremendous sums presents grave danger of disaster to our national economy. . . .

"All of us are used to spending money for things we want but which are not absolutely essential. We will all have to forego that spending. Because we must put every dime and every dollar we can possibly spare out of our earnings into war bonds and stamps. . . .

"The price of civilization must be paid in hard work and sorrow and blood. The price is not too high. . . ."

4

AT CAMP ROBERTS, California, Private Wayne Harris spent his month's pay on a telephone call to his sweetheart in Los Angeles. A Columbia, South Carolina, wife telephoned the draft board: "Please, oh, please, take my husband into the service. He wants to fight all the time and I am not able to." Another South Carolinian asked for a new sugar ration card to replace one kept by his wife when she turned him out. A Los Angeles official suggested that the city hang flags in front of the homes of night workers in war plants to keep peddlers away during the day so the workers could sleep. Edward Brentlinger of Overbrook, Kansas, was so eager to join the Navy, that he rode twenty-eight miles on his bicycle to a recruiting office.

The British Government of Burma abandoned Mandalay; anti-British uprisings were growing. With the letup of winter, the Nazis and the Reds were at it again. The R.A.F. blasted Hitler bases in Norway and Germany.

Since mid-April, MacArthur had been sending raiders on a 4,000-mile round trip to bomb the Japs in the Philippines. The spectacular aerial thrusts were in keeping with the general's pledge that he would "return to Bataan." While the MacArthur forces returned by air, Lieutenant General Wainwright and his men held on at Corregidor Fortress. It was a hopeless stand. Clark Lee, in Australia, was not permitted to accompany the MacArthur bombers. He got the story of what happened from Colonel J. H. Davies, who led one of the groups. He reported Davies's own words:

We smacked hell out of 'em in the Philippines and gained at least a little revenge for members of our squadron who fought in the front-line trenches at Bataan. We had hoped to get there in time to relieve our friends, but Bataan already had fallen and many of our old companions already were missing, killed, or captured by the time we arrived. That only spurred us on to try and cut down the score a little.

Our group downed at least one and possibly two seaplanes at Davao and sank one large ship and numerous smaller ones. At Cebu we plastered to bits the shipping and the water front. We surprised them. We picked out the targets and let them have it. Some of the Japs were standing on the water front, but they scattered in a hurry when the bombs started to fall. They opened attack, but it was too late to hurt us.

The next day we went to work on Davao. We dropped full loads on the ships in the harbor while they had their guns ablaze. I sighted a Japanese seaplane just taking off. I called the bombardier over the telephone.

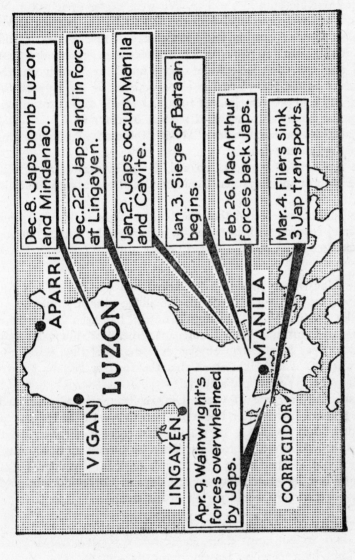

Dec. 8. Japs bomb Luzon and Mindanao.

Dec. 22. Japs land in force at Lingayen.

Jan. 2. Japs occupy Manila and Cavite.

Jan. 3. Siege of Bataan begins.

Feb. 26. MacArthur forces back Japs.

Mar. 4. Fliers sink 3 Jap transports.

Apr. 9. Wainwright's forces overwhelmed by Japs.

APARRI

VIGAN

LUZON

LINGAYEN

MANILA

CORREGIDOR

Map 21—The story of the defense of the Philippines ended May 6, 1942, when General Wainwright surrendered his forces and the island fortress of Corregidor. By holding out for five months, they had lessened Manila's strategic importance to the invaders. Above map tells how it happened.

"Hub," I said, "see that baby? I'm going down to give you a crack at him."

I put our big ship into a dive. We were doing some 300 miles an hour when we came level with the Jap to let the bomber shoot. Our midship guns opened up and I saw pieces of fuselage tearing out of that Rising Sun Jap plane, which was less than one hundred feet away. I also saw what looked like smoke until I realized it was the rear gunner in the two-place Jap plane popping at us. I upped the throttles and told our rear gunner to cut loose. He did, shooting one wing off the enemy ship, which dived out of control.

I called to the bombardier: "What's the matter? I didn't hear you shooting at that fellow."

He replied: "Doggone it, colonel, I was so excited at getting a chance at those monkeys that I couldn't get this gun into the right slot."

On landing we found that the bombardier's hands had been skinned and covered with blood as he had poked his gun from one slot to another in an attempt to get proper aim.

The MacArthur bombings "smacked hell out of 'em" in the Philippines, but did not prevent the inevitable—the capitulation of Corregidor Fortress. The "Battling Bastards" had been driven there from Bataan Peninsula. With Lieutenant General Wainwright, they held the fortress longer than anyone ever expected they could. So gallant was the Wainwright stand that the fortress became known its last days as "Wainwright's Rock."

Dean Schedler, one of Clark Lee's colleagues, had remained with the Bataan forces after Lee moved on to Australia. He stayed as long as he was permitted. He was the last correspondent to leave. For days, he was given up for lost. Then he turned up in an Australian hospital. He had made a 2,000-mile dash for freedom. From his hospital bed, he wrote about the last days of Corregidor and told as much as censorship would permit of his escape:

The story of "Wainwright's Rock" is the story of men who held on and fought until their endurance was stretched beyond human limits by a merciless blasting from the air and from massed artillery.

Japanese heavy cannon, firing approximately three miles from the Cavite area and six miles from the Bataan shore, hammered the island's gun positions until it seemed that nothing but utter wreckage would be left. When I had to leave, Corregidor had already been subjected to weeks of vicious pounding by shore batteries and bombers. But the men on the rock told me: "The American flag will fly topside as long as we are able to load the artillery and pump out loads from anti-aircraft and machine guns."

I left the fortress under instructions of Lieutenant General Jonathan Wainwright. I said to him: "You should be leaving, not me." He replied, harking back to one of the battle songs of Luzon: "I am one of the 'Battling Bastards of Bataan,' and I'll play the same role on the Rock as long as it is humanly possible."

All his men described him as "The most front-going general" of the war, and I guess they were right. So he ordered me to leave and I left. I was told to get around the Japanese forces that were surrounding Corregidor and meet Captain Charles Sneed and Lieutenant Parry L. Franks, both of the U. S. Army Air Force, at a secret air field on Luzon. I made it. There, under cover of darkness, we took off from a shell-pocked runway in an old two-seater trainer biplane of the Philippine Army. Captain Sneed and I crowded into the rear seat and Lieutenant Franks was at the controls.

North of (censored) we sighted a concentration of Japanese vessels. They opened fire and tracer bullets climbed under our wings. To gain altitude we threw out revolvers, cushions, instruments and everything else removable, and succeeded in evading the fire at 10,-000 feet, where we shivered from the cold.

At dawn we were flying over the open sea, having been blown off the course during the night. With gasoline running low, Franks sighted a small island through heavy ground fog. He didn't know whether the island was Japanese-held but had no alternative except to land. He banked over the trees and set the plane down on the curving beach. The plane ran several hundred feet and nosed over in a patch of soft sand. All three of us were pitched onto the sand, scratched and burned. We saw no immediate signs of life and were too exhausted to investigate. We crawled into a palm grove for several hours' sleep, not even knowing whether the island was in the hands of friends or enemies.

At noon we were awakened by Filipino children cautiously approaching the plane. When they saw the white stars on the wings, they ran away shouting "Americano aviators," and soon returned with adults from a nearby village. The men were friendly and spoke some English. They gave us coconuts and righted our plane, which had one wing torn, a bent propeller, and a bent tail rudder.

After camouflaging the plane, we slept on the floor of a nipa hut. Next morning we were starting repairs when a Japanese bomber flew over. Sneed worked on the engine, taking out sand and water, and patching the damage. His only tools were a bolo and a small screw driver.

Natives, gathering from as far away as twenty miles, said they could get gasoline. But none of us put much faith in the promise because there were no automobiles on the island. We had located an old map and discovered that we were 200 miles from the nearest friendly base—all across water.

On the third day everybody had a terrific scare when an unidentified launch was seen approaching. The natives quickly gathered their few belongings and took to the hills, with us behind them. But a small boy soon brought word that the launchmen were friendly. They were Europeans from a nearby island and they offered us transportation in the launch if we were unable to get gasoline. They also gave us food and coffee.

Later that afternoon the Filipinos appeared rolling a fifty-gallon drum of aviation gasoline plainly marked "Cavite Navy Yard." The natives said it had washed ashore. We strained the gasoline through a handkerchief into the plane's tank. Then Franks, who had been exploring in a native outrigger, returned with word that our plight had been spread by bamboo wireless to a nearby Japanese-held island, making immediate departure imperative.

Franks and I got in the rear and Sneed climbed into the pilot's seat. The plane raced down the runway, full throttle, zigzagging all the way. At length it got into the air after clearing the coral rocks by a few feet. We were all so scared we had no strength to look back. The bent propeller was unable to pull the plane above 2,000 feet, where it rattled like an old car. After a half-hour the headwind grew stronger and an ominous cloud, coming rapidly closer, increased our anxiety to reach a shore line before dusk.

We flew for an hour and as darkness approached we saw an island. Sneed circled low and we peered over the side at high waving palms without an open space in sight. It was raining harder and harder. Sneed said we had ten minutes more gas left with which to try to find a cove and set the plane down in the water. We tightened our "Mae West" lifebelts. Franks tied a safety belt around his right leg and my left leg, since it was not large enough to encircle both. Sneed reached back, shook hands with both of us, and said: "Well, this is it."

He flew gradually lower, the engine barking and spitting fire. He skimmed along beautifully until the prop hit the water, then he cut the engine that was so hot that we feared an explosion. The plane hit easily. Then, as the nose sank, it flipped over. We were hanging with our heads in the water. Sneed was thrown clear. Franks and I loosened the safety belt and made the surface, where we all clung to the wings.

I had a flashlight, and Franks, who was unable to swim, told me to dive into the sinking cockpit. I rescued a can of corned beef. We started paddling to the shore 500 yards distant. But the life preservers were incorrectly fastened and kept choking us. After an hour's fight through high waves and outgoing tide, I made shore and climbed the rocks to shine a beacon light for Sneed and Franks.

At dawn friendly natives came to the beach and gave us food, including overripe eggs and a few cans that native divers had salvaged from the wrecked plane. We managed to hire a fishing boat and made a slow day-long trip to the Island of Panay, where we were informed that eight Japanese ships were en route to make a landing, probably the next morning.

We had a hearty meal with United States Army officers, but at dawn the next day we were told that the Japanese already were landing only four miles distant. We went to the airfield and found an old plane that had been condemned as unflyable six years before, but had been reconditioned. Six of us crowded into that old plane and it got into the air with Major W. R. Bradford, of San Antonio, Texas, piloting. We flew over the city of Iloilo where we saw Japanese boats tied up at the piers unloading tanks, automobiles, and troops. The Japanese didn't open up, apparently believing the plane was Japanese.

It was a "heart-in-mouth" flight to another island, skimming over the water in the hope of avoiding detection by Japanese patrols. Major Bradford landed the plane as three Japanese dive-bombers swept down the field. We scattered for cover and no one was hurt.

From now on all of us are living on borrowed time. . . .

5

THAT was not all of Schedler's story of how he managed to reach Australia. The remainder was withheld in order to protect others who later used the same tortuous route.

The British occupied the French Island of Madagascar—im-

portant position along the supply route around Africa to the Far
East. The interest of some strategists turned toward India. The
Nazis and the Italians continued their attempt to push eastward
through the Mediterranean. The Japs were mopping up Burma in
their push toward the west. India might become the battleground in
a gigantic pincers thrust. In anticipation of what might happen in
India, additional correspondents either were there or en route.
Daniel De Luce was there. He had arrived after a perilous jaunt
through Burma in an army "jeep." He told about Allied forces that
were falling back to India to escape the Japanese. He also told
about his trip and what he encountered:

Drunk with weariness, slogging afoot in desert dust and the
oozy slime of dank teak forests, and swimming muddy, swollen
streams, the last companies of the British and Indian armies of
Burma are fighting on toward the mountains of India in the tough-
est withdrawal of this war.

Thirteen hundred miles and thirteen days back I left them, and
drove a U. S. Army jeep from Shwebo to Calcutta over trails fit
only for goats, mules—and jeeps. No other type of motor vehicle
in Burma could have made the trip. The exhausted remnants of two
Imperial divisions that have been continuously in action during the
whole Burma war must walk.

Harassed by enemy fighters and bombers which for nearly
seven weeks have been supreme over Burma, knifed from ambush
by blood-crazed bands of native traitors, the haggard British rifle-
men, tank crews, and wiry Sepoys from the Indian units, are now
within a few score miles of the rugged Assam border, which must
be held against the invader.

Back there in Burma the cruel lesson that something more than
willingness to muddle through is needed to win this war is still
being taught. Boys with matchless courage are being slaughtered
because they are inadequate in numbers, ill-trained, poorly equipped.
The last tired companies of what four months ago were proud and
smart battalions are still in a galling retreat.

In a downpour before dawn, past the ramshackle school where
the bomb-wounded lay groaning on bare tables, I drove out of
Shwebo, temporary British Army headquarters. I had been warned
that Japanese patrols might already have cut my cross-country track
toward India. Along the railway, continually attacked by Japanese
planes, headquarters and wounded were moving the same morning

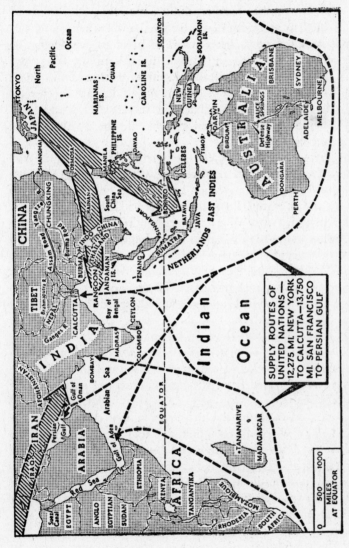

Map 22—As Japan advanced, the pattern of her strategy began to appear. One of her thrusts aimed at the East Indies, the other pointed through Burma to the Allied supply lines. Would this thrust also meet the expected German drive across Iran? Would Japan take the French island of Madagascar off the east coast of Africa and thereby cut British ship lines? The British acted quickly to forestall this latter threat and early in May, 1942, moved against the island in a well-engineered coup.

200 miles up country to Myitkyina, halfway from Shwebo to the eternal snows of Tibet.

The Imperials, never trained for jungle fighting, have learned it the hard way. Burma has been a school where they either learned the jungle or died in ambush. In spite of half a century of British rule, Upper Burma has never been linked to India by even one good road. If there had been one, the Burma disaster might have been averted. Instead of one lone battalion, sent to Burma from India by air after the loss of Rangoon, there might have been several divisions hurried by road to throw back the reinforced Japanese. Instead of sacrificing their motorized equipment, the British might have saved every vehicle.

Leaving Shwebo, I struck to the northwest on a new trail hacked out of the jungle, and followed the Chindwin riverbed mile after mile, thankful that the monsoon had not yet filled it with more than a few inches of water. I got the jeep ferried the last six miles of the Chindwin to Kalewa, where the trail ended. A supposed highway from Assam extends to Kalewa, but actually it is just a boggy cart track. Kalewa is a bedraggled, sodden river town, with cholera, smallpox, and malaria raging, and thousands of civilian refugees fleeing through it in the past months. Sick Indian mothers, clutching nursing babies, huddled under grass-thatched lean-tos in a driving rain. Skinny, white-bearded Tamil coolies begged help from the roadside.

A middle-aged English matron was the only European woman in Kalewa. She was the wife of a district official and so long as she stayed on the Indian water front the laborers did not rush in panic toward the frontier.

Forty miles onward, in the dripping village of Kangyi, the English manager of vast teakwood holdings told me that $4,000,000 worth of teak was lying in the highland forests, and that the rains would sweep the logs downriver, either to be lost or to be caught by the Japanese. A million-dollar herd of elephants was employed in this district, some transporting evacuees over the most difficult part of the route. A convoy of them preceded my jeep out of Kangyi. Swarms of mosquitoes and leeches covered my hands as I dug the jeep out of the mud, and rain drenched me from head to toe to give me a taste of what the British Army then was encountering far to the south without even the occasional shelter and freedom from attack that I was enjoying.

My jeep passenger, a wounded British captain, helped on frequently needed repairs and plodded in the mud on an infected foot to salvage bolts from an abandoned motorbus after the jeep's engine had jarred off its frame. Crudely-refined gasoline clogged the carburetor time after time. But the four-wheel drive enabled the jeep to climb slippery ditches and to push on through the stickiest swamps. Keeping the jeep going seemed the most important thing in my life.

Red-skinned Naga ex-headhunters, leaning on picks and shovels, gazed in amusement as we jolted into India on the emergency mountain road. The Nagas, with rings in their ears, brass bangles on their knees, black hair cut in mush-bowl shape, and tiny breechclouts their only clothing, were a friendlier race than the Burmese bad-hats with their long knives.

Now a Calcutta streetcar bangs past my hotel room in a city that never heard the ear-splitting crash of enemy bombs and never saw women and children smashed to pulp by high explosives. It seems like an unreal world—a world I had almost forgotten in four months of covering the Burma campaign. It is well-fed, comfortably bedded. It goes on dancing and drinking.

Yet, back in Upper Burma, dwindling columns of dirt-caked, khaki-clad troops are still fighting for their lives—one day tortured by thirst, the next nearly drowned by torrential rain. They have been fighting like this ever since January, when they were given the impossible job of defending Burma's wide-open eastern frontier against an enemy more numerous, more skilled in jungle warfare, and regularly reinforced by land, air, and sea.

What happened in Burma is a military tragedy for the United Nations, as bitter as those of Singapore, the Indies, and the Philippines. For the handful of Imperial soldiers who lost Lower Burma and for the few understrength Chinese divisions who stemmed the Japanese conquest for more than a month in Central Burma, there can be nothing but praise. They were ordered to do the impossible. Their casualties were appalling. Most of the stocky, singing Britishers whom I saw hiking into the Salween line in January and the smiling Chinese legions deploying around Toungoo in March, were killed in combat. Some cut their way out of the death pockets and always there was a temporary new line established farther back. Always it was weaker than the last one. For hundreds of miles it was fight, withdraw, fight again. Every mile backward the air support faded until in April there was virtually nothing left. The enemy and the traitors increased until thousands liberally equipped with mortars and tommy guns were thrown into the push.

The fall of Rangoon on March 8 doomed Burma and the British knew it, officers and men. They kept on fighting, for surrender was not in their vocabulary.

Back along the Irrawaddy two weeks ago I gave a sick Tommy from Yorkshire a ride to a field hospital. The same day the Japanese raided Shwebo and scored a direct hit on the bungalow where I had messed, killing the wife and mother.

"The bloody Japs are running us out of Burma," said the Tommy, "but we're coming back, that's sure. We won't keep on doing things wrong forever; someday we'll wake up and get smarter than the other bloke. Put that in the papers, sir. All the troops in Burma tried hard."

6

MAIN U. S. activity was off Australia. The Pacific Fleet was in the Coral Sea. On May 9, came the naval engagement the U. S. had been seeking with the evasive Japanese. First word of the battle came from General MacArthur's headquarters in Australia. McDaniel reported all available details:

The greatest naval battle of the war is in progress in the Coral Sea directly east of Australia, with the immediate fate of this continent depending on the result.

Allied headquarters disclosed today that eleven Japanese battleships already had been sunk and that five were badly damaged. U. S. bombers are playing a major part in the attack.

The battle is in its fifth day and still raging. First reports described it as perhaps the biggest naval engagement in American history and rivaling in magnitude the celebrated Battle of Jutland on May 31, 1916, between the British and German Grand Fleets.

The action started last Monday off the Solomon Islands and swept westward to the Coral Sea, flaming across hundreds of miles of the South Pacific. Australia waited tensely for the outcome, realizing that the fate of the Commonwealth may hinge on victory or defeat.

Australia's prime minister, John Curtin, declared that the action was of crucial importance to the whole conduct of the war in the Pacific zone commanded by General Douglas MacArthur.

The next day MacArthur announced that the action had "temporarily ceased." Other than confirmation of Jap losses, there still were few details. MacArthur said that huge Allied bombers were relentlessly pursuing the Japanese ships.

Again there was a period of waiting for details. Again too much information might have aided the enemy. But the full story came later. The only American correspondent to witness the momentous battle was Stanley Johnston. He represented the Chicago *Tribune,* a member of The Associated Press. He was aboard the aircraft carrier *Lexington,* who herself was sunk. He had been a war observer for the *Tribune* since 1940. Long before that he had had four years of World War I with an Australian artillery unit in Flanders. The time lag placed by Washington's release of the story gave him ample time to digest all details into one of the outstanding chronicles of the war:

From the deck of an aircraft carrier which was bombed, machine-gunned, and torpedoed, I witnessed the Battle of the Coral Sea. For five full days I lived with the American heroes—airmen and seamen alike—who there won a magnificent victory.

Now, five weeks after the battle, its story, filled with dramatic details of deeds of valor as thrilling as any in American history, can be told. The veil of official silence can be lifted.

It was the first great naval defeat ever dealt Japanese Fleets— and ironically enough it was fought entirely in the air. The battle was scattered over 400,000 square miles of tropic seas. The surface fleets that fought the battle never saw each other, and during most of the fighting were from 80 to 180 miles apart. There were, of course, other sides to the entire Coral Sea engagement. In these, General MacArthur's bombardment squadrons, based on Australian soil, pounded Japanese installations in and around New Guinea. I was, however, at sea, and my story is the Navy's story.

First of all this was an engagement of aircraft carriers—two American against three Japanese. It disclosed how completely the carrier has displaced the battleship in importance in modern war. It was a battle of dive-bombers, torpedo-bombers, and fighter pilots. It also was a battle of anti-aircraft gunners. When it was finished, two of the Japanese carriers had been sunk and the third was out of action. As for our own forces, the gallant old U. S. S. *Lexington,* one of the famous old "twin" carriers that laid the foundation for all the Navy's aircraft carrier operations, was our only loss.

In addition to their carriers, the Japanese also lost four heavy cruisers, three destroyers, one seaplane tender, four gunboats, three troopships, and supply vessels ranging from 10,000 to 20,000 tons each, and a host of auxiliary craft. Our airmen and ship gunners shot down more than 140 Jap airplanes, 120 of these falling to our pilots. We lost 25 airplanes in air duels and perhaps 60 more went down with the *Lexington*. We have no way of knowing how many Japanese planes were lost with their carriers.

For me the commencement of the Coral Sea epic was a notification last April 16. It came from the Navy and reached me at the Moana Hotel at Waikiki. It told me to report for sea duty. I was to be at Pearl Harbor at 7 A.M. the next day, typewriter, bag, and toothbrush. I reported on time and to my delight was led aboard the *Lexington,* then barren of aircraft and strangely empty. I couldn't understand why we were leaving without the planes.

"Are we going without our planes?" I asked the ship executive officer.

"They'll pick us up at sea," he grinned.

And they did, hours later, when we were hitting a fast clip southward. They came out of the sky in practice dives, aiming light smoke bombs at a target sled towed 1,000 feet back on our foaming wake. Then a scout bomber appeared, towing a sleeve target at which all the ship's gunners fired live shells. It was my first look at the high-speed automatic cannon with which this ship bristled. The pound and roar of the guns shake your very teeth. When this was over, the ship's little monoplane fighters came along, dived on the now-shattered sleeve, and finished by shredding it with their .50-caliber gun batteries.

"Looks like we're sharpening our teeth," I observed.

"Sure, for Japs," a senior officer said.

Later I learned what we were getting into. It seems that in order to take Port Moresby and invade Australia, the Japanese had established land-based aircraft on New Guinea at Salamaua and Lae; on New Britain at Gasmata and Rabaul; on Deboyne Island (eastern end of the Louisiade Archipelago), and in the Solomon Islands. To control the Coral Sea they had sent two powerful naval striking forces. One force moved south from the big Jap base on the Isle of Truk, 720 nautical miles north of Rabaul, New Britain. It was to control the Jomard passage—the only channel from north and south through the coral reefs at the southeastern tip of New

Guinea. The second moved southeast of Truk and took the long open sea passage around the Solomon Islands to the east into the Coral Sea.

These two fleets were intended to be a pair of pincers, nipping any American naval forces that might be in this area. Finally the pincers were to be assisted by occupation forces, cruisers, destroyers, troop and supply ships concentrated at Deboyne Island and Tulagi harbor. We didn't know all this at the time, but that was the situation when our task force arrived in the Coral Sea area on the 1st of May.

Our force from Pearl Harbor had consisted of the *Lexington* and a retinue of cruisers and destroyers. Throughout our two-week voyage we had our air scouts ranging the seas for 200 miles or more on all sides of us. When we joined forces these scouts were augmented and on the afternoon of May 3 an aviation ensign spied 15 enemy craft, warships, and transports in Tulagi harbor.

Rear Admiral Frank J. Fletcher, who had assumed command of the entire force, laid his plans as darkness descended that night. We turned northward, steaming hard, and at dawn lay south of Guadalcanal Island, 100 miles due south of Tulagi. This position was taken to screen us from possible enemy scouts.

We were up before dawn, airplane motors turning over on the flight deck of the carrier. Scout planes were off in the predawn dark. Soon they were reporting the enemy still in position, unsuspicious of our presence. Immediately dive-bombers and torpedo planes took the air, and in less than thirty minutes were roaring down on the Jap ships.

Surprise was complete. The first anti-aircraft fire came only with the second wave of bombers. Our boys unloaded, came home, loaded again, and flew off. A few fighters accompanied the second wave and liquidated the minor Jap opposition (five seaplane fighters). The bombers came back for a third trip and when they had dropped their last missiles, fourteen of the fifteen Jap ships were sunk or beached and burning. Photographs and pilots' reports indicated enemy loss of life here must have been terrific, particularly on the crowded troop ships that were blasted from above and below.

On the afternoon of May 6, our scout planes had exciting news. They had located, north of the Isle of Misima, a Jap carrier and cruiser force. We didn't know it then but this was the enemy spearhead bound for Jomard passage. Rear Admiral Fletcher ordered our force northeast. At dawn on the morning of May 7, we were standing eastward of the island of Tagula, and about 180 miles southeast of the second Jap force. Again we caught them by surprise, our dawn scouts reporting their planes still all aboard their carrier.

The Japs had nine fighters in the air when our striking force of torpedo planes and dive-bombers arrived, but obviously they did not expect attack. Their carrier, believed to be of the biggest and newest type, turned into the wind to launch planes as our dive-bombers started down. This was a fatal move, for it kept the Jap carrier on a steady course, presenting a perfect target.

Back on our carrier, anxiously awaiting the outcome, I crowded into the wardroom with officers on duty. Loud-speakers were connected with the *Lexington's* receivers, which were turned to the communication circuits of the planes in the air. There was a jumble of orders and meaningless calls between the planes until suddenly Lieutenant Commander Bob Dixon, skipper of the scout bomber squadron, identified himself to the carrier.

"Scratch one flat-top—scratch one flat-top," he said, and abruptly signed off.

The ship's loud-speaker system carried the message to the entire crew and the craft. There were cheers. The men knew that Dixon was reporting the total destruction of the Jap carrier. Our own losses were only two scout dive-bombers.

Our flyers shot down twenty-three planes in widely scattered engagements, and later in the day learned that a heavy cruiser was sunk at the same time. Our luck, it seemed, was extraordinary.

We had even more extraordinary luck that evening. At dusk, as our last patrols were gliding out of rain squalls and curtains of low clouds, nine planes, certainly not from our carrier, approached us. We were at battle stations with every gun manned for a raid when to our amazement all nine flashed on landing lights. The men at the guns on our carrier recognized them as enemy planes, even though the leader of the planes was flashing a landing signal with his light. Our gunners opened up and the destroyers around us took up·the barrage.

Almost with a disdainful air the Japs doused their lights and flew off in line astern. We learned by following them that a Japanese Fleet similar to our own was then only 30 miles away, hidden from our sight in the darkness and rain. The Jap pilots had mistaken our carrier for their own!

The information was electrifying. We expected a night action but in the darkness the fleets never met. Nevertheless, this incident opened the final twenty-four hours of the *Lexington's* career, forecasting,, if we had known it, her doom.

All night we maneuvered so as to be in the vicinity of the enemy for an early morning attack. It was one of those still, perfect tropical dawns. The black night had faded swiftly into gleaming torrid day. Our force swished along, the gray ships spaced around us, sliding quietly about their ominous business. Aboard the *Lexington* we went about our business, the air crews warmed up their planes, breaking the silence with the engine roars.

But all of us were tense inside. The pilots were jumpy as they gathered in the ready room, like athletes before a big contest. Even the stewards who passed around coffee showed the strain. This time we knew there would be no surprise. We had already been blessed with too much good fortune. Now we would have a fight. The two fleets would swing knockout blows at one another. It was a question of who connected first.

The whole fleet crouched, like a runner on his mark, awaiting the first "contact" report. When the primary search—an area of fifty miles around the *Lexington*—had been finished, we relaxed somewhat. Engines were stopped and pilots and off-duty officers had breakfast. Meanwhile, the scout flyers began a systematic hunt over the sea surface in a circle with a 250-mile radius around us.

At 8:10 A.M., Ensign Smith, who had gone out on a segment of the hunt that took him to the northeast, reported "contact." He reported the enemy was about 190 miles northeast of us and roughly forty to fifty miles southeast of Tagula Island in the Louisiade Archipelago. Five minutes later our pilots were in their cockpits with radio men and gunners. Engines were turning again. But the admiral, fearing there might also be a closer Japanese Fleet, delayed the departure order. His problem was to determine whether the reported Japanese were the only enemy naval units within striking distance.

Time passed slowly and tension increased. Lieutenant Commander Bob Dixon, who had been flying in a scouting segment near Ensign Smith, flew over to the latter's area and also made "contact" with the enemy. Dixon reported the Japs in great force with two big carriers, many cruisers and destroyers. He also could see the enemy had most of their aircraft aboard. Hardly had this information arrived when a huge column of smoke was sighted about five miles off our port beam. A fighter pilot radioed that he had shot down another of the big four-engined Jap Kawanishi patrol boats. It was obvious that the Kawanishi had seen our fleet and likely that its crew had reported our presence before crashing.

At 9:30 A.M. the real striking forces of our fleet got off. They consisted of fifty-four dive-bombers, twenty torpedo-bombers, and sixteen fighter planes. These forces were combined units from the *Lexington* and another carrier, the name of which must not be mentioned for reasons of military security.

As protection for our two carriers, our cruisers and destroyers, a unit of sixteen fighters and some scout planes were retained. These were distributed in various sectors of the sky from 20 to 150 miles from our ships which were steaming at 20 knots toward the northeast—a straight course for the enemy designed to reduce as much as possible the distance of the return journey for our striking air fleet.

Rear Admiral Aubrey W. Fitch, who had been given command of the *Lexington* group for the anticipated attack by the Japanese, disposed his fighters at high altitudes and the scouts at low altitudes.

From one of our scouts came a radio call about 10 A.M.: "Twelve unidentified planes approaching. Still 160 miles away on course to intercept you."

We reasoned that our scout had seen part of the Japanese carrier-borne air fleet soon after it had taken off to attack the *Lexington*. Captain Fred C. Sherman of the *Lexington* (recently promoted to rear admiral) and our air officers said they believed the two air blows—ours against the Japs and theirs against us—had been "fired"—that is, the planes on both sides had taken off at almost the same time.

Battle stations for the fleet kept the *Lexington* and the other carrier surrounded by a double line of cruisers and destroyers. Any torpedo planes coming in low to strike at either of the important carriers must pass through the anti-aircraft barrage of the protecting vessels. Our cruisers were perhaps a quarter mile off our beam on either side and destroyers about half a mile away.

"Katie to carrier," came the next radio warning from our scouts at 10:50 A.M. "Big force coming in from right ahead. Sixty miles away."

Immediately we knew we were in for a real battle. The *Lexington* turned into the wind at once, launching all the reserve fighters and scouts that had been waiting for this moment. Then things

happened fast and furiously. The timetable of the assault is
extremely important to give the true picture of the speed of such
attacks. I will give it, just as I scribbled it in my notebook while
standing on the *Lexington's* open signal bridge throughout the
battle.

"Enemy planes, 17,000 feet, four groups of nine each. Two
groups of dive-bombers, each protected by Messerschmitt-109's and
Zeros," Lieutenant Commander Paul Ramsey, skipper of the defensive fighters aloft, reported. "I'm at 14,000 about 12 miles northeast of you, climbing hard. They're going awfully fast. Doubt if I
can intercept."

Almost simultaneously we got a call from our scouts:

"Enemy torpedo planes spilling out of a cloud eight miles off.
They are at 6,000 feet in a steep dive. We're intercepting now."

I can fix the action of the next few minutes accurately from
my notes as follows:

11:14 A.M.—The *Lexington* was turning back into the defensive formation of ships. On its port side there was only one screening vessel, a cruiser.

11:16 A.M.—Suddenly we saw guns aboard our screening
cruiser belch smoke and flame, and a moment later, heard the thun-
derclap of the shots.

11:16½ A.M.—"Here they come," sang the lookouts. "Enemy
torpedo planes coming in port beam."

"Hard starboard," said Captain Sherman in a conversational
tone to his helmsman. This maneuver was to present only the stern
to the torpedo. But a ship, even a fast ship like the *Lexington,*
moves at a snail's pace compared with planes.

And as the captain spoke, the Japanese aircraft hove into view,
slim silver monoplanes, low, spreading out fanlike, diving in directly
toward our port side at high speeds. As soon as they came into view
all the 100-odd guns on the valiant old *Lexington* broke into flame.

There was the sharp "wham, wham, wham, wham" of the
5-inchers, the slow bark of the 1.1-inchers, and the stutter of the
smaller weapons. A hellish chorus, uneven and jerky, but with a
power that left us, there on the bridge, gasping in partial vacuums
created by the blasts.

More action from my battle notes expanded from the few
words I wrote at the moment:

11:17 A.M.—The Japs were so low that I saw two lead planes
pull up to skim over our protecting cruiser. In an instant one was

obliterated in a flash of flame—it must have been a direct hit from the cruiser's guns. The other kept right on coming.

The *Lexington* was still swinging, however, and because only her slender stern was presented the Japanese changed her course, paralleled us, and, when abreast, turned once more toward our left side. They were flying right into a hail of tracer bullets from our small weapons. They were close, only 800 to 1,000 yards away and we could see clearly as they began dropping their torpedoes.

11:17½ A.M.—Eight of those Japs braving our fire dropped their "fish," then they continued straight in toward us. The leading pair were right down on the water, so low that they zoomed up to get over us. Both would have passed right over the fore part of the deck.

Our forward 1.1-battery had the range of the first Jap. I could see their shell-bright crimson tracer, tearing through the wings and fuselage. This plane wavered, began a slow roll to its left, and veered off just enough to pass in an inverted position just under our bow. As it passed, I saw flames coming from the tail and the machine dived into the water fifty feet off our starboard bow.

The 5-inch forward battery, manned by Marines, laid its fire on the second Jap. As this plane zoomed to cross almost directly over the Marines' guns they hit it squarely with a shell. The plane flew to bits. Its engine plunged into the water, almost at the foot of the battery, shreds of its wings and tail surface slithered along the carrier's deck. The other Japanese flyers were trying to pass astern. There, similar fusillades of fire were concentrated on them.

11:18½ A.M.—The *Lexington* shuddered under our feet, and a heavy blast flashed in a spout of water on our port side, forward. It was a torpedo.

The wakes of others could be seen streaking toward us. Some of these torpedoes were porpoising, nosing up out of the water and then diving deeply as though their control mechanism had been damaged.

11:20 A.M.—"Wham"—another torpedo hit. Almost at the same place forward. Another spout of flame enclosed in sea water. While we were staggering under the lurch as the *Lexington* flinched under the blow, a lookout called: "Dive-bombers!"

Looking out, I saw the first dive-bomber flattening out, having released its bomb. "Boom"—a blinding flash on the port forward gun gallery. A 1,000-pound bomb had hit among these 5-inch guns, wrecking the battery and starting a fire. And more torpedoes were swerving toward us.

11:21 A.M.—"Baloom!"—another torpedo hit. Also on the port side, almost amidships.

All around the stricken vessel, huge spouts of water were rising. They were caused by the explosions of near-misses by bombs. One light bomb hit the top of the *Lexington's* funnel on the left side, killing or wounding several men firing a .50-caliber anti-aircraft machine gun.

In the midst of all this, doing my best to see everything going on, I suddenly had the illogical thought: "There's so damned much noise right here I can't hear any single explosion. It's almost like a silence."

"Wham," "boom," "tat-tat-tat-tat," "bang, bang, bang," went our anti-aircraft. Then the prolonged "whaaaaaaaaaaa" of the Japanese dive-bombers coming right down on us, all guns blasting as they came. We could see their tracers lacing past, many of them too high. I remember thinking then: "These fellows don't dive-bomb like our men. They aren't coming straight down, only about fifty degrees."

As I was thinking that, I saw a black-blue shape whip across between the bridge island and the funnel, a space of about fifteen feet. It cleared the rail by inches, hit the water, and blasted. It was a Japanese 1,000-pound bomb that would have removed all of us on the bridge island—the main control center for the entire ship—had it been a little closer. In passing, it had struck the siren lanyard housing causing the big whistle on the funnel to begin to howl.

11:22 A.M.—"Wham!"—Once more the *Lexington* lurched beneath our feet. The fourth torpedo hit.

11:22½ A.M.—"Baloom!"—Now the fifth torpedo, all on the port side, amidships and forward. Looking off the bridge, I could see the water foaming and laced with torpedo trails. They seemed to be coming from all directions and in unlimited numbers. I looked out to starboard to see how the rest of the ships were faring and counted five planes burning on the water. Japanese planes going away were being followed by our starboard guns that trailed tracers into and after them.

The dive-bombers still were coming down, only a second or so apart. Most of their bombs were falling toward the after-end of the ship, close but not quite hitting.

I looked up. I could see the Japanese machines diving in a

chain. As I watched I could see a bomb leave a plane. The plane would continue down, gradually flattening. Its machine guns and wing cannon would wink momentarily, it would sweep over the *Lexington's* deck and then would become a tiny shape, swiftly diminishing in size as it sped away.

11:25 A.M.—"Seven more torpedo planes," the lookouts called again. "From the port side."

The anti-aircraft fire was so hot that the pilots in those planes were anxious to get away. They dropped their torpedoes while still at a 45-degree glide and more than 200 feet above the water, then turned away, never coming closer than within 1,500 yards of the *Lexington*.

Again we swung to avoid the torpedoes. To the starboard again, to present as little target as possible. The Japs came in, fanned out over a wide arc. All the torpedoes seemed to be porpoising badly. Two among the first group disappeared, and when they reappeared they were on the ship's other side, having made their porpoising dive deep enough to pass underneath us.

"Hold her steady, captain, hold her steady," cried Commander Duckworth, the ship's air officer. He was out on the navigation bridge dancing up and down with excitement and with his hands out as if to press torpedoes away. "We've got three that are exactly paralleling us, if we turn we'll collect one sure!"

11:27 A.M.—Five more torpedo planes appeared in the center of the fleet. They singled us out, spread out, and bored in toward our starboard side. With the entire fleet firing at them, they dropped their "fish" a long way out. The old *Lexington,* still charging ahead in spite of her wounds, turned once more and all missed.

Two planes with torpedoes slid in through the fleet fire. These turned aside from the *Lexington,* passing astern of us, and dropped their "fish" at the cruiser on our port quarter. The ship swung, avoiding the torpedoes. The cruiser's gunners got a direct hit on one of the two planes. The plane disappeared in a clap of thunder and flame.

11:32 A.M.—The last of the dive-bombers swung by, raking us with his gunfire as he passed. The bomb fell close by, missed, and suddenly there was silence.

In all this furious action our fighters and scouts had not been idle. One hundred and three Japanese planes came over. Forty-three or more fell in a twenty-mile radius around us, downed by our planes and ship's guns. The guns in all took nineteen, an all-time high for a fight of this kind. Our pilots, heroes everyone, got twenty-four.

Right through the hurricane of bombing and torpedoing came a small yellow life raft—the kind that all our airplanes carried. On it was a pilot who had been shot down in air combat. He was drifting, but the fleet, speeding along at 20 to 25 knots, passed all around him so that for a few minutes he was in the heart of our formations.

Not a vessel stopped—to stop at such a time was suicidal. But our lookouts reported him to Captain Sherman. I looked at him through binoculars and saw that he was waving and cheering each ship as it went past him. He was not calling for help. I learned later that Captain Sherman signaled the last destroyer trailing the fleet to pick him up.

The *Lexington,* in spite of all her beating, was keeping up with the fleet. She had a 6-degree list to the port side.

I overheard some of the telephone conversation on Captain Sherman's side of the bridge. One orderly got a call from an inspector who was below reporting on a torpedo hit. The conversation was as follows:

"I'm in frame so-and-so, there's a hole in the waterline, a big one."

"Well, why don't you plug it?"

"Can't, it's too big. I can see a cruiser through it."

"Then shut the door and forget it."

I stood there on the signal deck of the gallant old *Lexington* and watched her crew fight off the Japanese and make desperate efforts to save her. But internal fires, started by the explosions, engulfed her even after the Japanese had been driven off.

When it finally was obvious to all that she could not be saved, when it appeared that another blast at any minute might hurl every living man aboard into kingdom come, with her officers and men I slid fifty feet down hemp lines into the sea. I was picked up by one of the United States vessels that rescued everyone who survived the air combats. And later, safe on the deck of another vessel, I saw an American destroyer approach and torpedo the *Lexington.*

"She never wavered. She kept her head up and went down like the lady she always was."

That was what one of the *Lexington's* executive officers said to me as we watched her sink slowly into the dusk of the South Pacific.

The *Lexington's* crew came home aboard three Navy ships, two cruisers and a transport. It was not, however, a retreat. It was only a temporary lull in battle, for the men came home to take over a new carrier, *Lexington II*.

Of course, we didn't know it would be this way the night of May 8 as we watched the old ship sink, hissing clouds of steam as the cherry-red plates of its flaming hull slid beneath the long Pacific Ocean swells, but next morning Captain Fred Sherman—now Rear Admiral Sherman—called together the 800 of us who had gathered on a smart new cruiser.

"Men, I've got news for you," he said. "I've asked the Navy Department to hold us all together as one crew and to put us aboard a brand-new aircraft carrier. And I have recommended that this new carrier be called the *Lexington II*, so that we can carry on together right from here."

7

THAT Battle of the Coral Sea staved off an attempt of the Japs to invade Australia. Bomber pursuit of the fleeing Nippon survivors accounted for another two or three ships. That raised the count of Jap casualties to at least twenty-three. United Nations around the world were heartened.

Churchill warned Hitler against using poison gas in Russia—said Britain would retaliate in kind. General Timoshenko's Russian Armies launched an offensive against Nazi-held territory in the Ukraine. The Axis opened its sixth Libyan campaign with a drive toward Tobruk. Axis submarines sank U. S. vessels in the North Atlantic and the Gulf of Mexico. French warships were immobilized at Martinique. Rationing of gasoline began in seventeen Eastern States and the District of Columbia.

Roosevelt's recent statement that an A.E.F. was spreading around the world was truer than ever. More men were sent through the Pacific toward Australia. More thousands were convoyed across the Atlantic to Ireland. They represented a young, vigorous army. On May 18, thousands of them landed at a Northern Ireland port to join others who had preceded them months before. There, the U. S. was building one of the most powerful bases in the history of warfare. Former New York ship news reporter, Johnny Moroso, was with the new contingent. His story of the crossing came back by cable:

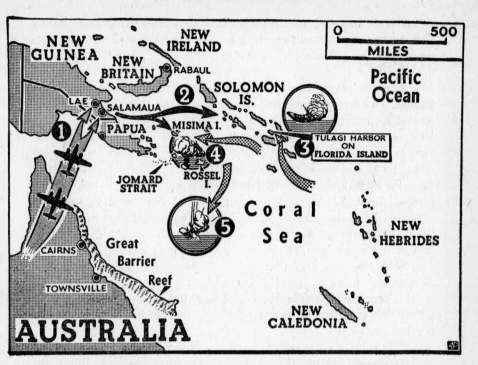

Map 23—The 400,000-square-mile battle of the Coral Sea staved off a Japanese attempt
to invade Australia. Early in March, 1942, Australia-based aircraft had bombed the Japs
at (1), delaying their advance toward (2). On May 4, the U. S. Navy virtually annihilated
a Jap fleet near Tulagi (3), and then on May 7 American planes attacked the main Jap
force near (4). U. S. losses in the battle following at (5) included the aircraft carrier
"Lexington," but the Japs withdrew after sustaining much heavier losses.

I have just crossed the Atlantic with a huge American convoy that outfoxed enemy submarines all the way. We had to "push the periscopes down," almost all the way of our 2,400-mile voyage of daring and skill.

The destroyers and planes delivered thunderous depth-charge attacks. In convoy work the job is to get the troopships through. You don't have time to investigate attacks or run the enemy down. You blast him when you think he is near and keep sailing. The vicious explosions left no doubt in our minds that some more strangers would have breakfast in hell.

No torpedoes were fired at us. Neither were we bombed by planes, although our eager gunners prayed for an attack as they crouched by their guns night and day. This eagerness was one of the cheering things during the voyage. Our Yankee kids have the utmost confidence in their ability to knock down planes.

So thousands and thousands of cheering Yankee soldiers— mechanized men of America's new world-girdling army—have arrived here after their dangerous and fog-ridden journey. With these jaunty lads came the millions of dollars worth of battle tools—ready for instant use.

The value of our convoy and its ultimate effect on the war are like the operational details of our trip—military secrets. But I am allowed to say that it was the largest yet to arrive here. The soldiers of this war are better equipped and prepared than the lads who rushed overseas in the last conflict. They have a new type of helmet that affords more protection. Their rifles shoot harder and faster. Their food is more plentiful and scientifically planned. They are sturdier, healthier, and as cheerful as kids at a circus. Some grew homesick at times. Others got seasick, but all carried on. One exuberant gang nicknamed their freighter the "Berlin Express."

And, of all things, we had a stowaway on the crossing. His name is Private George F. Duval, Jr. He is 29 years old and is from Chelsea, Massachusetts. He was discovered esconced in a bunk after we were well out to sea. He had come aboard, gear and all, while dock police were looking the other way. He is now under technical arrest, but likely will be absorbed into a military police unit. He had served one three-year hitch in the Army before being drafted. But he had not been selected to come along on this jaunt.

"Hell," he said, "I wanted action and this was the best way I could figure out to get it—quick!"

CHAPTER 20

The Axis' Inner Front

May 15–May 29, 1942

I

WARTIME censorship in this country goes back to the conflict between the states. Once a Civil War correspondent with the Yankee forces submitted a dispatch for the blue pencil before hurrying it to the telegraph office. He was one of the better correspondents. His story, completely verified, was that Lee was moving north on Pennsylvania.

"Sorry," said the censor, "but it can't go."

"Why not?"

"Because it gives information to the enemy."

The correspondent tried reason.

"But, colonel," he asked, "don't you suppose the enemy already knows what he himself is doing?"

The censor finally got the point.

The art of censorship—the art of war correspondence, as well —had progressed materially by the time World War II came.

John Evans is a man who knows as much as any individual about censorship. For most of his adult life he was a European correspondent. For eight years he has been chief of foreign service at the terminus of communications systems that dump the dispatches of all his correspondent colleagues on his desk. Since August 28, 1939, a grist of 40,000 to 50,000 war words from around the world has passed through his hands daily. With World War II at its height, with censorship in one form or another at work in every embattled nation, he wrote:

Censorship frequently impedes, but seldom prevents the essential truth from getting out. There was nothing new about it on

383

September 1, 1939, when Germany invaded Poland. Spain and Russia, notably, already had it very much in force.

Spain, having had a long Civil War, kept the native press under firm control. She forbade foreign correspondents to report certain troubled problems such as differences between Church and State and the rumblings of unrest. Russia alternately tightened and loosened her censorship. Once, in theory, she removed all restrictions, but that did not last.

When the war started, Britain and France immediately took control of all communications. From that beginning, it took a year for England to develop a well-ordered control that sought only to suppress military information. Toward the beginning of 1942 there was added a prohibition against sending abroad any news that might create dissension among the United Nations. In reality, neither of these restrictions greatly hampered the flow of honest, factual news.

France's censorship was hastily organized and erratically imposed. It sometimes had its humorous aspects.

One day an American correspondent walked into the office of the censor in Paris. His face was familiar; he had been there before. The censor handling the telephone switchboard tapped him on the arm:

"Say! Mind taking over here for a few minutes while I have some lunch?"

Before the surprised correspondent could explain his identity, the official was off. The correspondent took over.

No sooner had that censor returned than another—the one who read and blue-penciled the dispatches of all American correspondents—likewise tapped him on the arm. Would the obliging fellow take over for him for a few minutes?

The correspondent sat on the desk and fingered the copy of some of his rival correspondents. He could have done anything he wished with their stories. He also could have sent out anything he himself might have cared to write. The second censor finally returned. The correspondent identified himself.

After that there were at least two censors in Paris who knew that Roy Porter was a war correspondent!

The other day I heard two intelligent people discussing censorship.

"Just what is censorship, anyway?" one of them asked. "Tell me in words of one syllable."

The man who replied had a tough job on his hands, but he did rather well with it:

"In time of war a country feels that it must be careful that information will not get out that might be of military value to the enemy, or that might endanger morale. The country arranges to look at all dispatches and decides what should or should not be published. To do this, it appoints a staff of censors. The men set up a system of passing on all news copy based on principles laid down by the government. Some of them are well-informed and intelligent. Others, untrained for what they are supposed to do, frequently get bogged down by instructions they cannot understand, or take the easiest way and try to prevent the publication of almost everything. By doing that, they feel they stand less chance of getting in trouble with immediate superiors, or with the government itself."

The first man said: "I gather you do not feel that censorship as it is practiced is all that it might be. What would you do?"

His questions were getting tougher.

"Well," the other replied, "I am one of the first to admit that there must be some sort of check on information during war. At the same time I would modify censorship as it is known today in most countries. I would lay down certain principles for all correspondents; then I would not censor every story before it went out. If a correspondent offended, I would take steps. The real war correspondents today are intelligent men. They know what is military information of value to the enemy, and what is not. Frequently they know it even better than some military men because they are trained to know facts and their implications. Occasionally, under my system, they might come across stories about which even they could not be sure. To meet this situation, I would have one high authority to whom they could go. He would be available at any hour of the day or night, and he would be able to give them a quick answer. But then, maybe I am entirely wrong. You see, I believe that the people are entitled to just as many facts as possible."

The most effective censorship today is the drying up of news sources. In Germany, before the U. S. entry into the war, American correspondents were permitted to talk freely with almost any official, and to send out what they got without physical censorship. But the officials had their orders and they didn't tell all they knew. Correspondents frequently got around this by getting as much information as possible outside of official sources. For what they sent, Germany held them responsible and clamped down on those who were considered unfair.

In Russia, the embargo on official talk has been strict for years and nothing specific could ever be said about armament or the inside of politics. Even now, when Americans as Allies are given much freedom, there is no real relaxation in this censorship at the source.

The value of competent censors was shown most strikingly by British troubles early in the war. Foreign correspondents and the British press joined in protests against bad practices, and the government kept changing the guard until censorship now works fairly smoothly, with occasional blunders acknowledged and usually remedied.

Most important point of all is the demonstrated fact that vital news always gets out. Details may be suppressed for a time, but the essential news is obtained by correspondents and they manage to send it.

The notable exception to this was failure to tell the world of the tremendous Soviet armament. That, however, was a state secret that Russia managed to keep even from military attachés stationed in Moscow, including the Germans themselves. The Nazis had a year in which to find out—during the Soviet-German alliance. All of them reported that the Soviets had good military displays in Red Square, but that the munitions industry was inefficient because the shoe, textile, and other businesses seemed poorly handled. The truth appears to have been that the Soviets were making soldiers' boots instead of civilians' shoes, and bullets instead of butter.

One day the American division of the Ministry of Information in London arranged a big cocktail party to provide personal contact between the censors and the American correspondents. Shortly after the party began, the censor at the Western Union cable telephoned one correspondent with whom he had had a protracted argument the night before. He said in a conspiratorial stage whisper:

"Look, old boy, have you got anything hot you want to send? The Ministry has invited every bloody censor but me to this party and I have to stay on the job. If you want to send something over, I'll pass it. They can't do this to me!"

2

CORRESPONDENTS may have disliked censors generally, but they probably had a minimum of trouble with the Englishman who wasn't invited to the cocktail party. He had a sense of humor.

There were even worse things than censorship. There was in-

ternment in enemy countries. By mid-May, 1942, some of the men
who had been interned since December, 1941, were finally getting
out. They were "exchanged" in deals between the U. S. and Germany and Italy. They were conducted out of enemy countries and
headed for home—or other war assignments.

Alvin J. Steinkopf was one of those interned at Bad Nauheim, in Germany. He told about the life he and his colleagues had
led as "guests of the Gestapo":

Five months in German internment produced in all of us—
correspondents, diplomats, and cute little embassy stenographers—a
feeling of utter futility. Sometimes reason itself came dangerously
near to tottering.

There was nothing to do. One heard nothing. For months on
end our boredom was unrelieved by a single hint that America or
the German government was aware of our existence. We were forgotten men—and a few women. Nobody cared, no one loved us. It
was enough to drive one to drink, but there was precious little to
drink—and that little so bad and so expensive it didn't seem worth
while.

A sedate diplomat took to whittling out little wooden windmills that he set on his balcony. A few misguided internees (including, I am happy to say, only one AP staffer) started growing
mangy-looking beards and bragging about them. An American
naval officer, hard and mean enough to bite nails, started writing
poetry.

We published a newspaper for a while. Ernie Fischer, Eddie
Shanke, and Louis Lochner were reporters. Angus Thuermer was
the mechanical department, turning the crank of the hotel mimeograph machine. I was the sheet's "idea man," a sort of an executive
assistant to Ed Haffel of the New York *Herald Tribune,* who was
editor. As "idea man," I had to produce assignments, and one of
my brilliant notions led to the paper's untimely end. I suggested
an inquiring reporter stunt, soliciting answers to the question: "If
you ever get free, would you return to Bad Nauheim sometime to
have a look at it under happier circumstances?"

Most of the persons questioned said that Bad Nauheim and all
Germany, for that matter, gave them a feeling of nausea, and
that if they never saw it again, it would be far too soon. At this
point, censorship hit us. The American leadership decided we
shouldn't publish such matter because the Germans, who would

be sure to see the paper, might be offended. The official American attitude was that, under the circumstances, we couldn't afford to be sassy.

That dictum didn't please the correspondents. Their attitude was that, for some years, they had been bucking censorship, had endured it because they had to; that their Bad Nauheim paper was a labor of love; that they would do it without censorship, or not at all. Besides, Angus had cranked all our paper through the machine, and getting more was a problem. So our little publication folded. Its circulation at its peak was 186 copies, including numbers filed in the Library of Congress and in our memory books.

We didn't eat very well, as we have revealed in many dispatches. The Germans provided no cigarettes or tobacco, and soap only during the last two months of our detention. For the smokers, there were weeks of deprivation. But these matters seem unimportant now. The lasting recollection is that of the appalling boredom. We read until eyes tired. We played poker and bridge until the spots were rubbed from the cards. One did foolish, time-wasting things. The energetic Mr. Lochner memorized the U. S. Constitution, studied civics and got so full of the subject and a sense of mission that he organized a class and imposed civics on such members of our groups as needed to know something about America. The civics class became part of "Badheim University," which taught strange subjects, including tap dancing, French literature, and the theory of Diesel engine operation,

Phil Whitcomb, our AP Paris stringer, was president of the "University," and he functioned with great industry. Fischer and I became star pupils in a class on Bible history, and dabbled in phonetics, being rarefied speculations on the theory of language. Thuermer tried many courses, flunked in French. Shanke spurned education, and nothing we could do would induce him to improve himself. He was too busy with two other projects. He had smuggled in a little battery-set radio and, locked in his room, fished the air for such news as might be ethering about. Late in the evenings, he and such of us as he tolerated, could hear British broadcasts. It was a daily thrill, disturbed often by atmospherics.

Eddie's other time-killing project was a secret for a long time, but our curiosity was intrigued by the fact that he was always borrowing and stealing paste. Then, one day, the great revelation. He and a commander of the U. S. Navy had built a kite. They took it to the banks of the Usa brook, which flowed past the hotel and

along which we were permitted to walk occasionally. The kite flew
dandy, but the Gestapo was thoroughly alarmed. One got an
impression that Himmler himself took a serious view. Eddie was
scolded to within an inch of his life, and we all had to initial a
typed statement in which it was pointed out that kite-flying damages vegetation, and that it isn't allowed in wartime Germany.
Now Eddie is in London, doubtless writing about bigger kites that
are flying over Germany.

Of our group, Fischer was perhaps the most depressed by confinement. Often he was silent for hours, those staring blue eyes
fixed on a distant vision. None of us could quite see what he saw,
but one day he confessed to me that the mirage that troubled his
fancy was faraway Texas. Then he told me, exchange or no exchange, he was lighting out if we were still imprisoned June 17.

Why June 17? Well, said Ernie, that's Negro Emancipation
Day in Dallas, and that day suited his temperament just fine for
the emancipation of a correspondent. Two hundred kilometers to
Switzerland. Or, if we could get across the Rhine, a nice inviting
border in the direction of Luxembourg. He almost had me per-
suaded that June 17 would do as well for the emancipation of a
Minnesotan.

We hoarded some corned beef. We had some little maps. A
maid told us where a coal train stopped for water. We had a lot of
German passes which might fool the rural cops. We had some
food ration tickets.

The Swedish ship *Drottningholm* got us out before Negro
Emancipation Day, which may be just as well.

3

MONTHS of internment gave at least a few of the correspondents plenty of time to reflect on the causes and effects of war in
the countries in which they had worked. In addition to teaching
civics in that "University-in-Exile," which he and fellow internees
had organized, Louis Lochner mentally phrased his reaction to Germany's declaration of war on the U. S. It was the first story he
cabled after reaching Lisbon, Portugal. He could not have sent it
from Germany. It said:

Hitler committed the greatest blunder of his career when he
took upon himself the odium of declaring war upon the U. S.

That is the opinion held by those of us who lived in Germany and believe we understand German psychology.

The Fuehrer completely flabbergasted the German people. Apparently he also so effectively stunned even his own intimate followers that Paul Joseph Goebbels, propaganda minister, hitherto a master mind at propaganda, for once failed correctly to estimate German psychology. For weeks and months the Nazi slogan in response to unfriendly acts by the U. S. had been: "We won't let ourselves be provoked."

Even after Japan attacked the U. S., German friends and acquaintances in every walk of life insisted that Hitler would merely offer a declaration of solidarity with Japan but would not go beyond that. He had been able to "sell" his war to the German people by claiming:

That the Poles seized the Gleiwitz radio station before German troops moved. That the British and French declared a state of war existed with Germany. That the British already were on their way to Norway when, for "protection of Denmark and Norway," he sent his forces into those countries. That Holland, Belgium, Greece, and Yugloslavia plotted against Germany and were already on the move when he forestalled them. That the Russians were already mobilized against the Reich when, at the eleventh hour, he parried with a counterstroke.

The rank and file of German people—even those millions who do not approve his policies—thought Der Fuehrer too "smart" to declare war. President Roosevelt was represented especially as a man already in his dotage. Give him a little more rope—so the Germans were led to believe—and he would hang himself. Above all, don't play into his hands, was the watch cry. He wants war, it was said—in fact "Roosevelt is running after war—so don't do him the favor of giving him a war."

And then on December 11 the astounding, the amazing, the unbelievable thing happened—Hitler declared war. This was like an ice-cold shower to the German people. Their leader was slipping.

Although he had promised the "completion of the greatest victory in history during 1941," which every Teuton interpreted to mean a victorious peace after but two years of war, he now told the people to get ready for a prolonged conflict.

Incidentally, this conflict to date, according to best estimates available, has meant 2,500,000 casualties for Germany, of which three quarters of a million are dead.

Psychologically, too, Hitler was slipping. We American journalists were guests of the Gestapo while the Fuehrer spoke to the Reichstag on December 11, 1941, hence, we didn't hear that oratorical effort. We were genuinely surprised, however, when one of our guards next day, in return for cigarettes, slipped us a copy of a Berlin daily containing his text and we noted how the German dictator ended his speech, not with a pep talk to fire the nation, but with dire threats against saboteurs at home. We had hitherto considered Hitler a better psychologist.

Correspondents who consider themselves acquainted with German psychology also believe it was a grave error to present the German people with the fable about the heart disease of Field Marshal General Walther von Brauchitsch as a Christmas gift.

Large sections of the German people look to soldiers of the old school of which von Brauchitsch, a disciple of the late Colonel General Werner von Fritsch, was an outstanding representative as their last hope to stave off the worst aspects of Nazi domination over an enslaved people. Von Brauchitsch's "resignation" and Hitler's assumption of the supreme army command acted like a bombshell. The removal of the marshal further put the German people in the doldrums.

Besides, the older generation remembered but too well how the U. S., in 1917, gave the decisive turn to the last World War. Would history repeat itself? That was the question on millions of lips.

The answer by party spellbinders that this was a new type of war didn't seem convincing. The very fact that this is chiefly a mechanical war raised the gravest doubts of German victory in the minds of the common people in the Reich when America's participation was insured by Hitler's war declaration. For every schoolboy in Germany knows that America is tops in mechanics.

As if that were not enough, the talkative little Doctor Goebbels felt impelled to inject himself into the situation with two radio addresses to the German people on December 20, 1941, and on Christmas Eve. If ever he struck a wrong note, it was in those two speeches. At a time when people in Germany were freezing for want of coal and when no more "real" wool was available and furs were almost unobtainable, Goebbels four days before Christmas asked the nation to give up pelts and other warm things and have them shipped to the Russian Front. The German people couldn't believe their ears.

Only a few weeks previously a newsreel had been brought out

showing how soldiers were being furnished with everything needed for the winter. The newsreel even then was running in thousands of smaller houses which received their film later than metropolitan theaters. Clearly, somebody, somewhere was lying. Goebbels and his newsreel didn't jibe.

In an address he blamed the winter for the unusual appeal. That again was a contradiction of something he had said in his own ministry. Only shortly before, Otto Dietrich, Reich press chief, who holds the title of secretary of state in Goebbel's ministry, had appeared before the press directly from Hitler's general headquarters to bring information, as it were, from the horse's mouth. Winter cuts no figure, Dietrich shouted into the hall where we were assembled. Hitler had foreseen everything, including the rigors of a Russian winter. Far from being an ally of the Russians, it would prove a friend of the Germans, Dietrich averred. And now winter was suddenly deserting the little doctor and compelling the German people to give up precious furs and woolens!

His appeal was accompanied by a stern decree imposing the death penalty upon anybody who enriched himself by keeping warm articles given for the soldiers. Incidentally, the decree threw an interesting light on Hitler's estimate of the honesty of his subordinates, for it was they who did the collecting.

Goebbels's Christmas Eve oratorical effort showed a similar failure to gauge feelings of his compatriots correctly. Admitting that gifts were scant and scarce and the traditional candles were missing because all available supplies had been sent to the Russian Front, Goebbels suddenly warned the people not to forsake their leaders and the fighting troops as they had done in 1918. It was decidedly poor psychology to remind Germans of their defeat in 1918 so soon after the declaration of war on the U. S. It was even worse psychology to admit the possibility of a recurrence of 1918.

Hardly were the Christmas days over when a further blow to German morale was delivered by the Reich's sports leader, who urged every patriot to surrender his skis. Only 376,000 pairs of skis were donated as a result of this appeal to a nation extremely fond of slipping over snow on boards. So the government got busy jerking sluggish patriots out of their lethargy. A public announcement was made that no public conveyances could accept skis for transportation. Not even streetcars or city busses were permitted to take anybody with skis. Subsequently, all ski competitions were called off.

From early 1942, and until our departure in mid-May, one depressing fact after another was disclosed to the German people by Hitler and his lieutenants. The Ukraine, according to the German press on February 25, wouldn't yield tangible agricultural results until 1943. Before the Russian campaign every German had been led to believe that grain and other raw materials would pour in from the Ukraine from the moment of its conquest.

Speaking on the German Memorial Day, March 16, Hitler told his people the Russians would be definitely beaten this summer. A month and ten days later, in an address to the Reichstag, he promised that German transportation in the East would be better next winter than last. This was a wet blanket for millions of Germans and seemed to indicate that Hitler expected to face another Russian winter.

The Reichstag speech was a blunder in another way: It disclosed even to the most obtuse how far gone was all personal liberty and how one man arrogated to himself not only all legislative and executive powers, but even all judicial prerogatives. Even annual vacations would be taken from them at the Fuehrer's demand. As though to rub this fact in, the Reich's labor leader, Robert Ley, in a May Day proclamation, demanded more work, more sweat, more effort.

4

In subsequent dispatches, Lochner told more about conditions in Germany:

Life is as cheap in interior Germany as it is at the front. Death sentences are imposed by Nazi judges as easily as an American police court levies fines for minor offenses. Severe sentences and high monetary punishments were the order of the day as we left the Reich.

No sooner had the Nazi regime issued an appeal to civilians in late December to give up their furs and woolens than Hitler issued a decree imposing the death penalty on anybody found guilty of stealing these offerings. By January 12, one man, Karl Sachs, of Fulia, had been executed for pilfering furs. On February 15, we learned of the execution of Johann Walter, a Vienna clothes thief. Two persons who aided him were sentenced to fifteen and twelve years' hard labor, respectively. The next day the press announced the execution of seven Germans who committed thefts during blackouts.

There followed an announcement that two Berlin captains of industry had been yanked into a concentration camp because they assigned laborers in their munitions plants to do chores for them in their private homes. There was also published the story of a Frankfurt merchant whose safe was robbed of 18,000 Reichsmarks. He was fined 18,000 marks and sentenced to three months for hoarding money.

Hitler's widely advertised superhighways may prove an important factor in the undoing of the German war machine. The longer the war lasts, the more evident it becomes that Hitler bet on the wrong horse in solving the nation's transportation problem through the construction of highways rather than upkeep of Germany's railway system.

Hitler's military strategy may be summed up in the word that has become common to every language since 1939—"blitzkrieg." As long as that idea worked, Hitler was right in honeycombing the country with splendid highways, unexampled in Europe. Work was given to millions, and provision was made for the movement of troops to any frontier at a speed that no other country could match.

But when the war became one of years, the reverse side of the picture turned up: Fuel grew scarcer, the air force claimed the best gasoline, lubricants became a major problem, and cars wore out faster than they could be produced or seized in conquered countries. It became evident that the much-maligned railway was a far more economical mode of transportation for long hauls than the motor truck. The farther the German army moved from its home base, the more essential the railway became.

No matter how well an army, navy, or air force leader may know Der Fuehrer, no matter how completely in his confidence he may believe himself to be, the German dictator takes no chances. Hence, before anybody can come into his presence, he must park his pistol, his military belt, or his saber in the anteroom.

The erstwhile corporal of the first World War loves the game of war more than he loves anything else. Filled as he is with military ambition, he can tolerate no other gods besides himself. The late Colonel General von Fritsch, the father of the present German

Army, had to resign because he dared criticize Hitler's acquiescence in Field Marshal Werner von Blomberg's marital mésalliance in 1938.

General Beck, chief of the German general staff, became "ill" just before the outbreak of the present war. He opposed Hitler's policy of frightfulness.

General Halder, the present chief of general staff, has been promoted only to colonel general, while a dozen of his colleagues were made field marshals, simply because he is forever warning the dictator that this or that contemplated move involves more risks than the undertaking is worth.

General Blaskowitz, widely publicized as the hero of Warsaw, has gone into the discard. He objected to the brutal methods of the SS in occupied Poland.

To estimate the relation between Hitler and his generals, one must remember the tradition in which the men in their fifties and sixties, who now hold the responsible army positions, grew up. They are leftovers from the imperial regime. They rose to high military ranks. Hitler to them will ever remain the World War corporal. True to their oath as soldiers, they obey Der Fuehrer as the commander in chief of all the military forces. But they often wince at his decisions and, when strictly among themselves, criticize both his strategic plans and their moral implications.

Take the keynote speech that Hitler delivered to assembled military leaders in his Berchtesgaden mountain retreat a few days before the invasion of Poland. It caused no end of shaking of heads and whispers of dismay. One officer, sitting in the rear of the large room, scribbled the text of this brief but blood-curdling address in shorthand on the cuff of his shirt. In it, Hitler put himself on record as favoring total war in which women and children can be as little exempted as can civilian populations generally if caught between sections of the retreating army. He stated bluntly that he didn't mind being called Ghengis Khan or Attila the Hun; history recorded these names as those of great doers. He urged the generals to be tough.

The Polish campaign proceeded with a brutality unequaled hitherto, but Hitler was not satisfied. He wanted the soldiers and their officers not only to fight battles, but also to make short shrift of the Polish population. The Army balked at this. So Hitler sent his uncompromising SS men to Poland to "clean up." They did—

and countless are the stories told me by German officers of acts of inhumanity committed by the Black Guards.

The brutality of the SS in Poland is not the only objection which the regular Army has against this special formation of Hitler bodyguards. The regular forces resent the preferred publicity given the exploits of the SS in the daily communiqués, and they resent the "break" given the SS always to be in the final skirmish of a decisive movement. I need not quote a general on that—even the buck private feels that way about it. Here's how a German boy who was drafted at the very beginning of the Hitler compulsory service program stated it to me after the Polish campaign:

"We'd fight and fight, with hell popping 'round about us, until we thought we were ready to take a certain town or other locality. Suddenly there was a halt. At first we couldn't understand the reason—everything seemed to be going favorably. Well, we learned soon enough by experience: The SS troops were due to arrive to take part in the final skirmish and to share in the glory. It certainly made us sore."

Neither this lad nor anybody else denies that the SS troops fight doggedly, and that casualties among them are great. But the regulars object to the constant "horning in" by the SS men on jobs that bring glory or publicity.

It would be all gravy for the Hitler boys if Der Fuehrer should win the war. The Nazi party would be in more complete control of the country than ever, and the party button would open the doors to all positions, all graft, all swag. There would probably be one grand purge first, during which all those members who have rendered mere lip service to the regime would be ousted as dramatically as were Ernst Roehm and other Nazi leaders during the famed purge in June, 1934. But whoever survived and remained in good standing might look forward to a life of power, plenty, and possession.

During the first two years of the war the Army seemed temporarily to eclipse the party and its formations. But Hitler was quick to see this. His top men, like Goebbels and Himmler—jealous of the party's power—were even quicker to sense it. The Army, with its thrust through Poland, its blitz victory in the west, and its conquest in Yugoslavia and Greece, appealed more to the public imagination than the brown-shirted, rather pot-bellied Nazi ward heeler who remained at home.

It came to the point that some Nazi party officials deemed it wise no longer to wear their party uniforms except on festive occasions, lest they be spotted as slackers. No sooner did the top men notice how the party was slipping than they began to play up exploits of party functionaries in the Goebbels-controlled press. There were articles to prove that the majority of the Brown Shirts were playing a heroic role at the front, that the black-uniformed SS was in the vanguard in every military undertaking requiring courage and fearlessness, that the party was taking upon itself the thankless role of unostentatious heroism at the home front.

Reich's Justice Minister Hans Frank, who is also governor general of Poland, on more than one occasion has stated that, in Germany, two kinds of justice prevail—for the man or woman who belongs to the party or one of its numerous subsidiaries, and for the hapless individual who hasn't embraced the Nazi faith. The latter, like the Jew in Nazi Germany, is usually out of luck. Party domination has become so great in the daily life of the German citizen that he speaks of "vitamin B" as a prerequisite to success. "B" stands for Bezugschein, or pull with the party.

There was a time when Hitler's sensibility in feeling his way with the crowds was nothing short of uncanny. I have seen him address soldiers, women, agricultural workers, party functionaires, little tradesmen. I have seen him stand before high-brow academicians and before hundreds of thousands of common folk. Invariably I was impressed by his ability to be all things unto all men. He played with his audiences as an orchestra conductor plays with the members of his musical ensemble. His meetings often reminded one of the old revival meetings. Even the most hard-boiled seemed to "get religion," i.e., the Nazi religion of blood and toil.

The whole stage management for these meetings contributed toward this mass psychology—the martial music played during the hour or two before Hitler's arrival, the challenging slogans on huge banners, the gradual arrival on the stagger principle; of the second line of Nazi leaders, then of the top men like Goebbels, Goering, Hess, Himmler; and, finally, the dramatic entry, with searchlights playing upon his lone figure, of Hitler himself.

After Hitler became chancellor and later chief of state, he could seldom extemporize but had to read important pronouncements from prepared copy. Yet these speeches, too, during the first six or seven years of his dictatorship, showed a remarkable psychological understanding of the people.

During one of my interviews some years ago I said to the German dictator: "We are all aware that you owe a great part of your success to your ability to win over the masses of the people by your personal appeal in extemporaneous speeches. Now that you are the head of government you write out most of your pronouncements. Does that not cramp your style?"

"Not at all," he replied. "When I compose a speech I visualize the people. I can see them just as though they were standing before me. I sense how they will react."

That was some years ago. Today his speeches don't have the same compelling power with his hearers. The explanation seems to lie in the fact that Hitler now lives in a cloud world of his own, high up on Mount Olympus, and that his contacts with the real world are carefully filtered by the coterie of confidants about him. In short, Hitler no longer sees his people through his own eyes but through the strongly colored spectacles of his underlings.

These underlings permit Hitler to hear only what they think he should hear. One German ambassador, returning from his post, told Hitler all that seemed interesting about the country in which he was accredited. Then, before leaving, he presumed to put in a good word for a friend who had been taken to a concentration camp by the Gestapo.

"Why, the man has already been released," Hitler replied, obviously surprised.

"Sorry to say, no, mein Fuehrer," was the diplomat's rejoinder. "All our efforts to get him liberated have failed thus far."

When the ambassador reached the anteroom, the SS guard on duty spoke to him harshly.

"If you dare once more to discuss matters with Der Fuehrer that are not on the agenda," he shouted, "your career is finished."

The diplomat then realized that the Gestapo listens in even on Hitler's discussions with visitors.

Air raids increasingly are striking terror into the hearts of German civilians, lowering their morale and cutting war production. This may be said in spite of the fact that on no other factor of the war, perhaps, is it more difficult to obtain authentic information than on the results of R.A.F. bombings. There is an ironclad rule in Germany that bombing repairs take precedence over all others;

as a result, in an incredibly short time bombed districts are made to appear normal, at least outwardly.

A casual visitor in a bombed section, thus, on the first morning, will find areas roped off so that he cannot determine the extent of damage at first hand; by the second morning he may be able to pass by without noticing much of anything untoward. When large factories are hit, Propaganda Ministry officials may even conduct groups of foreign journalists on tours in an effort to prove that nothing of moment has occurred. But such plants may be composed of many buildings. It is easy, as at the Siemens works outside Berlin, for instance, to take a correspondent over a large area and to show him many undamaged buildings. Yet, he may pass within 100 yards of a vital subplant devoted to turning out some delicate precision instrument which for months may have been incapacitated by a bomb, and he may never be the wiser.

Only occasionally, when the truth simply cannot be concealed, is public mention of serious damage made. Thus, every German knows that Münster was bombed with frightful results late last summer. But only those who have relatives and friends there are aware that whole blocks were razed. Kiel, Hamburg, Bremen, Luebeck, and Rostock also figured in war communiqués because the damage was so great it could not be concealed.

Once the authorities decide to admit a raid, propagandists under Goebbels get busy to assert that virtually only cultural objects, which should be the property of the entire civilized world, were destroyed. The public mind is then prepared for Hitler's next retaliation move which, by the Fuehrer's own declaration, should be ten times worse than the raid suffered by the Germans.

Hitler is fighting the established Roman Catholic and Lutheran Churches just as relentlessly as he ever did, although outwardly there appears to be a truce. The Church leaders of both faiths haven't been fooled. They know that Alfred Rosenberg, Hitler's "ideological leader," has prepared a secret memorandum, of which a copy is in their possession, in which he demands, in substance, that after the victorious ending of the war nobody who still clings to membership in the Christian Churches shall be allowed to hold any government job whatsoever—not even that of messenger, or charwoman.

One always must remember, in dealing with the German Church situation, that the dyed-in-the-wool Nazi regards the

Christian religion as a Jewish product. It is, therefore, anathema to him. The rallies of the Hitler Youth Organization are arranged for the very hour when Christian believers flock to their churches. The little boy who nevertheless goes to church is a "sissy" to his classmates. If he persists in ignoring the Sunday rallies, he is thrown out of the organization and as he grows up this fact is held against him wherever he applies for a job.

A Protestant farmer in the Brandenburg area told me how the local Nazi farmers' leader tried to counteract the churches by summoning farmers under his jurisdiction to conferences and meetings during churchtime on Sunday mornings.

"We all ganged up against him," this farmer assured me, "and so he didn't get away with it. But if there had been any waverers in our midst, the story might have been a different one."

Whenever soldiers insist, they are assigned an army chaplain. But unless such a demand comes, religious services are not held. Clergymen are forbidden to visit the sick in state-owned institutions. Important festival days, if they fall within the week, have been called off "because of the war." Ministers and priests are forbidden to conduct religious instruction in the schools. Catholic and Protestant kindergartens, where working mothers could leave their children during the day, now have been eliminated. It's Nazi kindergartens only, for everybody. The religious press has virtually ceased to exist. Religious editors were told there is such a shortage of paper that church papers must cease publication.

During the last year the Gestapo has seized an untold number of religious institutions. The Jesuits, Franciscans, and Benedictines suffered especially. Nuns, priests, and lay brothers generally were forced to leave their homes overnight, with only a few personal belongings. The property seized was used.

The Christians of both faiths are just as determined to save their country from the proposed "National Church" as Hitler and his cohorts are set up wiping out the last vestiges of Christianity.

I recall a talk I had with Hitler almost half a year before he came into power. It was in August, 1932. He expressed the opinion that it takes about one generation until a people is weaned away from its former religious and political faiths. Then taking up religion specifically, he asserted: "Every leading religion runs for about 2,000 years at the outside; after that it has lost its appeal and something else takes its place."

When Hitler seized power in 1933, there were three men upon whom he relied more implicitly for loyalty than anybody else. They were Roehm, head of the brown-shirted SA troops, the only Nazi to whom Hitler addressed the familiar "du"; Hess, his trusted personal secretary and later deputy fuehrer; and Goering, his political right-hand man who is fond of calling himself, "Hitler's most faithful paladin."

Roehm was executed during the purge of June, 1934, for conspiring to depose Hitler and set himself up in his place. Hess flew to England under dramatic circumstances in May, 1941. Goering remains as field marshal, chief of the air force, president of the Reichstag, premier of Prussia, head forester of the Reich, and director of the gigantic German four-year plan for economic self-sufficiency.

The Roehm revolt lies too far back to be remembered by the German people in these fast-moving times. Besides, Roehm was a dissolute character, and while the purge bewildered many people, not many tears were shed over Hitler's Number 1 friend.

The Hess escape had a far more profound repercussion. Here was a man who was always regarded as his master's shadow, a partisan who had no other ambition than that of serving Hitler. He never appeared to have had an idea of his own; his job was that of executing his master's will. Suddenly he fled. Was it as bad as all that with Nazism? the masses asked.

Goering, alone of Hitler's three main props, remains. So does Goebbels, but Hitler has never trusted him as completely as he did the other three; he uses him because he is "gescheit" (clever, brainy). So does Heinrich Himmler, the sinister head of the Gestapo and in fact of the entire German police, but Hitler probably fears him more than he trusts him.

It is well known that Goering from time to time is in the doghouse. He and Hitler have spats. Now it is the luxury with which Goering likes to surround himself that irks his master. Hitler doesn't mind his boys enriching themselves, only they mustn't put it on too thick. Goering makes no secret of the fact that he thinks the second man in the Reich—meaning himself—is entitled to live off the fat of the land. The storm blows over and Hitler and Goering are shown shaking hands in the weekly newsreels.

General opinion among those who have watched Goering is that he is by no means wedded to the Nazi faith in the bigoted sort of way that Goebbels professes to be, and that Hess truly was—until his defection. It is also known that relations between Goering and Himmler are strained, and that the Reichsmarshal is by no means in harmony with all Gestapo practices. It is also known that his wife, Emmy, intervened for many hapless Jewish artists and that Goering himself once said, when confronted with the fact that one Jewish kapellmeister continued to conduct at the state opera: "It is I who determine who is a Jew and who not."

Furthermore, Goering is an officer from imperialist days. He always has remained a monarchist at heart. He has never broken off his connections with the former ruling families of Germany. On one occasion, to my knowledge, an American in Berlin was visited by a man claiming to represent Goering. The question he put was: Would the American administration have the same objections to Goering at the head of the German Government that it has to Hitler?

Watch Goering, is all that the trained observer of German politics can say to inquiring compatriots.

5

WHILE Lochner was reporting on Germany, one of his colleagues was surveying Italy. He was Richard Massock, free after five months of Italian internment. He had had an even less comfortable time than those interned in Germany. At first, he had been jailed with common prisoners in Rome's Regina Coeli (Queen of Heaven) prison. Then, along with others, he was moved to a better cell block in the same prison. Mussolini learned that Italian correspondents in the U. S. had not been interned in prisons. He ordered that Massock and the others be moved again. This time they were taken to a shabby, fourth-rate boardinghouse and kept under police guard. Finally, they were transferred to a hotel in Siena, north of Rome.

Massock's first cable from Lisbon said:

Italy is an Axis ally of questionable value, a hungry land with no love for her war partners, rife with defeatism and disillusion, ridden with hardship and unrest. Her war with the U. S. is clearly unpopular. In fact, Americans who languished in Italy for five months after Mussolini sent Italy into war with the U. S., believe that declaration dealt his home front a stunning blow.

Yet, with Italy propped up by Germany, virtually occupied by about 200,000 Nazis from one end of the peninsula to the other, and with no sign of effective opposition to Fascism, neither an Italian collapse from a food shortage nor an economic breakdown seems imminent.

But the elements are lacking to make Italy an ally of predictable worth to the Axis. Mussolini has apparently become a virtual gauleiter under Hitler, and as the Nazis tighten their hold on the country, the Italians' deep-seated antipathy for the Germans grows more intense.

As for the Japanese, there is some admiration for their swift successes, but Mussolini himself once characterized them as a barbarian menace to Western Civilization and some Italians profess shame that Il Duce later told them it was a "privilege" to fight side by side with "heroic Japan."

A steady flow of picked German fighting men, chiefly airmen and submarine sailors, and many Gestapo agents, are keeping the Italians in line with the Nazi program. One phase of the discontent is the view that the war with the U. S., although it means a long, hard struggle, encourages the widespread hope of German defeat. Indeed, some say that half the Italian people would like to see Americans and British invade Europe as a means toward crushing Nazism and lifting Italy from the oppressive yoke of the Germans.

While I was in Italy, Americans were regarded as friendly enemies. There was not one anti-American demonstration in all Italy since the declaration of war. Although inured to privation, the Italians are beginning to feel sharply the shortage of food, clothing, and fuel. Another winter may begin to take a toll of deaths from cold and hunger.

Having depleted her insufficient stocks of essential raw materials—iron, copper, and other metals, as well as oil, rubber, and some textiles—Italy has had to pay with great quantities of home-grown food to get these materials from Germany. Fruits, vegetables, and canned goods, once plentiful, are scarce. Even in good years, Italy must import wheat to meet her needs, but now Greece and Dalmatia look to her for some of their food. That explains in part why the bread ration was cut one-fourth last March, leaving a daily allotment of three one-ounce rolls.

Along with this, a "black market" has flourished for those Italians who can afford such prices as $2.16 for a dozen eggs, $1 for a pound of chicken or butter, $25 for a pound of tea or a ham.

These are for the rich and the Fascist party racketeers only, and observers report widespread resentment. Even Mussolini's attempts to check the scandal have had little effect. The high cost of living is the nightmare of the Fascist war economy and Mussolini recently has been mainly concerned with a desperate attempt to halt inflation.

Since his warning April 26 that the lira would be maintained "with good means if possible, with force if necessary, to prevent at any cost, first, the depreciation of the money and, finally, its complete cancellation," Il Duce's experts have concentrated on the problem. Months ago Italians started a rush to buy everything from shoes to diamonds because they lacked faith in the stability of the lira's buying power. Millions were spent on jewelry alone and Mussolini denounced those "thoughtless, hysterical persons . . . who are rushing to buy the widest range of things from old daubs by unknown housepainters to every kind of vase."

The government is trying to suck the national income into its treasury by discouraging investments in real estate, securities, and luxury goods, by controlling prices and rationing consumer's goods. The enormous war cost is plunging Italy into debt at an estimated rate of 120,000,000,000 lire a year or, nominally, more than $6,000,000,000.

Two yearly loans combined yielded less than half the national budgetary deficit, so the government has resorted to other forms of borrowing, for instance, ordering employers to deposit certain reserves and then converting these funds into government bonds. In spite of the government's efforts to drain off excess purchasing power, however, past months have witnessed a new upsweep of almost all prices except those of a few pegged articles. As a result, further measures are enforced to check this inflation, which is real even though it has not yet reached the banknote printing press stage.

For the currency situation, as for almost everything else, the Italians have a joke.

A man in a food store asks the price of figs.

"One fig, one lira," the shopkeeper tells him.

"What!" exclaims the customer, "a fig isn't worth a lira!"

"You mean," the dealer replies, "a lira isn't worth a fig."

Italian respect for the Il Duce has dropped with the ascendancy of Nazi influence. The customary cheers for him are said to have grown half-hearted and he himself shows signs of ill temper in his rare speeches. But, with no organized opposition, his regime probably is secure, although the Italians' dissatisfaction with both Fascism and Mussolini is more pronounced than ever. Their attitude is marked more by resignation than by resolve to make a change.

King Vittorio Emanuele, although still generally esteemed, is widely viewed as politically impotent and Crown Prince Umberto, once the anti-Fascists' white hope, now commands an army group and seems to have made his peace with the Fascists. In the view of many, rebellion is likely to come only if it is reasonably sure of success with the aid of the Army, which now remains loyal to the royal house of Savoy, and possibly military support of the United Nations.

Newspaper propaganda against the "Anglo-Saxon-Judo-Democratic Plutocracy" and "High Priest Roosevelt" has failed to stir any noticeable bitterness against the U. S. At the same time, Fascism makes much of Black Shirt participation in war. Troops of the Fascist militia figure prominently in news reports of actions on various fronts.

Mussolini has called to the leadership of the party as its secretary a 27-year-old crippled veteran of the war in Spain, Aldo Vidussoni. This young man interrupted the study of law for service in the legions and was sent to Spain. He is still studying for his degree. Such a Black Shirt hero has not been able to inspire the Italians with fighting spirit. They prefer home to the battlefields of Russia or North Africa. That may be why Mussolini answered Hitler's repeated request for troops with only a few hundred thousand.

The Italians have a new conundrum:

"What is the difference between the Japanese and Italian Armies?"

"It is—the Japanese have taken Manila, the Italians have taken mai nulla (nothing)."

Regardless of which side wins the war, observers see little prospect of Italy gaining anything worthwhile. The Italians dislike and distrust their German allies more than any other people. So widespread is anti-Fascist defeatism that thousands have been arrested in roundups of recent months. They fill the prisons and concentration camps. Others are exiled from their homes to hill towns for terms of two or three years.

First outstanding evidence of Mussolini's growing unpopularity among Italians came last autumn when the Duce made his pep tour of Bologna and near-by cities. Social unrest had reached such disturbing proportions that underlings could not hide it from him. Mussolini went to Bologna, former hotbed of Socialism, to show himself to the workers and charm them into renewed loyalty with his dynamic, theatrical personality. He had intended going on to Milan for the same purpose. The crowds were apathetic if not openly hostile toward the man who had plunged them into the war.

"How about food for our babies?" women asked the strutting dictator. Unable to answer their demand, he was conveniently called back to Rome for "important affairs of state."

Since then, Mussolini has made few public appearances. When Fascist practice required that he utter his declaration of war against the U. S. from the balcony of his Palazzo Venezia in Rome, there was no enthusiastic cheering from the crowd that had been maneuvered into the square below. There was no blustering street demonstration by university students as there was when, just eighteen months before, Mussolini declared war on Great Britain and France.

Mussolini's addiction to the company of young women favorites has been blamed for part of his political decline. His affairs with two sisters, whom he installed in a villa on the outskirts of Rome, were common gossip for several years. Now it is said that he has replaced the sisters in his affections with a cinema actress. It is even said that a young man's appointment to high political position was a reward for his having taken one of the sisters off the dictator's hands.

Psychologists might find in Mussolini's persistent application to amatory prowess an aging man's attempt to maintain the illusion of youthful virility. Observers consequently predict that history will record Mussolini as a dictator who started strong but finished as an also-ran.

6

THERE were stories by other released correspondents as well. Angus Thuermer, one of Lochner's Berlin colleagues, told about the drafting of German children for work on the home front:

The children of Germany—from 10 years old on up—will be drafted this summer and fall as farm laborers. By thousands they will be rounded up from the large cities, herded together in Hitler Youth platoons and companies, and sent to camps in farm areas where they will be put to labor as hired hands.

In a tremendous effort to break one of Germany's greatest

bottlenecks, labor for farms, Hitler's all-powerful labor leader, Fritz Sauckel, asked for the child labor. He called upon Arthur Axmann, Hitler's Youth leader, to send out his 8,000,000 uniformed children to plant potatoes, plow, weed, and harvest the crops for Germany's fourth winter of war. This duty far from home, to which all German children are liable, except those found physically unfit, has been designated a "war honor service."

From April 15 and on until November 15 any German school child can be expected to be ordered willy-nilly from his class into the field anywhere in the Reich to work a day or all summer. The most they have been promised is a vacation of at least three weeks sometime during the summer work period.

Sauckel and Axmann arranged two types of this farm service for children: Short-term work on call, or long-term work distant from home. A farmer needing someone to keep weeds down in his potato patch will take his request to the village farm fuehrer who will order the necessary number of children out of their classrooms to do the job.

In other areas, where lack of farm hands is a general problem, whole battalions of children will be imported for summerlong work and will be quartered in youth hostels, Nazi party halls, barracks, labor camps, or singly in farmers' homes.

The necessary movement of great masses of youngsters will be directed by the Nazi party children's evacuation division, which heretofore has been engaged in sending children from bomb-endangered areas.

Voelkischer Beobachter's account of the program said that children in the work camps would be allowed Sunday as a day of rest, and would not be required at any time to walk more than two miles to their assigned fields.

7

STEINKOPF detailed the famous "Black Market" as it operated in Hitlerland:

Germany is a land of irritating shortages, but it would be idle to assume that the lack of many things of ordinary living comfort means the nation is on the verge of collapse.

While in internment at Bad Nauheim, an acquaintance of this

writer paid ten marks (about $4) for two pairs of shoelaces. Behind this extraordinary transaction lies the story of the so-called "Black Market" that flourishes today in Germany. A great number of commodities are not to be found in German shops, but they show up in the illegal black market that thrives in spite of the death penalty and other drastic efforts at suppression.

German economy is geared to the needs of war and inevitably overlooks many requirements of the civilians who find life increasingly difficult. The most casual shopping tour of wartime Berlin discloses that the citizen who is not at the front is getting along without many trifles which no one ever stopped to think were important to frictionless living. It is very hard to find shoelaces, tooth paste, buttons, thread, envelopes, paper clips, suspenders, dust cloths, floor wax, light cords, typewriter ribbons, or photographic film—to mention just a few of the little things one doesn't think about when speculating on the meaning of total war.

It would be false to assume that the blockade on internal needs has become so acute that Germany cannot manufacture hairpins or tooth paste. The Reich could make such things in abundance, but the supreme economic planners have simply decided that no labor or factory space must be devoted to anything that is not primarily essential to the prosecution of the war. So the manufacturer and merchant, willing to risk violation of the stringent laws, are making vast profits.

Economically, it is the story of U. S. prohibition all over again except that the penalties are much more severe than those which confronted the American bootleggers. The black market merchant may be an ordinary shopkeeper who does some stealthy undercover business with his favorite customers who don't mind paying prices far above the legally fixed limits. Or he may be someone you meet in a café who has French silk stockings or coffee.

The black market's highest price for coffee, quoted to this writer, was forty marks (about $16) per pound. There are purchasers even at such a price because price fixing and rationing have increased the amount of money in citizens' pockets and citizens in many instances are doubting whether saving is worth while in view of the certainty that the mark will explode like a rubber balloon if Germany loses the war. Thus the citizen does not mind paying too much for things he can enjoy now.

A curious feature of the black market is the large number of

Italians involved in the business. The housewife may not know where to buy jelly glasses, but the chances are that the thousands of Italian workers who have been brought into Germany can lay their hands on some. In spite of the stern laws controlling conversion of German money into foreign currency, the Italians know the devious ways of getting cash to Italy.

One of the current jokes in Berlin is that the best place to buy wines and liquors is at the Italian embassy. Deals are not made at the embassy itself, but a number of highly placed employees can arrange the deal on the outside.

Penalties for black market operations are severe and death sentences are frequent. A typical case in recent weeks was a special court action against Karl Winterling, owner of a factory at Rehau. He bought cowhides and tanned them without the requisite reports to the government and sold the leather to Heinrich Fischer, owner of a shoe factory at Selbitz. Fischer manufactured shoes and failed to pool them in what the German economists call "the whole reservoir of peoples' goods." He sold the shoes to merchants who retailed them outside the rationing system. Winterling was condemned to death. Fischer was sentenced to eight years' imprisonment and lesser terms were meted out to others involved.

Death penalties are passed out liberally to black market operators who divert rationed food from people entitled to it. For an offense of this nature, two nurses of the Bethesda Institution for Crippled Children at Angersburg, East Prussia, were turned over to the executioner. They were Mathilde Arndt, head nurse, and Anna Rudeck, in charge of the institution's kitchen. Testimony submitted at a special court at Königsburg indicated the women withheld food from the children in their charge and conducted what the court called a thriving business.

But the death penalties are imposed for less serious offenses against food regulations. The director of a munitions factory at Braunschweig—Eugen Nubing—was condemned to death because he took three or four kilograms of meat weekly from the factory cafeteria and kitchen. His private secretary, Alice Dettmer, who helped him smuggle meat out of the plant, was sentenced to six years' imprisonment.

So the executioner is hot on the heels of the illegal market operator, who perhaps is rightly regarded as one of the most dangerous enemies assailing Germany's inner front.

8

AMONG the many angles to conditions both in Italy and Germany, the matter of German equipment was significant. Edwin Shanke, who got into trouble for flying the kite at Bad Nauheim, answered some of the questions:

Hitler's problem no longer is one of staying ahead of the Allies' war output. Now he has a struggle to keep up with it. Five serious bottlenecks stand in his way—the chronic and growing shortage of raw materials, sabotage and the lack of man power, transportation and electric power.

A source with access to reliable information has put Germany's airplane production potential at between 2,200 and 2,500 planes a month. Her total of planes is believed to have risen from about 10,000, when the war started, to about 25,000 now. Yet the need for airplanes grew so urgent last fall that Reichsmarshal Hermann Goering ordered to the Eastern Front all planes reserved for testing and experimentation. Aircraft engineers who had been working on new designs were instructed to concentrate on boosting production. From one plant alone, it was said, one out of every four engines was being turned back for overhauling after only a few flights.

Submarines slid from the ways at a rate estimated at fifteen to eighteen a month. But Germany is building no capital ships because, say naval officers, she cannot and still keep up other needed naval building. Her only aircraft carrier, the *Graf Zeppelin,* is said to be lying in Goteshafen harbor, only 80 per cent completed.

There are no reliable estimates on tank production, but Nazi difficulties are indicated by the fact that two tank divisions, camouflaged with desert yellow for Africa, had to be repainted overnight and sent east last fall at the height of the 1941 campaign in Russia.

The windfalls of booty from conquered countries helped in the first two years. Now, however, vital tin is being scraped almost to the bottom, the loot from the Ukraine admittedly will not be available this year, and the entry of the U. S. into the war, along with the Allies' unexpected economic staying power, has pushed Nazi production to the very limit.

Hitler himself has shaken his fist at saboteurs, threatening to track them down and exterminate them. New decrees have threatened death even for false reports on raw materials, labor reserves, or needs in man power or supplies to fill war contracts. Gestapo guards watch every vital factory, bridge, waterworks, gas and electric plant. Gestapo trouble shooters are posted in apartment buildings and stores as a precaution throughout German cities. Workmen, especially foreigners, are watched closely in factories. Still, at least 1,000,000 shells shipped from Czecho-Slovakia to the Russian Front were reported to have been duds.

A prison camp at Moabit, in the center of Berlin, is filling up with prisoners accused of sabotage—both Germans and foreigners, but especially Czechs. There are daily notices in the newspapers and on official news pillars in the streets of persons beheaded for sabotage or "damage to the national economy."

9

LOCHNER, Steinkopf, Massock, Shanke, and the others were clear of Nazi Germany and Fascist Italy—countries in which they had watched the plague of a Hitler war engulf such meager freedom as Europeans had once enjoyed. They left behind a diseased continent in which the contagion of Hitler violence destroyed or pockmarked everything with which it came in contact.

Through force of habit the released correspondents—finally back in America—cautiously looked around, fearing they would be overheard, before talking with friends of earlier years. They marveled at the smiles of people in the streets. They ordered steaks, breathed the new air, and oriented themselves to an America to which they had become unaccustomed. They were free.

They asked about the fate of colleagues in other enemy lands—about those in Japan and Japanese-occupied territory. Soon after they were released came word that some of their interned colleagues in the Far East also were obtaining their freedom in an exchange of "nationals."

The correspondents in Japan had had an even less comfortable time of it. Most of them had come under the surveillance of the Japanese police—known, by American standards, to be among the most difficult in the world even in peacetime and even with their own people.

Max Hill, Relman Morin, Morris J. Harris, Vaughn Meisling, Joseph Dynan, James D. White, and others were among those released. Along with other American "nationals," they were transported to Lourenço Marques, in Portuguese East Africa, where the exchange was effected. Once free, they could write again. They had plenty to write about. The first story, cabled from Lourenço Marques, told of the exchange of Japanese and American internees. It also was a composite of the experience of internees generally. Portions of the story were omitted to conform with official requests from Washington that nothing be said that might interfere with the welfare or repatriation of other Americans (including some of their own colleagues) who still were in enemy territory. The first story said:

The first diplomatic transfer of nationals between the U. S. and Japan since the start of the Pacific war was completed here today, when more than 1,100 North and South Americans boarded the Swedish liner *Gripsholm* to take the places vacated by Japanese diplomats and their families brought from America.

The Americans arrived here on the liners *Conte Verde* and *Asama Maru*. They walked down the gangplanks of the two ships as the Japanese left the *Gripsholm* and the two groups moved along the quay in parallel lines to their new staterooms. A line of railway cars had been drawn up on the quay, separating the Japanese and Americans as they marched to their new ships. Soon after moving to the *Gripsholm*, the Americans were permitted to disembark and tour the city. The exchange was supervised by the Portuguese Foreign Office.

Some of the returning nationals reported that prisoners were threatened with the guillotine by Japanese authorities seeking to obtain admissions of guilt from men charged with espionage. There were no known cases in Japan of physical abuse of women or children, but some men were told their wives and children would be made to suffer if they did not confess to espionage charges.

There was a general food shortage in Hong Kong, and Americans and Canadians held there suffered from beriberi, pellagra, and other ailments caused by diet deficiencies. Some lost as much as sixty pounds in weight and the average loss was twenty pounds.

In the northern areas of the Japanese Empire, internees suffered from cold during the winter. Those in Korea and Manchukuo endured unheated cells and houses with temperatures below zero. There were no reports of deaths among Americans from mistreatment, but a number of British prisoners committed suicide.

A score of American priests, captured in Hong Kong on Christmas Day, said they were marched to a ravine for execution, then reprieved at the last moment. They were held in a garage for three days, tied in groups with insufficient water and food.

Relman Morin, who had been at Saigon, Indo-China, provided additional details about the 1,100 who were free again for the first time in months. He told how they felt when they steamed into Lourenço Marques and saw the Stars and Stripes flying above the deck of a rusty American tanker:

Americans can take it. Their propensity for wisecracking over personal ordeals and disasters was a noticeable feature of life aboard the Japanese liner *Asama Maru.*

A portly business executive, who had lost seventy pounds and almost died of malnutrition at Hong Kong, smiled ruefully and observed: "The part I really mind is the necessity of buying a whole new wardrobe."

After experiences like his and those the others endured, the passengers took shipboard life in their stride and laughed at having to launder their own clothes, sleep on deck, and line up at 6 A.M. for a few cups of water. Ranking diplomats, businessmen, and mission leaders voluntarily took steerage bunks, giving women and children the upper deck privileges. Those with cabin facilities made an afternoon social function out of the bath hour, inviting as many guests as possible daily. Mrs. Joseph C. Grew, wife of the American ambassador to Japan, entertained an average of five guests a day throughout the long voyage.

Tears flowed only once. Entering the narrows of this harbor, some far-sighted passengers yelled: "Hey, there's a ship flying the American flag!" She was a rusty salt-encrusted tanker, but the Stars and Stripes were flying at her masthead. Her whistle saluted as our ship approached. Handkerchiefs fluttered as some returned the greeting. Many dabbed their eyes at the sight of the national emblem.

Typical of the fortitude of all was the behavior of James Theron Ward who one day will have a complicated passport. James was born on board, of American parents. The ship was Japanese, technically under Swiss jurisdiction, and he was delivered during a howling storm in the middle of the Indian Ocean. None of the difficulties brought any but the usual wails from young Mr. Ward. Like his compatriots, he's no cry baby.

One American who underwent an ordeal is Edwin Koons,

Presbyterian missionary, who was imprisoned by the Japanese in Korea, where, he said, he received the "water cure," when other punishment failed to make him agree he had been engaged in espionage. The water cure is a method of forcing quantities of water down the throat of the victim until he is unconscious and in a semi-drowning condition. Koons said: "They tried it once and I fainted." Somewhat apologetically he explained that he had a chronic heart condition.

"A few days later," he added, "while beating my back and the soles of my feet with rubber hose, they said I needed more water, but at the last minute they decided otherwise. Well, sir, just to show them I wasn't scared, I said I really was thirsty after so much talking and asked for a small drink."

He said he had the satisfaction of overhearing his tormentors remark that that was the first time anybody ever actually asked for a drink in that chamber. He said he did not blame his inquisitors personally, that he believed they carried out orders from above, and that he hoped to return to his mission some day.

10

Jennifer White, wife of correspondent James D. White, told of life among British and American civilians interned at Santo Tomas University, in the Philippines, after the Japs captured Manila:

The Japanese guards at Manila's internment camp frequently asked us: "How can you Americans be so happy here?" Apparently they were unable to understand how 3,200 civilian internees were able to work cheerfully without showing fear or shame at being Japanese prisoners. The Japanese themselves contributed to this state of mind since we had the run of the grounds during the day and there were only ten guards. Once seven of these were ill with the result that only three soldiers were on guard over us. The Japanese imposed only the most general rules. Otherwise we were permitted to govern ourselves. That was the secret of our happiness in detention. We ran ourselves. The American way of life prevailed inside the camp. In five months of internment I learned more American history than in my school years. Some of it was made before my eyes and I participated in it. The disordered throng of 3,200 persons herded into the oldest university of the Orient became an organized community.

At random, the Japanese picked E. A. R. Carroll, a Manila insurance agent, as chairman of the camp's executives, but the other officers, including twenty-seven department heads, were chosen by the internees. We had our own police, more than 200, working twenty-four hour patrols and a sanitation and health department with more than 500 workers.

There was also a sizable hospital and a newspaper called *Camp Affairs,* published semiweekly and edited by Russell Brines, of The Associated Press; a central kitchen, a fire department, and a sports and music committee. There were college courses in everything from engineering to Chinese, and there was schooling for the children.

We converted a junk pile into a vegetable garden that eventually supplied two-thirds of the community's needs. The internees built a portable stage, weekly entertainments were held, a fund for indigents was established, and there were religious services for all sects. There even was a Rotary Club and a Junior League. If we needed anything we didn't have, we generally made it out of odds and ends.

The first internees arrived at Santo Tomas University on January 4. Originally the Japanese said we were called merely for the purpose of registration—which would be a matter of three days. This was an understatement. We settled down to a regular, simple life. Everyone volunteered for work for which he was best fitted. A sour-looking businessman enjoyed making building repairs; debutantes asked to scrub floors, and bankers volunteered for the garbage collection detail.

The camp had towns such as "Shantytown" and "Glamorville," the latter being regarded as choice real estate. Signs like "Fifth Avenue," "Broadway," "Market Street," and "Piccadilly" appeared and some nostalgic soul put up one saying, "Subway entrance." A prankster marked "Los Angeles City Limits" near the communal washing trough.

Generally we saw no Japanese except a few guards wandering about in slippers watching the businesslike doings of their incomprehensible prisoners. They insisted that we were held in protective custody, but any infraction of the rules brought definite retribution. Minor offenses resulted in the cancellation of privileges. Three British seamen escaped and were recaptured. They were executed.

A central kitchen served meals twice daily. Breakfast was

cracked wheat, rolls, and coffee, but by the middle of March the mill for cereal was reserved for the army and flour for rolls was exhausted. The dinner menu was meat stew once a week, beans, macaroni, sweet potatoes, rice, eggs, and green vegetables once a week. Desert was served twice a week. There was chicken on Sunday, and turkey on Washington's birthday. Usually there was plenty, but the diet was unbalanced and some pellagra and beriberi appeared.

I found it difficult to purchase necessities but was able to barter and once traded safety pins for a knife and fork.

II

VAUGHN MEISLING, interned in Hong Kong, described life in that one-time British possession after the Japs took over. Along with others, he had been thrown into Stanley Prison after failure by police to induce him to sign a statement saying he was being well treated. His story:

Hong Kong must be the world's most looted city. It has been pillaged by experts and amateurs. Only three days after the outbreak of hostilities, Chinese began ravaging Kowloon opposite Hong Kong Island which that day was being evacuated by British troops and police. Trucks were being used by well-organized and armed gangs from the very start, supplemented by foot "patrols" of pickets who robbed Americans and Britons fleeing for the safety of Hong Kong Island. Several saved their watches and money only by shooting their way through the picket lines. Many were threatened with being shot or having their fingers chopped off if they did not surrender their rings and other valuables promptly.

A light touch was lent by a looter who emerged jubiliantly from a British villa. He carried a gigantic bottle. Passing refugees noted the label—"Epsom salts." An example of the thoroughness of the looting of Kowloon was provided by Americans who revisited their former residence there. They returned with a clothes pin, the only property left.

Large-scale and systematic looting of Hong Kong Island got under way as soon as the colony surrendered. Rich residences in the exclusive peak district were rifled with the obvious connivance of servants. Supposedly secret hiding places were cleaned out immediately. Some valuables, however, remain buried in gardens, cached by the owners after the servants fled. While metal fixtures were taken for military purposes, other parts of houses, including floor-boards, doors, and window frames, were appropriated by Chinese for firewood.

Occasional execution of looters reduced the practice only momentarily. Much plunder was offered for sale in the streets and shops, including silver bearing the name of a former British police commissioner. Watches, radios, and fountain pens were advertised for sale. A repair service sideline was the removal of telltale initials from the stolen goods. The Japanese soldiers were especially fond of wrist watches, cameras, rings, and sweaters.

The occupation was followed by universal street gambling, with stakes as low as 1 cent. This was suppressed later. Public amusements soon faded out. A few beer halls remained open for the benefit of the Japanese military, serving a synthetic Japanese brew.

12

MORRIS J. HARRIS and James D. White had been interned in Shanghai. They combined to tell about conditions there:

Still maintaining their traditional "so-sorry-for-you-but-we-need-this" attitude, the Japanese have steadily tightened their grip on Shanghai's historic International Settlement.

Just to keep the record straight, the Japanese occasionally remind the public and themselves that perhaps the Settlement is still supposed to be international, but this in no way hampers them from doing or appropriating anything they wish.

Immediately after war was declared, the tentacles of Japanese control reached into the farthest recesses of the Settlement to control its daily existence. The tentacles represent agencies like the Army and Navy, the gendarmes and the consulate. These tentacles cling to commodities that are scarce in Japan and vital to her war effort.

The Japanese have gone slowly in Shanghai and it is believed that the main deterrent has been the fear of arousing to panic the city's 5,000,000 Chinese, who, though unarmed, still constitute a potential mob in the minds of high-riding samurai.

Without the slightest warning the city was wakened at dawn on December 8 (the day of the attack on Pearl Harbor, according to East Asia time) by the uproar of Japanese guns destroying the sole British gunboat remaining in the Whangpoo River—the *Petrel*.

The vessel refused to surrender promptly and sank in a roaring mass of flames. One British seaman died. The American gunboat *Wake* surrendered and her crew was interned with the *Petrel's*.

Planes showered leaflets on the Settlement announcing the war and the fact that the Settlement would be entered. They urged the residents to remain calm. Then truckloads of bluejackets, soldiers, and gendarmes poured in from Hongkew, plastering the area with printed posters, obviously prepared long in advance, which proclaimed occupation of the Settlement and instructed Allied nationals to register on the following day. The occupation was effected speedily and without incidents. German inhabitants provided some of the most ironical comment. One of them said: "Japan's action means the white man's end in the Far East." The Americans laughed in their faces.

The Japanese occupied buildings like the American Club, the American Navy Y.M.C.A., the American Country Club, and the British Shanghai Club and used them for various headquarters.

Fifty of us, living at the American Club, were allowed three hours to get out. Allied consulates were sealed, their personnel interned in hotels. Squads of soldiers, sailors, and gendarmes descended on all Allied property except private homes and thereafter spent days, weeks, and months sealing American and British offices and warehouse stocks involving all essential commodities.

They commandeered Allied stores and factories and wharves, parceling them out among themselves and the favored Japanese companies. Muted bickering over the spoils still continues. However, there was no unofficial looting or despoiling. Public utilities like the American Shanghai Power Company, the Shanghai Telephone Company, and the British Shanghai Gas Company were occupied and continued in operation by military and naval agents. Most of the stores had Japanese supervisors appointed and some reopened for business, which was necessarily limited. The Associated Press office was sealed the first day and never reopened.

American Red Cross supplies were confiscated and some later released. Allied banks were sealed immediately and later reopened. Gold balances are still frozen. Depositors, in theory, could withdraw 2,000 Chinese dollars a month from private local accounts, but payments were slow and erratic. On winter days we lined up for hours, standing with others waiting to withdraw money for living expenses.

While some firms were allowed to withdraw enough to pay off

their staffs, some 200 others, including The Associated Press, were unable to get any funds whatever. All essential commodities like metals, basic foods, and medicines, were confiscated or became subject to priorities rule. Allied automobiles were requisitioned in February and "receipts" were issued by the military authorities. The Japanese steadily tightened control of the Settlement administration. They kept all of its departments working, including the police, although many employees were British and American. Allied nationals were immediately ejected from the Chinese Maritime Customs Commission.

The French thus far appear to have escaped Japanese control but have no illusions about the future, feeling that they will be ripe for harvest when the time comes. Reciprocally the French receive small favors like fuel for buildings, which is denied the Settlement. But gendarmes enter and search homes and buildings in the French concession, sometimes ostentatiously accompanied by French police, who thus signify "co-operation" in the best Japanese sense of the word. The French remain friendly and helpful to Allied nationals whenever possible.

13

JOSEPH DYNAN, who had been at Tokyo, told about the Doolittle bombing. He didn't fare too well with Japanese authorities, was banged on the jaw, and his bridgework suffered accordingly. One of his dispatches from Lourenço Marques said:

General Doolittle's raid on Japan provided the thrill of a lifetime for a group of Americans at an internment camp midway between Tokyo and Yokohama. One of the U. S. planes flew directly over our camp and the music of its motors was sweeter than Beethoven's Fifth Symphony, which our phonograph was playing at the time.

It was shortly after noon on April 18 that the big thrill came. We were having coffee and toast when the police rushed into our camp excitedly and told us to extinguish the fires in the stoves and close the windows because there was an air raid. We thought it was only a drill—even when we heard two tremendous explosions in the direction of the Kawasaki industrial area.

A few seconds later, however, we saw a large twin-motored plane flying very low. Bursts of anti-aircraft shells were streaking after it. The raider dropped down 200 feet to skim rooftops and escaped. It flew overhead as a squadron of slow Japanese planes arose from a nearby training field and circled around looking for the Americans. But by that time this particular raider was far away over the Tama River valley, speeding toward Fuji, where it disappeared in the mists.

We even spotted two raiders far distant in the direction of Yokohama's docks, and that evening the radio told us of raids on Kobe, Osaka, and Nagoya. Our guards were very excited, and later we heard that plane factories in Nagoya were badly damaged. Kawasaki likewise was hard hit, and 350 workers were reported killed there. Three days later I noted a small item in the Japanese press telling of a mass burial of Japanese Marines at Yokosuka.

The night after the raid the sirens blew again but no planes appeared. The next day Japanese pursuit ships patrolled the air constantly. Aside from the reactions of individual Japanese, the tone of the press indicated that Japan was shaken considerably by the American thrust into Japan's supposedly invulnerable defenses. Japanese ministers presented themselves to the Emperor to apologize and it was rumored that one army officer responsible for Tokyo's defense shot himself.

Early in March police investigating Max Hill, The Associated Press' Tokyo bureau chief who was held in jail, came to quiz me concerning news items which I had taken from the Japanese Foreign Office's short-wave summary and passed on to Hill. The police threatened to move me into a cell, too. I could only tell the obvious source of our news channels, shrug, and reply to the threat: "That's your business."

Two weeks before my departure I was taken along with other correspondents to the Sanno Hotel where a luncheon was given us. The luncheon, the Japanese said, was under the auspices of "The Pacific War Relief Committee," a front for the Japanese Home Office. Our hosts first asked, then demanded, that we write statements on various assigned topics, mine being internment conditions in Japan. When I refused a Home Officer struck me twice, knocking out a dental bridge—which a Japanese dentist later replaced without charge. This undoubtedly was the method used by the Japanese to obtain fantastic quotations from other American prisoners. They threatened to keep me in Japan unless I wrote a statement.

I finally performed. Under duress, I told the Japanese police that internment conditions were "as well as could be expected."

Now, on my way back to the U. S., I can explain that I had no illusions about what could be expected. Long-time residents of Japan used to tell me: "This would be a hell of a country to be interned in." That was true. But in fairness, the Japanese difference in living standards and conditions was the main factor.

In the six months' confinement the Americans in our group organized their own routines, and furnished and cooked their own food. There was no help in this respect from Japanese authorities, but little interference either. The Japanese provided so-called Western meals, but these were mostly inedible and always unpalatable. Only our own efforts and purchases kept us alive and fairly healthy in that period.

On the morning when the Japanese attacked Pearl Harbor, radios were blaring patriotic marches, and I was more or less prepared when I returned from church and entered my house to find myself surrounded by police who themselves seemed surprised and dazed by news of the war. With Robert Bellaire of the United Press, I was held incommunicado throughout that day. All day the radio told of Japanese successes at Hawaii and the Philippines. The Japanese servants seemed unable to believe or comprehend the announcements.

I was awakened the next day by a policeman with a mimeographed sheet in English and Japanese announcing I was to be interned and instructing me to take enough food for three days and a change of clothing and blankets. At the camp we were read a list of rules, including the prohibition on trying to escape. The guards were told to shoot to kill in that case.

14

MAX HILL had been in Tokyo long before war was declared. He was sent there two years earlier because of the expectation that things would happen. He had covered the sessions of the Diet and had watched U. S.-Japanese relations inevitably go from bad to worse. Japanese censorship had been rigid the whole time, but months before the final break Hill had tipped his New York office of the situation by a subtle ruse.

Into New York one day came a cable "half a yard long" requesting a figurative boatload of supplies. Hill asked for canned goods, tooth paste, soap, razor blades, cosmetics, and a dozen and one other articles of everyday use. There was probably no doubt that he actually needed most of them, but to headquarters his cable also was eloquent information that he was preparing for a time when such a request could no longer be made. Finally free at Lourenço Marques, after months of internment, Hill told about Tokyo the day and night before the attack on Pearl Harbor:

The usually cordial voice of Ambassador Joseph C. Grew came cold and reserved over the telephone that sunny Sunday morning in Tokyo last December. (According to Tokyo time, the bombing of Pearl Harbor came the following day.) I had called to ask about a message I had just received telling of President Roosevelt's personal appeal to Emperor Hirohito to intervene to save the peace.

"There's nothing I can say; absolutely nothing at this time," he said. Actually, the call gave him the first inkling of the critical turn in the Japanese-American negotiations.

The Japanese military had played its usual calculating hand and stopped Washington's message to Grew telling him of the President's eleventh-hour action. But Japanese censors slipped somehow in permitting correspondents to receive theirs. The embassy's first message was received in Tokyo at 10 A.M., but was not delivered until 9 that night, short hours before Pearl Harbor was attacked. Thus did the war makers make sure that no last-minute effort by the U. S. could head off the conflict. It was a restless, nerve-shaking eleven hours that Grew spent from the time of the call from The Associated Press office until he finally received the State Department's pilot message stating an important message from the President had been sent to the Emperor. Lights burned brightly that night in the embassy offices and residence as Grew and Eugene H. Dooman, embassy counsellor, conferred in the envoy's walnut-paneled library. While Grew puffed at his pipe, Dooman called Foreign Minister Shigenori Togo's secretary. Dooman explained that an important communication had just come from Washington and that, regardless of the hour, Grew must see Togo that night. Polite surprise seemed to be the attitude of Togo's secretary.

An hour later—at ten o'clock—the secretary telephoned and said Togo would wait at his official residence until midnight for Grew. Code clerks labored, meanwhile, behind locked doors over the text of President Roosevelt's communications to the Emperor. They delivered a completed text at 11:45 P.M.

Grew and Dooman looked vainly for a chauffeur and finally the ambassador was driven through Tokyo's deserted streets to Togo's residence, just behind the Diet building, by Merrell Benninghoff of the embassy staff. Wearing a gray business suit, Grew entered slowly and gravely and shook hands with Togo. Greetings exchanged, they sat down in blue plush overstuffed chairs in a second-floor drawing room. The American ambassador then began reading the presidential message. He left in twenty-five minutes.

Most Americans in Tokyo were naturally unaware of the momentous developments. Besides missionaries and the embassy staff, only correspondents and National City Bank of New York and Standard Oil employees remained. Virtually all of them were quickly rounded up by gendarmes and police and marched off to prison for internment bright and early the next morning.

Hill's next dispatch told about his own imprisonment and his experiences with the Japanese police, who still had a penchant for using "espionage" as a charge against foreigners. Hill's story said:

"American! This is Japan!" That is the way a sullen guard, from the cold, drafty corridor of Tokyo's Sugame Prison, whispered to me his hatred of foreigners through the peephole of my cell the night of December 8.

I lay huddled on the floor, bundled in my overcoat and a blanket, trying to keep warm in the heatless cell. Five police had arrived at my home early in the morning and marched me off in military fashion to the district station, where I was told I was accused of sending stories detrimental to Japan's diplomacy. Then I was removed to the prison proper, where I was stripped, searched, and locked in solitary confinement.

In the fifteen days that followed I remained in solitary, knowing only that war was declared and hearing an unsubstantiated rumor that Pearl Harbor had been bombed. The guards were antagonistic the first night, but after that the attitude was not repeated and most prison officials were helpful and tolerant. There was constant cold, day and night, with ice forming on the water basin. I was naturally depressed over my fate and by the police insinuation that I would be accused of espionage, and I was additionally disturbed by the scanty and poor Japanese food.

Throughout my confinement the police used torture as their main weapon. Once I was told the gendarmes were taking me over, and that I would be court-martialed instead of remaining in the hands of the civil authorities. Finally on Christmas Eve, shuffling along without shoes, I was led from my cell into a smoky room where I was questioned briefly. Then I was returned to the cell without explanation and remained there until January 6, when formal questioning under Inspector Takehara began.

I lost weight rapidly in December and January. Breakfast was a small bowl of mixed barley and rice and a small cup of soup made of seaweed or turnip tops boiled in water. Lunch was the same. So was dinner. After a few days I was permitted to supplement this with two yen worth of outside food in Japanese style until February, when I was allowed to switch to foreign-style food costing five yen a day. The portions were small, with few vegetables and little meat, sometimes horse or whale, but the quality generally was fair. The officials did not permit me to eat the prison fare when outside food was delivered, in spite of the need of this additional food. They said that the outside food was sufficient.

The first day in the cell the guard confiscated my shoes, keeping them until April. Because I was trying to keep warm, I both wore and walked on a tatame (Japanese mat). It was early in January when, finally, I was confronted by Inspector Takehara, a squat bullet-headed man with two assistants. His brilliant and incisive mind was evident immediately. Although expressing personal sympathy with my plight, he was a relentless inquisitor, hammering me with questions, squinting his eyes and rubbing his close-cropped head until he became to me the incarnation of the devil himself.

A typical line of questioning was about Koh Ishii, who in the summer of 1941, was the official Japanese Cabinet spokesman, and the story of the American liner *President Coolidge*.

[NOTE: In August, 1941, the State Department at Washington disclosed that the Japanese had refused to grant clearance papers to the *President Coolidge* if she sought to remove the more than 100 American private citizens then in Japan.]

I was asked why I sent a story so harmful to Japan even though quoting a government official, and I was forced to admit that such information was useful to foreign governments. Thus a story obtained from a recognized source of news became one which would react against the Japanese.

A brief story describing the antagonism between former Foreign Minister Yosuke Matsuoka and Baron Kiichiro Hiranuma, a former vice-premier and home minister, became, in a similar manner, what the Japanese called world-shaking copy. The story, the

Japanese said, encouraged the Russians to oppose Japan and spurred the Chinese national government at Chungking to greater efforts, and also caused the U. S. to believe Japan's leaders were divided.

[NOTE: Actually, the story received little attention abroad.]

After a week of steady questioning, during which I was told flatly that unless my information was more satisfactory I would no longer be treated as "a gentleman," the case was concluded with the filing of formal charges. Then followed sessions with the procurator, after which I was tried by a court. I was taken to the court in a bus crowded with Japanese, handcuffed and tied together with ropes. I wasn't tied into the line, but Americans from Yokohama were imprisoned and subjected to this humiliating experience.

The court procedure was dignified and solemn in spite of the farcical nature of the charges, which seemingly was recognized even by the trio of Japanese police handling the case. The procurator recommended an eight-month sentence. I was returned to prison for two weeks. Then I was brought back and given a suspended sentence of eighteen months. Finally, I was taken to an internment camp until the departure of the liner *Asama Maru*.

The evident purpose in arresting Tokyo newspaper men was to fish for a spy ring which did not exist and to harass the newspapermen's Japanese friends and employees, who have been in a state of terror during the war and also have been months in prison.

I did not know personally whether there was any chance of leaving Japan and was resigned to imprisonment, perhaps for the duration of the war, until my release came. I was not told anything about being evacuated. When we mentioned it once to Police Officer Okada, the interpreter, who had been graduated from Northwestern University, he laughed and told the men not to be so optimistic.

"This is war," he said.

Words have not been coined that would express the relief and pleasure of walking down the gangplank of the *Asama Maru* onto the free Portuguese soil after months of suspicious and spy-conscious Japanese. Japanese newspaper men who arrived on the *Gripsholm* and wryly told American correspondents from Tokyo their hardships in the U. S., of their "confinement" in a White Sulphur Springs luxury hotel, having their mail delayed as much as a month and of being able to read only the New York *Times,* stammered and stuttered when they heard our imprisonment stories.

The newspapers *Asahi* and *Nichi Nichi,* the news agency Domei and other news organizations did their utmost to aid the imprisoned journalists, but, as they pointed out:

"You know the Japanese police."

Hill also told how a nice bit of Japanese propaganda and deception on the Doolittle raid on Tokyo backfired:

It was a good story at the time, but it's funnier than ever now, the story of how the Japanese sought to save face after the Doolittle air raid but didn't quite succeed, all because some doubting Japanese know wet paint when they see it. Somehow you can enjoy a joke more when you breathe the air of freedom.

Americans interned at Tokyo carry vivid memories of that April 18 raid by American planes, and nothing serves better to keep the memories alive than this story which circulated among us internees. The Japanese press, telling of the attack on Tokyo and other cities, said first that nine of the planes were shot down. Later this figure was more conveniently modified to one, and wreckage to give weight to the announcement was displayed in the Japanese capital.

That was all very well, but even this limited propaganda stunt backfired, so the story goes, when some curious spectators discovered that the red, white, and blue paint on the twisted wing covering was wet instead of dry.

Actually, I understand now, there were as many as sixteen planes in the raid, and while there is no available reliable estimate of the casualties, it is known that heavy damage was done in the industrial districts between Tokyo and Yokohama, where large areas of factories and homes were burned.

15

IF FRESH paint on a faked display of a downed American plane was the best the Japs could do as far as propaganda was concerned, they were not as subtle as their Axis partner. Over in Europe, German propaganda and Germans guns were equally pointed in World War II.

From the outset, Hitler had used propaganda for all it was worth against the British. He went into German universities. He stopped the regular curricula of 5,000 students. He assigned them the task of gathering material which would ridicule the enemy.

Students of philosophy turned to British philosophers. They sought quotations that could be used by the Nazis. The German literati studied English writers. They were looking for vituperative material. Law students pored over enemy law codes. All British newspapers on file in German libraries were sought out. Anti-British caricatures from the year 1600 to the present were aired. The students turned out more than 20,000 essays. They all dealt with the low and mean phases in British history.

Then, after Germany declared war on the U. S., a new phase of the propaganda campaign began. The students concentrated on America. Some of their conclusions may not have been new, but at least they were amusing. Ernest G. Fischer and Angus Thuermer, released from Germany, wrote about this latest campaign after they returned to neutral territory:

When the Nazi propaganda job was completed so far as England was concerned, the same German students were given new assignments.

Nazi propagandists, educated in American universities, served as advisers. It was their job to see to it that the "Yankee angle" was given due consideration in the preparation and release of propaganda blasts. Germans who had lived or traveled in the U. S. furnished up-to-date material while the students were delving into American history. In addition, several natives of the U. S., who chose to cast their lot with the Nazis, were enlisted in Hitler's propaganda corps.

This description of a "typical American woman" by a German propagandist, Dr. E. Ahlswerde, is repeated here as a sample of the material given the German public:

"She plays with married life and averages from two to seven divorces. At forty her nerves are used up and she winds up in a bridge club or a religious society. Born in the midst of skyscrapers, steam whistles, saxophones, boiler factories, and automobiles, she has an unbounded yen for noise, movement, and masses of humanity. She's always changing her residence, her friends, husbands, clothing, religion, and ideas. She is constructed quite simply and primitively and, like a cheap watch, only three or four cogs fit together, and she is as transparent as a windowpane. She is always in movement, usually on the wrong track, and lands nowhere. She's always talking, but says nothing, and has a real fear of rest and solitude."

On Americans in general, the doctor made these comments:

"They believe everything they see printed, including attacks on the U. S. by Mars and Germany. They all have the same views, and they all use snappy sayings. They keep grinning—'Keep smiling, boys!' They all chew gum. They all buy on the installment plan.

"They eat griddle cakes with syrup and grapefruit for breakfast. (Ouch, that still hurts, doctor! Because we remember in German internment breakfast consisted of two potato-meal rolls, twenty grams of whale-blubber butter, synthetic jam, and malt coffee.) Lunchrooms in downtown New York are crowded and food is thrown into the customer's face."

Maybe, as the German propagandists said, a lot of middle-aged American women were attending bridge clubs. But now many of those clubs were clubs where war work was being done. Maybe a lot of Americans were chewing gum. They were chewing it in plane and munitions and tank plants from one ocean to the other.

The American science of mass production—unequaled in the world—was turning out airplanes and ships and other supplies in increasing numbers.

On the night of May 30, more than 1,000 R.A.F. planes were warming their motors at scores of secret British airdromes. Their noses were pointed toward Cologne, Germany—their motors roaring to go.

CHAPTER 21

... *Not with the End of Hope*

May 30–July 4, 1942

I

FIELD MARSHAL ERWIN ROMMEL and his Nazi Armored Army of Africa were on the offensive against British mobile forces in Libya. Hitler's troops moved cautiously in Russia, with reinforcements coming up, on their attack against Sevastopol, in the Crimea. The British lost the cruiser *Trinidad* while convoying supplies to Russia. Their submarines retaliated by sinking 12,000 tons of Axis shipping in the Mediterranean. Jap bombers were making sporadic attacks on Port Moresby, north of Australia. And "Hangman" Heydrich, of the Gestapo, lay fatally wounded in a Prague hospital, victim of the fury of Czecho-Slovak resentment even more bitter than it had been at the time of "Munich."

That is a quick résumé of the war situation the night of May 30, when more than 1,000 R.A.F. planes warmed their motors at English airdromes. It was a Saturday night. The week end had held no promise of unusual action on any front. But the drone of those planes foretold a story the like of which no war ever had known.

No correspondents were permitted to accompany the fighter planes across the English Channel. They got details when the last plane was back and the government told what had happened. Robert E. Bunnelle, in London, got the story of how the greatest air armada in history zoomed down on Cologne, one of Germany's big industrial centers:

The grass grew neatly to the edge of England's flare-lighted runways with the peaceful lushness of a country club lawn. But there peace ended, for it was 8:08 P.M.—and take-off time for the greatest raid in all aerial warfare.

In the soft dusk of England's spring, dozens of heavily loaded bombers squatted at the top of the line. Their propellers beat an impatient rattle awaiting the green light from the control tower. And the same thing was happening at hundreds of hidden bomber bases over England. Already the sky was filled with the roar of planes from the other fields, all getting ready for the 1,250-bomber party at Cologne—the world's first four-figure air raid.

The best way to describe the unprecedented battle perhaps will be to describe what happened aboard one of those planes. It was a feat that was being duplicated by all the others.

The captain of a four-motored Stirling in one group of waiting ships suddenly heard an anxious voice on the intercommunicating telephone.

"Captain," the voice said, "if we have to wait much longer, we'd better switch off. Engine three's getting hot."

But before the captain could reply, the green light flashed from the control tower. The big plane began to move. The raid was on.

The crew in the Stirling looked to the left. In the flickering light of flare-path number two, they saw the others taking off—plane after plane like streetcars leaving a terminal. The Stirling moved faster. As it began to lift, a voice on the interplane phone sang: "We're off to see the Wizard, the wonderful Wizard of Oz." The field dropped swiftly away and the Stirling circled to set its course. The crew suddenly felt a mighty bump—but it was only the slipstream from another Stirling that roared near by.

Before the planes reached the coast they were climbing through clouds. A dejected voice on the Stirling's phone complained: "Just our luck to find ten-tenths cloud (thick clouds) at Cologne." But the clouds began to break and soon dykes and towns in Holland loomed in the moonlight. The moon was to the starboard and straight ahead was a rose-colored glow in the sky.

"It's probably something to do with the German-Dutch frontier searchlight belt," somebody said. But just then the captain broke in on the plane's phone to warn the Stirling's three gunners: "We're in the danger zone now. Keep your eyes skinned for any aircraft of the enemy."

The front gunner spoke up quickly.

"Fight ahead to port," he reported.

All eyes turned to the front, just in time to see a sudden shower of incendiaries, apparently jettisoned by a bomber under attack by a Nazi night fighter. Soon they saw the burning wreckage of a plane on the ground. Disaster had struck in the soft moonlight. By this time the Stirling was in the searchlight belt and in the blue streaks piercing the sky the crew saw other planes—some traveling their way and others headed back for England. The going was rougher now because the captain was dodging and weaving the ship to avoid lights and flak that sailed up from the ground like white mushrooms.

The front gunner broke the tenseness. "Keep weaving, captain," he shouted on the plane's phone. "The flak is getting so thick you could walk on it."

"There's a plane on our tail," cut in the rear gunner, then, half disappointedly, he added: "Hell, it's only one of ours."

The rose-colored glow was still ahead and the captain came on the phone again.

"How much longer before we're there, navigator?"

"About ten minutes," replied the navigator.

"Well, we don't need you any more. That light's Cologne. The fellows have built up quite a fire."

By this time the sky became so full of flak, tracers, shell bursts, and spotlight streaks that it was like the fireworks at the county fair. The Germans were throwing everything they had at the attackers. From the bomb aimer's hatch, Cologne glowed like a big cigarette end in a blackout. Then the plane was directly over the fires and the captain ordered: "Bomb doors open!"

"Bomb doors open," came the reply.

The captain spoke again. He said: "Hell, wait a minute. No use wasting stuff on burning buildings. Let's look for a black spot."

Block after block of the town was blazing under the craft, smoke drifting past the flame-outlined wings. In the blaze could be seen what appeared to be white-hot skeletons of steel framework.

There were Wellingtons, Halifaxes, Manchesters, more Stirlings—in fact, about everything but helicopters—flying above, below, and on either side of the Stirling. All were silhouetted against the towering flames of Cologne. And all were dropping their loads on Cologne. While the town blazed like a furnace, the blasts of high explosive bombs continued to hurl the walls of buildings across the flames. From time to time, in the outer dark spaces, showers of incendiaries poured down in platinum-colored flashes that turned slowly red.

One tiny dark spot showed on the Rhine river's glowing west bank.

"That might be Elektra Stahldraht Fabrik (a steel wire plant)," said the captain. "Let's try it."

There followed an anxious moment of leveling off and moving right and left to get on the target. Then the bomb aimer pressed the button and the plane gave a lift from the release of the heavy bomb cargo. A piece of flak tore through the ship six inches above the pilot's head and for a few minutes everybody was busy with the guns, rudders, and cameras as the Stirling wove its way out of a blazing curtain of anti-aircraft fire. The ship slipped through the flak, and the rear gunner shouted: "We got it! I saw the white flash of debris flying, then red and yellow flames shooting up."

There were shouts of elation on the ship's phone. The job had been done. The Stirling's bombs had found their mark. The Stirling skirted the city, setting a homeward course. The burning area had increased tremendously in the eight minutes over the target. New fires were springing up everywhere. About ninety miles from Cologne, the captain turned in a complete circle to take another look. From this distance, the three major fires had merged into one immense volcano of flame.

The Stirling dodged and spiraled on to England, trying to confuse Nazi night fighters and ground observers.

"Can't anybody see our coast yet?" the captain asked.

"Not yet," the phone said. Then—with obvious relief—came: "Yes. There it is and you can still see Cologne."

"Well," said the captain, "throw the navigator overboard. We won't need him any more tonight!"

It was a breeze from there on to the home station. The Stirling radioed in and the flare-path control informed the pilot he was fourth in and gave him the height at which to circle for a landing. As he rounded the field awaiting his turn to land, a Wellington fluttering from the opposite direction, nipped past one wing.

"What's wrong with that idiot!" growled the navigator. But he quickly added: "Sorry, looks like he had a rough trip."

It turned out later that the Wellington was short-cutting home with a badly wounded crew.

Three planes ahead of the Stirling were shepherded in quickly without incident—one every three minutes with timetable precision —and within a few moments after the Stirling touched ground she was in the hands of a ground crew hurrying to heal her battle wounds.

The bus that took the cheerful crew to quarters for interrogation by intelligence officers also carried others just back from Cologne. One lanky pilot with sun-reddened face and white eyebrows said with a laugh:

"Well, that was the only time I enjoyed being over Cologne—and this is my fifth trip. God, what a pretty fire!"

"Damned good show," another agreed.

Interrogation finished, the crews went off to eat bacon and eggs—a special treat.

One of the R.A.F.'s fastest reconnaissance planes was back over Cologne in broad daylight to photograph the wreckage—but couldn't because of a pall of smoke rising to 15,000 feet. So he dropped a couple of bombs through the smoke at 7:45 A.M. just for luck and then scurried home. The Air Ministry's prosaic communiqué on the raid was typically British in its understatement:

"Last night a force of considerably over one thousand bombers attacked targets in the Ruhr and the Rhineland. Cologne was the main objective. Full reports are not yet available, but preliminary reports of crews indicate the attack was an outstanding success. By dawn fires and smoke were visible from the coastline of Holland and reconnaissance early this morning reported a pall of smoke was rising to a height of 15,000 feet over the target. During this operation other aircraft of the bomber command and aircraft of the fighter, coastal, and army co-operation command attacked enemy airdromes and enemy fighters which attempted to intercept. Forty-four of our aircraft are missing from all these operations."

That was the first official word on the 1,250-plane attack on Cologne. Later the British estimated the smash devastated 300 acres in the heart of the city and seriously damaged more than 250 factory buildings. The world's largest mass air raid also smashed railway communications in the Ruhr, made fifty or sixty thousand persons homeless and set back war production in Germany's "Pittsburgh" for two or three months.

The raid was no spur-of-the-moment undertaking. Instead, it was a masterpiece of perfect planning that had behind it six weeks of hard work by every branch of the R.A.F. and its feminine auxiliary—the W.A.A.F. The "brains" was tough, stocky Air Marshal Arthur Harris. Details on how the attack was carried out remain a secret because the system is going to be needed again and again—and the United Nations don't want Germany to know too much about it. But the tense hours and some of the toil that went into the attack can be divulged.

Harris believes that mass plane raids will win the war. After he had worked out the master plan, he personally called in his aides who command groups of bomber stations scattered throughout Britain. The group commanders got their first orders on May 26. Station commanders were to cancel all leaves, muster every serviceable plane, and make ready to receive flocks of "Coocoos" (airmen brought in temporarily to strengthen force units). They were told to make ready for "a really big show."

The next morning a sealed envelope marked "Most Secret" was on the desk of each bomber group commander. It contained an order detailing a raid by 1,000 planes to be made that night, or the first suitable night thereafter, on one of two targets. By that afternoon, headquarters knew just what it could expect, and was ready. But the weather wasn't—and the attack had to wait.

The next day—May 28—the word went out that the zero hour would be that night. But bad weather again interferred and the raid was canceled. The same thing happened May 29. By this time every bomber crew, mechanic, and clerk knew something big was in the wind. And each was growing impatient. May 30 came and the tension sharpened. At noon the weather turned bad and a decision was delayed. But at 5:25 P.M. the bomber command signaled the raid was on.

At one station hidden away in Britain's hills the crews piled into the station command room. The same thing was happening at other stations over England.

"You may have guessed there is something special on tonight," the station commander started. "Well, this is what it is. Target for tonight is Cologne, and we are bombing Germany with over a thousand aircraft."

His voice was drowned by the cheers of the men who had been keyed up for days. The crews filed out cheering and shouting.

"Hope I get a smash at that Schlebush explosive works," cried one bomb aimer. "What a bang it would make!"

"I want that big Diesel plant," shouted another.

"I'll take the Ford plant at Niehl," chorused others.

When the raid was over the operations officer parried with a grin an inquiry on just how 1,250 planes could fly over Cologne within an hour and a half, drop bombs and get back with only forty-four losses.

"It was just an ordinary raid," he said.

And, as a matter of fact, it was almost that simple. Planes got a given route to follow in and out at a specified angle. The first groups went in comparatively low to saturate defenses so every German gunner had so many targets he didn't know which to chose. It was like a gunner who finds himself in the middle of a hustling covey of quail with a single-barreled shotgun. That was a new tactic, as was the covering operation of sending light bombers and fighters to harry the Nazi night-fighter stations in Holland and the Ruhr.

What followed was really old stuff—that of showering incendiaries to light up the target, then medium explosive bombs followed by incendiaries to fan the flames, and finally two-ton bombs for the real job when the target was fully lighted.

The Air Ministry regarded the raid as so important that a number of senior officers made the trip—among them Air Vice-Marshal J. E. A. Baldwin, who is now helping to break in America's new generation of sky fighters in this war. The Rhineland metropolis was flattened by 6,000,000 pounds of bombs.

The astronomical proportions of the assault—far greater than anything the Germans ever let loose upon England—were indicated by authoritative estimates that 100,000 men at scores of airdromes made possible this flight by 6,000 of Britain's best airmen. Arriving on schedule six seconds apart in a masterwork of co-ordination, the bombers concentrated their hail of blows in a whirlwind raid that left the defenders overwhelmed by the sheer weight of numbers.

In a message read at the bomber stations before the crews set out on their mission, Air Marshal Harris told his men:

"Press home your attack on this night's objective with the utmost determination and resolution in the full knowledge that if you individually succeed, the most shattering and devastating blow will have been delivered against the very vitals of the enemy."

A "very high" proportion of the bombers each carried a cargo of 8,000 pounds of bombs. The 44 lost planes were downed by the immense concentration of 500 large and small anti-aircraft guns and 120 searchlights ringing Cologne and the many fighter squadrons that got into the air. In view of the large number of planes participating, the British considered these losses small, but it meant that many of the 6,000 British, Australian, and Canadian airmen would not come back.

Watching "every step" of the vast operation were American Air Force observers who are preparing to join their own offensive with that of the British. Among the four Canadian squadrons that took part were American flyers, and among their planes were American-made Boston bombers.

2

NAZI propagandists at first had a different version of the Cologne bombing. They said a comparatively few planes killed some civilians and wantonly destroyed cultural centers. Later, they changed their story.

The R.A.F. continued its work the next day. It attacked German-occupied territory in Norway and France. Then, the night of June 1, greasy, grinning ground crews by the thousands sang "We're off to bomb the Jerries" as they loaded another 6,000,000 pounds of explosives into 1,036 planes. Again the giant armada streaked across the Channel. This time the objective was Essen. The Nazi stronghold housed the Krupp munitions works. Again fires and explosions did their damage. Only thirty-five British planes were lost. The next night they repeated the procedure—over Essen again.

A wave of cheer swept Britain, elation that the R.A.F. could repeat such great mass bombings in short order. The whole Western Hemisphere also reacted. At last Britain appeared on the offensive. Long before this the English had proved they could take it. Now they were proving they could give it.

Mexico declared war on the Axis. The Nazis claimed the annihilation of an entire British unit and the capture of 3,000 prisoners in Libya.

Observers who knew Japanese psychology said that the Nipponese would do something to avenge the humiliation of the attack on Tokyo. Their prediction came true on June 3. Jap fliers bombed the U. S. naval and air base at Dutch Harbor, Alaska. They damaged American installations, though the damage was regarded as small in relation to what the Japs undoubtedly had in mind. It was the first time the North American continent had been attacked from the air. There was speculation as to whether the Nipponese would hit again at the far-flung Aleutians, which pointed menacingly toward their own islands.

The attack on Dutch Harbor was followed quickly by a development of much greater importance. On the morning of June 4, the last U. S. outpost in the northwest Pacific—Midway Island—appeared asleep in the early dawn. Then, bounding off stealthy aircraft carriers, Japanese planes approached. Behind them stood two huge fleets—one mainly of transports and the other a strong battle force. The Japs expected to occupy Midway. They had come prepared. If they should occupy Midway, they could move on Hawaii, little more than 1,000 miles away. But Midway was not another Pearl Harbor. Midway was prepared. A U. S. scouting plane had made "contact" with the Jap Fleet. Midway knew what to expect.

What followed was the biggest Pacific battle since Coral Sea— a thrilling continuation of the desperate struggle for control of the Pacific. Fifty to 100 enemy planes pounced on Midway. Marine and Navy fliers met the attack. Anti-aircraft fire cut loose from the island stronghold. Flying fortresses went after the Jap aircraft carriers. The land-based planes roared off Midway, carried the fight to the enemy, then returned to refuel and pick up more loads of bombs.

Walter Clausen, aboard "A United States Fighting Ship," obtained the first account of what the Marines did on Midway that morning of June 4. He got the story from Captain Jean H. Buckner, a 28-year-old former University of California football player. Here are the high lights of Buckner's story:

We received word the Japs were coming in at 6 A.M. on June 4. They were sighted at 6:20, several miles at sea. We were ready for them. All our planes were in the air when they came in three waves of bombers at ten thousand feet.

I saw that Marine force pilots already had taken off and watched them attack the Jap bombers, downing four or five of them fifteen or twenty miles at sea. After that contact, the Jap force circled north and came straight in a horizontal formation for the initial attack. Anti-aircraft fire caught two more before they got in bombing range. They dropped their first bombs, then peeled off and started dive-bombing and strafing both islands—Eastern and Sand Islands. There were twenty bombers and about forty fighters in this attack.

During the actual attack, six or eight more Jap planes were brought down by our land fire. Completing this attack, the Jap planes flew out at a low altitude to a rendezvous in the southwest for a start back to their carriers. As far as we know they never got there. We replenished our ammunition and stood by for another attack which never did materialize because of damage delivered to the Jap carriers by Navy and Marine dive-bombers and torpedo planes and Army bombers.

The biggest bombs the Japs dropped at Midway were 500-pounders. I figure there were forty to seventy planes in the attack. Some say there were a hundred. Five 500-pound bombs landed within 125 yards of our battery position. The Japs apparently had certain objectives, most of which they missed—we think because of our heavy ground fire. Our men were doing everything that possibly could be expected of them—they were good Marines.

One Jap bomber exploded in the air about four to five hundred feet above us. Another landed and burned. One crashed in flames on Eastern Island. Several fell into the lagoon. All Japs aboard these planes were killed.

The Battle of Midway lasted four days—most of it at sea. Walter Clausen got another eyewitness story. It came from a man who saw much of the battle from the very surface of the rolling Pacific. It was from a downed flier who watched the drama unfold as he floated helpless on the wreckage of his plane:

The first eyewitness account of the Battle of Midway Island, detailing its most violent stages, was related today by a wounded American naval aviator who told of floating in the sea and watching a line of burning Japanese ships pass by.

He told of a thunderous—and highly successful—attack by American dive-bombers and torpedo planes on Japanese aircraft carriers. And from his "fish-eye" view he watched the desperate circlings of Japanese naval planes, unable to settle on their blazing and battered mother ships. The story was told by Ensign G. H. Gay, 25-year-old torpedo-plane pilot of Houston, Texas. His wounds were not serious.

For ten hours the pilot, careful to conceal himself from vengeful Japanese flyers by hiding his head under a cushion from his wrecked plane, drifted in the sea and obtained one of the most amazing stories of a major naval engagement.

Ensign Gay occupied what naval men called "a fish-eye view" of the attack on three Japanese carriers. His squadron met fierce enemy fighter plane opposition while driving home a torpedo assault on one of the larger Jap carriers. It occurred early on June 4, opening day of the battle. He was the only one of the crew of three to survive the crash of his ship.

Taking off from his fleet carrier with his squadron, Gay approached the objective in midmorning. Visibility was unlimited. Below lay three Japanese carriers, less than ten miles extending between the first and last of the enemy ships that were screened by a considerable force of cruisers and destroyers. Gay took stock of the drama below him. Two Kaga class carriers had been taking on their aircraft. Another smaller carrier lay between them, also receiving planes. One of the larger carriers already burned fiercely, while enemy cruisers and destroyers wheeled around it waiting to rescue personnel.

Twenty minutes later the American dive-bombers rocketed into view. In the face of terrific anti-aircraft fire and enemy fighter attack, they leveled for the assault. Gay heard his machine gunner say he had been hit. But the approach continued. Near the great Japanese carrier, Gay launched his projectile, then swung sharply over the target and sped astern as fast as his plane could carry him.

Suddenly an explosive shell from a Zero fighter ripped through his torpedo plane's rudder controls. The detonation seared Gay's left leg. Almost simultaneously a small-caliber bullet struck his upper left arm. Coolly, he brought his heavy plane into a stall and pancaked into the sea several miles astern of the enemy carrier. His gunner was dead, and in the emergency landing his radioman was unable to pull free.

At 11 A.M. Gay, alone, watched the tail surfaces of his plane disappear. Then a bit of luck held with him. Out of the sinking wreckage floated the bag containing the deflated rubber life raft—and a black cushion on which the bombardier kneels while working. Gay figured his chances quickly and accurately. There had been reports of Japanese strafing helpless pilots bailing out by parachute, and of machine-gunning of men in such life rafts as had floated clear of his own plane. He declined to offer himself as such a victim. He ducked under the cushion as enemy fighters swarmed overhead. Not knowing the extent of his wounds, he felt cautiously at his arm. The bullet, which apparently had struck him at the spent end of its trajectory, dropped out in his hand.

"For some reason," Gay recalled, "I put it in my mouth. Maybe I wanted a souvenir. Anyhow, I lost it before long."

He bandaged his injured leg under water. Then from his fish-eye view, he saw two other Jap carriers hit squarely by U. S. bombers. Tremendous fires burst from these vessels. Great billows of smoke churned upward with the flames billowing from the apex in dark columns. Internal explosions sent new gushes of smoke and fire belching from the carriers. As the ferocious Pacific Fleet attack ended, the second Kaga class carrier was on fire from bow to stern.

Surface craft gave Gay some narrow brushes. One enemy destroyer appeared to be driving straight at him as she sped to aid a stricken carrier. He thought she would run him down, but at the last instant she plowed past. A heavy Jap cruiser steamed by less than 500 yards away. He saw her crew lining the rail, their white uniforms gleaming against the battle paint, grimly watching the destruction of their force.

As the afternoon waned, the Japanese made frantic efforts to stem the damage. An enemy cruiser sought to stand alongside a crippled cruiser, but seemed unable to approach close enough. Gay observed this vessel's big guns commence to rake the wounded carrier, presumably to scuttle her. Sometime later a destroyer managed to come alongside the still-floating carrier to remove survivors. Overhead, Japanese planes appeared to be circling in a vain attempt to land on the smashed carrier. They would pass above her, then soar out of sight and return.

Darkness fell, and Gay never learned what became of them. In the twilight, "maybe a little earlier than was wise," he inflated his life raft from his carbon-dioxide bottle. He said he had his fill of salt water. He had to make emergency patches on several bullet holes in the rubber boat before it would sustain him safely. He clambered in. The long night began.

Far to the north, great glowing patches appeared in the sky. Gay thought these might have been the searchlights of Japanese rescue vessels seeking to pick up carrier personnel. There didn't seem to be much else to do, so he "tried to catch a few winks of sleep." Toward morning, he was awakened by three explosions which he believed may have been demolition charges. Several hours after sunup a Navy patrol plane, winging out on a search, spotted his rubber boat and picked him up. A Navy doctor asked him what treatment he had for his burns and he replied: "Well, I soaked 'em in salt water for ten hours."

3

No one correspondent could obtain the complete picture of Midway because of the diversified attack. But the whole story slowly unfolded. Wendell Webb was aboard one of the participating cruisers. He saw most of what happened at sea, was with the Fleet

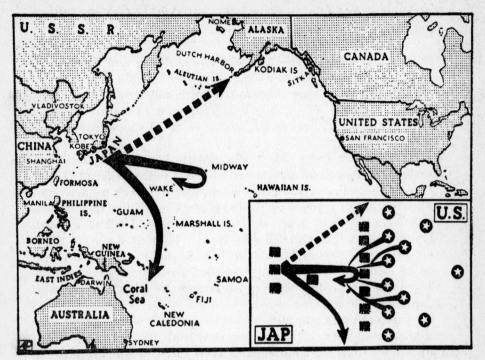

Map 24—U. S. forces operated like a smart football team (inset diagram) when the Japs attacked Midway Island on June 4, 1942. The Americans had not let themselves be diverted by the Japs' right-end try (lower black arrow) into the Coral Sea or by their aerial attack (broken arrow) on Dutch Harbor on June 3. Instead, they met the Japanese attack at the center and turned it back with crippling losses.

as she chased the Japanese back toward the Land of the Rising Sun. He reported the battle day by day:

June 4—First Day—A trail of fire, death, and destruction streaked across mid-Pacific today.

There were blazing ships to the north and west of us. There were pilots of the Rising Sun dying for want of a place to land. If the Battle of Midway is not already won, its course now is unmistakable.

Tonight the Pacific Fleet is headed straight for the scattering survivors of Japan's attempt to carry the war to the Occident. There is no one story that would give the whole of this day's engagement. One might tell of bombs and flaming planes that fell like rain around the cruiser on which I am writing. Another could tell of a game ship winning a fight to quell fires from a Japanese bomb. A third story—a long one—might show in humble part the skill and heroism of these pilots, living and dead. But a retrospective picture of the grim drama strung out over 100,000 square miles of ocean will have to come at a later time.

From the time Japanese planes assaulted Midway Island this morning until the last tired gunner laid aside his work, this area, 3,000 miles from the United States West Coast, was the scene of a battle that well could be all-decisive.

We do not know tonight that all the would-be invaders are retreating, but as nearly as can be determined there were three great tentacles of power reaching for strategic Midway. It now appears that two of them are withdrawing to the west with whatever they have left to withdraw.

The action today against planes, carriers, battleships, cruisers, and destroyers, hurled back at least the vanguard of the enemy push. His chance to get at Midway now is gone. As far as the Japanese were concerned, they had planned only an offensive. Tonight the tables are turned, and what started out defensively for the men from Pearl Harbor has turned into a pell-mell race to destroy.

June 5—Second Day—A dazzling Victory V shot into clear skies tonight to climax one of the most dramatic episodes of this far-flung encounter at sea. It was flashed as a guide to naval bombers returning from the west where a major Japanese force was harried and crippled, and striving desperately to beat its way back home.

Our ships' regular lights were on in defiance of any lurking challenge and the entire Fleet was hot on the chase. It hoped to close in at dawn near Midway. Carrier planes had gone out early in the evening for one last assault before dark. They were roaring in by twos, threes, and sixes. We counted and cheered as their wing lights broke the clouds. There were cheers, too, with each safe landing. But the darkness deepened fast and our count was incomplete. We wondered what was wrong. It was then the searchlights flared their V.

Minutes later more planes swept in and circled for their mother ships near by. There were few if any missing then. One faltered and crashed. His wing must have hit the water. It was too dark to see what had happened. A light flashed on the waves. He was alive and a destroyer picked him up. The Fleet plowed on.

All the lights are out now and there's blackness that only a night at sea can show. This has been a daring action, but big dividends have come from such bold, decisive strokes. It took planes to do it and cool skill and courage to bring them in.

June 6—Third Day—A blazing warship was abandoned by the Japanese 500 miles west of Midway tonight. Word of the abandonment was flashed by naval dive-bomber pilots, who had a field day over fleeing enemy forces, but the flyers' radioed conversation indicated they wanted no part in strafing the helpless survivors.

"We ought to take those Japs in the lifeboat but I don't go in for that stunt," one flyer was heard to comment.

"I agree with you on lifeboat," was the reply of another flyer.

The scene they were witnessing was the grand finale of a three-day battle that wrought destruction or damage to a large part of the attacking Japanese and apparently wiped out its sea-borne air power.

The radio conversation of several American pilots told the windup of day-long assaults on the now-scattering enemy ships.

"Oh, baby," said one, "did we put that destroyer on fire!"

"It looks like the battleship is burning."

"Hit him again."

"They'll never get that fire out."

"Did you see where your bomb hit?"

"Mine hit on the fantail."

"Okay, some of you hot-shots. There's a perfectly good cruiser back here."

"Go over and get that boy."

"Put them right smack on the bottom."

"That one blew up, too."

"Looks like he's turning over."

"Let's get a couple of those destroyers."

"Atta boy. There's a hit on a cruiser."

"Today's a field day, boys."

"That was a beauty; right down the stack."

"There goes another hit. We got her right on the bow."

"Boy, he sure exploded below decks, I betcha."

"Look! They're firing anti-aircraft. That destroyer is sure putting it out."

"I wish I had one more bomb"

"Do you see any gas coming out of my plane? There's no fuel on the gauge."

"Yeah. You got a hole in your tank."

"Report the result of your attack."

"Attack complete; heavy cruiser gutted, afire; battleship and cruiser afire and heavy explosions; one ship's nose is heavy."

And so it was that the Navy's wish came true, for it was in mortal combat with the enemy in its own backyard. Some of the officers of the cruiser were discussing recently the possible progress of the war, and one of them said: "It's too much to hope for, I guess, but I believe we'd gain a tremendous advantage if the enemy would come over on our side of the ocean."

While the score of this battle is not yet in, there's no doubt about the "tremendous advantage" being realized. This fleet chased units of the retreating Japanese all last night and today. Time after time the carrier-based fighters and bombers blasted ships fleeing far ahead of us.

The Battle of Midway apparently is over, and the pilots of the cruiser's scout planes watched enviously as carrier wingmen roared away to the attack. Crews of this ship's main batteries were disappointed because no enemy surface craft came within range of their fire. But the gunners had plenty of action when machine-gun bullets splashed over the ship's superstructure and enemy torpedo-bombers flashed in to attack.

Enemy aircraft were in the vicinity of this ship for thirteen consecutive hours. There are none in sight today, however, for our carrier planes rule the air.

June 7—Fourth Day—"In the flush of victory let us not be hasty to take all the credit, but humbly give thanks to Almighty God over us for all good things."

It was with deep reverence—reverence born of faith, of thanksgiving and of sadness over those who died—that the officers and men of the Pacific Fleet listened to these words today. The chaplain was speaking at services at mess quarters.

"Let us give thanks," he said, "that you are here upon this earth, and let us say a prayer for those who have given their lives in this battle that their country might live. Today, just six months after Pearl Harbor, the 'Pacific situation has changed, thanks to courage, to skill, and to devotion."

A hymn, a prayer, and the services were ended. Another week of war was under way.

4

THE current gag sweeping Honolulu after Midway was this: "Japs lose pants trying to save face." Japanese losses were placed at two or more aircraft carriers and a destroyer sunk, eleven warships sunk or damaged, thirty-five planes downed or badly damaged, and probably 10,000 killed. U. S. losses were officially announced as one destroyer sunk and an aircraft carrier damaged. Officials in Washington viewed the outcome of the battle as speeding the day when the United Nations would be able to launch an "all out" offensive.

Six months to the day after Pearl Harbor, Coast Guard recruits in hundreds of cities took their oath of office via radio, the first time such a mass swearing-in was ever attempted. It worked. While Mr. and Mrs. Fred Lutt went to nearby Wane, Nebraska, to buy a new supply of matches, their farmhouse burned to the ground. Eight Brooklyn riveters, working on a war project, rang up a new world record by banging in 2,563 rivets in seven hours and fifteen minutes. On June 8, the U. S. Senate voted a pay increase to $50 monthly for army privates. Roosevelt asked Congress for $39,-000,000,000 more for the Army and $11,000,000,000 for the Army Air Corps.

British bombers attacked the Nazis in the Ruhr Valley and Holland. They also raided the Italian naval base at Taranto. Eighteen thousand Japs were reported killed in three days at Chuhsein, with the Chinese still holding out. U. S. ship losses had cost insurance companies $46,486,068 in the first five months of the U. S. war.

The list of Nazi reprisals was getting longer. It is conceivable that reports of some of them were exaggerated. What happened on June 10, however, offered little ground for doubt. The Nazis themselves told the story of what they did to Lidice, in Czecho-Slovakia.

Lidice was a village about eighteen miles from Prague. It was there that Reinhard Heydrich, Gestapo scourge of Nazi-occupied Europe and "protector" of Bohemia-Moravia, met nemesis. He was fatally wounded by Czech patriots. Reprisal executions had begun when he was attacked on May 27. By the time he died on June 4, at least 187 Czechs had been executed, including three women—and retaliation continued.

The latest Nazi act came on June 10. On that day, the Gestapo wiped out the entire village of Lidice. Every man in Lidice was killed, every woman forcibly removed to a concentration camp, and every child placed in an institution. The village itself was destroyed and left a mass of rubble. Even the name of the community was obliterated.

The official Berlin radio ratified the story:

"The investigation of the murder committed on deputy Reichs-protector for Bohemia and Moravia, SS Uppergroupleader Reinhard Heydrich, revealed beyond doubt that the population of the township of Lidice near Kladno gave shelter and assisted the murderers.

"In addition, evidence was found of hostile actions committed against the Reich, subversive printed matter as well as arms and ammunition dumps, illegal radio transmitting stations, and huge supplies of rationed commodities were discovered.

"In addition, the fact was ascertained that inhabitants of this township were in active service of the enemy abroad. After ascertaining these facts, all male grownups of the town were shot while the women were placed in a concentration camp, and children were entrusted to appropriate educational institutions. The township was leveled to the ground and the name of the community extinguished. The inhabitants of Lidice, near Kladno, numbered 483."

5

A Springfield, Illinois, taxicab driver who found a wallet containing $2,700, turned it over to police with the request that his name should not be published because his friends might consider him a chump. A man in an Eldorado, Kansas, hospital said he looked forward to emerging into a world of cuffless trousers because he had broken his hip when he caught his left foot in his right cuff.

On June 11, Russia and the U. S. signed a "mutual aid" pact. They also agreed on a "second front" for 1942—perhaps a U. S. invasion of Europe which would take some of the pressure off the Reds' Eastern Front. Word of a somewhat similar agreement between Britain and the Soviet came the same day.

But something more positive came out of the Pacific in mid-June. The Japs landed on the Aleutian Islands off Attu and Kiska. The islands were far-flung outposts of the U. S. They were stepping stones to Dutch Harbor. If Jap hopes materialized, they were also stepping stones to the mainland of North America. Attu, in U. S. hands, was a threat to Japan because it was only 700 miles from her nearest territory.

For most of the year the islands of Attu and Kiska are enveloped in fog and mists. That situation was rather typical of the news that came out within the next few days. But the uncertainty cleared somewhat. It was acknowledged that the Japanese had occupied both islands. Their ships rode at anchor in the fine harbor at Kiska, and U. S. planes, attacking whenever the fog lifted, continued to exact a heavy toll.

Russia reported the annihilation of 15,000 in three days. The Axis took Bir Hachiem, in Libya. One American ship was shelled, rammed, and sunk by a Nazi submarine near Cuba. Four U. S. bombers landed in Turkey after raiding Rumanian oil fields and had their crews interned. Nazi Propagandist Goebbels threatened "extermination" of German Jews in reprisal for British air raids. He also promised "worse than Dunkerque" if the Allies invaded Europe. The Nazis claimed the taking of 20,000 Russian prisoners on the Kharkov Front.

American citizens were doing all sorts of things to aid the war effort.

In Prescott, Arizona, a gasoline station proprietor who had disposed of old auto tires by rolling them into a canyon 1,000 feet deep, hired eight youngsters with burros to bring them back. Result—eight tons. Near Kansas City, Missouri, the proprietor of a trapshooting park began scraping an inch of top soil from his six-acre tract to recover an estimated 125 tons of shot metal. In Seattle, Washington, a shoe repair man got the idea that the government could use old rubber soles and salvaged 12,110 pounds.

And from faraway New Delhi, India, came word about one of the war correspondents:

During two years in the war zones, Associated Press Correspondent Preston Grover was bombed more than 100 times by the British, Germans, and Italians. He was repeatedly under artillery, machine-gun, and snipers' rifle fire. He was on a bomber raiding enemy territory. Twice he was pitched into the Mediterranean from attacked ships. He wasn't scratched.

Today he was nursing two ribs, broken when he slipped on a piece of soap in his bathtub.

6

NAZI reinforcements were driving harder than ever in Russia, Libya, and Egypt. Hitler, pooh-poohing the possibility of a second Allied Front, was intent on finishing off Russia and pushing on through the Suez Canal to meet Japan somewhere east of Suez.

The Russians held on desperately. Hard-pressed British forces at Tobruk, in Libya, tried to stave off German and Italian troops under Field Marshal Erwin Rommel. A big United Nations convoy fought its way through the Italian Fleet in the Mediterranean, trying to get sorely needed supplies to Malta and Tobruk. There was an unusual feature to this latest Mediterranean struggle. Big U. S. bombers were in the fight. By June 17, they had scored thirty-five direct hits on two Italian battleships. They had set one cruiser afire and damaged a destroyer.

The convoy got through to Malta after suffering losses. The Nazis claimed they sank two British cruisers, one destroyer, and four or five convoy vessels. The British denied the losses were so high. They countered with a claim they had sunk three Italian warships and damaged six others.

But the supplies were too late for Tobruk. On June 18, the famous old stronghold was surrounded by Rommel's divisions. The British were falling back toward the Egyptian border. Another great British fortification had finally been taken. Edward Kennedy reported the fall of Tobruk on June 21:

Striking with the suddenness and fury of a desert sandstorm, German and Italian panzer forces captured today the British Libyan fortress of Tobruk in one of the most stunning setbacks suffered by Great Britain in the war. Haggard and shell-shocked survivors arriving from the blasted port gave fragmentary descriptions of the swirling battle in which the Axis columns smashed the fort in less than twenty-four hours.

"It was worse than Dunkerque," said a young truck driver who added that he had seen both. He declared that the real assault on Tobruk started early Saturday morning. By dusk the fortress was a roaring inferno of exploding shells and of fighting within the town itself. He reached an advanced British base only after a tug and mine sweeper had been shot from under him and he had been picked up by a British torpedo plane.

In smashing Tobruk within twenty-four hours, the Nazis eclipsed the mark set by General Archibald Wavell in January, 1941. Then the British chief's army took Tobruk and some 30,000 Italians in a day and a half. And Wavell's victory was considered a swift and brilliant feat.

The fall of Tobruk ended seventeen months of British occupation of the Libyan port. The British first took the town on January 22, 1941, in General Wavell's drive that carried to Bengasi. But a German counterattack shoved the British back and on April 12, 1941, Tobruk was surrounded and put under siege. The siege lasted until December 10, eight months later, when a British Army rolled back the Germans and relieved the garrison.

The surrender of Tobruk was a sweet revenge for the Axis. For in the ruined city they took some 25,000 trained desert fighters, the cream of the British Libyan Army. And vast supplies which the British had too little time to destroy also fell to German General Erwin Rommel, along with many Nazi tanks taken earlier in the fighting by the British.

But not all of the supplies in Tobruk fell to the Axis. Shiploads of munitions and oil were destroyed by two anonymous heroes who gave up their lives to keep the supplies from the Nazis.

From far out in Tobruk harbor, Army and Navy men aboard a mine sweeper saw the pair standing on the opposite end of docks loaded with supplies. Together, they set off five tons of explosives under the wharves.

"There was a blinding flash, the loudest roar I ever heard, and everything around the harbor went up in bits, including the two boys," one soldier said.

The lightning blow against Tobruk reduced the fortress so rapidly that it stunned the British defenders. Many of them had never a chance to offer any real resistance. The Germans—for the first time in the African campaign—used parachute troops in clouds.

They were supposed to mop up the British and frustrate the destruction of their supplies before they could fall into Axis hands. Floating down from big Junkers transports, they were picked off like clay pigeons as they hit the ground.

But where the 'chutists failed, the tanks succeeded. Once Tobruk's outer defenses were pierced, the Nazi tanks made straight for the water front. Their blazing guns sank most of the ships fleeing the port, but a few managed to escape.

High British quarters acknowledged the fall of Tobruk was a "crushing blow." And they conceded that the setback might even imperil Allied plans for a second front. Too, it left Egypt and the Suez within dangerously close reach of the Axis columns. Military observers, seeking the cause of the collapse, believe the tide in Libya turned when Nazi General Rommel lured General Neil Ritchie's armored forces into a trap in the Knightsbridge area southwest of Tobruk. In this action, Rommel pulled the British tanks into an ambush and inflicted heavy losses on them with 88-millimeter guns. Many of the British tanks knocked out were the U. S.-made General Grants, or 30-ton types.

The Germans did not have more material in bulk than the British did, but theirs was better selected, better co-ordinated, and better applied.

For his amazing victory, General Rommel was quickly advanced by Hitler to the rank of a full field marshal.

7

LIBYA represented a great Allied loss. With that country overrun, Hitler's forces planned the same fate for Egypt. By June 27, Axis tank columns were 115 miles beyond the Egyptian border. Egypt, stepping stone to the Middle East, was imperiled. Russia, more than ever, needed help. The whole Allied situation in Europe and Africa was desperate. U. S. bombers reached Egypt, though in insufficient numbers. Blockade of supplies was a big problem. Both the British and the Americans promised aid to Russia.

World War II was in full blast. The battlefronts extended two-thirds the way around the globe. World War I paled beside it.

The new A.E.F., increasing in thousands almost daily, was moving to positions wherever there were conflicts. Men in American uniform were fighting side by side with the British in North Africa. Other U. S. troops were put through their paces in Ireland. American bomber squadrons were ready for attacks on Germany and German-occupied areas of Europe. American forces helped guard Australia and New Zealand. The U. S. Fleet continued to blast Jap ships out of the Pacific.

Roosevelt's promise of 60,000 planes in 1942 was coming true. Tanks and guns in untold numbers were rolling off tireless assembly lines. Aircraft carriers—unknown in World War I—were a new and potent weapon. They had proved their worth in the Pacific conflict. More of them were being built.

America was assuming her role as the bulwark of democracy in a downtrodden, bewildered world.

8

TODAY, as this line is written, it is July 4—166th anniversary of the Declaration of Independence. Not even on such a holiday is there a letup in U. S. war effort. The traditional celebration is significantly quiet and sober—ominously busy. Millions of men and women in war industry—ordinary, everyday people—are at their jobs. Fireworks displays are curtailed. Gas and tire rationing has thinned holiday motor traffic. Roosevelt himself has just said:

On the desert sands of Africa, along the thousands of miles of battle lines in Russia, in New Zealand and Australia and the islands of the Pacific, in war-torn China and all over the seven seas, free men are fighting desperately—and dying—to preserve the liberties and the decencies of modern civilization.

And in the overrun and occupied nations of the world, this day is filled with added significance, coming at a time when freedom and religion have been attacked and trampled upon by tyrannies unequaled in human history.

Never since it first was created in Philadelphia has this anniversary come in times so dangerous to everything for which it stands.

We celebrate it this year, not in the fireworks of make-believe, but in the death-dealing reality of tanks and planes and guns and ships. We celebrate it also by running without interruption the assembly lines which turn out these weapons to be shipped to all the embattled points of the globe.

Not to waste one hour, not to stop one shot, not to hold back

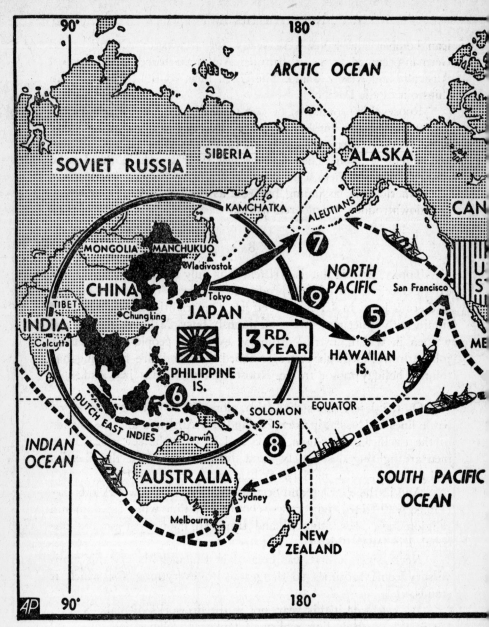

Map 25—Here is a summary of World War II as it neared the end of its third yea[r]
gium, Luxembourg, and France (1) and began all-out bombing of Britain. In the seco[nd]
(3). The fighting in Libya (4) grew fiercer when the hard-pressed Italians got Germe[...]
brought the U. S. into the war. While her neighbor Russia was locked in a bitter strugg[le]
the Dutch East Indies (6) and occupied U. S. Aleutian Islands at (7). Smashing air-nav[...]
striking hard from lands under its domination (black areas), while Finland (striped [...]
R. A. F. raids against Axis Europe and the fact th[...]

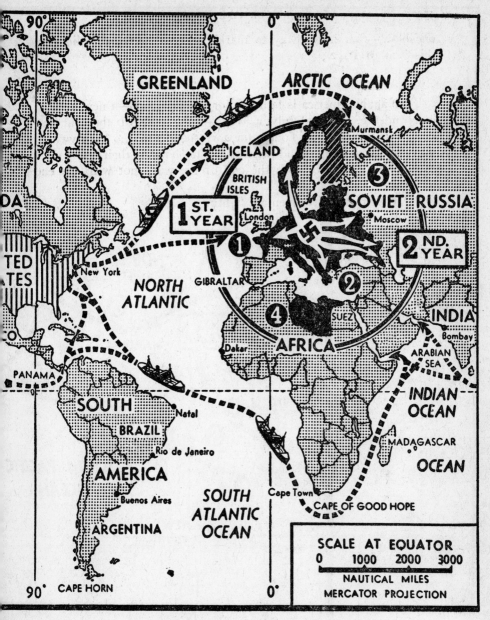

SCALE AT EQUATOR

0   1000   2000   3000

NAUTICAL MILES
MERCATOR PROJECTION

uring the first year the Germans conquered Poland, Denmark, Norway, Holland, Bel-
ear Germany, with nominal Italian help, drove into the Balkans (2) and invaded Russia
id against the British. The third year saw Japan's sneak attack on Hawaii (5) which
vith the invading Germans, Japan moved against the Philippines, Malaya, Burma, and
ictories for the United Nations resulted at Coral Sea (8) and Midway (9). The Axis was
vhite) warred against Russia. But bright spots were the mounting fury of U. S. and
upplies were streaming from the U. S. to its Allies.

453

one blow—that is the way to mark our great national holiday in this year of 1942.

So again America is fighting for independence—a new kind of independence. Today—July 4, 1942—this story of the war has caught up with events. Today, the correspondents who have written it are still deployed around the world. This book of theirs now must come to an end—not with the end of the war—not with the end of hope.

On all fronts, free men are fighting.

New York, N.Y.
July 4, 1942

About the Correspondents

LARRY ALLEN—He shattered British Admiralty tradition in the summer of 1940 when he talked his way into a regular assignment to the Mediterranean Fleet. He couldn't swim, but that didn't seem to bother him. His travel aboard British vessels had approximated 100,000 miles when, on December 16, 1941, he nearly lost his life in the torpedoing of the cruiser *Galatea.*

Allen was born at Mount Savage, Maryland, in 1908. His father, a coal operator, died virtually penniless when Allen was eleven. His mother took in sewing and he sold newspapers to earn his way through school. He had to wear his sister's shoes to school, stopping en route to rub mud over the tops so other children wouldn't see that they were girl's shoes—and laugh at him.

He got his first newspaper job on the Baltimore *News.* Later, he worked on the Charleston, West Virginia, *Daily Mail,* the Washington, D.C., *Herald,* the Portsmouth, Ohio, *Morning Sun,* and the Huntington, West Virginia, *Evening Herald.* He won the 1941 Pulitzer Prize for distinguished foreign reporting. As this sketch went to press, word had just been received of his capture by the Italians in Libya.

GLENN BABB—He is a recognized authority on Far East affairs. He went to Tokyo in 1915 as a reporter and later was news editor of the Japan *Advertiser.* He had had earlier experience on the St. Joseph, Missouri, *Gazette* and the New Bedford, Massachusetts, *Standard.* He returned to the U. S. in 1917 and served two years in France as a lieutenant of Infantry. He became a foreign correspondent in 1924 in Tokyo. He has known personally most of the outstanding figures in Oriental life of the last twenty years. His beats on the military rebellion in Tokyo in 1936 attracted wide attention. He reported the assassinations of five premiers or ex-premiers of Japan; scores of disasters, flood, and famine in China; earthquakes, typhoons, and tidal waves in Japan. He has been cable news editor in New York since 1936. He was born in Columbia, Missouri, in 1894, was graduated from the University of Missouri.

CLARKE BEACH—Son of a Washington dentist, he began his career at the tender age of two by crawling over the knees of Champ Clark, former Speaker of the House, and asking questions while Clark was waiting his turn in the dental chair. He was born in Washington, D.C., in 1905 and studied law for two years. After that, he was successively a deep-water seaman and a California cowboy. He had his first news experience on the Baltimore *Sun*.

RUSSELL BRINES—He was born in Denver, Colorado, 1911, was graduated from Pomona College. He then worked on the Hilo *Tribune-Herald* and the Honolulu *Star-Bulletin*. He became a foreign correspondent in 1933.

ROBERT E. BUNNELLE—He went to London in 1939, and three and half months later was in the midst of World War II. He was born in 1903 at Urbana, Ohio, spent a year at Wittenberg College in Springfield, Ohio, and two years at Northwestern University. He landed his first newspaper job on the Chicago City News Bureau, then worked for the Chicago *American*. Several years on Southern newspapers followed—managing editor of the Briston, Tennessee-Virginia, *Bulletin*, telegraph editor of the Lynchburg, Virginia, *News*, news editor of the Fort Smith, Arkansas, *Southwest American*, and reporter for the Asheville, North Carolina, *Times*.

EUGENE BURNS—He was born in Moscow, Russia, in 1906, and became a naturalized American twenty-three years later in Seattle, Washington. Before beginning his newspaper career he was a forest ranger and a teacher of English at the University of Idaho and Albany College. He also studied at Munich, Germany. He was graduated from Ellensburg, Washington, Normal College in 1925; received his B.A. at the University of Washington in 1929; and his M.A. at Harvard University in 1932. Prior to becoming a foreign correspondent, he worked on the Hilo *Tribune-Herald* and the Honolulu *Star-Bulletin*.

HENRY C. CASSIDY—If he had taken the advice of a Harvard vocational adviser, he would have been a schoolteacher instead of a war correspondent. The adviser said he was "too bashful" to be a newspaperman. Cassidy lined up a job as a teacher of English and French in a Maine preparatory school, then rebelled at the last minute. The more he thought about it, the more determined he was to become a correspondent. He landed a job on the Boston *Traveler*. He helped to cover the events leading to the outbreak of World War II and the first months of the fighting before going to Moscow in 1940. He was born in Boston in 1910. He thinks the Harvard adviser was wrong.

WALTER B. CLAUSEN—In 1910 and 1911 he was adviser to the Chinese Republic Movement. In 1918 and 1919 he was in public information duty for the U. S. Government. His news career was begun on the San Francisco *Examiner* when he was sixteen years old, and continued on the *Post, Chronicle,* and *Call,* in the same city; later he worked with the Los Angeles *Examiner,* the Fresno *Republic,* and the Los Angeles *Express*. He is now in Honolulu. He was born in San Francisco in 1890.

R. P. CRONIN—A newspaperman of much experience in the U. S. before he was assigned to Manila in 1935. He was born in Pittsburgh in 1893. His first newspaper job was with the old Tri-State News Bureau in that city. Later he worked on the Huntington, West Virginia, *Advertiser,* where he rose to the position of managing editor. He has been with The AP since 1915.

DANIEL DE LUCE—He has been in the thick of things since going to London in 1939. He was the only American newsman in Iran when the Allies took over that country in August and September, 1941. He arrived at Teheran, Iran's capital, ten days in advance of the invasion, and was all set when it came. He went to Burma in January, 1942, covering the fighting there until the Japanese advances forced him back into India. Born in 1911 at Yuma, Arizona, he got his first newspaper experience on the Los Angeles *Examiner*. He was graduated from the University of California.

JOSEPH DYNAN—Several of his teeth were knocked out by the Japs when he was interned in Tokyo at the beginning of the war. He would not sign a statement admitting that his activity as a reporter had included espionage. He was born in Chicago in 1913 and was graduated from Rockhurst College. He worked in Kansas City, San Antonio, and Oklahoma City before going to Honolulu on the staff of the Honolulu *Star-Bulletin*. He became a foreign correspondent in Tokyo in 1941.

JOHN EVANS—He saw service in many countries of the world before returning to New York in 1936 to take over the post of foreign news editor of The Associated Press. He was born in Des Moines in 1883 and was educated in private schools. He had his news experience on the Des Moines *Capital,* the Chicago *Inter-Ocean,* and the Washington *Times.* When Lindbergh came out of the sky at Le Bourget in May, 1927, Evans was at the field to report the wild scene. Originally he was going to be a restaurateur, but changed his mind. Now he knows foods around the world equally as well as he knows news around the world.

ERNEST G. FISCHER—He was born in Bartlett, Texas, in 1902. He decided on a newspaper career early in life. He peered through the window of a weekly newspaper, saw a linotype machine in operation, and that decided him. He landed a job as "printer's devil." Jobs in mechanical departments of newspapers helped him through the University of Missouri. His first reportorial experience was on the New Orleans *Item-Tribune.* Later he worked on the Del Rio *Evening News,* the Marshall *News Messenger,* the San Antonio *Express,* the Houston *Press,* and the Corpus Christi *Caller,* all in Texas. He was also with The United States *Daily.* He was assigned to Berlin for two and a half years.

CHARLES FOLTZ, JR.—He was born into a newspaper family in Lancaster, Pennsylvania. His father published the Lancaster *Intelligencer-Journal.* When he got out of college, he wanted to see the world. He took a look at a big part of it. Then he settled down for a time in England and in France. He has been working for The AP since 1933. In 1935 he was sent to Paris, and later he covered the Spanish Civil War.

J. WES GALLAGHER—He lost thirty-five pounds during a two-year swing through sixteen European countries and four different wars. His first goal was the Finnish-Russian war. Then the

Germans moved into Denmark and Norway, and so did Gallagher. From there he went to Rumania in time for the Russian invasion of Bessarabia. Most impressive of all to Gallagher, however, were the Greek-Italian-German campaigns during which he traveled with the half-starved Greek Army. When he left Greece in 1941, he said natives were digging for roots in vacant lots. He said at least 2,000,000 were expected to die of starvation during that year alone. His next assignment was London. He was born in Santa Cruz, California, in 1911. He got his first foreign assignment in 1939.

EDDY GILMORE—For five years before he was assigned to cover the war in 1941, Gilmore wrote about the lighter side of Washington. He went to London with Wendell Willkie and covered Willkie's inspection of the British defenses. Bombs were dropping, but the English were smiling through it all, and Gilmore stayed. In Washington he had turned out dozens of humorous stories, such as Walter Johnson's project to hurl a silver dollar across the Rapahannock River and the Bureau of Fisheries' campaign to educate people on how to tell male from female goldfish. Gilmore's first newspaper work was selling the *Times-Journal* in Selma, Alabama, where he was born in 1907. He attended the Carnegie Institute of Technology and later worked on the Atlanta *Journal*.

PRESTON L. GROVER—He got the itch to become a war correspondent as soon as World War II started. His chance came in 1940. He was born in 1900 at Farmington, Utah, was graduated from the University of Utah in 1924, and worked on the Salt Lake City *Deseret News*. For three years he wrote a daily AP column, "The Washington Daybook," from the nation's capital. Prior to leaving for Europe, he wrote this in a sketch about himself: "His principal claim to special attention is that accidents frequently happen to him—automobile wrecks, airplane crashes, horse spills—and he does not get hurt. He left for Europe hoping that this situation would continue."

DANIEL WITT HANCOCK—After London, to which he was assigned in 1936, he went to Moscow in 1939. A year later he was transferred to Istanbul, Turkey, and from there to New Delhi,

India. In January, 1942, he went to Batavia to cover the Japanese invasion of the Dutch East Indies and has been missing since March, 1942.

He was born in Bluefield, West Virginia, in 1909, and was graduated from Davidson College. He worked on the Hickory, North Carolina, *Daily Record,* the Bluefield, West Virginia, *Daily Telegraph,* and the Henderson, North Carolina, *Dispatch.*

MORRIS J. HARRIS—He covered virtually all the major events in the rebirth of China and the resurgence of Japan until his internment. He was born at Columbia, Missouri, in 1897, was graduated from the State University there. He worked on the Japan *Advertiser* from 1920 to 1923 and later on the Manila *Bulletin.* He became a foreign correspondent at Shanghai in 1927.

THOMAS F. HAWKINS—He became a foreign correspondent in London in 1939—just in time to help cover World War II. He saw service in Copenhagen, Stockholm, and Budapest, and then was sent to Bern, Switzerland. He was born in 1908, in Elliott, Iowa. He went to junior college in Creston, Iowa, where he studied speech culture, dramatics, and the piano. His first news experience was on the Creston *Advertiser.*

LYNN HEINZERLING—He has spent three and a half years covering Europe's hot spots. The first time he went to Europe was in 1927, when he toured with a college orchestra. Later he was graduated from Ohio Wesleyan University. After a decade of newspaper experience, he returned to Europe in 1938—this time as a foreign correspondent.

He was sent from Berlin to Danzig in July, 1939, when Polish border "incidents" were becoming frequent and bitter. He was there the morning of September 1, when the Germans opened up against a small Polish garrison on the Westerplatte. That was the start of the war.

He was born in Birmingham, Ohio, in 1906, and attended Akron and Ohio Wesleyan Universities. He had his first newspaper experience on the Cleveland *Plain Dealer.*

HENRY TAYLOR HENRY—He avoids name trouble by bylining his news stories "Taylor Henry."

He was born in Mineola, Texas, in 1910, and was graduated from the U. S. Military Academy in 1933. Newspaper work was a stronger lure than the profession of arms, and, after holding a commission for a short time, he resigned to become publisher of the Palestine, Texas, *Press*. He also worked on the Austin, Texas, *American* and the Blackwell, Oklahoma, *News-Tribune*. He began his foreign assignment in Paris in 1938.

MAX HILL—He was interned by the Japanese on December 7, 1941, the day of the attack on Pearl Harbor. Before that he had been a correspondent in Tokyo for almost two years. He is the author of *Exchange Ship*, forthcoming book on the Far East. He was born in Colorado Springs, Colorado, in 1904, was graduated from the University of Colorado. He was on the staff of the Denver *Post*, and later spent six years with the AP in New York.

TOM HORGAN—At seventeen he was a cub on the Boston *Traveler*. He worked in twelve cities during his first three years of newspaper work. After World War I he gained further experience with the INS, the UP, Hartford *Post*, Boston *American*, Miami, Florida, *Herald*, and Lord Northcliff's Cross-Atlantic News Service. He was born at Ponkapoag, Massachusetts, in 1898.

WILLIAM J. HUMPHREYS—He worked for the Baltimore *Evening Sun*, *Newsweek*, New York *Daily News*, and the New York *World-Telegram*. He was born in Salisbury, Maryland, in 1905, and was graduated from Annapolis College. He became a foreign correspondent in Paris in 1940. He is now with the New York *Times* in London.

CLAUDE A. JAGGER—He is Financial Editor of The Associated Press. He reported the final gasps of the frenzied bull market of 1928 and 1929. He was among the outstanding American correspondents at the World Economic Conference in London in 1933. His surveys of business, articles on such developments as the collapse of the gold standard, the banking holiday, the trends of government and corporate finance, the price level, and efforts to spur employment, have made headlines throughout the country.

Born at East Palmyra, New York, in 1902, he was educated at Dartmouth College and Columbia University. After experience on newspapers in New York State and New England, he left the Providence *Evening Bulletin* to join The AP in 1927.

EDWARD KENNEDY—He has been in the thick of hot news abroad ever since 1937, when he helped to cover the Spanish Civil War. He has seen historic events take place in Hungary, Rumania, Yugoslavia, Greece, Italy, Turkey, Palestine, Syria, Libya, and Egypt. Born in 1905, in Brooklyn, New York, he studied architecture at Carnegie Tech before deciding on a journalism career. His first news job was on the Cannonsburg, Pennsylvania, *Daily Notes.* He worked on newspapers in New York and New Jersey, and with the Paul Block newspapers in Washington before becoming a member of the New York *Herald Tribune's* Paris staff in 1931. He returned to this country and worked for the Newark, New Jersey, *Ledger* until October, 1932, when he joined The AP. He was assigned to the Paris bureau in 1934 and worked for a short time in Rome before becoming a war correspondent at Valencia and Madrid in 1937.

CLARK LEE—Mud-covered and dog-tired, he staggered into the Manila bureau on December 25, 1941, and wrote the first eyewitness account of the Japanese invasion along the Lingayen Gulf. For days after the fall of Manila his whereabouts were a mystery. Then, on January 9, 1942, he sent a dispatch from Fort Mills, on the island of Corregidor—the first dispatch to be sent out by any American newsman since December 31. He comes by newspapering naturally. His father, his mother, and his sister are newspaper people. Born in Oakland, California, in 1907, Lee moved with his family to Maplewood, New Jersey, during World War I. Tall and rangy, he was a three-letter man in high school. He entered Rutgers in 1925 and was varsity third baseman. He had his first foreign assignment in Mexico in 1933. He went to Honolulu in 1938—then to Tokyo. He married Liliuokalani Kawananakoa, daughter of the late David Kawananakoa, who was created a Prince by the last king of Hawaii, Kalakaua.

LLOYD LEHRBAS—His newspaper experience began on the Salt Lake City *Tribune*. While he was studying at the University of Wisconsin, the U. S. entered World War I and Lehrbas entered the Air Corps. Awaiting orders, he worked for the Chicago *Tribune*. Later came service with the San Francisco *Chronicle,* the Chicago *American,* the Manila *Bulletin,* the Shanghai *Evening Star,* Hearst Services, and Fox Movietone News.

He covered diplomatic, Army and Navy affairs at Washington, and the Sino-Jap War, saw the bombing of Warsaw, and scored a beat on the killing of Premier Calinescu at Bucharest.

He is now a colonel of General Douglas MacArthur's staff in charge of press relations in Australia. At MacArthur's reception in Melbourne on March 21, 1942, the general spotted him and shouted: "How the hell are you, Larry?" Lehrbas was born at Montpelier, Idaho, in 1899.

LOUIS P. LOCHNER—He probably knows more Germans—and more about them—than any other American newsman. He was a correspondent in Berlin from 1924 until he was interned at Bad Nauheim in December, 1941.

He was awarded the Pulitzer Prize for distinguished foreign reporting in 1939. At that time he said: "I regard it as a solemn obligation always to interpret the news to the American public impartially and fairly."

He has had many great news stories and has covered many sensational beats, among them: an exclusive interview in 1925 with Paul von Hindenburg, then a presidential candidate; the first authentic story of Marshal Pilsudski's 1926 coup d'état in Warsaw; the dirigible *Hindenburg's* first U. S. flight; interviews with the Kaiser; an exclusive interview with Adolf Hitler in August, 1932, a contact which led to one of the frankest interviews ever given by Hitler as Fuehrer in 1934; the first inside stories on Germany at war with the U. S. in 1941-1942. He is the author of *What About Germany?*

Lochner was born 1887 in Springfield, Illinois. He was graduated from the University of Wisconsin in 1909 with Phi Beta Kappa honors. When World War I broke out, he was on the way to a peace conference at Vienna and was the only American to see the first British arrive in France en route to Belgium. Later as peace secretary to Henry Ford, he was prominent in the famous peace ship venture.

J. NORMAN LODGE—In his latest stretch as a foreign correspondent he packed more into into those fourteen months than most newspapermen could in forty-one. He covered the war in fifteen countries.

He ran away from home at the age of fifteen to join General Pershing's punitive expedition into Mexico in 1916. An expert rifleman, he was detached from the regular army to act as small arms instructor for the Massachusetts National Guard during and after the border mobilization. He went to France in 1917, in advance of the 26th Division, to establish a cantonment at St. Nazaire. For ten months and four days, he was on front-line duty and took part in six major engagements, during which he suffered leg wounds and gassing. He was awarded the Croix de Guerre for a successful liaison job as a volunteer runner after two others had failed to contact a short-firing artillery unit at Château-Thierry. Three times he was cited for exceptional service. After twenty-eight months in an army hospital he joined the Lawrence, Massachusetts, *Sun* as reporter. He also worked on newspapers in New London, Connecticut, and Lowell, Massachusetts. He was born at Methuen, Massachusetts, in 1899.

DEWITT MACKENZIE—At 5:30 A.M. daily a New York train pulls out of suburban Bronxville, and aboard it is the tall, heavily built, steel-gray-haired man who writes "The War Today," the most widely-read commentary on foreign affairs. The man is DeWitt Mackenzie. His column appears in 900 daily newspapers.

To make early afternoon editions, the column must start clicking over a nationwide news wire by 8:45 A.M. daily. Mackenzie arrives at his desk at six; pores over news reports of the preceding twelve hours; divines their between-the-lines meaning; and picks out the precise phraseology that will convey this meaning in a few hundred words.

Mackenzie spent nearly twenty years abroad as a correspondent, beginning with World War I. He was one of two American reporters among the "Big Seven" attached to British General Headquarters in France. Later he covered the Versailles Peace Conference. Mackenzie has written three books, all published in England. They are: *The Awakening of India, The Girl in the Mask,* and *Hell's Kitchen.*

Born in West Burke, Vermont, in 1885, Mackenzie was employed at various stages as farmhand, schoolteacher, woolen mill hand, and traveling salesman. He worked his way through Syracuse University leading an orchestra. He started his newspaper career on the Syracuse *Post-Standard*.

FRANK L. MARTIN, JR.—A veteran of Far Eastern reporting, Martin has been in Africa covering the desert war since early in 1942. He was born in Columbia, Missouri, in 1912, and was graduated from the University of Missouri. He made his fourth trip to the Orient in 1939 and joined The AP staff at Shanghai in 1940. He traveled to Chungking and Hong Kong, and made a trip over the Burma Road before covering Indo-China while it was under Japanese occupation. Prior to beginning his foreign experience, he worked for the UP in Chicago, INS in New York, the Minneapolis *Star,* the Sedalia, Missouri, *Capital,* and the Salt Lake City *Tribune.*

RICHARD G. MASSOCK—He covered many of Europe's hottest news stories for ten years prior to his internment at Rome in December, 1941. In France, he reported the Stavisky financial scandal; the February, 1934, riots, in which he was wounded slightly, and the assassinations of King Alexander of Yugoslavia and French Foreign Minister Barthou. In Spain, he reported the Civil War. In Russia, he reported the purge of 1937-1938, when Soviet citizens disappeared in record numbers. In Italy, he reported the crisis over Czecho-Slovakia, the death of Pope Pius XI, the coronation of the new Pope, Italy's occupation of Albania, and the many other events precipitating World War II. He has just written a book on his experiences in Italy.

Born in 1900, at Blue Mound, Illinois, he studied law at the University of Illinois. He worked on the Springfield, Illinois, *State Journal*. He became a foreign correspondent in 1932.

C. YATES McDANIEL—Slim, grave, prematurely gray, he was the first American correspondent to arrive in Singapore—and the only one left to witness the heroic last-ditch stand of Singapore's outmanned defenders. He probably got some of his outward calm from the Chinese children with whom he played as a child in Soochow, China, where his parents, the Reverend and Mrs. Charles G. McDaniel of Blackstone, Virginia, operated a Baptist mission.

He was born there in 1906. Like most missionaries' sons, he was sent to the U. S. for his college education. He attended the University of Richmond.

He had newspaper experience on the Sarasota, Florida, *Morning Herald* and the Durham, North Carolina, *Herald*. Then he returned to China in 1929 to work for Shanghai papers. He became a foreign correspondent in 1935.

WILLIAM McGAFFIN—He began his foreign assignment in London in August, 1937—to report "the human interest side of European life." A native of Polk, Nebraska, he was graduated from the University of Nebraska and worked successively on the Nebraska State *Journal,* the Lincoln *Star,* the Omaha *World-Herald,* and the Columbus, Nebraska, *Telegram.* He was the first Nebraskan to receive the Gilbert M. Hitchcock scholarship for a year of postgraduate study at Columbia University.

VAUGHN F. MEISLING—A native of Denmark, born in 1902, at Copenhagen, he was one of the newsmen interned by the Japanese at Hong Kong. He had worked on papers in Philadelphia, where he became a naturalized American, Los Angeles, Richmond, Virginia, New Orleans, and San Francisco. He went to China on the staff of the North China *Daily News* at Shanghai, joined The AP at Peiping in 1940.

DREW MIDDLETON—Months before World War II started, he reported Britain's preparedness—from the April conscription through the August mobilization. He pleaded and cajoled until he was assigned to the British Expeditionary Force. He wallowed in the mud of Northern France during the first winter of the war, went back to London because there was no action, returned to France after the May invasion, and stayed until the correspondents were ordered back to London—just before Dunkerque.

Middleton was born in New York City in 1913. He was graduated from Syracuse University. He was sports editor of the Poughkeepsie, New York, *Eagle-News,* and later of the Poughkeepsie *Evening Star.* He is now a member of the London staff of the New York *Times.*

HAROLD MILKS—He's in the Army now, but for the three years previous to May, 1942, he reported Latin-American affairs and events in New York, Buenos Aires, Argentina, and Bogota, Colombia. He paid his tuition at Lombard (Indiana) College by working as a railroader, and got his news experience on the Kendallville, Indiana, *News-Sun,* and the Fort Wayne, Indiana, *Journal-Gazette.* He was born at South Milford, Indiana, in 1908.

RELMAN MORIN—Extensive travel through China and Japan, after graduation from Pomona College in 1929, prepared him for his first foreign assignment in Tokyo in 1937. He was born in Freeport, Illinois, 1907. His first news assignment was that of a Hollywood columnist. Later he worked on the Shanghai *Evening Post.* He is the author of a forthcoming book on the Far East.

JOHN A. MOROSO, 3rd.—He specializes in the subject of sea warfare, a job that he held down for two and a half years before joining the Atlantic Fleet as a war reporter in April, 1942. He was born in Charleston, South Carolina, in 1910, and attended the University of South Carolina. After spending considerable time as a seaman aboard a freighter, he worked on the New Rochelle, New York, *Standard Star* for several years.

NOLAND NORGAARD—He came by his unusual surname from Danish grandparents and his equally unusual given name from a remote Scotch-Irish ancestor. Born at Gypsum, Colorado, in 1905, he started newspaper work at the age of twenty on the Grand Junction, Colorado, *Sentinel.* He became a foreign correspondent in 1941.

ROBERT OKIN—War, death, and violence are woven through his news career. Okin covered the Hauptmann execution in 1936 and handled the story on the flaming explosion of the dirigible *Hindenburg* at Lakehurst, New Jersey, in 1937. He cut his war teeth as a correspondent in the Spanish Civil War, the preview of World War II. At the Spanish war's end in 1938, he began news tours that took him into Algeria and to London. When World War II came, he followed the tide of battle from Belgium, Copenhagen, Paris, and Vichy. Okin was born in 1911 at Hackensack, New Jersey, graduated from Rutgers University in 1932, and had early news experience with the Hackensack Bergen *Evening Record*.

J. REILLY O'SULLIVAN—In his earlier days as a newsman he covered many important events, including the plane crash that killed Knute Rockne, Notre Dame's famous football coach, and the Kansas City Union Station massacre. He worked on newspapers in Oklahoma City, Sioux Falls, Kansas City, Chicago, Indianapolis, and St. Louis. He was born at Kansas City, Missouri, in 1898. He became a foreign correspondent in 1939.

ROY PORTER—He covered negotiations between the Czecho-Slovak and German governments prior to the Munich conference. Later, he arrived in Danzig an hour ahead of the German motorized forces. He was in Paris when the German Army occupied that city. Born in Chicago in 1907, he was graduated from the University of Iowa. He had early experience on the Des Moines *Register* and *Tribune*, the Chicago *Herald-Examiner*, and the Los Angeles *Herald*. He is the author of *Uncensored France*.

J. M. ROBERTS, JR.—He is foreign news editor of The Associated Press, was born in 1902, at Elkton, Ky., and attended Davidson College and the University of North Carolina. He had early newspaper experience on the Durham *Herald*, Asheville *Citizen* and Charlotte *Observer*, in North Carolina. Foreign affairs became a hobby for him under the kindly tutelage of the late William Jennings Bryan, who was a neighbor after resigning as secretary of state during World War I, and the hobby had become a profession by World War II.

DEAN SCHEDLER—He was born in Stillwater, Oklahoma, in 1914. He went to Manila in 1936 after attending Oklahoma A. and M. and Georgetown University. He worked for the Manila

Bulletin and edited a mining magazine. He became a correspondent at Manila in 1941. He escaped to Corregidor Fortress, at the entrance to Manila Bay, when the Japanese occupied Manila. He was missing for two weeks or more after the Battle of Bataan, but finally turned up in Australia.

EDWIN SHANKE—He learned to speak, read, and write German as a boy in his home town of Milwaukee, Wisconsin, where he was born in 1910. This stood him in good stead when he was assigned to Berlin in 1937. He had ample opportunity to make use of it for the next five years, during which time, except for a few brief assignments in Central Europe, he remained in Germany. He was graduated from Marquette University.

KIRKE SIMPSON—He is the man who wrote the famous Unknown Soldier stories. Because of them he won the Pulitzer Prize in 1923, the first press association man ever to receive the award.

Born in San Francisco in 1880, as a youngster he volunteered for service in the Spanish-American War. In 1906 he went to Nevada and ran the Tonopah *Sun* for two years. In 1908 he joined The AP in San Francisco, where he worked on the desk with red-headed Sinclair Lewis, another AP man, who became a famous novelist.

He went to Washington where he covered the War and Navy Departments and later the State Department. During World War I, and afterward, he was a major in the Intelligence Service Reserve of the U. S. Army. He knows official Washington as few men do, attends the meetings of Roosevelt's Cuff-Links Club on the night of the President's birthday.

ALVIN J. STEINKOPF—He has been at the front in two world conflicts—as a soldier with the 32nd Division of the U. S. Army in World War I and as a correspondent in World War II. From 1917 to 1919 he served with the A.E.F. Mustered out, he spent five years on the St. Paul *Pioneer-Press* and six years on the Milwaukee *Sentinel* before joining The AP in 1931.

He became a foreign correspondent in Vienna in 1934. After

Vienna was enslaved in 1938, he went to Budapest and again had a front seat in Hitler's war drama. When Nazi domination of Hungary became complete, he moved on to Berlin in 1939. He was the first American correspondent to view Warsaw after its fall. He returned to Berlin and predicted a new front. Within a few weeks the Nazis marched into Russia.

He was born on a farm in Sibley County, Minnesota, in 1897, was graduated from Marquette University.

ROBERT ST. JOHN—In the Balkans he was wounded by German machine-gun bullets. He fled before the Nazi advance in Yugoslavia and Greece. He escaped in a small boat and after four weeks turned up in Egypt. He was born in Chicago in 1900. He ran a weekly newspaper in Cicero, Illinois, fought Al Capone editorially, and was beaten up by gangsters. After experience on newspapers in Illinois, Pennsylvania, Vermont, and Connecticut, he went to the Balkans. He reported such news as the overthrow and flight of King Carol of Rumania and the uprising and suppression of the Iron Guard. He is now with NBC in London. St. John is the author of last year's *From the Land of Silent People*.

MILO M. THOMPSON—A city editor in Joliet, Illinois, gave him his first news assignment. He had to ask Negro clergymen what they thought about a prize fighter named Jack Johnson. His newspaper career included training in Boston, Atlanta, Boise, Des Moines, and other cities, with time out for army service during World War I.

He became a foreign correspondent and a European news executive in 1937, now is president of La Prensa Asociada, The AP Latin-American news subsidiary. He was born in Joliet, Illinois, in 1894; was educated at Harvard.

ANGUS M. THUERMER—He became a foreign correspondent at Berlin when only twenty-two years old. That was in 1939. Previously he had worked on the Champaign, Illinois, *News Gazette* and the *Daily Illini*, the latter while attending the University of Illinois, from which he was graduated in 1938. He was born in 1917 at Quincy, Illinois.

RICHARD L. TURNER—He has covered political conventions as well as war news. His first newspaper experience was on a Skowhegan, Maine, weekly, following which he worked on the Chester, Pennsylvania, *Times,* the Boston *Herald-Traveler,* and the Providence *News.* He was born at Laurel, Delaware, in 1901, attended the University of Pennsylvania.

FRED VANDERSCHMIDT—He had his first foreign assignment in London in 1937. He was there when war was declared. Born in 1906, his first job was on his home town paper—the Leavenworth *Times.* He also worked on the Wichita *Beacon.*

HUGH WAGNON—He is a blond, cheerful chap who hails from Oklahoma. He became a foreign correspondent in London in 1939, where he remained for two years. He had much early newspaper experience in Oklahoma, Missouri, and Kansas. He covered Governor Alf M. Landon's unsuccessful Republican campaign for the presidency. Now he is in charge of AP service in Pennsylvania. He was born in Calvin, Oklahoma, in 1904.

ALFRED E. WALL—He became a foreign correspondent in 1940. He had thirteen and a half years of news experience in Denver, Cheyenne, Oklahoma City, Tulsa, Chicago, and New York. He was born September 18, 1901, at Indianapolis, was graduated from the University of Colorado.

WENDELL WEBB—Blue-eyed, blond Webb covered the news in many American cities before he became a foreign correspondent. He went to Honolulu when the U. S. entered World War II. Born at Conrad, Iowa, in 1905, he attended Cornell College, Iowa State Teachers' College, and Drake University. He had news experience on the Des Moines *Register* and *Tribune,* the Omaha *Bee-News,* the McMinnville, Oregon, *Telephone Register,* and the Salem, Oregon, *Statesman.*

FRANK I. WELLER—From farm editor to political correspondent—that's the story of Frank Weller. Born at Vincennes, Indiana, March 11, 1900, he had his early experience on the Seymour *Democrat,* the Seymour *Republican,* Columbus *Dispatch,* all in Indiana; the St. Petersburg *Times,* the Springfield *Register,* and the International News Service. Then he decided that he wanted to be a political correspondent. He went to Washington, where he felt there would be a springboard. There was, but he spent several years there as AP farm feature editor before he realized his ambition.

WADE WERNER—He is the man who got out the first news on the Nazi killing of Chancellor Dollfus in Vienna in 1938. He received a tip from a confidential source and dashed to the barracks where Nazis, clad as Austrian officers, were assembling to ride on the Chancellory. All civilians were barred from the Chancellory, but Werner got through anyway. He ran, under cover of guns, to the doubtful shelter of one of Chancellory doorways and got away alive with details of the assassination. He became a foreign correspondent in 1929, covering the early days of the Nazi movement. He was born in 1893 in the Chicago suburb of Harvey, was graduated from the University of California. His early news experience was with the Los Angeles *Herald* and the Prescott, Arizona, *Courier.*

JAMES D. WHITE—He was the first foreign correspondent to reach Marco Polo Bridge in the vicinity of Peiping in July, 1937, when the "China Incident" began. He was born in 1907 near Appleton, Missouri, and was graduated from the State University in 1932. Later he had two years of graduate study at Yenching University, Peiping. He managed and edited the Yenching *Gazette* and was correspondent for the *Christian Science Monitor* until 1936, when he joined The AP.

WILLIAM W. WHITE—He helped to cover the bombings of London in 1940 and 1941. Early news experience was on the Denver, Colorado, *Rocky Mountain News* and the Boulder, Colorado, *Daily Camera.* He was born in Boulder, Colorado, in 1908, was graduated from the University of Colorado School in 1932. He is now on the London staff of the New York *Herald Tribune.*

MELVIN K. WHITELEATHER—He is a native of Damascus, Ohio, was graduated from the Ohio State University, and received his early newspaper training at East Liverpool, Youngstown, Pittsburgh, Cleveland, and on the Paris (France) *Times*. He was born in 1903, had his first foreign assignment in 1930.

When the Nazi troops marched into Sudetenland, after 1938's "Munich," Whiteleather accompanied the high command that took possession of the "Schoeber lines" of fortifications. He now is with the Philadelphia *Bulletin*.

RICE YAHNER—He was born in Munhall, Pennsylvania, in 1905 and has been a newspaperman since he was sixteen years old. He went to Northern Ireland as correspondent with the American Expeditionary Force in January, 1942, previous to which he had served as field correspondent with the U. S. Army covering camps and maneuvers in Tennessee, Texas, Louisiana, and the Carolinas. He joined The AP in 1933 after working on the old Tri-State News Bureau at Pittsburgh, the Pittsburgh *Press* and the *Post Gazette*.

TOM YARBROUGH—He is a native of Chickasha, Oklahoma. He attended the University of Oklahoma, where he received his first newspaper training on the Oklahoma *Daily*. In 1932, after graduation, he went to work for the Oklahoma City *Times*. He arrived in London only a day or so before the outbreak of World War II. Since then he has had assignments around the world.

Index

475